WOMEN'S RIGHTS

Natasha Thomsen

Foreword by Kathryn Cullen-DuPont

An imprint of Infobase Publishing

To the memory of Rosa Parks (1913–2005),
who personified the human right to self-develop.

GLOBAL ISSUES: WOMEN'S RIGHTS

Copyright © 2007 by Infobase Publishing

Facts On File, Inc.
An imprint of Infobase Publishing
132 West 31st Street
New York NY 10001

ISBN-10: 0-8160-6809-7
ISBN-13: 0-978-0-8160-6809-8

Library of Congress Cataloging-in-Publication Data
Thomsen, Natasha.
    Women's Rights / Natasha Thomsen.
        p. cm. — (Global issues)
    Includes bibliographical references and index.
    ISBN 0-8160-6809-7 (alk. paper)
        1. Women's rights. 2. Women's rights—United States. I. Title.
    HQ1236.W652525 2007
    305.42072—dc22   2006028650

Facts On File books are available at special discounts when purchased in bulk quantities for businesses, associations, institutions, or sales promotions. Please call our Special Sales Department in New York at (212) 967-8800 or (800) 322-8755.

You can find Facts On File on the World Wide Web at http://www.factsonfile.com

Text design by Erika K. Arroyo
Cover design by Salvatore Luongo
Diagrams by Jeremy Eagle

Printed in the United States of America

MP KT 10 9 8 7 6 5 4 3 2 1

This book is printed on acid-free paper.

CONTENTS

Foreword by Kathryn Cullen-DuPont **vii**

List of Acronyms **xi**

PART I: At Issue

Chapter 1
Introduction   **3**

Chapter 2
Focus on the United States   **50**

Chapter 3
Global Perspectives   **94**

PART II: Primary Sources

Chapter 4
United States Documents   **134**

Chapter 5
International Documents   **185**

PART III: Research Tools

Chapter 6
How to Research
the Women's Rights Movement   **238**

Chapter 7
Facts and Figures   **250**

Chapter 8
Key Players A to Z   **255**

Chapter 9
Organizations and Agencies   **273**

Chapter 10
Annotated Bibliography   **298**

Chronology   **342**

Glossary   **371**

Index   **381**

Foreword

The global significance of women's rights has never been clearer than at the beginning of the 21st century. When the United States prepared to strike Afghanistan in the wake of the September 11, 2001, attacks, President George W. Bush stated that Afghanistan's Taliban-run government would be punished if it did not turn over al-Qaeda members within its borders. After the U.S.-led military attack, First Lady Laura Bush also delivered a speech—a speech on the importance of women's rights and the Taliban's failure to support those rights.

The Bush administration's wartime discussion of a country's women's rights record is but one example of the issue's global significance and impact. Female genital mutilation, once considered a private matter, has been debated in legislative halls worldwide; currently outlawed in many developed and developing countries, it has been grounds for refugee status in Canada, Great Britain, and the United States. The European Commission, in evaluating Turkey's candidacy for full admission to the European Union, has raised concerns, among other things, about Turkey's women's rights record. The United Nations's eight Millennium Development Goals, dedicated to eradicating the worst ravages of poverty throughout the world by 2015, lists the promotion of gender equality and the empowerment of women as central to achieving that goal. At a time when the global significance and impact of women's issues have never been clearer, however, the issues themselves—and especially the way these issues are viewed by women through the prism of their own countries' histories and cultures—are not always clearly understood.

Global Issues: Women's Rights addresses this. It presents a thorough, global overview of the struggle for women's rights, an overview that makes clear not only the significance of this struggle but its long history and international character. It then examines how that struggle has been experienced in five different countries: the United States, Denmark, China, Afghanistan, and Kenya. These five case studies illuminate, in detail, the different contexts in which women have sought recognition of their rights and their varying, culturally informed views of what those rights might entail.

The global overview begins with a discussion of the issues understood to be involved in women's rights: women's suffrage and their right to stand for election; civil rights, including property ownership and inheritance rights; access to education; social, employment, and economic rights; enrollment in the military; family health and sexuality; atypical gender roles; traditional practices such as female genital mutilation (also known as female circumcision and female cutting); violence against women; and religion and spirituality. Each discussion is a full one. The section on violence against women, for example, examines both the free-speech and violence-inducing arguments concerning pornography, as well as the World Health Organization's studies on rape and domestic violence, the intersection of war and violence against women (particularly the use of rape as a weapon of war), female infanticide, and human trafficking and prostitution. A narrative history of the international struggle for women's rights concludes this global overview. Beginning with British feminist Mary Astell's suggestion for a women's college in her *Serious Proposal to the Ladies* (two parts, 1694–97) and concluding with the United Nations's four world conferences on women and the 1990s spread of women's studies programs into countries as diverse as Vietnam and the Czech Republic, the narrative places the women's rights movement's most important figures and achievements in a truly global context.

The United States is the first country to be individually examined in *Women's Rights*. The strategies and victories of the American women's suffrage movement and the women who led the 72-year campaign for the vote are clearly presented, as are American women's initiatives and progress in the areas of employment rights, education, reproductive rights, and other crucial areas. Moreover, these areas are presented against a backdrop of cultural history, allowing for understanding of the interplay between such events, for example, as the 1940s return of male soldiers from World War II and the subsequent decrease in the numbers of employed women and, decades later, Anita Hill's 1991 charge of sexual harassment against Supreme Court nominee Clarence Thomas and the subsequent increase in the number of women willing to come forward with sexual harassment claims.

Each of the other countries that is the subject of a case study is also examined in depth, beginning with a presentation of the issues, events, and matters of timing that led to the inauguration of each country's women's movement. Each movement is then presented against its country's particular political background and the specific challenges presented by that background. The current issues facing each country's women's rights movement are also evaluated, as are its ties with the international women's movement and its future goals.

Denmark's case study begins with an account of the translation into Danish of the British writer Mary Wollstonecraft's *A Vindication of the Rights of Women* (1792), the 1850 publication of Mathilde Fibiger's novel *Clara Raphael,* and the 1869 translation into Danish of John Stuart Mill's *On the Subjection of Women,* all of which served to stir public discussion of women's rights. As the case study progresses, it examines the Danish suffrage movement and women's initiatives and progress in such areas as education, employment, family life, gay rights, and religion. Issues particular to Denmark—such as those that arise in a country where adult prostitution and pornography are legal and where a formerly socialized medical system is adopting free-market features—are also discussed.

The discussion of the women's rights movement in China begins with an account of that country's women's suffrage movement and a consideration of women's property rights, educational access, and employment opportunities. It contains a balanced, objective discussion of how, as the author puts it, "cultural interpretation of the concept of rights differ[s] greatly from its meaning in the United States." The Chinese Communist Party's limitation of media discussion of topics such as lesbian rights and female trafficking is examined, as is China's 1979 one-child policy and the questions it raises regarding women's autonomy and an increase in female infant abandonment. There have been indisputable improvements for women as well, and they, too, are presented here. China's role as host for the United Nations's Fourth World Conference on Women in 1995 is highlighted, as are important improvements in legislation affecting women, including laws against domestic violence and the sale of women into marriage. Chinese women's participation in the fruits of country-wide advances—China's move from a country with a 90 percent illiteracy rate in 1949 to one that now has an almost 90 percent literacy rate is one example—is outlined as well.

Likewise, the consideration of women's rights in Afghanistan is set against the pertinent cultural background. It begins with Afghanistan's winning of independence from Britain in 1921 and its first constitution, which granted equal rights to men and women but withheld suffrage from women. Moving to the adoption of a reformed constitution that granted women's suffrage, educational access, and equal wage protection in 1963, *Women's Rights* then traces the subsequent empowerment of Afghan women. The 1979 invasion by the Soviet Union and the Taliban rule from 1994 to 2002—which sharply curtailed women's rights—are also closely examined. In describing women's rights and the environment for women's rights in Afghanistan since international forces ousted the Taliban, nuances of argument are not overlooked: Some Muslim feminists argue that it is the Western display of female bodies and not the privacy accorded it by the burqa that is objectifying, for example, and this and other such culturally inflected arguments are objectively and fully presented.

Kenya, home to the United Nations's Third World Conference on Women in 1985, is the final country considered. Again, nuances of culture and argument are not overlooked. Granted suffrage in 1963 soon after Kenya won independence from Britain, Kenya's women struggle for their rights in a traditional environment that includes unequal inheritance practices (outlawed by the Law of Succession Act of 1981 but rarely challenged in court) and female genital mutilation (performed on an estimated 38 to 50 percent of Kenya's women). Kenya's women have nonetheless created a broad-based network of women's rights organizations to work for improvement in women's health, property rights, employment opportunities, and other issues long recognized as central to women's empowerment: To date, Kenya's Ministry of Culture and Social Services lists more than 24,000 women's rights groups and relevant NGOs, including the League of Kenyan Women Voters, the Women's Political Caucus, and the National Council of Women of Kenya. Issues particular to Kenya, such as the existence of five different marriage systems (African, Civil, Christian, Muslim, and Hindu) and the interpretation of those systems in the courts, are also discussed.

Women's Rights also brings together primary-source documents relevant to the foregoing. The United States's 1848 Declaration of Rights and Sentiments; Denmark's 2002 Gender Equality (Consolidation) Act; China's 2002 Population and Family Planning Law; current newspaper "dispatches" from Afghanistan; the speech of Kenya's Dr. Maathias upon receiving the 2004 Nobel Peace Prize for her contribution to sustainable development, democracy, and peace; and the United Nations Convention on All Forms of Discrimination Against Women are but a few of the important and enlightening documents consolidated in this volume.

In addition, *Women's Rights* provides the reader with useful research tools. Biographies of each country's key women's rights figures, the relevant facts and figures, a thorough and well-annotated bibliography, a list of organizations and agencies, a chronology of the women's rights movement worldwide, and a glossary of the relevant terms are all provided.

Women's Rights is a perfect choice for any high school (or, indeed, college) student ready to begin research on the important subject of women's rights.

— Kathryn Cullen-DuPont
Brooklyn, New York

List of Acronyms

ACW	African Centre for Women
AD	active duty
AERA	American Equal Rights Association
ATA	Afghan Transitional Administration
AWSA	American Woman Suffrage Association
BLS	Bureau of Labor Statistics (U.S.)
BWOA	Black Women Organized for Action
CCDF	Child Care Development Fund
CEDAW	Convention on the Elimination of All Forms of Discrimination against Women
CIS	Commonwealth of Independent States
COYOTE	"Call Off Your Old Tired Ethics"
CSCE	Conference on Security and Co-operation in Europe
CPTP	Civilian Pilot Training Program
D&E	dilation and evacuation
D&X	dilation and extraction
DOB	Daughters of Bilitis
DOMA	Defense of Marriage Act
ECOA	Equal Credit Opportunity Act
ECPs	emergency contraception pills
EMILY's List	Early Money Is Like Yeast's List
ENDA	Employment Non-Discrimination Act
ERA	Equal Rights Amendment
EEOC	Equal Employment Opportunity Commission
EU	European Union
FACE	Freedom of Access to Clinic Entrances
FGM	female genital mutilation
FMLA	Family and Medical Leave Act
HIV/AIDS	human immunodeficiency virus/acquired

	immunodeficiency syndrome
IAW	International Association of Women
ICCPR	International Covenant on Civil and Political Rights
ICESCR	International Covenant on Economic, Social and Cultural Rights
ICPD	International Conference on Population and Development
ICW	International Council of Women
IED	improvised explosive device
IGOs	intergovernmental organizations
ILO	International Labour Organization
INSTRAW	United Nations International Research and Training Institute for the Advancement of Women
IUD	intrauterine device
IWSA	International Women's Suffrage Alliance
LDNs	least developed nations
MDGs	Millennium Development Goals
MULPOC	Multinational Programming and Operational Centre
MWPA	Married Women's Property Act
NACW	National Association of Colored Women
NAF	National Abortion Federation
NASA	National Aeronautics and Space Administration
NATO	North Atlantic Treaty Organization
NAWSA	National American Woman Suffrage Association (1890)
NBFO	National Black Feminist Organization
NCL	National Consumer's League
NGO	nongovernmental organization
NOW	National Organization for Women
NWP	National Women's Party
NWSA	National Woman Suffrage Association
OECD	Organization for Economic Cooperation and Development
OSCE	Organization for Security and Cooperation in Europe
PaCS	Pacte civil de solidarité (civil solidarity pact)
PICW	President's Interagency Council on Women
PPFA	Planned Parenthood Federation of America
PRC	People's Republic of China
STDs	sexually transmitted diseases
UIFSA	Uniform Interstate Family Support Act
UNDP	United Nations Development Programme
UNESCO	United Nations Educational, Scientific and Cultural Organization
UNICEF	United Nations Children's Fund
UNIFEM	United Nations Development Fund for Women

List of Acronyms

UPAA	Uniform Premarital Agreement Act of 1983
USAID	U.S. Agency for International Development
VA	Veterans Administration
VAWA	Violence against Women Act
VOCA	Victims of Crime Act
VTVPA	Victims of Trafficking and Violence Protection Act of 2000
WASPs	Women's Airforce Service Pilots
WCTU	Woman's Christian Temperance Union
WHO	World Health Organization
WILPF	Women's International League for Peace and Freedom
WITCH	Women's International Terrorist Conspiracy from Hell
YWCA	Young Women's Christian Association
YWHA	Young Women's Hebrew Association

PART I

At Issue

1

Introduction

WOMEN'S RIGHTS

The call for women's rights began at different times in different countries, often coinciding with the demand for other rights, such as political freedom or economic reform. Countries redefining their futures have repeatedly kindled women's aspirations, beginning in the early 17th and 18th centuries in Europe and the United States; followed in the 19th and 20th centuries in many African, Asian, and Latin American countries as part of their struggle for independence; and into the 21st century in some countries of the Middle East.

The issues women have been dealing with have been similar worldwide but varied by the pace of change allowed by political climate and cultural beliefs. What began as largely a political and legal awareness by women in the suffrage movement, who fought for the right to be represented by vote, evolved into social and economic rights that included the rights of employment and reproduction rights, and the balance of these two domains.

Political and Legal Rights

Women the world over have been foremost concerned with winning the right to vote in their countries. This basic power would then enable them to participate in elections of local officials and, in turn, have a voice on legislative issues that affected their lives. Although women have played a role in various wars throughout history—from Bodaceia in the first century c.e., to the French Revolution, through to World War II, and now in present-day Iraq—they did not have a significant part in the political process that caused or ended these wars.

SUFFRAGE

The privilege of political and legal equity has been hard won where it is in effect. In 1893, New Zealand became the first country to grant women the right to vote, yet in other countries the struggle for suffrage and the right to stand for elections as a candidate continues even today. Although most accounts of how suffrage movements succeeded describe peaceful protests—such as picket lines, marches, and peace rallies—in many instances women were the victims of perpetrators of violence. In Great Britain and the United States in the early 1920s, for example, hunger strikes turned into forced feedings and marchers shattered windows.

One of the first aims of the United Nations after beginning its existence after World War II was to extend suffrage rights to the women of all member nations. In 1952, the General Assembly adopted a resolution urging such action. By the 1970s, most member nations complied with the act, although subtle forms of discrimination persisted.

For example, although some countries in Asia and Oceania—such as Bangladesh, Pakistan, India, Indonesia, Sri Lanka, Philippines, and New Zealand—have had a large number of female heads of state and have enjoyed universal suffrage for decades, cultural barriers have often prevented women from fully exercising their voting privileges and penetrating political realms. In other countries, the right to vote has not always been continuously assured once it was won. The Taliban government in Afghanistan did not recognize women's suffrage during its time in power from 1994 until its fall in 2002 at the hands of international troops. Even now, warlords defend traditional views in rural areas of that country, making it difficult for women to reclaim their rights. An amendment to Kuwait's election law in a decision made in May 2005 enfranchised Kuwait's women over the age of 21 with the vote and the right to stand for election. The parliamentary elections were held in June 2006, and although none of the 27 female candidates was elected, 60 percent of the Kuwaiti electorate was female.

There are still countries that do not condone women's suffrage or allow women the vote. In the United Arab Emirates, where the parliament is officially appointed, neither men nor women have the right to vote or to stand for election. Women in Bahrain have been struggling to exercise their right to vote since the country's constitution was amended in 2002. In Saudi Arabia, men took part in the first local elections ever held in that country in 2005, but women were still not allowed to exercise the right to vote or stand for election even though the election law of Saudi Arabia does not explicitly deny them that right.[1] Oman restricts the privilege to vote to a certain number of citizens, mostly male. Brunei and Vatican City still do not allow women the vote. Restrictions in Bhutan (one vote per family) and Lebanon (optional voting for women, who must have attained a certain level of education) make it impossible for women to vote in large numbers.

4

CIVIL RIGHTS

With the establishment of suffrage for women, the next logical step was to demand civil rights in other areas of living: from property ownership and job opportunities to financial and social rights. Depending on the country, this effort has mushroomed into a range of issues that include family leave and access to medical care.

The idea of equal rights for men and women, although starting with a simple premise naturally ensuing from the right to vote, would prove to be difficult in its interpretation. For example, some women's rights activists in the United States consider the Equal Rights Amendment a threat rather than an advantage, believing that the act could be used to fight the need for special employment considerations for pregnant women and mothers. The Equal Rights Amendment was first introduced to Congress in 1923, but it was not passed until 1972. It failed to win ratification by its 1982 expiration deadline and has been reintroduced a number of times since then, but without success.

One of the first steps toward equal rights of men and women has often been the establishment of equal opportunities in employment, as seen in the United States with the amendment of Title VII of the Civil Rights Act in 1964 and the establishment of the Equal Employment Opportunity Commission (EEOC). Affirmative action, a policy to ensure equal representation by women, ethnic, or disadvantaged groups in the workplace, was put in place by the EEOC. It began when the then-president, Lyndon B. Johnson, issued two executive orders, 11246 and 11375, requiring government contractors and educational institutions receiving federal funds to "correct the effects of past and present discrimination."

In the United States, opponents have characterized affirmative action as "reverse discrimination." Many see enforced hiring of individuals, not for their skills, but for filling of quotas based on their sex or ethnicity, as counterproductive.

The concept of affirmative action was taken up by governments around the world as a way to obligate society to provide opportunities for minorities and women, especially within managerial-ranked positions. Denmark followed a more radical approach by adopting the 1988 Equality Act, which established equal rights of the sexes. Since 1997, the European Court of Justice has upheld the use of affirmative-action programs for women in the public sector, establishing a legal precedent for the nations of the European Union (EU). Since 2000, the EU has been concerned with the application of the principle of equality without regard to race or ethnic origin to the national law of member states.

Australia and Great Britain have also implemented equal employment legislation that is largely responsible for women's access to management-level positions.

PROPERTY OWNERSHIP AND INHERITANCE RIGHTS

The ability of women to own property is also a right applied with varying degrees of cultural acceptance worldwide. The adoption of the Convention on the Elimination of All Forms of Discrimination against Women (CEDAW) on December 18, 1979, by the United Nations (UN) General Assembly has been a driving force behind asserting women's property rights. This "Treaty for the Rights of Women" has received ratification, as of November 2006, by 185 of the 192 UN member countries. The United States has signed but not ratified the treaty.

In order to own property in some Arab and Islamic countries such as Saudi Arabia and Iran, women are required to have either male proxy representation or permission from a male relative. In Afghanistan, a woman's right to inheritance varies depending on the application of the Islamic law in different regions, from only the trousseau (personal possessions of a bride) to a portion of the father's land. On the other hand, under Islamic law, Muslim women have, for the most part, been able to retain their own belongings and could even specify conditions in their marriage contracts, such as the right to divorce if their husband takes another wife. In contrast, until the late 1800s women's property in Western societies was given to their husbands when they married.

Property ownership is also a central issue in Kenyan society, in which two-thirds of the population is rural. Land is a vital asset of family life and status, and seen less as a commodity than as a part of the social fabric of living. In Kenya, women receive the rights to land through husbands, fathers, and sons. Privatization during colonial rule in the 1950s led to land registration, making the process more difficult for a woman to exercise tenure over property registered in her husband's name.

In China, inheritance and property rights apply equally to men and women, but in practice they are dependent on various factors. Often, land is owned by the state but rights to its use is extended to a family, a right that becomes nebulous if the husband dies.

Access to Education

Education has been among the first priorities of the women's movement in most countries. In the United States and Europe, women's access to education was limited to primary schooling until the late 1800s, except among the rich. When political rights proved extremely difficult to attain, women rallied for the right to enter higher educational institutions. By the 1950s, women in

Europe and the United States had access to a college education, but domestic duties were still expected to be their priority. This emphasis shifted in the 1970s, as women won political and legal rights to the same jobs as men but were often required to have had more education than men.

Women from other nations joined this rally for the fundamental right to be educated as the movement increasingly became more international. By the end of the 20th century, women had access to higher education in most countries around the world with the exception of some Asian and African countries. Women's poverty, disease, and illiteracy in sub-Saharan, Asian, and Latin American countries have been perceived as a direct result of their lack of education, leading to the universal "Education for All" program within the Dakar Framework for Action and the UN Millennium Development Goals. The programs seek to ensure that "by 2015 all children, particularly girls, children in difficult circumstances and those belonging to ethnic minorities, have access to and complete free and compulsory primary education of good quality."[2]

By the dawn of the 21st century, girls' primary school enrollments had significantly improved, especially in some of the lowest-income countries of sub-Saharan Africa, and South and West Asia. Gender and educational quality measures are increasingly visible in national education plans. With improved access to education was a decrease of the illiteracy rate among women, giving them better employment, health, educational, political, economic, and cultural opportunities. Eradicating illiteracy is considered a strategy of human rights by Human Rights Watch, a privately funded nongovernmental organization (NGO) founded in 1978. Almost a fifth of the world's adult population, an estimated 771 million, is illiterate, and two-thirds of them are women.[3] The United Nations Literacy Decade (2003–12) is focusing on women's literacy as a crucial element in establishing gender equality and ending poverty and "gender apartheid."

Social, Employment, and Economic Rights

Today, more women are employed in the world than ever before in the history of humankind. In addition, the role of women substantially changed in the latter half of the 20th century because of wars, decolonization, and lifestyle changes. The decolonization that was achieved by the national movements of the 20th century led to reforms that often included the liberation of women from traditional boundaries of home and responsibilities and their right to take on duties as far away from home as the military front.

SOCIAL CHANGES

More women were being paid for work in the latter half of the 20th century than ever before, including married women who had children. One possible reason for this trend is the increase in job opportunities for women associated with greater educational attainment. The other is that men are not making as much as they did in the past, in proportion to the increase in cost of living, leading to the need for more income.

As women began to enter the workforce in greater numbers, their traditional role and duties did not adjust as quickly. Women struggled with the need to balance duties at home and in the workplace and to define themselves as either "housewives" or "working women."

Women's social roles have changed as a result of their new participation in the workplace, concerns about job discrimination, and managing of dual careers. By the same token, men's roles in many societies have also changed, expanding to include domestic responsibilities and gender awareness in nearly all aspects of living.

Some cultures are dealing with radical changes to custom because of the country's liberation or women's enfranchisement, and women stake out a variety of positions in response. For instance, the practice by Muslim women of wearing burqas has led to debates inside Muslim countries and foreign powers on the privileges of wearing them. When France passed a law in 2005 that forced young Muslim women and girls not to wear their traditional head scarf to schools, it stirred heated public debate, as many women argued that a woman should have the right to choose the customs she wants to follow. Meanwhile, in Afghanistan, where women had to wear the burqa by law under the Taliban, the debate is around women not having to wear them, if they so choose. Conversely, women who are not required to wear them may want to.

Another area of social change involves the choice of using a married or "maiden" (also "birth") name. In most Muslim countries, women have traditionally been allowed to keep their own surnames after marriage. But in countries where this right is dictated by common law and does not require legal action, such as England, the United States, and much of Canada, choosing to keep one's birth name was rare until the mid-19th century. The act itself has grown to be more of a practical issue with the emergence of the professional woman who uses her maiden name professionally and her married name socially. This trend shifts as each generation of women reconsiders its social and professional priorities. In one informal survey among women in the United States in 2005, 81 percent of respondents took their spouse's last name, up from 71 percent in 2000. Meanwhile, hyphenated surnames dropped from 21 to 8 percent.[4] Chinese and Korean women keep their maiden names after marriage, although Chinese women who live abroad might insert their husbands' surname as a middle name. A married woman in Taiwan also uses her maiden name and appends her husband's name only when she wants people to know her marital status.

Most countries consider age 18 the legal minimal age for marriage for both men and women, which is also upheld by the UN Committee on the Elimination of Discrimination against Women. However, in some countries the legal minimal age is ignored as a result of poverty and traditional customs. The tradition of early marriage is most common in South Asia and sub-Saharan Africa. For example, according to UNICEF, 51 percent of girls in Bangladesh and 50 percent of girls in India were married by the age of 18 in 2000,[5] even though it is illegal in both countries for girls under the age of 18 to be wed. In Niger, where marriage is governed by custom and many communities begin to marry their children at puberty, 76 percent of all girls were married by the age of 18.[6]

THE "WORKING WOMAN"

Although women have been part of the labor force since humankind began, a woman's role has traditionally been largely associated with domestic duties of family care and child rearing. This perception began to change with industrialization, as women began to spend part of their time at paid work outside the home. The role of the so-called new woman at the end of the 19th century in Europe and the United States continued to evolve at a rapid pace during World War II and the 1950s.

In 1972, the assertion of Title VII of the Equal Employment Opportunities Act in the United States made it clear that employers could no longer discriminate in their hiring and employment practices on the basis of sex. Meanwhile, opponents of this act argued that problems with children were rising because of mothers who were no longer "on the job."

The idea of the "working woman" did not become an accepted notion in China until after 1949, when the socialist government began implementing measures to assist mothers with the double burden of home and work. With increased mobility, women—even in rural areas—are today participating more in industry and having a greater say in family decision making.

The urban, skilled, and educated woman who arose in Afghanistan in the 1950s and 1960s suffered a series of severe setbacks with the Soviet invasion in 1979, the subsequent civil war, and the establishment of the Taliban government in 1996. Even today, since the removal of the Taliban by international security forces in 2001, professional women are challenged by strict Muslim rules that tend to safeguard tradition.

African nations such as Kenya have known a different trajectory, being under colonial British rule until 1963. Kenyan women were disempowered by lack of property rights and education under colonial and native rule. Here, women have known a largely rural lifestyle, with limited professional opportunities within a patrilineal and patrilocal community.

Of the 2.8 billion workers worldwide in 2003, 1.1 billion, or 40 percent, were women. This is an increase of nearly 200 million women in employment in the past 10 years. However, women still face higher unemployment rates, receive lower wages than men, and represent 60 percent of the world's 550 million working poor.[7]

When looking at what occupations women now hold, the picture varies widely in different parts of the globe. Although agriculture remained the primary sector of employment for 40 percent of the world's population in 2005, this percentage is declining (except in Asia) and shifting toward the service and industry sectors, which are currently 39 and 21 percent, respectively, of global employment opportunities. Within the service sectors, women still primarily perform community, social, and personal services while men secure the better-paying jobs in finance, business, and real estate. The potential for women in industry to thrive on better wages and skill development is also limited by the fact that employers still prefer to hire male workers. Now, less than 10 years off from the UN Millennium Development Goal (MDG) of achieving parity by 2015, many estimate that most regions in the world will not reach this goal.

According to a 2006 report by the International Labour Organization (ILO), the trend of women's activity in the labor market varies by country. Overall, the trend of increased rates of young women's labor force participation noted in the 1980s and early 1990s has slowed in the non-EU countries of central and eastern Europe; the Commonwealth of Independent States (CIS) countries of Armenia, Azerbaijan, Georgia, Kyrgyz Republic, Moldova, Uzbekistan, and Tajikistan; East Asia; and sub-Saharan Africa; and even stopped in regions of Southeast Asia and South Asia. The number of working women increased in Latin America and the Caribbean, as well as in the Middle East and North Africa, where female participation grew from 25 percent of the labor force population in 1995 to about 30 percent in 2005.[8]

In most economies, women still tend to earn only 70 to 90 percent of what men earn for the same job. In industry, women might earn 75 to 79 percent of what male workers earn, depending on the country. In many economies, male teachers or health care workers might earn between 6 and 21 percent more than women earn for the same job, even though these professions are generally considered typical for women.[9] Furthermore, women on average occupy more of the lower-level positions and work in lower-paying industries, a pattern that leads to a significant wage disparity between the sexes.

Alongside these changes evolved different perceptions of the working woman, with her expectations growing beyond just equal pay and social benefits. She was also seeking stature. Although women still represent a small portion of management levels and few receive high salaries equal to those of their male counterparts, they are nevertheless more present in the workforce than ever before worldwide.

Beginning in the 1980s, women in management have been most noticeable in industrialized nations. In the United States, England, and Australia, more women have been able to make their way into management positions under enforced equal opportunity laws, but not without being challenged by office politics and status quo management. Issues such as sexual harassment and difficulty in achieving a balance with home management and child rearing have also contributed to the slow rate of growth.

In the United States, 46 percent of managerial positions were held by women in 2002, while within the European countries women held 26 to 41 percent of managerial positions. Most European Union countries have enacted legislation for equal opportunity, but the level of enforcement varies by country.[10] Still, high-profile positions, such as network news anchors, are starting to become available to women all over the world, and this trend may lead to more opportunities for women to hold influential positions.

At first, it was believed that women's lack of access to managerial positions was due to their absence of work experience in general. Now that women have over 25 years of exposure, it has become apparent that the problem has more to do with entrenched customs. Women's ability to share and delegate power, a skill developed from raising families, has even been cited as a reason why they may make naturally good managers. Still, women's enrollment in business schools in the United States has plateaued at 30 percent since 2000, while the numbers have peaked at 44 percent in medical and law schools. One reason more women are not pursing degrees in business may be a lack of female role models, incompatibility of careers in business with work/life balance, lack of confidence in math skills, and a lack of encouragement by employers, according to one study.[11]

SEXUAL HARASSMENT

In hand with increasing employment has risen the opportunity for discrimination against women in the workplace. As women have fought to establish themselves within the workplace, they have also had to define inappropriate behavior that affects them physically and emotionally as sexual harassment. In spite of legislation to protect women against sexual harassment, a pattern has emerged by which women often do not report cases because of fear of losing their jobs or positions.

The ILO recognized the implications of sexual harassment as a labor condition that negatively impacted women and their work performance in a 1985 Resolution of the International Labor Conference. Since then, sexual harassment is considered a form of violence, discrimination, and health risk, defined in CEDAW's General Recommendation 19, Article 11, to include

11

such unwelcome sexually determined behavior as physical contact and advances, sexually colored remarks, showing pornography and sexual demand, whether by words or actions. Such conduct can be humiliating and may constitute a health and safety problem; it is discriminatory when the woman has reasonable grounds to believe that her objection would disadvantage her in connection with her employment, including recruitment or promotion, or when it creates a hostile working environment.[12]

In spite of international support from the ILO and the UN, many countries still regard sexual harassment as a taboo subject even with national legislation in place to address it. About a third of industrialized global economies had laws on sexual harassment by 1992, while others classified sexual harassment under wrongful dismissal, tort, and criminal laws.

Australia, Canada, Denmark, Ireland, New Zealand, Sweden, the United Kingdom, and the United States are among countries that have equal employment opportunity laws. In the United States, where the Equal Employment Opportunity Commission has jurisdiction over sexual harassment cases, this issue won center stage in the 1990s as a series of high-profile sexual harassment cases made their way into the public eye. One poll in the United States indicated that four of 10 women were being victims of some kind of sexual harassment at work and nearly half of all women said they could perceive evidence of it at some point during their professional careers. This is about on par with similar reports of an estimated 40 to 50 percent of employed women in the European Union.

This percentage is lower in Denmark, where the Equal Treatment Act has been in effect since 1978 and the Gender Equality Act since 2003 to reinforce the protection. There, an estimated 15 percent of women have experienced some form of sexual harassment on the job.

In China, although a law exists to deter sexual harassment, a woman's fear of losing her job frequently overrides her legal right to report incidences. This is also true of women in most countries.

Japan, Switzerland, the United Kingdom, and the United States have applied tort law—a legal wrong for which the court usually offers remedy, such as monetary damages—to sexual harassment cases.

Criminal law in some countries applies to extreme cases of sexual harassment, such as assault or indecent behavior. France is among the few countries to have passed a criminal law related to sexual harassment.

WORKING MOTHERS AND CHILD CARE

With improved day care facilities and job protection under family leave legislation in many developed countries, marriage and children seem to have less of an effect on the percentage of women who are paid workers today than they had in the 1950s. As a result of the growth of the labor market, competitive trade, and increased pace of industrialization, this trend has now become global, radically changing women's lives the world over. Women are increasingly dependent on child care services and maternity benefits.

Beginning with the French *école maternelle* at the turn of the century, and the Russian model for state support to working mothers during World War I, today day care services range from sophisticated ones in Scandinavia and continental western Europe to basic and mediocre ones in the United States, Canada, the United Kingdom, and Japan. The quality of available care is often tied to economic factors, which include the total salary the two parents earn to be able to afford better care.

In most countries, women's maternity benefits are left to private enterprise and some legislation at the government level. Child care is often an essential component of government-based health care systems in nations with a social welfare tradition—including the former Soviet Union (USSR), Europe, Latin America, and Asia—where child care and working women are supported by politics, family, and society. Women in Canada are protected by a government-based medical system that gives them up to 18 weeks of maternity leave with employment insurance maternity benefits for 15 weeks, depending on the province. Most European countries, especially the Scandinavian countries, also offer paid leave. Women in Denmark receive up to 60 weeks' paid leave compared with 16 weeks in France, Netherlands, and Spain.[13] By comparison, the United States requires only 12 weeks of unpaid leave. In addition to Papua New Guinea, Lesotho (South Africa), and Swaziland, the United States has no national maternity program.

INDEPENDENT CREDIT

While cultivating their roles as a provider, women were finding fewer reasons for being declared a dependent of family or spouse and began seeking financial independence. Women's desire to do business and be self-reliant also meant having access to and control over their own credit and bank accounts.

In the 1970s, women around the globe began to organize themselves into associations of entrepreneurs or bankers in order to enhance their economic status and have an impact on economic policies. The right to have their own credit cards and bank accounts without a husband's approval was granted to married women in the United States in 1974. The ability to borrow money for investment led to economic improvements for women and often to positive social change in general as women used their newfound economic freedom to the benefit of their families. "Women's banks"—whereby women are encouraged to put their funds in a bank that will support fellow women's investments in small businesses—were started in the 1970s in different parts of the globe. Implementation of women's banks was especially successfully in India, where female trade union workers and poor self-employed women were forming their own banks. The successful paradigm in India was later implemented in Africa in the 1990s. One experience in a small suburb in the Republic of Benin saw its bank membership grow in 1992 from 15 women to 2,000 women, with a combined $20,000 in savings and $40,000 in loans, and a 99 percent reimbursement rate.[14] A similar trend arose in Japan in the late 1990s as an alternate mode for women whose needs to finance businesses were overlooked during times of recession or in the name of traditional banking approaches. Another example is Women's World Banking, founded by the former World Bank executive Nancy Berry. It has made a difference to many women, including a farmer in Kenya who now exports roses and a Bosnian woman who now owns three food shops. With some 18 million women worldwide receiving microfinance loans, the United Nations dubbed 2005 the Year of Microcredit.

The African Centre for Women (ACW) organized a meeting in Kampala, Uganda, in 1994 to evaluate the establishment of an African bank for women. The meeting was attended by high-level experts invited from Burundi, Cameroon, Ghana, Kenya, Mali, Nigeria, Sierra Leone, Uganda, and Zimbabwe. Their expertise ranged from finance and banking to economic planning and improvement of women's access to financial resources. Observers from the United Nations Development Programme (UNDP), the United Nations International Research and Training Institute for the Advancement of Women (INSTRAW), and the Lusaka-based Multinational Programming and Operational Centre (MULPOC) also attended. The feasibility study conducted during the meeting helped to establish the base for a financial institution that could cater to specific needs of African women at all economic levels, defined the mode of operation, and identified financial sources for getting it started.

ENROLLMENT IN THE MILITARY

Women's involvement in the military was not part of international discourse until 1961, when the first North Atlantic Treaty Organization (NATO) Conference of Senior Women Officers of the Alliance with delegates from Denmark, the Netherlands, Norway, the United Kingdom, and the United States took place in Copenhagen, Denmark. Since then, the committee has grown with the NATO alliance, in which 25 nations are represented today. Iceland is the only country missing since there is no military in that country.

Since the end of the cold war era in the early 1990s, many nations have considered doing away with male-conscription armies and maintaining volunteer armies of men and women. In the countries where military personnel include females, women often occupy noncombatant roles as physicians, lawyers, pilots, paratroopers, military police, air traffic controllers, heavy equipment operators, photojournalists, and forklift operators.[15] Canada, Belgium, Denmark, and Norway began allowing women to choose their occupations in the army in the 1990s. In Britain, women were allowed to join air and sea combat units, but not ground units.

Debates turn around women's ability to fight, gender integrated training, provocation of discipline problems among male members by the presence of women, and the question of whether women add to or detract from a nation's virile image and the capacity of its armed forces. The issue of equal rights becomes enmeshed with issues of military strategy.

Italy was the stage for a conference about this topic in 1992 as it was the only NATO country at the time to prohibit women from active duty (AD), although they were allowed to participate in the other roles mentioned. Italy is still reluctant to allow women to serve in combat within the armed forces. In 2005, 1 percent of Italy's armed forces were women.[16] The U.S. Department of Defense defines AD as full-time duty soldiers and sailors. Members of the reserve components and national guard may serve on AD or training duty but are considered separate parts of the military.

In recent years, women's enrollment in military service academies for officer training and service in active combat has sparked public debate in several countries, including the United States, Australia, Canada, Algeria, Zimbabwe, and Nicaragua. Although women traditionally had to fulfill military service requirements in Israel, they can be exempted for religious, physical, or psychological reasons.

The way wars are fought is changing, however, with the added element of terrorism, which does not discriminate by gender. In the more recent conflict in Iraq (2003 to present), enough American female soldiers have suffered casualties that they are being trained to handle firearms while they do their "support" jobs as drivers, medics, and the like.[17]

Family Health and Sexuality

HUMAN RIGHTS

The core right of a person to own his or her body is taken for granted in many countries now. However, not so long ago women were thought of as property, or "chattel," of their fathers or husbands. This notion persists in some nations and is upheld by tradition in many African cultures. Some, such as the Taliban in Afghanistan, defend the tradition in the name of protecting women and girls from societal pressures or defacement.

Whether women should have a choice over the destiny of their bodies is also still very much debated. A woman's ability to choose whether to experience childbirth, end it prematurely, or use her reproductive capacity as a means of income and/or to benefit others, as is the case with surrogate motherhood (often referred to as "womb for hire," but sometimes involving family members or friends without financial remuneration), varies not only from country to country, but also according to cultural and religious preferences.

DEFINING ROLES WITHIN THE FAMILY AND THE WORKPLACE

The family has evolved dramatically in developed countries since the 1970s, causing gender roles to be redefined. Higher education and increased job opportunities have caused both women and men to delay marriage. Smaller households, delayed childbearing, declining birth rates, increased divorce and single parenthood, and family mobility are all contributing factors as well. In eastern Asia, western Europe, and most developed countries, there are few early marriages (below 2 percent of the population), with the average age for first marriage between 25 and 30 in 2000. In transitional economies in eastern Europe and central and western Asia, most women are marrying in their early 20s, a trend that has been maintained since the early 1990s.[18]

With the increasing number of women in the workplace since the latter part of the 20th century, the role of man and woman, or husband and wife, in the family setting has changed dramatically since the 1950s. As women have increasingly occupied the workplace, they have expanded their roles from child rearing to sharing the identity of "breadwinner," or earning income outside the home, with men. By the same token, men are participating more in child rearing, albeit still not to the same extent as women. This transition has been more evident in some countries than in others. For instance, Denmark leads the way as a model for the modern couple's equal division of labor. There, nearly 50 percent of men today are responsible for 26 to 50 percent of the housework in households where both adults work full time.[19]

As a result of these changes, comparing male and female behavior and physical gestures became a topic for scientific, social, and economic study that often centered around the question of whether it is a person's (biological) sex or (socially determined) gender that shapes his or her behavior. At the start of the 21st century, men's studies developed into a formal academic area of study in Western countries, focusing on men's roles in the workplace and family as well as men's health and masculinity.

The UN proclamation of 1994 as the Year of the Family around the theme "Family: Resources and Responsibilities in a Changing World" was largely an attempt to preserve some of the values of family structure, while bearing in mind the need for gender roles to evolve. These issues were explored at the International Conference on Population and Development in that same year.

ACCESS TO MEDICAL CARE

An issue that moved to the forefront in the 1990s and early 2000s for women around the globe is access to health care. This ranges from access to basic care such as immunizations and screenings for pregnancy, human immunodeficiency virus/acquired immunodeficiency syndrome (HIV/AIDS), and other sexually transmitted diseases (STDs), to more sophisticated tests to diagnose heart disease, breast cancer, and bone density.

The economic consequences of women's low access to health care have been magnified in developing countries, where many women are living with HIV/AIDs and in poverty. In 2005, 17.3 million of the 38.6 million adults living with HIV worldwide were women.[20] Nearly three-quarters of these women were in sub-Saharan Africa, where they made up nearly 57 percent of adults living with HIV. High prevalence rates were also occurring in heavily populated countries such as India and China, where the number of people living with HIV infection in 2005 was estimated at 5.7 million and 650,000, respectively.[21] UNICEF reported in 2005 that worldwide, about 1 percent of pregnant women were HIV-positive, with a 35 percent chance that their child would be born HIV-positive if no prevention measures were taken. On its current course, international population researchers are expecting the incidence of AIDS to kill 31 million people in India, 19 million in China, and 100 million in sub-Saharan Africa by 2025.[22] This outlook may modify if the current strategies of routine blood screening for the presence of HIV and provision of antiretroviral prophylaxis therapy to HIV-positive pregnant women to prevent mother-to-child transmission persist. The other consequence of AIDS has been the increase in the number of orphaned children, who then experience malnutrition, illness, abuse, and sexual exploitation such as child trafficking.

Countries that have been conservative in acknowledging the presence of AIDS, regarding it as taboo for public discussion, such as in the Caribbean and Latin America, are beginning to emerge with public campaigns and greater support from churches. These countries are coming to terms with having one of the highest rates of adults and children living with HIV in the world, at 330,000 and 1.6 million, respectively, in 2005. AIDS is considered the primary cause of mortality for adults under the age of 50 in Caribbean countries.[23]

The problem also exists in developed countries. In the United States, 1.2 million people live with HIV, and the rate of infection among women is increasing, with one in four new cases the result of injecting drugs in addition to having unprotected sex. African-American and Hispanic women in the United States, who represent less than one-quarter of all women in the United States, account for 80 percent of AIDS cases reported among women in 2002, according to the U.S. Center for Disease Control and Prevention. AIDS has become the leading cause of death among African-American women age 25 to 34.[24] Similarly, a growing proportion of new infections are occurring in women in Canada and Europe as a result of unprotected sex.

Prevention and education can make a marked difference in outcomes involving HIV and AIDS. A pregnant woman can decrease the chances of passing on HIV to her baby by 50 percent by taking antiretroviral drugs. Her receiving the drugs thus has a disproportionate effect on preventing the suffering among children.

While high-income countries rate ischemic heart disease, cerebrovascular disease, lung cancer, lower-respiratory disease, and breast cancer among the 10 leading causes of death and disability for women, low- and middle-income nations report these and HIV/AIDs as the leading cause of death.[25]

The quality of medical care and access to it varies from country to country. Additionally, women's access to health care services is influenced by social customs. In most countries, their access to health care and benefits is largely related to economic stature. Health disparity—or the unequal treatment of women based on social, economic, and ethnic background—is being discussed on an international scale by the World Health Organization as it seeks accountability for the global 70 million women and their newborn babies who are uncared for annually, or the over 500,000 maternal deaths each year worldwide from preventable conditions.[26]

SELF-DETERMINED REPRODUCTIVE RIGHTS: ACCESS TO CONTRACEPTIVES

The development of contraceptives and access to them has allowed women of reproductive age across the globe to exercise their rights to reproduce and have children or abstain from having them. With the advent of safe and efficacious methods of family planning since the 1960s, the use of contraception—including female sterilization, the intrauterine device (IUD), and oral contraceptives—has steadily risen to 61 percent among married and partnered women worldwide.[27] The initial reservations of the 1970s about the Pill and the IUD have been relieved by decades of research from the pharmaceutical industry, governments, and independent organizations, which are now moving in the direction of offering increased options to women. This trend has, in turn, been perceived as a means for empowering women by giving them better control over their lives.

On the other hand, heavily populated areas, such as Africa, India, and China, have also introduced contraception as a coercive means to control the population. Women's groups rallied for greater emphasis on strategies that encouraged people's participation in programs to exercise their voluntary rights to use contraceptives. Curiously, the 1994 International Conference on Population and Development in Cairo, Egypt, did not emphasize contraceptive use, in spite of the growing AIDS epidemic. Condoms, for instance, are considered an important and effective measure in HIV prevention.

Between 1995 and 2002, contraceptive use by women who were married or in a partnership varied dramatically by region and wealth distribution within the region. As many as 201 million women worldwide were still lacking access to contraceptives in 2005.[28] Contraceptive access has been slow, if not stagnant, in the world's least developed nations (LDNs)—largely made up of sub-Saharan, Asian (including Afghanistan), and Oceanian countries, and Haiti; as a result, the fertility in these countries averaged 119 births per 1,000 women ages 15 to 19 compared with the global rate of 56 births for that age group.[29] In Europe, anywhere from half to three-quarters of the female population of reproductive age used contraceptives.[30]

A major factor in contraceptive use is wealth. On average, the poorest women are four times less likely to use contraception than the wealthiest. Access to contraceptives, however, is also tempered by cultural and religious beliefs both within the United States, where an estimated 95 percent of women have used some form of birth control during the course of their life, and worldwide. Several new methods are being developed, including male hormonal products, that are adding to the choices available in wealthier nations.

INVOLUNTARY EUGENIC STERILIZATIONS

Another means of controlling reproduction is sterilization. In women this procedure is usually done by tying the fallopian tubes (tubal ligation). Although the right to choose sterilization as a form of birth control is an issue in some countries, it is involuntary sterilization, usually employed by the government as a means to control birth rates, that has received public scrutiny.

In the United States, the issue of forced sterilizations was highly publicized in the 1920s with the case of *Buck v. Bell*. In 1924, the state of Virginia adopted a statute authorizing the compulsory sterilization of the mentally retarded for the protection and health of the state. Carrie Buck was a dependent in the care of the state of Virginia. In 1927, the Supreme Court decided that it was in the state's interest to have her sterilized. Virginia's eugenics law was partially repealed in 1974 and completely repealed in 1979, but *Buck v. Bell* has yet to be overturned.

During the reign of Indira Gandhi (1917–84), India used forced vasectomies, a form of sterilization, on fathers; that policy led to public resentment of family planning in that country that persists today. Family planning has since focused on women, with sterilization and contraception programs, but educational campaigns have been hampered by illiteracy and poverty.

SURROGATE MOTHERHOOD

Ten to 15 percent of married couples worldwide are unable to have children. As a solution to being unable to reproduce an offspring, surrogacy, also known as "womb for hire," has become one of many assisted reproductive technologies. Surrogate motherhood dates back to biblical times, when Sarah, the wife of Abraham, could not have children in the first decades of her marriage. She gave her handmaid, Hagar, to her husband to produce a child.

Assisted reproduction has become a field of science that includes the technologies involved in surrogate motherhood. The act of a woman's bearing a child for an infertile woman or couple is slowly gaining acceptance. Ethical issues are numerous: from the pros and cons of using excess embryos from medical research, to the possibility that the surrogate will decide to keep the baby, to the legal question of handing over a child after delivery for a fee.

In the United States, surrogate mothers are paid between $10,000 and $15,000 for their services, in partial payment if they miscarry, and nothing if they withdraw from the agreement. Commercial surrogacy is illegal and states have different laws about the way surrogacy is regulated.[31] In the case concerning "Baby M" in 1987, the New Jersey Supreme Court upheld the maternal right of a surrogate mother who refused to surrender her baby and ordered that custody and visitation be arranged as if following a divorce. With this decision, limits on surrogacy contracts and custody rights were defined.

European countries also have specialized laws to cope with surrogate motherhood. Italy considers the mother to be the woman who gives birth to the child, regardless of the source of the egg. A similar law in the Netherlands makes it difficult for commissioning parents to have custody over their surrogate-born child.

In 1995, Israel's High Court of Justice overturned a 1987 law barring surrogate motherhood and now allows it with strict supervision. Restrictions include that the surrogate mother must be a full citizen of Israel, preferably not married, and not a relative of either of the commissioning parents.

Opponents of surrogacy feel that bearing a child for others in exchange for large sums of money may be an attractive option for poor women. They perceive surrogacy as a form of baby selling that takes advantage of a women's economic situation and should be banned.

ABORTION RIGHTS

The earliest documented right to abortion dates back to the 1327 Twinslayer's Case and 1348 Abortionist's Case in England, which helped establish a common law authorizing termination of a pregnancy at any time, when the judges—in pre-Reformation England all Roman Catholic—refused to make causing the death of a fetus a legal offense. Abortion before the "quickening"—when the fetus moves or kicks in approximately the 21st week—was never punishable under English common law, nor considered a moral problem.

In mainland Europe and the United States, abortion was not regulated by the state until the 19th century. In the United States, opponents of abortion and birth control have accused Margaret Sanger, the nurse who pioneered family planning and founded birth control clinics in the early 1900s, with eugenicism and racism. The 1973 *Roe v. Wade* case was the first court case decided by the U.S. Supreme Court to establish a woman's constitutional right to an abortion in the first trimester of pregnancy, and it is still being debated today. The decision, written by Justice Harry Blackmun and based on the residual right of privacy, struck down dozens of state antiabortion statutes, but the right to abortion has been meeting resistance in other ways.

An ongoing concern of women's organizations in the United States is how the Supreme Court might handle abortion cases in the future. In 1976, the U.S. Congress barred the use of federal funds to reimburse the medical expenses involved in abortions under its Medicaid program, except when the woman's life is endangered by a full-term pregnancy or in the case of rape or incest.

In the same year *Roe v. Wade* was decided by the Supreme Court, abortion became a bargaining chip when discussed in the context of foreign aid. Congress amended the Foreign Assistance Act, sponsored by Republican senator Jesse Helms from North Carolina, prohibiting the use of U.S. foreign aid funds for abortion. In August 1984, at the International Conference on Population in Mexico City, the U.S. delegation, headed by James Buckley, announced that the United States would not authorize funding of foreign NGOs that provide, refer, counsel, or advocate for abortion. The executive branch policy stayed in effect until 1993 and became known as the Mexico City Policy, later dubbed the "Global Gag Rule" by its opponents. The ruling has affected family planning services around the globe, including clinics in Kenya that depended on abortion as a way to control multiple births in Kenyan families. Of concern in Asia, Africa, and Latin America is the one in 10 pregnancies that will end in unsafe abortion.[32]

In China, on the other hand, the government encourages the use of abortion as part of its one-child policy to control the population increase, leading to resentment among people who view the government's policies as an imposition on their lives.

According to the Guttmacher Institute, family planning and reproductive health have lost priority as development issues since the International Conference on Population and Development in 1994. Reproductive health was noticeably absent from the eight goals discussed at the UN Millennium Development Conference in 2000.[33]

ATYPICAL GENDER ROLES

Gay rights have moved beyond the social arena into political and legal fields with sufficient success that legislation establishing civil rights has been awaiting ratification by the courts in many countries since the latter half of the 20th century. Although a variety of sexual orientations—bisexual, transvestite, and transgender—are publically known, no others have tried to establish civil rights in the same way.

Still considered taboo in many countries for even a public debate, gay rights have moved to the news in other countries as supporters have fought for the right to same-sex marriages and other sociopolitical and economic benefits afforded to opposite-sex couples.

Same-sex marriage affording the same legal rights and benefits as marriages between heterosexual partners was now recognized in Belgium, Canada, the Netherlands, Spain, the U.S. state of Massachusetts, and South Africa, by the end of 2006. Civil unions and other forms of partnerships for gay couples have been legally established in many different countries and with varying amounts of benefits.

In 1989, Denmark became the first country to introduce civil partnerships, establishing for same-sex couples the same privileges as for married heterosexual couples, with few exceptions, including adoption. This paved the way for other European nations to allow civil unions for same-sex partners. In France, the National Assembly passed an equality law in 1999 known as the civil solidarity pact (*pacte civil de solidarité*, or PaCS). It permitted same-sex partners to be joined in a civil union contract in order to organize their common life. The couple is required to register a common declaration with the local court where they are resident. The contract makes them eligible for joint taxation benefits after three years. The tenant's lease can be transferred to one partner if the other leaves their common home or dies. A partner who does not have social protection (health benefits) may enjoy the other partner's social protection. The law does not address lineage, adoption, or custody roles.

In the United States, political activism for lesbian rights first emerged around 1970, in the wake of the feminist movement, which then divided over whether to associate women's gay rights with its campaign. The Stonewall uprising of 1969 is considered the initiating act of the modern gay rights movement. Youths protested on June 27 by throwing bricks at local police during a routine raid of the Stonewall Inn, which catered to gay and lesbian customers in the Greenwich Village area of New York City. The fact that gay rights are now part of the platform of the National Organization for

Women (NOW) has helped, however, to make the movement more main-stream, so much so that it is today a subject of television plots and films. Activism for sexual freedom and basic legal, political, social, and economic rights has led actors and politicians to reveal their private lives in the name of making a difference.

On the other hand, gay marriage or civil unions are challenged by tra-ditional and fundamentalist views in Asia and Latin America, where religion has a greater influence over society. In the United States, states have been amending their state constitutions to ban same-sex marriage. Nevertheless civil unions are permitted in Brazil and Argentina. In India, homosexuality is still considered illegal. A zero-tolerance policy by the Chinese government means homosexual practices are treated as a mental illness. Since the late 1990s, Chinese psychiatrists have debated the classification of homosexuality in the Chinese Classification of Mental Disorders. After the People's Republic of China's (PRC's) rise to power in 1949, any open display of or discussion about gay or lesbian orientation was suppressed. Urban life has evolved somewhat to accommodate gay nightclubs, and the Internet has provided some room for discussion, but still with much restraint. Although the Chi-nese parliament has proposed same-sex marriage legislation since 2003, as of 2006 the bill had not passed.

TRADITIONAL PRACTICES: FEMALE GENITAL MUTILATION

Female genital mutilation (FGM), also known as female circumcision and female cutting, is the practice of cutting any part of the female genitalia for cultural (rather than medical) reasons. There are three kinds of FGM:

1. Clitoridectomy: the cutting of the "hood" or tip of the clitoris, leaving the muscles and nerves intact.
2. Excision: the cutting away of the entire clitoris and the labia minora. This ensures that because of the destruction of muscle and nerves, the woman does not experience pleasure during the sexual act. However, the entrance is not restricted.
3. Infibulation: the entire clitoris, the labia minora, as well as at least two-thirds of the labia majora are cut away. The two sides of the vulva (external genitalia) are then sewn together, leaving just enough room for a match-stick to pass through. If a finger can pass through, the hole is considered too large.[34]

Over 40 Muslim and non-Muslim countries—mostly the sub-Saharan Africa countries of Egypt, Sudan, Somalia, Ethiopia, Kenya, and Chad—prac-tice some form of circumcision of men and women for cultural, social, and economic reasons. FGM is perceived as a cultural custom among various religious groups and is not itself a religious rite. Clitoridectomy and exci-sions are practiced in Chad, countries of West Africa, Kenya, and Tanzania. Excision is most common in Kenya and much of Africa, often done without anesthesia and with a blunt knife or a razor blade, by a woman. According to the Kenya Demographic and Health Survey of 2003, the Somali, Kisii, and Masai women have the highest percentage of female circumcision among the 20 or so ethnic groups residing within Kenya.[35]

Medical consequences of a practice perceived by many as a violation of women and girls that adversely affects their health and well-being include infection, hemorrhaging, trauma, and death, not to mention the psychologi-cal trauma that lives with them for the rest of their lives.

As immigrants move to the United States, they take with them their customs. According to the Centers for Disease Control and Prevention in Atlanta, Georgia, an estimated 168,000 girls and women in the United States had been circumcised as of 1990. The U.S. Congress and several states have outlawed the practice of infibulation since 1996. Similar laws have been passed in Europe, New Zealand, and Australia, as well as in a number of African countries.

Violence against Women

Violence is a major and growing public health problem across the world, takes many forms, and is subject to cultural interpretation. International organizations such as the World Health Organization (WHO) have played a key role in addressing the connection between women's development and violence, especially during wartime and with domestic partners. The adop-tion by WHO of Resolution WHA49.25 in 1996 drew attention to the serious consequences of violence—in both the short term and the long term—for individuals, families, communities, and countries and stressed the damaging effects of violence on health care services. The UN Resolution of December 17, 1993, on pornography was another opportunity to evaluate the connec-tion between violence and women.

PORNOGRAPHY AS FREE SPEECH

The word *pornography* is derived from Greek and means "writing about prostitution." Pornography as an act of free speech is complex and polarizes around several viewpoints, ranging from consent and self-choice, to preven-tion of violence.

Antipornography laws have been advocated by religious fundamental-ists and feminists who believe the public portrayal of women in explicit sexual conduct provokes violence toward women and is socially demeaning, thus violating their civil rights. Those who support antipornography laws see pornography as a form of violence that "glamorizes the degradation and maltreatment of women and asserts their subordinate function as mere receptacles for male lust."[36]

In the literature and research studies on the topic, the definition of what constitutes pornography and the way it is measured vary. The definition ranges from explicit sexual images to coercive images.[37] The only link research has consistently shown between violence against women and pornography are the common elements of sexual repression and aggression. Whether the violent act was committed as a result of the sexual fantasies that were inspired by the pornographic images or was a result of unrelated emotional or psychological causes has not been measured consistently. For example, a 2006 study in Denmark using 200 randomly selected young Danish adult males (100) and females (100), aged 18–30 as a representative sample, suggested that violent pornographic material did not induce changes in the experimental group when compared with the control group. Attitudes toward women, sexism, rape, myth acceptance, acceptance of interpersonal violence, and gender stereotypes did not change as a result of watching hard-core pornography, although doing so did cause emotionality and negativity.[38] The United Nations has encouraged further evaluation of the bearing of pornography and prostitution on men's violence against women.

The legal boundaries for pornography involving children are more established, including the universally accepted Convention on the Rights of the Child (1989, ratified by all countries except Somalia and the United States) and its Optional Protocol on the Sale of Children, Child Prostitution and Child Pornography (2000, signed by 115 countries as of December 2006).

GENDER-BASED VIOLENCE: RAPE AND DOMESTIC ABUSE

The World Health Organization reports that 10 to 69 percent of women worldwide have been physically assaulted by an intimate male partner at some point in their life.[39] Within Japan alone, 10 percent of women reported physical abuse by a close relation and 57 percent suffered a combination of physical, psychological, and sexual abuse. In other countries, such as Mexico, over 50 percent of physically assaulted women were also sexually abused by their partners. In Nicaragua, 40 percent of women of reproductive age have experienced violence by a partner, of whom 31 percent reported its occurrence during one or more pregnancies.[40] A 1995 study by the Pan American Health Organization of 500 women and 1,000 service providers in 10 countries in Latin America, called La Ruta Crítica (Critical Path), identified two factors that led women to seek help: recurrence or severity of violence and fearing for one's life or that of the children. Economics was an important factor as well, in whether women felt they could support themselves.[41]

A 2005 landmark study on domestic violence sponsored by WHO, which began interviewing more than 24,000 women in 1997 from rural and urban areas in 10 countries (Bangladesh, Brazil, Ethiopia, Japan, Namibia, Peru, Samoa, Serbia and Montenegro, Thailand, and the United Republic of Tanzania), is the first survey of this scope to be done outside North America and Europe.[42] The survey found that 25 to 50 percent of all women physically assaulted by their partners suffered physical injuries as a direct result. These abused women were twice as likely as nonabused women to have poor health, including physical and mental problems, even years after the violence took place. Symptoms included suicidal thoughts and attempts, mental distress, and physical symptoms such as pain, dizziness, and vaginal discharge.

Although this issue may have been present since the dawn of time, it is only recently that women have created means by which to litigate against it in some countries. In most countries, there are still cultural as well as legal barriers that prevent women from seeking protection against physical violence and rape.

Acts of violence against women include rape and sexual assault. In the United States, which has one of the highest rates in the world, it was estimated that as many as 89,000 women were forcibly raped in 1999. Under the Victims of Crime Act (VOCA), 3.8 million people reported themselves as victims of violence in 2003, 49 percent of whom were victims of domestic violence; the majority of cases took place at home.[43]

There was an increase in legislation to protect women during the 1990s and law enforcement has taken a more active role in domestic disputes in some countries. There has also been an increase in the number of women's and children's shelters and rape crisis hot lines.

In the United States, rape is treated as a violent felony and tough sentences await repeat offenders. Since 2004, under the Crime Victims' Rights Act, domestic violence is also punishable as a federal offense, thereby mitigating against previous weakness of state-based jurisdictions.

WAR AND VIOLENCE AGAINST WOMEN

War, or armed conflict, as a form of collective violence, is a context for a variety of forms of violence against women, from rape, forced labor, death, and exposure to communicable diseases such as HIV/AIDS and infections. Nearly 19 percent of global violence-related deaths, or 301,000 deaths in 2002, resulted from war, in which the majority occurred in low- to middle-income countries.[44] Sixty to 70 percent of those deaths were among people not engaged in fighting and included women and children.[45]

Rape was frequently used as a weapon of war in recent civil wars in the latter half of the 20th century to terrorize and break up communities. Conflicts in Somalia, Bosnia-Herzegovina, and Kashmir have caused human rights activists to watch closely and insist that rape cases not be dismissed as private crimes or as commonplace. An estimated 10,000 to 60,000 women were raped in Croatia and Bosnia-Herzegovina alone between 1992 and 1995. Bangladesh, Liberia, southern Sudan, and Uganda have also reported high incidences of war-related rape cases. As many as 250,000 to 500,000 women were raped during the 1994 genocide in Rwanda.[46]

Given the psychological impact on those who survive and their families, much has been needed in the way of developing programs to cope with displaced families and women. UNIFEM has been implementing training programs for law enforcement officials in handling rape crimes, and NGOs in war-torn areas have been active in providing remedial action, but more efforts are needed on an international scale.

FEMALE INFANTICIDE

Infanticide, mutilation, abandonment, and other forms of violence against children date back to ancient civilizations. In some countries, the pressure to control populations has led to illegal means of killing female babies. In China, where the one-child (Planned Birth) policy is in effect, and India, where sterilization is encouraged after birth of a third child, the perception is that male children provide more revenue for the family. The act of female infanticide—the abandonment and killing of female infants—has been increasing in South Asia as a way to alter the man/woman ratio. The World Health Organization has identified a pattern of fatal abuse of children that is more prevalent in low-income countries.[47]

The issue of female infanticide was raised at the Beijing Conference in 1995 and has continued to garner interest as one form of child abuse. The practice continues in India and China and among the Inuit of Canada and North America.

HUMAN TRAFFICKING AND PROSTITUTION

Human trafficking is defined as "the recruitment, transportation, transfer, harboring or receipt of persons, by means of the threat or use of force or other forms of coercion, of abduction, of fraud, of deception, of the abuse of power or of a position of vulnerability or of the giving or receiving of payments or benefits to achieve the consent of a person having control over another person, for the purpose of exploitation," by the Protocol to Prevent, Suppress and Punish Trafficking in Persons, Especially Women and Children, which supplements the United Nations Convention against Transnational Organized Crime. Involuntary trafficking is illegal in most countries and 117 countries have signed the treaty since its adoption in 2000 and enforcement in 2003. According to 2006 estimates, humans are trafficked from 127 origin countries for exploitation in 137 destination countries, making it a global problem.[48]

Sexual trafficking is especially prevalent during wartime violence and economic difficulty, when women are deceived, coerced, or kidnapped and enslaved into prostitution. The greatest incidence of trafficking occurs in Asia, for origin, transit, and destination, with China and Thailand ranking highest. Africa is a significant source of origin for victims of trafficking. Central and southeastern Europe are origins for women who are then exploited in western Europe. The Commonwealth of Independent States (11 former Soviet Union countries) and Latin America are significant providers of the international traffic that takes women to western Europe and North America. Oceania (New Zealand and Australia) and the United States are mostly destination countries for the international slave trade.

Trafficking is distinguished from prostitution, a profession in which a person offers to provide sexual services in return for money. Prostitution is legal in many countries, including in the Netherlands, where prostitutes are taxpaying and unionized professionals. On the other extreme are countries such as Iraq, where prostitution carried the death penalty until the United States–led invasion in 2003. The liberal laws tolerating prostitution in some western European countries have made it difficult to distinguish traffickers who exploit young girls and women in global networks against their will from prostitution rings. The protocol implicates prostitution in trafficking in the following way: "Exploitation shall include, at a minimum, the exploitation of the prostitution of others or other forms of sexual exploitation, forced labor or services, slavery or practices similar to slavery, servitude or the removal of organs."

Although no accurate numbers exist, the estimated number of women and young girls who are trafficked worldwide is in the area of 700,000 to 2 million a year annually, with profits of between $5 and $7 billion a year. As of 2006, as many as 50,000 girls were taken into the United States each year. In eastern Europe, 500,000 women have been forced into commercial sex.[49] Of the 114 countries that reported features about trafficked victims, women (87 percent) and girls (54 percent) were the majority of victims being trafficked, while others reported that boys (14 percent) and men (10 percent) also were among those being trafficked.[50]

Religion and Spirituality

The relationship between women and religions is complex. Reflecting women's general status in society all major religions were traditionally male dominated, and many religious leaders have contributed to the spread of misogyny, the hatred of women. The adherence to sacred texts and customs, and their traditional interpretation, has also made it difficult for women to modify the way they are treated by religions. Beginning in the 20th century, the possibility of religious freedom took on several forms, from the stance of choosing not to adhere to a faith (agnostic or atheist), to a modification of traditional religious modalities (freethinkers), to adoption of an individual or gender-based spirituality, better known as "new age." All major religions have had remarkable spiritual woman leaders such as Rabia al-Adawihay (712–801), a great Sufi mystic; Hildegard von Bingen (1098–1179), a German nun renowned for her talents in mathematics, science, medicine, music, and theology; Muktabai (d. 1297), a Hindu saint; and Mother Teresa (1910–97), an Albanian nun who founded the Missionaries of Charity in India.

The women's movement has been supported by some religions more than others. Protestant sects sympathetic to female emancipation—primarily Quakers and Unitarians, who believe in the equality of men and women before God—gave rise to many of the leading women suffragists in Europe and the United States. Mary Wollstonecraft, author of the *Vindication of Women's Rights,* was influenced by the Unitarian Church in Europe. Susan B. Anthony, Lucretia Mott, and Alice Paul were all raised as Quakers.

Women's role in all the major religions of the world has improved significantly over the past few decades. The efforts have concentrated on gaining access to leadership roles, analyzing and reinterpreting religious history and sacred texts, and creating innovative forms of religious and spiritual practices.

LEADERSHIP ROLES IN RELIGIOUS WORSHIP

Some scholars argue that male dominance in world religions may have been a relatively recent development considering the role of women in mythology and antiquity. A gradual decline in the importance and status of women has been documented for the Judeo-Christian tradition, Hinduism, Buddhism, and Islam.

Lucretia Mott was recorded as a Quaker minister in 1821, and Antoinette Blackwell was ordained a minister by the First Congregational Church in 1853. It was not until the United Methodist Church began to ordain women in the 1980s, however, that female clergy began to serve in numbers. The Anglican and Episcopal Churches followed suit in the 1990s. By 2001, over 1,000 women were serving as ordained ministers in the Southern Baptist Convention. The authorization of female priests and bishops by the Methodist Church is evidence of women gaining more power within the church.[51] Nevertheless, women in the clergy have been faced with issues similar to those in other domains, namely, unequal pay and requirements, as women have often had to have more education to do the same task.

U.S. federal labor statistics indicate that the number of women who describe themselves as "clergy" increased from 16,408 in 1983 to 43,542 in 1996. As of 1996, one in every eight members of the clergy was female in the United States.

The percentage of female graduate students at 229 North American Christian schools of theology rose from 10 percent in 1972 to 30 percent in 1997. In some schools of theology, more than 50 percent of the students are women.[52]

Within the Lutheran Evangelical Church, the national church of Denmark, 40 percent of all priests were women by 1995, the year the first woman became bishop.

The Roman Catholic Church, the faith of about 25 percent of the U.S. population, continues to bar women from ordination worldwide.

Although Orthodox Judaism does not permit female rabbis, more liberal Jewish movements have begun to allow them in recent years. Reform movements in Judaism have also put in question traditional rituals that separate women from men in prayer. In the United States in 2006, Dina Najman was made spiritual leader—not as a rabbi, but as a *rash Kehillah* (head of congregation)—of a modern Orthodox community in New York City that adheres closely to Jewish law.

Within Buddhism, it was believed that Buddha not only established an order of *bhikhsu* (monks) but, albeit reluctantly, one with female *bhuksuni* (nuns). In instituting the order, he affirmed that women could attain spiritual enlightenment, an unusual concept for its time. At the same time, however, he imposed rules on the *bhuksuni* that were designed to maintain their subordinate status within the Buddhist religious community. Buddhists of diverse traditions and schools from around the world joined together in 1998 for an international and ecumenical ordination in Bodh Gaya, India. One of the goals of the ceremony was to reestablish the order of nuns in Sri Lanka, Thailand, Tibet, and India, where no nuns had been ordained for over eight centuries.

In recent years, some Muslims have argued that women should be able to lead mixed congregations as well as single-sex ones in prayer; they support their arguments with passages from the Qu'ran and the hadith. Most Islamic schools allow women to lead a congregation of women; however, women are currently not allowed to lead mixed congregations. In 2005, the Islamic scholar Amina Wadud led a mixed congregation in prayer in New York, the first time such an event garnered international attention. In response, the Assembly of Muslim Jurists in America reiterated the traditional view that women cannot deliver the Friday prayer.

FEMINIST SPIRITUALITY

Women's spirituality became popular in the late 20th and early 21st centuries, in what is often called the "new age" movement. The term describes alternative spiritual practices that combine Eastern and pre-Christian Western traditions and were developed in response to the restrictive tenets of established religions. Popular practices include meditation, channeling, reincarnation, use of crystals, psychic experience, and holistic health.

As part of the movement, Neopaganism, or new religious movements, has also gained in popularity. The largest Neopagan belief in the United States is Wicca, an Earth-based faith that depends on celebrations of the seasons and recognizes divinity in the female form. Its contemporary origins are attributed to Gerald Gardner, a civil servant in Great Britain, whose activities in the 1930s caused the movement to spread to many parts of the globe and to include men.

RELIGIOUS SCHOLARSHIP AND HISTORY

Around the same time, women scholars within the major religious traditions began to reconsider the scriptures, interpretations, and practices of their religion from a feminist perspective. Religious history has largely been preserved through sacred texts, which recount the prophesies, tales, and founding philosophies upon which a religion or spirituality is based. The impact of sacred and religious texts on gender roles has been considerable worldwide. Men have been key players in creating these texts, both oral and written, and maintaining the knowledge of the original language in which they were written. In the few pre-19th-century religious texts authored by women, such as Catherine of Siena in 14th-century Italy, the Indian saint Mahadeviyakka in the 10th century, and the Arabic poet Rabi'ah (c. 644), wisdom is often couched within folklore myths, poems, dialogues, and letters.

Feminist theology has been particulary strong in the Christian and Jewish traditions. Among its goals have been reinterpreting sacred texts, changing the language and images used to describe God, studying female religious leaders in history, and increasing the role of women among the clergy and religious authorities.

Monitoring Women's Rights

The contemporary women's movement has expanded its agenda from the early focus on the freedom to vote within each nation to a new emphasis on holding governments accountable for the hard-won freedoms and rights.

These freedoms are liberties that need to be protected with care. Holding countries accountable for signed treaties and agreements has become an important issue. The ability to monitor progress for the welfare of women and men is subject to the capacity and willingness of countries to report data accurately.

During the 1995 UN conference on women, the Beijing Declaration and Platform for Action highlighted the importance of the ability to monitor countries' commitments; participating countries agreed to provide yearly reports to the United Nations and to allow human rights and women's advocacy groups as well as the United Nations's own Department of Economic and Social Affairs to monitor their activities.

Strengthening the ability of countries to gather and report statistical information continues to be one of the key goals. The results from the 1995–2003 period have caused concern: Among the 204 countries that reported statistical information, only 100 to 160 countries were able to supply some data about wages, birth, and death by sex. Europe had the highest ability to submit data and Africa the lowest.

Where Is the Women's Movement Headed?

That women have not been newsmakers for the majority of time that life has been recorded by books, newspapers, magazines, and movies indicates that people have still much to discover about women's history.

The women's movement evolved largely around a variety of causes—decolonization, national liberation, civil rights for all races and creeds, world peace, gay and lesbian rights, educational access, equal employment and pay are some—that contributed to the movement as a whole. Much of the emphasis so far has been on establishing those rights, something that is still happening today in different parts of the globe. *Gender mainstreaming* is now a strategy that encompasses the women's movement and promotes gender equality.

Other aspects of the struggle now are fulfilling the rights that have already been achieved and finding a voice that fits with being a woman in these times. The rights women seek are also for children and men, and are expanding to what women wish to safeguard in the world. Many organizations—including the Girl Scouts—are calling out to girls and women to consider careers and lifestyles in which they can influence, or change, public policy by the choices they make.

INTERNATIONAL HISTORY OF WOMEN'S RIGHTS

The demand for women's rights first became vocal in the late 17th century and 18th century, but it did not become a visible part of life until the 19th century revolutions in Europe. Although the movement arose separately in the United States and Europe, the common goal of achieving women's independence caused woman in these countries to appreciate each other's efforts and coordinate efforts to make a greater impact.

One of the earliest women who attempted to "move" other women about rights was the British author and feminist Mary Astell (1668–1731). She pleaded for greater opportunities for women in her *Serious Proposal to the Ladies,* written in two parts between 1694 and 1697, which offered a scheme for a women's college, an idea that turned out to be before its time and subject to public ridicule.

During the American Revolution in 1776, Abigail Adams admonished her husband, John, then vice president of the United States, to include women's rights in the new republic, else "there will be another revolution." It was not until the 1789 French Revolution that women rallied in support of women's rights.

In 1792 in England, Mary Wollstonecraft published *A Vindication of the Rights of Women,* which was translated into several languages and gave impetus to the movement worldwide. She addressed political emancipation for women when others around her limited their demand for rights to men. Although this stirring text opened the door for the women's movement, women's suffrage did not become the focus of the movement for another 50 years. One reason why liberal and socialist groups generally opposed women's suffrage was the claim, mostly by men, that women would vote conservatively. Conservatives, in turn, viewed suffrage as being entirely incompatible with the "women's sphere."

The First International Movement

The 1830s and 1840s was a time of social and radical reform, and leaders of the movement in Europe and the United States began to demand voting rights for women. However, the movement's agenda diversified quickly as it became evident that there were other issues that could be addressed in the short term, including economic independence for single women and improved legal position of married women.

In Europe, the rise of the Saint-Simonians and Fourierists in France inspired women to be *femmes libres,* or free women, believing they would lead the world into social and sexual freedom. This movement was opposed by some feminists, who said they would find their path to emancipation through religion, not sexual freedom. In Germany, the feminist Mathilde Franziska Anneke (1817–84) stated that her fellow feminist Louise Aston (1818–71) was exiled from the country for rejecting the religious faith, yet men were treated much less harshly for their resistance. The Chartist movement petitioned the vote for all men in England in the 1830s and 1840s and stimulated the same notion in women, yet while the men's movement was tolerated, the women's demand was not.

In the United States, Ernestine Rose (1810–92), a rabbi's young daughter who advocated married women's property rights, and Lucretia Mott (1793–1880), a promoter of racial equality and international women's rights, were early voices in the movement in the 1830s and 1840s. Mott was denied entry to a conference on antislavery in the United Kingdom because she was female. This pushed her onto the path of demanding equality for women and minorities. Public speeches by Frances Wright (1795–1852) and the Grimké sisters—Angelina Grimké Weld (1805–79) and Sarah Moore Grimké (1792–1873)—were conscious raising, as were publications by women: Mathilde Franziska Anneke's *Women in Conflict with Social Conditions* and Louise Otto's (1819–95) *Song of a German Maiden* among them.

A series of revolutions in 1847 and 1848 across Europe released a fury of women's rights activities. During this time, feminists began to reach out to one another for inspiration and help, mailing articles and books to each other across the ocean and translating each other's works into their native languages. By 1847, several hundred women considered themselves feminists, propelling the international women's movement into existence.

Elizabeth Cady Stanton (1815–1902), a judge's daughter with a flair for dramatics and a belief in coeducation, and Mott stood up to the limitations placed on them. They planned what came to be known as the first Women's Rights Convention in Seneca Falls, New York, in 1848. For that occasion, *Declaration of Sentiments* was drafted by Stanton to describe the key grievances of the day, including "the duty of the women of this country to secure to themselves their sacred right to the elective franchise."[53]

Stanton's high profile among women suffragists attracted Susan B. Anthony, who was then a schoolteacher and working with the temperance movement; they met in 1851 and developed a lifelong friendship of mutual support, often with Anthony taking care of Stanton's nine children so the latter could concentrate on speechwriting. Anthony's organizational and strategic strengths, which caused her to be nicknamed "Napoleon," complemented Stanton's eloquence in public speaking.

Along with suffrage, women focused on establishing economic independence and property rights. Together, Stanton and Anthony secured the first laws in the New York state legislature guaranteeing women rights over their children and control of property and wages, which gave impetus to the movement in other countries over the next two decades. In 1856, the British women Barbara Smith Bodichon (1827–91) and Bessie Raynor Parkes (1829–1925) advocated women's property reform through their newspaper, the *English Women's Journal.* The German feminists Louise Dittmar (1807–84), Louise Aston, and Anneke took radical positions on property and other rights in 1865 in the General Association of German Women. Canadian women began to lobby for similar rights. Canada's first suffrage groups—the Woman's Christian Temperance Union (WCTU), founded by Letitia Youmans (1827–96) in 1874, and the Toronto Women's Literary

Club, led by the physician Emily Howard Stowe (1831–1903), in 1876, and later by her daughter, Dr. Ann Augusta Stowe-Gullen (1857–1943)—were moving beyond charitable and religious work to focus on suffrage. The Toronto Women's Literary Club became the Toronto Women's Suffrage Association in 1883, then the Dominion Women's Enfranchisement Association in 1889, paving the way for and inspiring women's leagues in other Canadian territories.

Preparing for the Next Wave

In the United States, the Civil War of 1861–65 subdued the focus on women's rights as energy was put into preserving the Union and defeating a secession attempt by slave-owning states. In 1863, Anthony and Stanton coorganized the Women's National Loyal League to support Lincoln's government and emancipation policy during the war. American women served in the conflict as nurses or spies. The Thirteenth Amendment, ending slavery throughout the United States, was passed in 1864 and ratified in 1865. The Fourteenth Amendment, stating that "[a]ll persons born or naturalized in the United States . . . are citizens" and extending suffrage to black men, was passed in 1866 and ratified in 1868. Anthony and Stanton opposed granting suffrage to freed men without also giving it to women, and many woman suffrage sympathizers broke with them on this issue.

In 1869, Anthony and Stanton organized the National Woman Suffrage Association (NWSA). Three years later, Anthony led a group of women to the polls in Rochester, New York, to test the right of women to the franchise under the citizenship clause of the Fourteenth Amendment. Anthony's arrest, trial, and conviction on charges of unlawful voting received front-page attention, as did her refusal to pay the sentenced $100 fine.

Meanwhile, other factors were fueling the movement. An early supporter of women's liberation was the English philosopher and economist John Stuart Mill (1806–73). As a member of the British parliament, he advocated women's right to vote in the name of proportional representation. He addressed the rights of women in his 1869 book *The Subjection of Women* and wrote articles on the subject for the press. His work was translated into Danish, inspiring the movement in Denmark.

Women were applying for higher education by the mid-19th century, following pioneers like the British-born Elizabeth Blackwell (1821–1910), who, in spite of being turned down by 29 medical schools, was finally admitted to the medical department of Geneva College in upstate New York. She graduated from Geneva and attained full status as a physician in 1849. Universities had been associated with men and monasteries since the 12th century, and women were admitted only to colleges, often single-sex schools.

Nielsine Nielsen (1850–1916) was among the first women to apply to and be accepted in medical school at the University of Copenhagen in Denmark in 1874. Women were required to take an entrance exam and could obtain degrees at the university in most subjects, except theology.

Through the late 19th and early 20th centuries, the women's rights movement emerged with renewed intensity from the seeds of previous attempts and expanded in a ripple effect throughout Europe. In 1868, the activist Maria Goegg (1826–99) founded the International Association of Women (IAW) in Geneva, Switzerland, which then grew to have divisions in Italy, Portugal, France, Germany, England, and North America. Women's suffrage and better education for girls and women were IAW's priorities. At the same time in France, the Society for the Amelioration of Women's Condition was pioneered by Léon Richer (1824–1911) and Maria Deraismes (1828–94) to create better access to education, divorce, and property rights for married women. Both Danish and Swedish women also founded organizations to solidify rights for women.

These endeavors were not without resistance, however. IAW collapsed in France after the defeat of the Paris Commune in 1871; the new conservative government associated women's rights with a socialist regime. Another attempt by French feminists in 1878 to convene as the International Women's Rights Congress in Paris turned into a decision to deny women suffrage by the 220 mostly male delegates.

The International Council of Women (ICW) was founded in Washington, D.C., in 1888, formed by Anthony and Stanton with contacts made while in Europe, to work on women's issues on a broad front. However, the ICW's leader from 1893 to 1899 and from 1904 to 1936, the Scot Lady Aberdeen (1857–1939), was reluctant to advocate women's suffrage, believing women's household duties were primary.

Twentieth Century: Women Network

During a conference of the ICW in Berlin in 1904, a special organization, the International Women's Suffrage Alliance (IWSA), was founded to focus on the struggle for suffrage across the globe. It hosted meetings in Copenhagen (1906), Amsterdam (1908), London (1909), Stockholm (1911), and Budapest (1913) before World War I. By then, it had added labor, prostitution, world peace, and equal rights to its agenda.

In the early years of the 20th century, although national movements were occurring separately, women were making contact with one another individually, inspiring and influencing each other. Events that occurred in the United States involving female factory workers who marched against substandard conditions in New York City in 1857 drew the attention of the second International Conference of Socialist Women in Germany in 1910 through the German labor leader Clara Zetkin (1857–1933). The conference designated International Women's Day in recognition of women's fight for universal rights (but the United Nations did not decide upon the specific date of March 8 until 1975, during International Women's Year). A women's uprising in Russia along the Afghan border in the 1920s inspired Afghan women to commemorate the occasion on International Women's Day many decades later.

The British suffrage movement was a radical model for the women's movement leading up to World War I. The English suffragettes Hertha Ayrton (1854–1923) and Emmeline Pankhurst (1858–1928) and her two daughters, Christabel (1880–1958) and Sylvia (1882–1960), applied near-violent pressure for women to vote on Winston Churchill, the prime minister of England at the time, upsetting "the whole orderly conduct of life."[54]

The French suffragists Madeleine Pelletier (1874–1939) and Caroline Kauffmann (1840–1926), riled by their experience in British demonstrations, resuscitated the movement in France. Pankhurst's American friend (and suffragist daughter of Elizabeth Cady Stanton) Harriot Stanton Blanch (1856–1940) invited Annie Cobden-Sanderson (1852–1944) to speak of her experience of imprisonment in British jails, which no doubt influenced American suffragists Alice Paul (1885–1977) and Lucy Burns (1879–1966). Paul and Burns participated in the British suffrage demonstrations and were both arrested in London. Undeterred by the experience, they applied the same techniques to the American struggle when they returned home. The South American Bertha Lutz (1894–1976) also tried to take militant techniques to Brazil from her visit to London, where women marched in picket lines, chained themselves to fences, or endured hunger strikes in prison in the name of winning the right to vote.

By contrast, Carrie Chapman Catt (1859–1947) used a more missionary style as she traveled with Dr. Aletta Jacobs (1854–1929) from the Netherlands through the Philippines, Palestine, Indonesia, and Burma in 1911 and 1912, trying to induce suffrage movements in developing countries.

Despite these efforts, when World War I began in 1914, few women in Europe, other than in Finland and Denmark, were allowed women's suffrage. For the next several years, women's rights organizations put their efforts into supporting the war and filling jobs vacated by men at war. Women in the United States and western Europe, each in their own way, questioned their limited rights in democratic societies that claimed they were going to war for democracy. The founding of the Women's Peace Party in 1915 by Jane Addams (1860–1935) was also part of a trend in which several women's organizations rallied for peace during the war. Jacobs helped found with Addams the International Congress for the Future Peace. The journalist and lawyer Crystal Eastman (1881–1928) established the National Civil Liberties Bureau to protect conscientious objectors to the war.

One of the larger European organizations—the International Conference of Socialist Women—and the Euro-American International Women's Congress met in 1915 to advocate peace. Women from 12 countries met in the Hague, the capital of the Netherlands. U.S. delegates campaigned for America not to enter the war, and it did not until 1917. In 1919, the delegates from the International Women's Congress formed a new organization, the Women's International League for Peace and Freedom (WILPF), in Geneva, Switzerland, led by Addams.

By the war's end in November 1918, women had been moving into white-collar jobs as secretaries, postal service clerks, and telephone operators, as well as such trades as plumbing. Public perception of women's ability, dress, and appearance shifted dramatically. Women were finding out about contraceptives as an option for sexual freedom and self-determination. Although women would soon be again alienated from job opportunities as men returned to the workforce, countries initiated suffrage in record numbers after the war.

After the war, women had the opportunity to meet with the 14 allied country representatives at the Paris Peace Conference in 1919 and to provide proposals for the newly formed Covenant of the League of Nations and ILO. This set a precedent for women's organizations to observe the intergovernmental agencies at work regularly and provide recommendations, helping them to gain experience in international affairs and networking. The covenant included statements about reasonable working conditions for men, women, and children and the prevention of human trafficking. It also specified equal opportunity for employment within the league. For the ILO constitution, women proposed statements that were radical for the time, including an eight-hour workday, an end to child labor, and equal pay and minimum wages.

The movement that was formerly dependent on middle-class women in North America and Europe now began to accommodate a more diverse social and multicultural population of women. African-American women, impacted by racism in the United States, formed their own alliance in 1920, the International Council of Women of the Darker Races. In the same year, Ayrton and Pankhurst befriended the two-time French Nobel physicist Marie Curie (1867–1934), who returned their support by lending her name to petitions to free suffragists from British prisons. While British property-holding women over the age of 30 had gained suffrage in 1918, it would not be until 1928, with the second passage of the Representation of the People Act, that suffrage was granted equally to men and women in Britain.

Women gathered in countries such as Egypt, India, China, and Japan to form their own organizations. Delegates attending IWSA conferences were raising issues that were of concern to Muslim women. South American and Pacific Rim countries also began to host movements. The first Pan-American Woman's Conference was called by the IWSA president Catt in Baltimore, Maryland, in 1922. Organized by the Pan-American International Women's Committee, the Mexican Feminist Party cofounder Elena Torres (unknown birthdate), the Brazilian activist Bertha Lutz, and the Chilean Amanda Labarca (1886–1985) were among the 2,000 delegates, who included Canadians and Americans, to be inspired from the conference for the next two decades. The Brazilian Women's Suffrage Alliance and the Pan-American Association for the Advancement of Women emerged in the wake of this occasion.

Latin American women also united with Spanish women to form the International League of Iberian and Hispanic-American Women in the 1920s. Led by Paulina Luisi (1875–1950) from Uruguay, the league represented the sentiment that South America did not depend on missionary feminist zeal, as portrayed by Catt.

Women tried very hard to use their newfound voices for world peace. The WILPF grew to 50,000 members by 1926 and was advocating control of fascism and imperialism through pacifism, an approach, others argued, that would not be effective.

Throughout the 1920s and 1930s, women persisted with campaigns to be sure their rights would not be neglected by the League of Nations, which gradually implemented international legal protection of rights for specific minorities, including women. During this period, many of the international NGOs that would later play an important part in the forming of the United Nations were formed. The League of Nations ended with the outbreak of World War II, as did, temporarily, much of the contact among different women's movements.

During the 1930s, Joseph Stalin in the Soviet Union and Adolf Hitler in Germany found ways to limit women's rights through governmental rule. In Russia, abortion was banned, and, although women had previously won the right to vote, the one-party system did not allow them to exercise their voice. National Socialism in Germany was vehemently opposed to women's rights. Although it tried to limit the number of women in the workforce, the men's call to arms required that women take on their jobs, even in civil service positions.

World War II (1938–45) transformed women's working experience. In the United Kingdom, unmarried women were drafted into the military. The United States implemented a women's auxiliary for the armed forces. Germany's voluntary labor service also drew out young women from the home. By the early 1940s, an estimated 90 percent of unmarried women and 80 percent of married women were employed in some form of service in the United States and Europe. Shift work, day care, and increased pay rates were policies new to the workplace to accommodate needed women workers. Social equality was first felt, finally, in a time of crisis.

As a result, women were given suffrage toward the end and after the war in Russia, Germany, France, Hungary, Italy, Portugal, Croatia, and Romania. At the same time, the return of men from war and the need to find jobs for them led to an emphasis on family values and women in the home. During the 1940s and 1950s, two trends emerged: Unmarried women began working in "female" jobs such as nursing and teaching. In the United States, these professions were considered "male" jobs until the mid-1800s, when women began to assert their stature and access to educational training. On the other hand, married women often left the workforce to have children and returned on a part-time basis, if at all. Although the particulars varied by country, the trend to reemphasize domestic priorities for women was global.

Women's Rights: A Global Affair

From its inception, the women's rights movement has been fostered by national and international influences. After World War II, the founding of the United Nations in 1945 as a mediator for world peace was expected to include women's participation. Yet, of the 51 founding member states, only 30 granted women equal voting rights with men or allowed them to hold public office. On the other hand, the United Nation Charter specified equal rights for men and women in a way that no previous international legal document had.

In 1946, the UN Commission on the Status of Women was established to secure equal political rights, economic rights, and educational opportunities for women throughout the world. U.S. delegate Eleanor Roosevelt's (1884–1962) authorship of the Universal Declaration of Human Rights to the General Assembly in 1948 was one example of women's new presence at the forefront of the international scene. It was also an early example of the as yet futuristic concept of gender balance.

During the first 30 years of the United Nations's work on women's rights, it struggled with some of the same issues that the women's movement in general faced, mainly the challenge of expanding the concept of gender equality from a minimal and basic legal and civil right into a socially and politically accepted idea. By the 21st century, countries also needed to establish mechanisms to gather data on the status of women around the world, a task that is still being worked on today.

Over time, it became increasingly apparent that laws, in and of themselves, were not enough to ensure the equal rights of women. Although the ILO adopted a convention for equal pay for women in 1951 for enforcement in 1953, the resolution would be ignored for another two decades. The Equal Remuneration Convention ratified nations to enforce among all men and women workers the principle of equal remuneration for work of equal value. The convention has been ratified by 162 nations, including most of Europe, Canada, South America, and the United Arab Emirates in 1997, but not the United States, which is still cautious over how comparable worth of work between men and women is to be measured.

In the 1960s and 1970s, the women's movement flourished at national levels, beginning in the United States alongside the Civil Rights movement, then spreading to Europe, where it gained momentum with the trade unions. University students began to call for a change to the status quo in all aspects of life, and the rebellious character of the young people manifested itself in demonstrations and riots in 1968. Many marched against the U.S. involvement in the Vietnam War, advocating peace. Women, still considered supporters and not leaders in this wave of change, began to take independent positions, demanding social and economic liberation and recognition. This took the form of the women's liberation movement, which, in turn, grew at an international pace, involving women from all social and economic strata.

WOMEN AND THE UNITED NATIONS

As the movement became international, the United Nations responded by designating 1975 International Women's Year and holding the first of what would evolve into four world conferences on women, in Mexico City (1975), Copenhagen (1980), Nairobi (1985), and Beijing (1995). These international conferences empowered the movement by strengthening the web of communication. The exponential increase of conference attendees was another indication of the growth of the movement into a global one.

In Mexico City, 6,000 women from NGOs and 133 government delegations (113 were led by women) attended. One focus of discussion was the effects of colonialism, which was reflected in the World Plan of Action. It was here that INSTRAW and the United Nations Development Fund for Women (UNIFEM) were established. The Mexico City conference also led to the proclamation of 1976–1985 as the UN Decade for Women.

At the time of the UN world conference on women in Copenhagen, the cold war and apartheid preoccupied the program. The Copenhagen conference adopted a World Program of Action calling for women's participation in politics and decision making, and for the elimination of discrimination in law and policy. It encouraged governments and international institutions to conduct more research and to collect gender-based data. It also introduced

CEDAW to the 1,326 delegates from 145 states and 8,000 women who attended as NGOs. The convention, which had been adopted at the end of the previous year by the General Assembly, provided strategies and set specific goals aimed at improving women's participation in social, economic, and political activities.

The women's movement was redefining itself as one for global gender equality with the Third World Conference on Women, in Nairobi, Kenya, in 1985, marking the end of the United Nations Decade for Women. Among the 15,000 women from NGOs and 157 government representatives, the sentiment was that, although many gains had been made during the past decade, statistics indicated that these benefits were only reaching a minority of women. Action statements concerning new approaches to the same problems—equality, development, and peace—were drafted and issued as the Nairobi Forward Looking Strategies for the Advancement of Women, focusing on three areas: constitutional and legal steps, equality in social participation, and equality in political participation and decision making.

By the time of the Fourth UN World Conference on Women in Beijing, China, in September 1995, it became clear that the focus needed to be on gender equality and human rights, a position that would draw international attention to itself and make use of the new World Wide Web, the Internet.

In addition to the 5,000 representatives of 2,100 NGOs and 189 government representatives, 30,000 women participated through the independent NGO Forum '95, and many thousands more took part through the Internet. All told, 47,000 people participated at this landmark event.[55]

The conference unanimously adopted the Beijing Declaration and the Platform for Action as an agenda for empowerment, highlighting three main areas: economic advancement, equal rights and access to health care and education, and violence against women and girls. Women's involvement in armed conflict and access to health care was of critical importance at the time. The Platform of Action also called to public awareness the important economic role that women migrant workers play, including domestic workers, who contribute their remittance to the economy of their country of origin and participate in the labor force of the country of destination.

The platform identified 12 critical areas for action:

- Poverty
- Education and training
- Health
- Violence against women
- Armed conflict

- The economy
- Women in power and decision making
- Institutional mechanisms for the advancement of women
- Human rights of women
- Women and the media
- Women and the environment
- The girl child

In 1997, the 15 EU nations adopted the Amsterdam Treaty, which confirmed equality of men and women as a fundamental right in the EU. Both the treaty and any legislation toward "gender positive action to compensate for discrimination against women"[56] were intended to assert women's rights for "effective equality" and "obligation of result" in the newly expanding EU.

To give momentum to political commitments to achieve women's empowerment and gender equality, a UN special session was scheduled in June 2000 by the General Assembly and the Division for the Advancement of Women, entitled "Women 2000: Gender Equality, Development and Peace for the Twenty-first Century." Also known as "Beijing+5," the special session reviewed the progress made in the five years since the Beijing Platform of Action was adopted. It provided the opportunity for governments and participants to share strategies and study obstacles encountered in the implementation of the Beijing Platform for Action.

Between September 6 and 8, 2000, heads of states and governments gathered at the United Nations Headquarters in New York to reaffirm their faith in the organization and its charter "as indispensable foundations of a more peaceful, prosperous and just world," in what has become known as the Millennium Declaration.

Certain fundamental values were asserted by the countries present, including freedom and the right to live "in dignity, free from hunger and from the fear of violence, oppression or injustice." A major step for all nations was to agree explicitly on the value of equality: No individual and no nation must be denied the opportunity to benefit from development. Finally, the equal rights and opportunities of women and men were to be, in some manner, assured.

That equality for women was now perceived as a vehicle by which a nation could measure its development for both genders gave it new legitimacy. The assembly ratified this notion in 2000 with the following statement: "To promote gender equality and the empowerment of women as effective ways to combat poverty, hunger and disease and to stimulate development that is truly sustainable." It was here that the member nations pledged to combat all forms of violence against women and yet again to implement the CEDAW, established in 1979.

On October 31, 2000, the United Nations Security Council passed Resolution 1325 on Women, Peace and Security. Women's organizations and peace groups around the world made it clear that governments needed to be held accountable and to honor commitments made through this and previous resolutions. The UN International Day for the Elimination of Violence against Women is now observed on November 25 in countries worldwide. Although it is overshadowed in the United States by the Thanksgiving holiday, it is often used to publicize local work at the community level with women in other countries. In the latter half of the 20th century, women's movements in all parts of the world found a voice through events like Women's Day.

The Dakar Framework for Action adopted at the World Education Forum in 2000 also highlighted the role the United Nations Educational, Scientific and Cultural Organization (UNESCO) could play in eradicating poverty and achieving the Millennium Development Goal of universal primary education by 2015 by joining its agenda with the movement for gender balancing.

GENDER MAINSTREAMING

A conference commemorating the 10th anniversary of the fourth UN world conference on women was held in Beijing in March 2005 to review advances and objectives since 1995 globally and in China. At "Beijing+10," member nations declared solidarity with "gender mainstreaming" and planned to take recommendations of this conference to the Millennium Summit 2005.

At the convening of the General Assembly in September 2005, further goals were stated in the Millennium Document, adding the promise of education, especially for females: "for eradicating illiteracy, and [to] strive for expanded secondary and higher education as well as vocational education and technical training, especially for girls and women."[57]

Member nations were explicit about their positions of continued support of the 1995 Beijing conference as well as pursuance of gender equality in education and other areas such as property ownership, equal access to reproductive health, employment, and "productive assets and resources" such as land, credit, and technology. The 2005 World Summit promised to eliminate all forms of discrimination and violence against women and "the girl child," especially during and after armed conflicts. Another area that was featured was the "increased representation of women in government decision making bodies, including through ensuring their equal opportunity to participate fully in the political process."[58]

THE MOVEMENT EVOLVES

During the two decades following its passage in 1979, CEDAW would be ratified by 185 countries and become the subject of outreach by over 190 national NGOs. Known as the "Treaty for the Rights of Women," or the international "Bill of Rights" for women, it shaped the passage and enforcement of national laws in many countries. The treaty consists of a preamble and 30 articles that define what constitutes discrimination against women and set an agenda for national action. The treaty requires regular progress reports from ratifying countries, but it does not impose any changes in existing laws or require new laws of countries ratifying the treaty. It lays out models for achieving equality but contains no enforcement authority. In December 1999, an Optional Protocol to the Convention was entered into force, enabling women victims of sex discrimination to submit complaints to an international treaty body and making the convention as effective as other international human rights instruments by providing individual complaints procedures. As of November 2006, 84 states had become party to the Convention's Optional Protocol.

The United States is one of only eight member states—and the only developed country—that has not ratified the treaty. Opponents of U.S. ratification of CEDAW have raised fears about the ways it might affect the United States's ability to grant or withhold rights to its citizens. Some believe ratification would give too much power to the international community, with treaty provisions superseding U.S. laws and violating U.S. sovereignty.

The enforcement of women's rights is now closely watched through a variety of international agencies and NGOs. The United Nations holds member nations accountable through statistics-gathering efforts and regular meetings of the Commission on the Status of Women, which has focused on two "emerging issues" every year since the implementation of the Beijing Platform for Action.

Amnesty International and Human Rights Watch also appoint delegations to monitor on-site elections and to provide testimony to the implementation or absence of women's rights in countries around the globe.

International women's organizations, such as WILPF, continue to advocate enhanced participation and development of women, including equal participation of women and men in decision-making processes at all levels. They send delegates to attend and address meetings of the Commission on the Status of Women at the United Nations every year.

The efforts of women's movements are continuing in countries where these rights are only now seeing the light of day, such as Afghanistan, where women have been fighting to keep their rights under the threat of conservative Islam. In the United States, the emphasis is on equal pay, and protecting reproductive rights, social security, pensions, and secure employment. Meanwhile, domestic violence is a growing concern across the globe, made visible by a 2005 report from the World Health Organization.[59] The severe and continuing problem of violence against women was newly underscored by the UN's October 2006 presentation of the Secretary-General's in-depth study on all forms of violence against women.

WOMEN STUDYING WOMEN

The growth of women's studies programs paralleled the growth of women's conferences. Beginning in the late 1960s and early 1970s, courses formalized into degree programs in the United States and Europe, soon followed by women's studies programs in Australia, New Zealand, Taiwan, India, South Korea, the West Indies, and Japan. With the international conferences, the field of women's studies moved across borders in the 1980s into other parts of the world, including the Philippines, Thailand, South Africa, Puerto Rico, the Dominican Republic, China, and eastern Europe. By the 1990s, it had reached Malaysia, Vietnam, the Czech Republic, Slovakia, and Uganda.

The programs have helped to dispel the image of a monolithic women's movement and have proved invaluable for observing the evolution of the women's movement from one about women's rights into one about gender equality. In the past few years, some programs have been changing their names to reflect this shift in perception. In addition, programs have helped bring about accountability that is outside of the political arena and offered another market for statistics gathered by international organizations and NGOs. Women's history classes have also become part of some public school curricula in the United States.

One common element to most programs, whether a course, an undergraduate degree, or a doctoral program, has been the analysis of power and ways it is handled by gender and ethnicity within any given country. More important, women's studies programs have helped women to understand that "every issue is a woman's issue," a concept inspired by the U.S. congresswoman Bella Abzug (1920–98) and, in some way, a wedge to keep progressing forward.

---

[1] Amnesty International. "Women Denied Right to Vote in Saudi Arabia." *The Wire* (December 2004). Available online. URL: http://web.amnesty.org/web/wire.nsf/print/December 2004Saudi_Arabia. Accessed May 15, 2006.

[2] Christopher Colclough, et al. "Rights, Equality, and Education for All." EFA Global Monitoring Report 2003/4, UNESCO, 2003, p. 44.

[3] Colclough, et al. "Rights, Equality, and Education for All." Executive summary.

[4] Amanda Bower. "It's Mrs., Not Ms. In a Return to Tradition, More Brides Are Taking Their Husband's Name." *Time*, May 29, 2005.

[5] "Child Marriage Factsheet." *UNFPA State of World Population 2005*. Available online. URL: http://www.unfpa.org/swp/2005/presskit/factsheets/facts_child_marriage.htm. Accessed June 19, 2006.

[6] "Child Marriage Factsheet." *UNFPA State of World Population 2005.*

[7] "Global Employment Trends for Women." Report, International Labour Organization, March 2004, p. 3.

[8] "Global Employment Trends Brief." Report, International Labour Organization, January 24, 2006, p. 3.

[9] "Global Employment Trends for Women." Report, International Labour Organization, March 2004, p. 13.

[10] United Nations Statistic Division. Table 5f—Women Administrative and Managerial Workers (April 22, 2005). Available online. URL: http://unstats.un.org/unsd/demographic/products/indwm/indwm2.htm. Accessed January 25, 2006.

[11] "Study Finds 'Opportunity Gap' for Women in Business Schools." Press release, Center for the Education of Women and Catalyst Business School. University of Michigan, Ann Arbor. *The University Record Online.* May 22, 2000. Available onine. URL: http://www.umich.edu/nurecord/9900/May22_00/8.htm. Accessed January 21, 2006.

[12] UN Division for the Advancement of Women. "General Recommendations Made by the Committee on the Elimination of Discrimination against Women" (May 19, 2006). Available online. URL: http://www.un.org/womenwatch/daw/cedaw/recommendations/recomm.htm. Accessed June 20, 2006.

[13] "Maternity Benefits—European Study Shows Wide Variations." Press release, Mercer Human Resource Consulting, May 10, 2006. Available online. URL: http://www.mercerhr.com/pressrelease/details.jhtml?idContent=1221340. Accessed June 5, 2006.

[14] Mauricette Mongbo. "Low-Income Women's Bank in Benin: Social and Economic Empowerment." Brandeis University, Waltham, Mass. Available online. URL: http://www.gdrc.org/icm/wind/benin.html. Accessed January 30, 2006.

[15] The following Web site lists male and female personnel available for military service by country: The World Factbook, 2005. Central Intelligence Agency. Available online. URL: http://www.cia.gov/cia/publications/factbook/fields/2105.html. Accessed May 16, 2006.

[16] "Percentage of Military Service Women in NATO Countries Armed Forces, 2001–2005." Datenquelle: Office on Women in the NATO Forces. December 4, 2006. Available online. URL: http://www.nato.int/issues/women_nato/perc_fem_soldiers_2001_2006.pdf. Accessed December 9, 2006.

[17] Tim McGirk. "Crossing the Lines." *Time,* February 27, 2006, p. 38.

[18] United Nations. *The World's Women 2000: Trends and Statistics.* New York: United Nations, p. 24.

[19] Karen Sjørup and Gyldendal Leksikon. "Gender Equality." Denmark.dk—The Official Window Web Site. Available online. URL: http://denmark.dk/portal/page?_pageid=374,477789&_dad=portal&_schema =PORTAL. Accessed November 15, 2005.

[20] "The Global Coalition on Women and AIDS." Press release, UNAIDS, June 1, 2006.

[21] UNAIDS. "2006 Global Report on the AIDS Epidemic." Report, annex 1: Country Profiles, pp. 333 and 374.

[22] Terry Leonard. "AIDS Toll May Reach 100 Million in Africa." The Associated Press, June 3, 2006.

[23] UNAIDS. "2006 Global Report on the AIDS Epidemic." Report, Executive Summary, chapter 2: Overview of the Global AIDS Epidemic, p. 38.

[24] UNAIDS. "2006 Global Report on the AIDS Epidemic." Report, Executive Summary, chapter 2: Overview of the Global AIDS Epidemic, p. 46.

[25] Etienne G. Krug, Linda L. Dahlberg, James A. Mercy, Anthony B. Zwi, and Rafael Lozano, eds. "World Report on Violence and Health." Report, World Health Organization, 2002, p. 286.

[26] Wim Van Lerberghe, Annick Manuel, Zoë Matthews, and Cathy Wolfheim. "The World Health Report 2005: Make Every Mother and Child Count." Report, World Health Organization, 2005, p. xiv.

[27] María José Alcalá. "State of World Population 2005." Report, United Nations Development Fund, p. 41.

[28] Alcalá. "State of World Population 2005," p. 41.

[29] Alcalá. "State of World Population 2005," p. 41.

[30] United Nations Department of Economic and Social Affairs. "The World Women's 2005: Progress in Statistics." Report, Statistics Division, 2006, p. 130.

[31] Grayce P. Storey. "Ethical Problems Surrounding Surrogate Motherhood." Report, Yale–New Haven Teachers Institute, 2000.

[32] Alcalá. "State of World Population 2005," p. 35.

[33] Duff G. Gillespie. "Whatever Happened to Family Planning and, for That Matter, Reproductive Health?" *International Family Planning Perspectives* vol. 30, no. 1 (March 2004), pp. 34–38.

[34] Joanna Francis. "Making a Wave." *Template Times*, February 1, 2006, p. 2.

[35] "Kenya Demographic and Health Survey 2003." Report, Central Bureau of Statistics in partnership with the Ministry of Health, December 2003, p. 30.

[36] Mrs. Coomaraswamy, UN special rapporteur on violence against women. "Human Rights: Women's Violence." United Nations Department of Public Information, DPI/1772/HR, February 1996.

[37] Neil M. Malamuth. "Pornography and Sexual Aggression: Are There Reliable Effects and Can We Understand Them?" *Annual Review of Sex Research* vol. 11 (2000), pp. 26–91.

[38] Gert Martin and M. Hald. "The Effects of Exposure to Pornography: An Empirical Contribution to the Porn Debate." *Journal of Sex Research*, University of Aarhus, Denmark (February 2006).

[39] Krug, Dahlberg, Mercy, Zwi, and Lozano, eds. "World Report on Violence and Health," p. 89.

[40] Kajsa Asling-Monemi, Rodolfo Pena, Mary Carroll Ellsberg, and Lars Ake Persson. "Violence against Women Increases the Risk of Infant and Child Mortality: A Case-Referent Study in Nicaragua." *Bulletin of the World Health Organization* vol. 81, no. 1 (2003), p. 11.

[41] Krug, Dahlberg, Mercy, Zwi, and Lozano, eds. "World Report on Violence and Health," p. 109.

[42] Claudia García-Moreno, Henrica A. F. M. Jansen, Mary Ellsberg, Lori Heise, and Charlotte Watts. "WHO Multi-Country Study on Women's Health and Domestic Violence against

Women: Initial Results on Prevalence, Health Outcomes and Women's Responses." Report, World Health Organization, 2005.

[43] Jamie Whaley. "Report to the Nation 2005: Fiscal Years 2003–2004. Office for Victims of Crime. U.S. Department of Justice, 2001, p. 8.

[44] Krug, Dahlberg, Mercy, Zwi, and Lozano, eds. "World Report on Violence and Health," p. 10.

[45] Krug, Dahlberg, Mercy, Zwi, and Lozano, eds. "World Report on Violence and Health," p. 218.

[46] Krug, Dahlberg, Mercy, Zwi, and Lozano, eds. "World Report on Violence and Health," p. 218.

[47] Krug, Dahlberg, Mercy, Zwi, and Lozano, eds. "World Report on Violence and Health," p. 60.

[48] United Nations Office on Drugs and Crime (UNODC). "Trafficking in Persons—Global Patterns." Report, 2006, p. 17.

[49] United Nations Population Fund. "Trafficking in Human Misery." Available online. URL: http://www.unfpa.org/gender/violence1.htm. Accessed June 2, 2006.

[50] United Nations Office on Drugs and Crime (UNODC). "Trafficking in Persons—Global Patterns." Report, figure 37: Profile of Victims, Gender and Age, 2006, p. 77.

[51] Michael P. Harris. "Hour of Decision for Women Priests—The Church of England Considers the Ordination of Females." *Time*, March 2, 1987.

[52] Caryle Murphy. "A Chorus of Amens as More Women Take over Pulpit." *The Washington Post*, July 25, 1998, p. B.01.

[53] E. C. Stanton, S. B. Anthony, and M. J. Gage, eds. "Seneca Falls Declaration." *History of Women's Suffrage*, vol. 1, 1887, p. 70. Available online. URL: http://usinfo.state.gov/usa/info usa/facts/democrac/17.htm. Accessed December 20, 2005.

[54] Denis Brian. *The Curies: A Biography of the Most Controversial Family in Science.* New York: John Wiley & Sons, 2005, p. 149.

[55] "The Four Global Women's Conferences 1975–1995: Historical Perspective." United Nations Department of Public Information Bulletin. DPI/2035/M, May 2000. Available online. URL: http://www.un.org/womenwatch/daw/followup/session/presskit/hist.htm. Accessed February 1, 2006.

[56] Antoinette Fourquet. "Women's Rights and the European Union." Women and Law in Europe. January 1997. Available online. URL: http://www.helsinki.fi/science/xantippa/wle/wle13.html. Accessed November 30, 2005.

[57] Office of the Spokesperson. "Message from Mr. Koïchiro Matsuura, Director-General of UNESCO, on the Occasion of the International Day for the Eradication of Poverty" (October 17, 2005). UNESCO. Available online. URL: http://portal.unesco.org/en/ev.php-URL_ID=30221&URL_DO=DO_TOPIC&URL_SECTION=201.html. Accessed May 25, 2006.

[58] "2005 World Summit Outcome." United Nations General Assembly, September 15, 2005, p. 18.

[59] García-Moreno, Jansen, Ellsberg, Heise, and Watts. "WHO Multi-Country Study on Women's Health and Domestic Violence against Women: Initial Results on Prevalence, Health Outcomes and Women's Responses," 2005.

2

Focus on the United States

HISTORY OF THE WOMEN'S RIGHTS MOVEMENT

The establishment of political rights for women in America, Europe, Australia, and New Zealand in the early part of the 20th century set a precedent for the rest of the world. This pattern persisted with women's pursuit of higher educational, employment, and social rights in the middle of the 20th century, which women of the 21st century are now seeking ways to enforce. The concerns are far more diverse now, as industry and technology spawn issues never before considered, from access to advanced forms of health care screening and contraceptives to the policing of live pornographic feeds over the Internet.

Women in America are now aware of the interdependence one issue can have with another, whether it is poverty, health, violence, or equal pay. They also are becoming more aware of the impact one country can have on another and global issues. By the same token, women elsewhere are struggling with and discovering new identities, yet retaining their independent cultural features.

Early Stirrings

The rights described in America's first Constitution, written in 1776, were intended for men; women were denied most legal rights and expected instead to be treated according to social custom and English common law. Although unmarried women had the right to own property, that property usually passed to their husbands upon marriage. They could not vote, keep their own wages, or even have custody of children.

Abigail Adams (1744–1818), the wife of the then–vice president, John Adams, and Mercy Otis Warren (1728–1814) pressed for the inclusion of women's emancipation in the Constitution, but the issue would not be considered seriously for another 45 years. Women began, one by one, to break the barriers of public silence in the early 1800s; they spoke out on property and civil rights, suffrage, and education. The historical event that contributed most to the initiation of the women's movement in the United States was the Seneca Falls Convention of 1848, when Elizabeth Cady Stanton (1815–1902), Lucretia Coffin Mott (1793–1880), and other women met at Seneca Falls, New York. There, they issued a declaration of independence for women, called *Declaration of Sentiments*, demanding full legal, educational, and commercial opportunity; equal pay; the right to earn an income; and the right to vote.

The Sentiments were modeled after the Declaration of Independence and just as the Declaration's authors had more than 70 years prior, the authors of the Sentiments highlighted 18 grievances. Grievances included married women's being considered legally dependent ("civilly dead") and women's not being allowed to vote or to have property rights (although they had to pay property taxes). Husbands had legal power over and responsibility for wives to the extent that they could imprison or beat them. Divorce and child custody laws favored men with the "ownership" of children, household belongings, and land. Most occupations, including all those in the fields of medicine, law, and politics, were closed to women, and when women did work, they were paid only a fraction of what men earned. Women were not allowed to receive an education, and colleges and universities would not accept women as students. The situation was even worse for African-American women.

Civil Rights

Frances ("Fanny") Wright (1795–1852) wrote *A Plan for the Gradual Abolition of Slavery in the United States without Danger of Loss to the Citizens of the South* in 1825 and became one of the first American women to lecture before "promiscuous audiences" (audiences that included both women and men). Maria Stuart (1803–79) advocated rights for black women of the North. The Grimké sisters from South Carolina began lecturing crowds in 1836 about slavery. Angelina Emily Grimké (1805–79), converted to the Quaker faith by her elder sister, Sarah Moore Grimké (1792–1873), became an abolitionist in 1835 and wrote *An Appeal to the Christian Women of the South.* With her sister, she began speaking around New York City and became an orator of considerable power. She was invited to lecture in Massachusetts, where she made three successful appearances before the legislative committee on antislavery petitions early in 1838. That year, she married Theodore Dwight Weld, who was also an active abolitionist. She discontinued her public work when struck down by bad health but continued to help Weld in his work.

Also a Quaker, Mott in her early activism focused on racial equality and international women's rights. She aided fugitive slaves, and in 1833, after a meeting with the American Anti-Slavery Society, she organized the Philadelphia Female Anti-Slavery Society. The refusal to recognize Mott and other women delegates at London's World Anti-Slavery Convention in 1840 fueled her actions in the United States.

Property Rights

Another area that gained early attention by women's rights advocates was property rights. The first-known advocate for women's land rights was the colonial Maryland landowner Margaret Brent (1601–71). An active businesswoman and lawyer, she pleaded legal cases on numerous occasions on behalf of Governor Leonard Calvert of Maryland and Lord Baltimore. In 1648, she made her mark as a suffragist when she argued that she should be awarded two votes for a voice in the colonial assembly's counsels—as a landowner in her own right and as holder of a power of attorney for another landowner—but she received neither.

Until the Married Women's Property Act (MWPA) in 1839, women who married in the United States automatically turned over all their property to their husband. Early activists such as Ernestine Rose (1810–92), the daughter of a rabbi who immigrated to the United States in May 1836, petitioned for married women's property rights in New York State, aided by Paulina Wright Davis (1813–76).

In 1839, Mississippi became the first state to pass MWPA, and Maryland followed soon after, in 1843. After 12 years of campaigning, New York finally passed the law in 1848. It became a model for many states because of the increased protection it afforded women from husbands' creditors. Ernestine Rose's campaign in New York led to a lifelong association with Elizabeth Cady Stanton.

Suffrage

Although women put their ambitions for suffrage on the backburner during the Civil War (1861–65) and focused instead on the campaign against slavery, they fully expected that women's right to vote would be part of the civil rights for which they were fighting. However, the Thirteenth Amendment, which prohibited slavery, and the Civil Rights Bill of the Fourteenth Amendment granted rights to slaves and citizens, but the right to vote was extended only to black men, not to white or black women.

Two women pivotal to the movement were Stanton and Susan Brownell Anthony (1820–1906). They met in 1852 and their relationship evolved into a lifelong commitment to each other's role in the movement. Stanton and Anthony formed the National Women Suffrage Association (NWSA) in 1869 to fight for amendments to the U.S. Constitution that would enfranchise women. In the same year, Lucy Stone (1818–93), Julia Ward Howe (1819–1910), and Josephine Ruffin (1842–1924) organized the American Woman Suffrage Association (AWSA) in Boston, Massachusetts, to promote change in individual state legislatures for women's suffrage. The AWSA membership base was more conservative than NWSA's and did not campaign on issues such as employer discrimination and easier divorce for women. In 1870, the AWSA founded the *Women's Journal,* a magazine edited by Lucy Stone.

Abby and Julia Smith (1797–1878 and 1792–1886, respectively), two Glastonbury, Connecticut, sisters in their 70s, received international publicity for their refusal to pay taxes unless they were given the right to vote in town meetings in 1869. Abigail Duniway's (1834–1915) weekly Portland, Oregon, newspaper, the *New northwest,* founded in 1871, also became a vehicle for women's suffrage.

With the text of the Fourteenth Amendment and a copy of New York State's constitution in hand, Anthony voted in the presidential elections on November 5, 1872, with other women following her lead. Three weeks later, she and three election inspectors were arrested and brought to trial, which lasted until 1874 and enabled the issue to become newsworthy as the trial of Susan B. Anthony. The trial also highlighted that women were not allowed to serve as jurists at the time.

Meanwhile, Virginia Minor (1824–94) had also tried to vote in the 1872 presidential election in Missouri. Her husband, Francis Minor, filed suit when his wife was turned away at the polls by the voter registrar. The couple petitioned for their case to be heard by the Supreme Court, and their appeal was accepted. The Court ruled that, although Virginia Minor was a citizen, the Fourteenth Amendment did not guarantee her right to vote. (The Fourteenth Amendment would not be interpreted as protecting women's rights until the Supreme Court's 1971 decision in *Reed v. Reed.*)

Congress passed a constitutional amendment that enfranchised women in 1878, but the act would not be ratified by the states for decades. The campaign labored on in the postbellum years, and many of the activities are recorded in a multivolume work, *History of Woman Suffrage,* authored by Stanton, Anthony, and Matilda Josyln Gage (1826–98), that was later published in 1881, 1882, 1886, and 1902.

Upon being admitted to the Union in 1890, Wyoming became the first state to grant suffrage, followed by Colorado in 1893, and Utah and Idaho in 1896. With the right to vote, women's insistence on access to higher education, trades, and professions, and married women's rights to own property were gaining public awareness and acceptance.

The two suffrage groups, NWSA and ASWA, united in 1890 as the National American Woman Suffrage Association (NAWSA). Carrie Chapman

Catt (1859–1947) was named its president in 1900. She left in 1904 to care for her ill husband and upon his death in 1905 became involved with the International Women's Suffrage Alliance. Meanwhile, Ida B. Wells-Barnett (1862–1931) organized a national movement for black women. Presidency of NAWSA was assumed from 1904 to 1915 by Dr. Anna Shaw (1847–1919), under whose leadership membership grew from 17,000 to 200,000 women.

Inspired by the British example, increasing numbers of African-American and working-class women joined the movement during the opening decade of the 20th century, leading to a more diverse movement, socially, economically, and politically.

A younger generation of suffragists, including Alice Paul (1885–1977) and Lucy Burns (1879–1966), picked up the struggle for a federal amendment to the constitution for women's suffrage with renewed energy after 1912. Largely inspired by the high media coverage of Emmeline Pankhurst's prison hunger strikes and protest marches in Britain, Paul and Burns organized a large-scale parade on March 3, 1913, in Washington, D.C., the day before Woodrow Wilson's inauguration. The parade of 8,000 women was the largest of its kind ever seen in the U.S. capital and was Paul's first attempt to arouse public support for women's rights on a broad scale, with floats and banners and an audience of a half-million people.

After trying in vain to coordinate her efforts with Chapman, who had returned to NAWSA, in 1913 Paul created the Congressional Union for Woman Suffrage, which was renamed the National Women's Party in 1916. Under Paul's leadership, picket lines, marches, and hunger strikes became prominent tactics used to pressure the government and President Wilson to grant women the right to vote. In the climate just before the nation entered into the throes of World War I, the tactics did not garner much public support.

Another influential woman during this time was Emma Goldman, who advocated free speech, birth control, women's equality and independence, and union organizations. She was imprisoned for two years for criticizing mandatory conscription of young men into the military during World War I. Deported in 1919, she participated in international social and political events, including the Russian Revolution and the Spanish Civil War, until her death in 1940.

In 1918, President Wilson endorsed the amendment allowing women to vote, pending ratification by two-thirds of the states (32 of 48 states). The 32nd state to vote for constitutional ratification was Tennessee. In a historic moment, the young state legislator from Niota, Tenn., Harry T. Burn, changed his intended vote to support the amendment, at the urging of a note from his mother. Ratification allowed 25 million women to vote and the Nineteenth Amendment to the Constitution to become law on August 26, 1920.

In 1919, when ratification of the Nineteenth Amendment seemed imminent, Catt had renamed the National American Woman Suffrage Association the League of Women Voters to educate women about their newfound voting freedom, especially pending employment legislation. Women were divided about which strategy to pursue: demanding equal standing with men or protective legislation that would control the number of hours women could work per week and prevent them from entering certain risky occupations. The Women's Bureau of the Department of Labor formed to gather information about women's conditions at work and to lobby for the protection of women workers from abusive and unsafe conditions.

After the ratification of Nineteenth Amendment in 1920, Paul continued to fight for women's equality in the United States and abroad. In 1938, she founded the World Women's Party, based in Geneva, Switzerland. Her international work included a demand for equality of the sexes in the preamble to the United Nations Charter. In 1923, Paul introduced a draft of the Equal Rights Amendment for the Constitution, called the Lucretia Mott Amendment, at the 75th anniversary of the Seneca Falls conference. Now that women had won suffrage, guaranteed equality under the Constitution was Paul's next goal. The amendment was finally passed by Congress in 1972, but it failed to win ratification.

Other Fronts

At first American women focused on property, civil, and voting rights, but as they became aware of how long it might take to effect change, they also turned their attention to other areas of life, from work opportunities, to quality of life, to birth control.

EMPLOYMENT RIGHTS

An important social activist who focused on employment rights was Florence Kelley (1858–1932). She began to advocate labor reform as early as 1894, when she persuaded the Illinois state legislature to change existing child and women labor laws and limit the workday for women to a maximum of eight hours. The Illinois Association of Manufacturers repealed the legislation in 1895. Kelley then established the National Consumer's League (NCL) in 1899; its main objective was to implement a minimum wage and limited working hours for women and children.

The idea of protecting women and children from labor exploitation through law eventually became a source of conflict with equal rights advocates, who thought a strategy that demanded special protection for women would ultimately backfire in the fight for equal access to labor opportunities.

EDUCATION

As efforts to gain suffrage were thwarted, some women began to focus on education as a way to advance change. In the early 19th century, girls and young women were allowed to attend grade school, academies, or seminaries but were not expected to go beyond that stage, having their domestic and marital duties to occupy them. The wife of a male school headmaster, Emma Willard (1787–1870), asked for funds from the New York State legislature in 1819 to open a women's college. The state refused her request, and she was forced to use her own funds to open the Troy Female Seminary, in 1821. Among its graduates was Elizabeth Cady Stanton.

In 1833, Oberlin College in Ohio became the first college in the United States to admit women, coeducating them with men. The first all-women college to offer a bachelor of arts degree in a variety of disciplines was Mount Holyoke in 1837 in South Hadley, Massachusetts, founded by Mary Lyon (1797–1849), a former assistant principal of Ipswich Female Seminary, which she had found limiting in its ambitions for women, given its missionary focus.

Access to education varied according to one's social, racial, and economic background. The Morrill Act of 1862 provided land grants for colleges where men and women could receive basic technical and agricultural training to pioneer the West. This happened along with generous land development accommodations from the Homestead Act, which granted 160 acres of public land to citizens who would purchase the land after living on it for five years.

Three private colleges in Ohio—Antioch, Oberlin, and Hillsdale (which later moved to Michigan)—and two public universities—the University of Iowa and the University of Utah (formerly Deseret)—admitted women before the Civil War. The war caused fewer male students to enroll, making some postsecondary institutions more amenable to admitting women.

By 1870, eight state universities accepted women. While coeducation was not allowed by the more established universities, expensive all-women colleges, called "sister schools," began to flourish in the late 1800s. They included Vassar in 1865, Wellesley and Smith Colleges in 1875, Radcliffe College in 1879, Bryn Mawr College in 1885, and Barnard College in 1889. By the turn of the century, 15 percent of college alumni were female. However, their limited access to specialized training in medicine, law, politics, and education, in turn, affected their ability to become physicians, lawyers, politicians, and college professors.

Women's demand for higher education was fueled by the appearance of some home appliances (such as mechanical carpet sweepers, kitchen gadgets, glass jars, canned food, and public laundries) and the development of electricity, which freed women from their full-time domestic duties. The phonograph, the radio, and the telegraph, alongside the increasing availability of reading material for women that informed them about the world, also stirred women's ambitions. The growth of primary schools led to a shortage of teachers that fed the demand for educated personnel. Another impetus to educating women was the increase in the range of jobs that women could pursue that began during the Civil War. Although it remained limited (including domestic servants, agricultural laborers, seamstresses, milliners, teachers, textile mill workers, and laundresses), the increase of the number of women in the workforce contributed to social awareness that education might better prepare them to work.

Women were finding ways to make their mark even though their contributions were slow to make it into history books. The cardiologist and pediatrician Helen Brooke Taussig (1898–1986) contributed to the field of cardiac surgery with her theories about "blue babies"—babies who lacked oxygen from arterial constriction between the heart and lungs and were often left to die. The surgeon Alfred Blalock performed the groundbreaking Blalock-Taussig shunt during an operation in 1945 using her groundwork, assisted by the African American Vivien T. Thomas. Taussig later earned the Medal of Freedom, the highest civilian honor bestowed by an American president, for this contribution.

The decades following World War II saw an explosion in the number of male students who entered higher education institutions due to the return home of veterans under the GI bill. As service benefits applied only to men, women's enrollment in colleges declined during the 1950s. During the 1960s and 1970s, all-male higher education institutions began to open their doors to women because of social and legislative changes. Women's colleges began to merge with all-male or coeducational institutions. Declining enrollment and financial problems in women's colleges caused some to close, as they could not keep up with the increased competition in higher education. Although the number of women's colleges decreased from over 200 in 1960 to 83 by 1993, women's enrollment in higher education regained momentum in the 1960s and 1970s. In 1970, 68 women enrolled for every 100 men, and in 1978, the ratio was 100 women for every 100 men. By the 1980s, female students outnumbered male students, 110 to 100.[1]

STANCE AGAINST ALCOHOLISM

The temperance movement spurred on by women's groups in the 1870s was a precursor to the Prohibition era of the 1920s. The Woman's Crusade of 1873–74 had opposed the manufacturing of alcohol and operation of saloons, forcing some owners to close their doors and engage in another line of work.

Catt noted at the time that the liquor industry was a powerful opponent of women's suffrage—with good reason.

Women who had gained the right to vote in 16 states were largely responsible for the launch of the Prohibition era, as in 1917 they used that power to pass the Eighteenth Amendment, banning the manufacturing and selling of alcohol in the United States.

THE BIRTH CONTROL MOVEMENT

Although the first birth control clinic was founded by a Dutch physician, Aletta Jacobs (1854–1929), in 1878, in Amsterdam, the birth control movement in America would have to wait for several more decades. In 1873, public morality had already culminated in the Comstock Act, which classified information about birth control—including rubber condoms, diaphragms, chemical suppositories, vaginal sponges, and medicated tampons as well as classical techniques of rhythm and withdrawal—as immoral. The notion of a woman's right to own her body and control her own reproduction and sexuality was a novel concept of the women's movement. One of the leading birth control reformers was Margaret Sanger (1879–1966), a public health nurse. She gave up her New York practice in 1912 to focus on the distribution of information about contraceptives. Arrested for distributing obscene material, she managed to flee to England, where she founded the National Birth Control League. During World War I, she returned to the United States, where she opened the first birth control clinic in 1916 but was arrested and received a 30-day jail sentence in a workhouse in 1917 because she was deemed "a public nuisance." Nevertheless, an American judge ruled in 1918 that contraceptive devices could be used legally to prevent disease.

The birth control movement emerged as a respectable cause once the drive for suffrage reached its culmination in 1920. This meant women needed to be educated about birth control methods such as contraceptive suppositories and the decision to become a mother. The National Birth Control League became the American Birth Control League in 1921 and later was renamed the Planned Parenthood Federation of America in 1942. Prior to that, a 1936 Supreme Court decision declassified birth control information as obscene material. Throughout the 1940s and 1950s, legal suits occupied birth control advocates, but the movement still made strides and resulted in the U.S. Supreme Court's striking down the last remaining state law (in Connecticut) to prohibit married couples use of contraceptives in 1965. (Unmarried women's right to contraception was recognized in 1972.)

The Stock Market Crash of 1929

The Depression era that was initiated in the United States by the stock market crash on October 29, 1929, caused the federal government to urge women to leave job opportunities to male heads of households. Nevertheless, during the administration of President Roosevelt (1932–45), the first lady, Eleanor Roosevelt, worked hard to represent women's rights in the workplace, often urging her husband to employ women in government positions. He made Francis Perkins (1880–1965) the first female cabinet member as secretary of labor. Mrs. Roosevelt also extended her support to minority men and women. Mary McLeod Bethune (1875–1955) became the Negro affairs director for the National Youth Administration during Roosevelt's administration.

World War II

The advent of another world war meant women were enticed back into the labor market to make up for the shortage of men in both civilian and military jobs. From 1939 to 1945, over 6 million women were estimated to be employed outside the home. Women's percentage in the workforce grew from 25 percent in 1940 to 35 percent in 1945 with nearly 19 million women employed outside the home by the end of the war. Of those, three-quarters were married, a majority were over the age of 35, and more than a third had children under the age of 14.[2]

Women now held nontraditional jobs in the blue-collar sector: in shipyards and airplane plants, as welders and crane operators. The famous Rosie the Riveter was the icon—inspired by real women—for Americans in the 1940s who assembled bombs, built tanks, welded hulls, and greased locomotives. As men were shipped to the front lines, women moved into assembly lines, enticed by higher wages and a propaganda poster featuring a muscle-bound Rosie the Riveter exclaiming, "We Can Do It!"

Almost 300,000 women served in the armed forces, mostly the army and navy, in noncombatant jobs as secretaries, typists, and nurses. However, some were involved in military activities, namely, the Women's Airforce Service Pilots (WASPs), who were responsible for ferrying airplanes to strategic points. Nancy Harkness Love's (1914–76) Women's Auxiliary Ferrying Squadron and Jacqueline Cochran's (1910–80) Women's Flying Training Detachment trained women to work within the United States and Great Britain. The Women's Army Corps tried to recruit women with the claim that it could offer 239 kinds of jobs for women, including radio repairing.[3]

Of the thousand or so women who enlisted in the flying programs, 38 women pilots in the WASP program were killed in service, while drawing $250 a month as army employees. Jacqueline Cochran wrote in her final report that this "was slightly less than that of a 2nd Lieutenant with flight pay." She also noted, "There was no promotion or advancement in pay depending on length of service," meaning veterans were paid the same rate as inductees.[4] During their flying careers in World War II, she and other women lived a military style of life and were expecting to be commissioned as officers in the Army Air Forces, an action that was never approved by the U.S. Congress.

In spite of the mounting evidence that women were competent in the workplace and in the battlefield, the American government promoted women's war work as a temporary response to an emergency.

The 1950s: The Silence before the Storm

War-weary Americans were eager for the resumption of traditional life. Although the women's movement did not disappear, it became more subdued. Several lesbian organizations in the United States were founded in the early 1950s, including the Daughters of Bilitis, a name inspired by a poem by the Frenchman Pierre Louys about women in love. Founded in 1955 in San Francisco, California, it had a growth in membership sufficient for a national convention in 1960. However, even by the time of its third convention in the 1970s the discussion of lesbian rights was still considered taboo and separate from women's rights.

Images of women's freshly found domestic bliss in television series like *Blondie* or *Father Knows Best* were offset by the reality of women's struggling to find work during peacetime. In further contrast to media images of traditional family life, the number of single mothers and divorced women also started to increase.

The 1960s and 1970s: Women Go Professional

In the 1960s and 1970s, feminism experienced a rebirth in the United States. Several influential leaders emerged to become icons for this second wave of the women's liberation movement (a term coined in 1968), including Betty Friedan (1921–2006), Bella Abzug (1920–98), Shirley Chisholm (1924–2005), and Gloria Steinem (1934–   ).

In 1963, Betty Friedan published *The Feminine Mystique,* which emerged from her survey of colleagues at a 20-year college reunion, inspiring women to seek fulfillment beyond their roles as homemakers. The best seller documented the impact that limited life options and emotional and intellectual oppression had on middle-class educated women.

Bella Abzug, a female politician from New York, founded Women Strike for Peace in 1961 and the reformist New Democratic Coalition later. Known for her wide-brimmed hats and New York chutzpah, Abzug vocally opposed the Vietnam War, made herself a bitter enemy of President Nixon, and became the first Jewish congresswoman. She was elected to the U.S. House of Representatives from New York in 1970 and became a leader of the House antiwar movement and a vigorous proponent of women's rights. Abzug founded the National Women's Political Caucus with Friedan and Chisholm in 1972.

After her loss in a Senate primary in 1976 and in a New York City mayoral primary in 1977, Abzug went on to found and head the Women's Environment and Development Organization and to take a more active role in international women's affairs.

Chisholm, the first black woman to become a congresswoman, was a founding member of the Congressional Black Caucus in 1969. She also became the first black woman to run for president in 1972. She addressed social, economic, educational, and political issues affecting black women through the National Political Congress of Black Women, which she also founded.

The media became a vehicle for the women's movement when Gloria Steinem founded *Ms.* magazine in 1971. When few women journalists were covering politics, Steinem took up the political beat. She also founded the National Women's Political Caucus, the Women's Action Alliance, and the Ms. Foundation for Women.

During that era, activism was also fueled by younger college women who participated in the antiwar and Civil Rights movements but found themselves hampered by domestic gender issues and legal and social barriers in education, political influence, and economic power. A component of the movement was the use of "consciousness-raising" as a tool, for example, by the Redstockings, who in 1969 combined education with social revolution to produce alternative think tanks and strategies toward winning women's rights, and the Women's International Terrorist Conspiracy from Hell (WITCH), which combined spontaneous street theater with protest to gain attention to women's causes.

Other organizations began to address the needs of specific subgroups, including those of blacks, Latinas, Asian Americans, lesbians, welfare recipients, business owners, aspiring politicians, tradeswomen, and professional women.

EMPLOYMENT

At the urging of Esther Peterson (1906–97), director of the Women's Bureau of the Department of Labor, in 1961, President Kennedy convened the Commission on the Status of Women and named Eleanor Roosevelt as its chair. The report issued by the commission in 1963 documented discrimination against women in virtually every area of American life. State and local governments quickly followed suit and established their own commissions for women, to research conditions and recommend changes that could be initiated.

Several federal laws improved the economic status of women at this time: The Equal Pay Act of 1963 required equal wages for men and women doing equal work; the Civil Rights Act of 1964 (Title VII) prohibited employment discrimination based on sex, race, religion, and national origin by any company with 25 or more employees; and a Presidential Executive Order in 1967 prohibited bias against women in hiring by federal government contractors.

Discrimination complaints were to be investigated by the newly established Equal Employment Opportunity Commission (EEOC). One of the issues the commission took up in its early years were the sex-based "help wanted" advertisements in newspapers. Under Title VII, it was unlawful for newspapers to have separate classified job advertising sections for whites and blacks, and the commission eventually found sex-segregated classified advertising unlawful in 1968, despite the strong protest of newspaper publishers. However, the ruling was not enforced until several years later, when the National Organization for Women (NOW) took the issue to the Supreme Court.

The proportion of women in the civilian labor force rose from nearly 34 percent in 1950 to 51 percent in 1980, representing an increase of 17 percentage points, while men's role declined from 86 percent to 77 percent in that same period. By 1978, 27 percent of women worked full time and year round. This percentage increased to 42 percent by 1997.[5]

Financial liberation also took place in the 1970s. With the Equal Credit Opportunity Act in 1974, married women were finally allowed to obtain independent credit without their husband's signature. This meant they could open bank accounts and hold credit cards in their own name. Interestingly, Citicorp appointed its first female vice president, Diana K. Mayer, in 1974.

NOW

The National Organization for Women (NOW) was founded by Betty Friedan and 27 other women at the Third National Conference of the Commission on the Status of Women, in Washington, D.C., in 1966. Friedan became its first president. Another founder, the Reverend Pauli Murray (1910–85), the first African-American woman Episcopal priest, coauthored NOW's original Statement of Purpose: "The purpose of NOW is to take action to bring women into full participation in the mainstream of American society now, exercising all privileges and responsibilities thereof in truly equal partnership with men."

Older, middle-class professional women joined the organization in large numbers and helped NOW to grow into an important organization that stood for civil and equal rights. NOW campaigned for changes through legislation in abortion rights, federal support of child care centers, equal access to funding for education, and employment.

EDUCATION

Title IX in the Education Codes of 1972 made equal access to higher education and to professional schools the law and prohibited discrimination based on sex. Women could now become doctors, lawyers, engineers, architects, and other professionals and attend graduate schools. However, perhaps its most visible impact has been on female athletes. An increase in female participation—one in 27 high school girls played sports in 1971 compared with one in three in 2004—affected girls and women from grade school to the Olympic Games.

AFFIRMATIVE ACTION

The EEOC established a commission in 1972 to enforce the establishment of racial and sex quotas, called *affirmative action*, a term first coined in 1964 when the then-president, Lyndon B. Johnson, issued two executive orders, 11246 and 11375, requiring government contractors and educational institutions receiving federal funds "to correct the effects of past and present discrimination." The policy sought to address the problem of unequal representation of women, ethnic, and other disadvantaged groups.

Charges of reverse discrimination challenged affirmative action in the late 1970s. In spite of several court cases, such as the *Regents of the University of California v. Bakke* (1978), and voluntary affirmative-action programs in unions and private businesses, the U.S. Supreme Court let existing programs stand and approved the use of quotas in 1979. In the 1980s, the federal government's role in affirmative action was considerably diluted. In three cases in 1989, the Supreme Court undercut court-approved affirmative action plans by giving greater standing to claims of reverse discrimination, voiding the use of minority set-asides where past discrimination against minority contractors was unproved, and restricting the use of statistics to prove discrimination, since statistics did not prove intent.

The Supreme Court further limited the use of race in awarding of government contracts in 1995 in *Adarand Constructors, Inc. v. Federico Pena, Secretary of Transportation,* when a firm contested being passed over for a contract, in spite of its low bid for a guard-rail highway contract, for another firm with ethnically diverse employees. The decision caused government programs to change their criterion for eligibility from race- or sex-based discrimination to a condition of being "socially disadvantaged." California and other states followed suit by prohibiting race and sex preference in state and local programs. A 2003 Supreme Court decision concerning affirmative action in universities allowed educational institutions to consider race as a factor in admitting students as long as it was not used in a mechanical, formulaic manner.

AFRICAN-AMERICAN WOMEN

The roots of black feminism go back to the late 19th century, when Mary Church Terrell (1863–1954), Josephine St. Pierre Ruffin (1842–1924), and Anna Julia Cooper (1858–1964) formed the National Association of Colored Women (NACW) in 1896, joining more than 100 black women's clubs.

By 1935, Mary McLeod Bethune organized the National Council of Negro Women, a coalition of black women's groups that lobbied against job discrimination, racism, and sexism, further carrying out the mission.

It would take several more decades, and the Civil Rights movement in the 1960s, for the women's movement to unite black and white women on issues common to both, namely, rights for all women, regardless of race or creed.

Black feminism gained prominence in the 1970s when black women perceived that their concerns about sexism and racism were not being addressed by the women's movement or the black Civil Rights movement. In May 1973, approximately 30 African-American women held an all-day gathering in NOW's donated New York offices. With no specific agenda other than mutual recognition, the women discovered their politics were diverse, causing them to form separate organizations. The National Black Feminist Organization (NBFO) was one of the organizations founded as a result of the meeting. Its first chapter was formed in August 1973 in New York City. Other chapters soon followed suit in other major U.S. cities. In addition to seeking change in the way black women were portrayed in the media, NBFO fought for minimum wage for domestic workers, raised consciousness about rape and sexual abuse, and worked with political candidates on black women's issues. By November, the first Eastern Regional Conference on Black Feminism was held, attracting a few hundred African-American women from around the United States. Among the objectives of the conference organizers was to address politics, racism, and sexism from the perspective of the black community and the larger women's movement. The national organization dissolved in 1977, but independent chapters continued to work at local and regional levels.

Other organizations were Black Women Organized for Action (BWOA) in San Francisco in 1973 and the Combahee River Collective in Boston in 1974, which later protested the murders of 12 black women in Boston in 1979. Black feminist scholarship grew, starting with the publication of *Conditions: Five—The Black Womens Issue* in 1979, and began to identify with women in developing countries. Black feminism became a field of study in the 1990s.

One of the leaders of the black feminist movement was Coretta Scott King (1928–2006), who pursued the goals of equality for minorities long after her husband, Martin Luther King, Jr., died in April 1968. While raising their four children, she was successful in establishing the federal King holiday in February and making it a day of action and service using the slogan "A Day On Not a Day Off." She helped secure social reform legislation, including the 1978 Humphrey-Hawkins Full Employment Act and the Anti-Apartheid Act of 1986, and supported campaigns for national health care and better funding for education. She also supported gay rights with the Employment Non-Discrimination Act (ENDA) of 1994, when she argued that "freedom and justice cannot be parceled out in pieces to suit political convenience."[6]

BIRTH CONTROL

Although the knowledge of how to make a contraceptive pill had been available since the 1920s, it was not until the 1950s that the "Pill" was developed by a reproductive scientist, Gregory Pincus; supported financially and morally by Sanger; and put on the market in the 1960s.

In 1965, a Supreme Court decision in *Griswold v. Connecticut* ruled that married couples in all states could obtain contraceptives legally, and in 1972, in *Eisenstadt v. Baird,* the U.S. Supreme Court found that the right of privacy recognized for married couples in *Griswold v. Connecticut* should extend to unmarried couples and their procreative decisions. These two decisions finally overturned the Comstock Law of 1873, which had ruled information about birth control as "obscene."

Opponents to birth control denounced the Pill as a way to control the population and limit births among certain races. Others proclaimed its unnatural effects, manipulative nature, and irreverence for what should occur naturally. Nevertheless, by 1982, about 54 million women of childbearing age (15 to 44) in the United States would use some form of contraception.[7]

However, in 1969, the medical journalist Barbara Seaman published *The Doctor's Case against the Pill,* in which she assembled evidence from physicians, medical researchers, and women who had used oral contraceptives that the Pill posed a serious health threat to women.

Simultaneously, African Americans became increasingly ambivalent about the motives of the U.S. government in making the Pill available to low-income black communities: In 1969, a violent protest by men in an African-American community of Pittsburgh, Pennsylvania, who opposed contraception as a potential means of population control, led to the closing of a Planned Parenthood Clinic. In response to the controversial closing, feminist writers such as Toni Cade Bambara (1939–95) touted the benefits of the Pill, arguing that it allowed women to make their own decisions about fertility.

Pill hearings in 1970 held pharmaceutical companies accountable for cancer-producing levels of estrogen and consequently led to the lowering of the dosage and a rise in prescriptions. The National Women's Health Network also used the occasion to demand an end to "white-coated" gods and their practice of not informing patients of all potential side effects or risks. This was the beginning of what evolved into a patient/physician partnership in decision making about patients' care.

ROE V. WADE

Soon after the Supreme Court recognized the right to privacy for unmarried couples in *Eisenstadt v. Baird*, it guaranteed in *Roe v. Wade* the right to obtain an abortion during the first trimester of pregnancy. The decision in 1973 represented freedom of choice for millions of couples and single women about terminating an unplanned pregnancy. In 1973, 616,000 legal abortions were performed. This grew to 1.4 million by 1990.[8] Legalized abortion generated a backlash of antiabortion and antifeminist activism.[9] Even though the number of abortions declined after its peak in 1990 as a result of more effective birth control methods, the right to obtain an abortion continued to fuel opposition.

THE EQUAL RIGHTS AMENDMENT

The Equal Rights Amendment (ERA), first drafted by Alice Paul in 1922, was passed by Congress in 1972 and sent on to individual states for ratification with a time limit of 1982. The wording of the ERA was simple: "Equality of rights under the law shall not be denied or abridged by the United States or by any state on account of sex."

Many women's organizations, including NOW and the League of Women Voters, supported the legislation. Others, however, opposed it. Stop ERA, founded by Phyllis Schlafly (1924–   ), was one of the chief opponents of the ERA; the organization was formed to demonstrate how ratifying such a measure would undo the work of protective labor laws. Other anti-ERA organizers, including fundamentalist religious women's groups, warned it would prevent women from being supported by their husbands, overturn privacy rights, obligate women to be drafted into combat, and allow widespread abortion and homosexual marriage.

When the deadline for ratification came and went in 1982, the ERA was just three states short of the 38 needed to amend the U.S. Constitution. Seventy-five percent of the women legislators in those three pivotal states supported the ERA, but only 46 percent of the men voted to ratify it.

Taken up as one of the top priorities of NOW in 2006, constitutional equality is still on the agenda in the 21st century. Its supporters argue that the ERA would serve as a permanent guarantee of women's rights in the United States.

CURRENT SITUATION

The early work to win the right to vote that culminated in the ratification of the Nineteenth Amendment in 1920 freed subsequent generations of women in the United States to express their political will. Generations of women have since enjoyed this right and others, such as property and educational rights. A second wave of feminists began in the 1960s and 1970s to focus on better access to education, political representation, reproductive rights, equality in the workplace, and the need to redefine the relationship between men and women. It led to many additional changes in legislation, as well as a cultural shift in ideas about family, gender relations, and father- and motherhood. A third wave of activists began in the 1990s to address the issues that have stubbornly persisted. They include fair pay, better access to high-level career opportunities, and fair representation of women in government and management.

However, areas of interest to the current generation of the movement go well beyond politics and economics and the borders of the United States. In addition to concerns about violence against women, women are seeking improved conditions for child care and kinship care, gay rights, reproductive rights, racism, and transnationalism. Among the Latina population in the United States, immigration rights are part of the agenda. How women are portrayed in television and film and the small number of meaningful, strong characters in movies are also themes that rally women. Adequate access to health care, health insurance, abortions, and screening for potentially deadly viruses, such as human papilloma virus (HPV), are now also included in the list of concerns. A more recent addition is the demand for additional research into the biological distinctions between women and men and their different reactions to medical treatments.

Political and Legal Rights

In the eight decades since women in the United States won the right to vote, women have gradually become educated about how to use the power of suffrage. Women have consistently been voting at higher rates than men in presidential elections since 1980, and the gap widens with each election as proportionally more women vote. In the 2004 presidential elections, according to the U.S. Census Bureau, women turned up at the polls at a rate of 60.1 percent compared with 56.3 percent for men. The 67.3 million women who voted, compared with 58.5 million men, for a difference of 8.8 million, is up from the 2000 elections, when 7.8 million more women than men voted. Women also outvoted men within all racial and ethnic groups—African American, Latino, Asian/Pacific Islander, and white.

Still, not all women are yet taking advantage of the privilege of voting. During the 2000 election, of eligible women, 29.7 percent were not registered to vote, 70.9 percent of women were registered, and 60.7 percent actually voted.

A balanced gender representation is needed within legislation, especially when it comes to women's issues, and yet the percentage of judicial, executive, and legislative seats held by women in the federal government continues to be limited in the United States. In the November 2004 elections, of 435 seats in the House of Representatives, 15.2 percent (66 seats) were held by women, and of the Senate's 100 seats, women occupied 14 percent.[10] This means the United States ranked 67th in the world in terms of women's representation in national legislatures or parliaments, out of over 187 directly electing countries.

Organizations like EMILY's List (EMILY stands for Early Money Is Like Yeast), a grassroots political network of Democratic Party women in Washington, D.C., are attracting and supporting pro-choice women who wish to occupy seats within the government.

Property and Financial Rights

Early English common law in America dictated that husband and wife formed one union or person, represented by the husband. Legislation from the 1830s to the 1890s helped to protect married women's legal right to property, particularly from husbands' creditors.

Property ownership has been less of an issue in the United States since 1974, when married women won the right to maintain credit cards and bank accounts in their own name with the passage of the Equal Credit Opportunity Act (ECOA).

Until the 1980s, most states opposed premarital agreements, as common law held that both husband and wife equally own property. But since 1983, half of the states have adopted the Uniform Premarital Agreement Act to protect an individual's property owned prior to marriage. The Uniform Marital Property Act of 1983 supports spouses' sharing equally in property acquired during the marriage.

Educational Rights

Since the time women were granted the right to equal access to education in the 1970s, the focus has shifted to fulfilling these rights and using them to influence girl's and women's behavior and life choices, from self-esteem to career choices.

Gender inequality was addressed by the government in the 1970s through a variety of measures. Title IX of the Educational Amendment Act in 1972 revolutionized the way universities and colleges could treat women. Until then, women could be denied access to the best libraries in the university or even the school cafeteria. The act excluded military academies, however. In 1970, of the 8.5 million people enrolled in colleges, women represented only 41 percent. By 1980, women represented 51 percent, surpassing men in higher education enrollment.

A current concern in the United States is the number of students who do not complete high school. In spite of the educational reforms from 1985 to

2005—including government-driven programs like "No Child Left Behind"— the number of male and female students who drop out of high school has grown to 25 to 30 percent and was about 50 percent among minorities such as Latinos and African Americans, in 2006.[11]

Of the 75 percent of all teenagers age 17 graduating from high school in 2004, however, women were as likely as, or more likely than, men to graduate, a pattern that has been consistent since data were collected in the late 1800s.[12]

Women high school graduates are also more likely to enroll in college than their male counterparts. As of 2002, 57 percent of students enrolled in higher education were women. Among the 2.7 million high school graduates in 2004, 1.02 million young women enrolled in college, versus 815,000 young men.[13] By 2005, 35 percent more girls enrolled in tertiary education than boys. [14]

Yet, the increase in the number of young women who enroll in college does not mean women are improving their options of what to train for, and they are largely still destined for female occupations as opposed to the traditionally male-dominated fields of science, mathematics, politics, and law. For example, although over 50 percent of law students are women, and more women than men graduate from law school today, only 30 percent of the 735,000 lawyers in 2004 were women, and even fewer females were partners in law firms.[15] Nevertheless, law is one of the seven occupations with the highest median weekly earnings among full-time working women, at $1,255 a week.[16]

In spite of their dwindling numbers, private four-year women's colleges confer a larger proportion of women's bachelor's degrees in mathematics, computer sciences, and physical sciences than private four-year coeducational institutions. Since the early 1990s, women have occupied nearly 70 percent of professional staff and faculty positions in women's colleges. The average salaries of full-time faculty members at women's colleges were also higher than those at similar coeducational institutions.

Overall, the number of women who have completed higher education has tripled in one generation. Nearly 33 percent of women ages 25 to 64 years held a college degree in 2004, compared with about 11 percent in 1970. Females represented over half of the total number of graduates from college and one-third of those awarded doctoral (Ph.D.) degrees as of 2000.

Social, Employment, and Economic Rights

Access to education has meant access to better employment opportunities and overall earnings. Women who graduated from college earned about 76 percent more than women with only a high school diploma in 2004. Nevertheless, women still faced the challenge of receiving equivalent pay to that of their male counterparts and accessing high-level jobs. On average, women with a four-year degree earned the same wages as men with a high school diploma.

THE WORKING WOMAN

Women increased their labor force participation from 43 percent in 1970 to 59 percent in 2000 according to the U.S. Census. Beginning with the need to replace men in the labor force who were going off to war, this trend continued in the second half of the 20th century.[17] Whereas one in three women was employed in 1950, three in five were employed in 1998. Between 1950 and 1998, the dramatic increase in the number of women in the workforce—especially women ages 25–34—more than compensated for the decline in men's participation, which occurred once disability and pensions became more available to men under the age of 50 (with an amendment of the Social Security Act in 1960) and men became eligible for Social Security benefits at age 62.[18] More women found themselves not leaving the workforce after they married and had children.

By the year 2008, married women could make up as much as 48 percent of the labor force, compared with 46 percent in 1998. Of the married women in their 40s who are not in the labor force, 58 percent are stay-at-home caretakers and 29 percent are retired.[19]

The age group of women most active in the workforce has shifted from the 16- to 24-year-olds (representing 43.9 percent of women their age) in 1950, to the 35- to 44-year-olds (representing 76.1 percent of women their age) in 1998.[20] Half to three-quarters of all age groups were active in the workforce in the early 2000s, with the exception of men and women age 65 and older.

Although women make up nearly half of the labor force today, they still do not receive equal pay. According to the Bureau of Labor Statistics, "female college graduates who were full-time wage and salary workers had median weekly earnings that were only 75 percent of those of their male counterparts in 2004, $860 versus $1,143." Most recent census findings in the United States found that women still earn less than men in all occupational groupings[21]: With median yearly earnings of $35,654 for women compared with $50,034 for men in 1999 in management, professional, and related occupations, women's earnings reflect 71.3 percent of men's earnings in this category.

Interestingly, parity most closely exists for wages earned by women and men in "blue-collar" construction, maintenance, and extraction jobs, which compose the second highest-paying occupational group for women ($29,000). Women in these professions earn about 90.6 percent of men's earnings.

The censuses of 1990 and 2000 also observed a new trend: the significant increase in the number of female workers in what were considered traditionally male-dominated occupations, such as the following:

- Police detectives and supervisors—360 percent increase
- Millwrights—315 percent increase
- Civil engineers—196 percent increase
- Automobile mechanics—177 percent increase
- Firefighters—174 percent increase
- Airplane pilots and navigators—167 percent increase

Until the late 20th century, women were denied access to these fields or deterred from studying for them. Trailblazing women such as Sally Ride (1951–), who became the first American female astronaut in 1983, have since made an effort to ensure that girls who have mathematic aptitude know their options include careers in science, math, and engineering. The Sally Ride Science Club reaches out to elementary and middle school girls, and Sally Ride Science creates science publications and educational programs for girls, teachers, and parents.

Although the employment gap is narrowing, women's pay rate ceiling is still quite low compared to men's, even accounting for factors such as occupation, industry, race, marital status, and job tenure. From 1979 to 2004, women's earnings as a percentage of men's increased by 18 percentage points, from 62 to 80 percent.[22]

One factor contributing to the unequal pay of men and women seems to be the difference in work patterns. On average, women spend fewer years in the workforce and work fewer hours per year. More women than men take on part-time work, and on average they leave the labor force for longer periods than men do. Industry, occupation, race, marital status, and job tenure are additional factors that account for earning differences.[23]

WORKING MOTHERS

The issue of juggling work and motherhood is as pressing today as it was for women 25 years ago. Women who continue to fulfill their traditional roles as caretaker—in effect, doubling up on tasks—and the lack of affordable day care in the United States have become key issues, spawning public debate over the different approaches taken in the United States, in contrast with more successful ones in European countries. American women are increasingly relying on statewide paid-leave measures to compensate for the absence of one at a national level.

Proportionately, more adult women today are doing "the balancing act," even though the number of weekly hours of paid work an employed woman must balance with other commitments has not increased substantially beyond what it was in 1980. The exception to this, however, is among married women who have children under the age of six. They have increased the average number of weeks they work, from 36 weeks out of the year in 1978 to 45 weeks in 1998.[24]

By the late 1980s, many European nations, especially Scandinavian countries, had systems of public funding of day care for between 50 and 95 percent of all children between the age of three and compulsory school age (ranging from ages five to seven).[25] Women's organizations in the United States lobbied hard to make affordable child care services available to low- to middle-income mothers and families. These efforts finally resulted in the Child Care and Development Fund (CCDF), federal legislation that provides state-level block grants to day care services since 1990. Nevertheless, with 60 percent of working mothers' children under the age of five in some form of day care by 1999, the problem of high-quality and affordable day care has persisted, largely due to the high cost of day care at an average of $85 per week, which represents nearly one-third of a low-income salary. By fiscal year 2004–05, CCDF funded $4.8 billion in block grants for low-income family child care in U.S. states, territories, and tribes.[26]

THE GLASS CEILING

Senator Robert Dole introduced the Glass Ceiling Act in 1991, and the U.S. Department of Labor created a 21-member, bipartisan Federal Glass Ceiling Commission in the name of Title II of the Civil Rights Act of 1991, with a mandate to study barriers to advancement of minorities and women within corporate hierarchies—a problem that would come to be known as the "glass ceiling."[27] The commission reported its findings and recommendations on ways to dismantle the glass ceiling in 1995:

> *While minorities and women have made strides in the last 30 years, and employers increasingly recognize the value of workforce diversity, the executive suite is still overwhelmingly a white man's world. Over half of all Master's degrees are now awarded to women, yet 95 percent of senior-level managers of the top Fortune 1000 industrial and 500 service companies are men.[28]*

The percentages are the same for Fortune 2000 industrial and service companies. The commission recommended that corporate America use affirmative action as a tool to ensure that all qualified individuals have equal access and opportunity to compete on the basis of ability and merit. The commission also asked that "organizations expand their vision and seek candidates from non-customary sources, backgrounds and experiences, and that the executive recruiting industry work with businesses to explore ways to expand the universe of qualified candidates."[29] Business leaders claimed that they often could not find suitable minority and female candidates because the networks from which they recruited male candidates—with the possible exception of the military—did not include them.

In March 1995, the commission prepared a fact-finding report, *The Environmental Scan,*[30] based on commission hearings, interviews, focus groups, panel discussions, and public and private research. According to this report, there are three kinds of barriers to women who want to make gains in the high-level management world:

- Societal barriers, "which may be outside the direct control of business"
- Internal structural barriers, "within the direct control of business"
- Governmental barriers: lack of monitoring and law enforcement, weak collection of employment-related data, and inadequate reporting on the issue

Improving stature of women in the workplace has made some gains in the United States, with more women in managerial or professional positions as of 2001 and over a quarter of companies owned by women by 2000.[31] A follow-up report released by the Equal Employment Opportunity Commission in 2004 indicated that 36.5 percent of officials and managers in the private sector were women.[32] The General Accounting Office's 2002 study of 10 major industries revealed that five (communications, public administration, business, entertainment, and diverse professions) had female management in proportion to the number of women employed in the industry. The data also showed that within seven of the 10 industries (entertainment, communications, finance, business, professional services, retail trade, professional medical services), the wage gap between male and female managers had actually worsened between 1995 and 2000, as women earned two to 21 cents less than every dollar earned by male managers.[33]

SEXUAL HARASSMENT

Sexual harassment in the workplace has always been an issue for women working outside the home, but dealing with its legal liability is a relatively recent issue. Defined by the Equal Employment Opportunity Commission (EEOC) as "unwelcome sexual advances, requests for sexual favors, and other verbal or physical conduct of a sexual nature . . . when submission to or rejection of this conduct explicitly or implicitly affects an individual's employment, unreasonably interferes with an individual's work performance, or creates an intimidating, hostile or offensive work environment," claims of sexual harassment, which violate Title VII of the Civil Rights Act of 1964, are dealt with by the EEOC. The specifics of Title VII apply to employers who have 15 or more employees, including state and local governments, employ-ment agencies, labor organizations, and the federal government.

Sexual harassment was not highly publicized at first. The first case under Title VII was not filed until 1976. Not until 1991—and the law professor Anita Hill's charges that the Supreme Court nominee Clarence Thomas had made unwelcome sexual advances while he was her supervisor at the EEOC in the 1980s—did it receive wide public attention. Thomas's appointment was subsequently confirmed, but Hill's testimony changed relations between men and women in the workplace from that point forward. Hill's testimony led to an increased sensitivity among employers and employees of both genders to all forms of aggressive discrimination against women in the workplace, which in turn accounted for the sudden increase in complaints. The number of claims received by the EEOC grew from 10,532 in 1992 to 15,549 in 1995 and has been declining slightly ever since. In 2005, the EEOC received 12,679 charges of sexual harassment, of which 14.3 percent were filed by males. The EEOC resolved nearly 50 percent of 12,859 sexual harassment charges in 2005 with the settlement of "no reasonable charge" and recovered $47.9 mil-lion in monetary benefits for charging parties and other aggrieved individuals (not including monetary benefits obtained through litigation).[34]

FINANCIAL FREEDOM

Compared with those in countries in sub-Saharan Africa and South Asia, fewer women live in poverty in the United States. However, women in the United States fare worse when compared to those of western European nations and Japan, Australia, and Canada, with an average of 10 to 15 percent living in poverty. In 2002, 87.9 percent of women lived above poverty level in the United States, where poverty is measured as a percentage of the average income.[35] The poverty rate is proportionally higher for minorities—African Americans, Hispanics, and Native Americans—at about 25 percent.[36] Single mothers are more likely than any other group to file for bankruptcy. One report indicates that nearly half of all single mothers live in or near poverty, and 53 percent are employed in service or administrative fields that tend to offer low earnings, few benefits, and little opportunity for advancement.

Adjacent to this has been the trend of fathers' not fulfilling child sup-port obligations. In the United States, state laws govern child support and vary from state to state. The fourth article of the U.S. Constitution empowers states with the final decision on child support matters, but it was not until the 1910 Uniform Desertion and Non-Support Act that fathers were held punishable by law for deserting and/or not supporting a spouse and/or child under the age of 16. Further measures were taken over the next century to ensure enforcement, resulting in what is known as the Uniform Interstate Family Support Act (UIFSA), especially with the increasing likelihood that a parent will move to a different state. In spite of increased federal and state government resources toward child support enforcement since the 1980s—including the 1984 Child Support Enforcement Amendments to Title IV-D of the Social Security Act enforcing women's ability to collect delinquent child support payments[37]—the proportion of single mothers who receive child support, at 59 percent in 2003, has remained mostly unchanged.[38]

The Bankruptcy Abuse Prevention and Consumer Protection Act law was passed in April 2005 and put in effect in October 2005. Prior bankruptcy law had protected women whose former husbands filed for bankruptcy. The child support and alimony owed could not be discharged by bankruptcy. Under the 2005 law, both child support and some credit card debts are non-dischargeable, thus making it more difficult for the former spouse to collect the child support. When the Senate voted to pass the bankruptcy reform bill, an amendment that would have extended protection to struggling single mothers was voted down.

The reforms being advocated by women's organizations include equal allocation of Social Security benefits between married partners. Less than 40 percent of women currently receive benefits as retired workers compared with 80 percent of men, although 60 percent of women receive some kind of benefit as a spouse of a retired, disabled, divorced (after 10 years of marriage), or deceased worker. Homemakers and working mothers tend to receive less than their working spouses even though they may live longer. Women made up 71 percent of beneficiaries over the age of 85 in 2005.[39] Since the program is intended to provide security to the family, women's organizations—the National Women's Law Center, for one—are guarding women's interests against government reforms that could leave women in poverty at an older age. Privatizing the system and reducing benefits, which are being proposed by the George W. Bush administration, run the risk of decreasing the Social Security benefits women receive under the current law for high- and average-income workers.

WOMEN IN THE MILITARY

Since 1973, when the government switched from all-male conscription to a volunteer force, women have been allowed to enlist in the armed forces. Women enlisted in large numbers during the Vietnam War, doubling their presence between 1972 and 1975, although the number of female officers remained virtually unchanged. Women's organizations were divided over the issue: Some were rallying against U.S. troops in Vietnam in the name of world peace, while others were seeing it as an opportunity for honorable employment.

In the late 1970s, the National Organization for Women (NOW) lobbied for women's equal access to the military. Nevertheless, a 1981 Supreme

Court decision, *Rostker v. Goldberg,* only required male 18-year-olds to register with the draft board, maintaining that the exclusion of requiring women to register was not a violation of the due process clause (Fifth Amendment) of the U.S. Constitution. The Selective Service law still does not require women to register for the draft because of the Department of Defense's policy of restricting women from direct ground combat.

After a prolonged court battle, a high school student, Shannon Faulkner, became the first woman to enroll in a military academy, the Citadel in South Carolina, in 1995. Although she remained there only for her first year of college, she set a precedent for four other female cadets to enroll in 1996. The 1995 Supreme Court decision in her case ruled that discrimination against women was illegal in state-supported military schools, such as the Citadel and Virginia Military Institute.

As with other hard-won rights, the legal battle proved to be only a first step. The military was slow to adjust to the new requirements, and physical assault and harassment made the first decade of coeducational military school a rocky one for the female cadets. At a 1991 convention of the Tailhook Association, a navy aviators' group, 83 female officers and other women were physically assaulted by 117 naval officers. The resulting lawsuit damaged the careers of 14 admirals and 300 aviators and instigated a zero-tolerance policy of discrimination and harassment within the U.S. Navy. In 2003, the Air Force Academy began investigating what turned out to be a decade-long list of sexual harassment allegations against cadets in the air force and overlooked by senior officers. A report issued in September 2004 highlighted several issues that would need to be addressed in the future, including female cadets' fear to report such incidents, lack of training of personnel to handle this kind of violence, absence of documentation and evidence about allegations, an overly strict application of the Privacy Act preventing follow-up on status of cases, and the added complexity of alcohol and consensual sex factors.

As of 2004, 37 percent of the permanent workforce of the army, 32 percent of the air force, and 30 percent of the navy were women.[40] The marines remains largely a male force. The majority of women's positions are in management and program analysis. Of the women in the armed forces, nearly half represent minorities.

Within the armed forces in 2004, 212,516 women were on active duty, 35,112 (17 percent) were officers, 174,929 (82 percent) were enlisted, and 2,115 (1 percent) were cadets or midshipmen. The largest age groups of enrolled women were ages 20 to 21 (7.55 to 8.2 percent) and ages 40 to 44 (5.66 percent).[41]

The debate continues as to what role women should play in the U.S. military. A Pentagon mandate prohibiting women from serving in ground combat units was loosened in 1994 to allow women to take on "supporting" combat roles. Although women have been involved as allied professionals, they are increasingly needed to supplement shortages of men in active militarized zones. Between 2002 and 2005, 33 women were killed in Iraq, five in Afghanistan, and more than 250 were wounded in action.[42] As of 2006, the number of women who died in Iraq grew to 48, representing 2 percent of the total number of U.S. troops killed to that date, and 300 had been wounded, which, although a small number, already exceeds the number of women wounded during the entire Vietnam War.[43]

The Department of Defense identifies 17.3 percent of the selected reserves (the highest status of reserves that is considered essential to wartime mission) as women, making up nearly one-quarter of the army and air force reserves, and 4.7 percent of the marines.

Associated with this has been the need for adequate Veterans Administration (VA) health care benefits for women. The VA estimates that by 2010, 10 percent of the veteran population will be women.[44]

Another sign of continued support for women (and men) in the armed forces has been the upholding of the Family and Medical Leave Act (FMLA) of 1993 among reservists' and National Guard members serving in support of national emergencies. According to a 2002 Department of Labor memorandum signed by President George W. Bush, uniformed service members' active duty time should be counted toward their eligibility to take time off from work under this act.

Access to Medical Care

With improved medical screening technologies, it has become obvious that certain diseases afflict American women in a more devastating way than was recognized before the 1990s, paving the way for a field of study now known as women's health. At the turn of the 21st century, heart disease was to be the number one cause of death in both men and women, followed by cancer and stroke.

However, women's symptoms of heart disease—including shortness of breath and weakness in muscles—are less dramatic than those typical in men, such as sharp chest pain. As a result, men and women have received disproportionate treatment. This condition is quickly changing with public awareness campaigns. Other diseases that have a high mortality rate in women in the United States include cancer, stroke, and chronic lower respiratory diseases; Alzheimer's disease; diabetes; accidents (unintentional injuries); influenza/pneumonia; and kidney disease.[45]

Adequate female and child representation in clinical trials and more accurate attention to symptoms in women that may indicate serious conditions are among the concerns of women about quality of access to health care.

Sex- or biology-based medicine, as a new field of investigation, garnered interest at the legislative level during the 1990s and was one of the issues lobbying for attention in Washington, D.C., before terrorism became the center of attention after the September 11, 2001, attacks on the United States.

The Society for Women's Health Research called attention to sex-based differences in 2001 by initiating the landmark study "Exploring the Biological Contribution to Human Health: Does Sex Matter?" for the Institute of Medicine. The report underscored the need for better understanding of the importance of sex differences and application of that knowledge in improved medical practices and therapies.[46]

Family and Sexuality

The rise in dual-income families during the latter half of the 20th century introduced new issues such as the need for leave of absence for caretaking of a child, parent, or other family member, a responsibility once reserved for homemakers. This issue is discussed in the section "Social, Employment, and Economic Rights."

As in many other countries, sterilization, the birth control pill, and a variety of contraceptives have become primary methods for family planning, making abortion a last recourse.

FORCED STERILIZATION AND LIMITING REPRODUCTIVE FREEDOM

In the early 1900s, the U.S. government founded a eugenics program in an attempt to perfect the gene pool of the population, envisioning a society without crime, mental illness, and homelessness. By the 1970s, an estimated 65,000 males and females had been sterilized, many without their knowledge.[47]

The case of Carrie Buck, a young, "feeble-minded," Virginia woman in the state's care who was forcibly sterilized to prevent her from having more children, set a precedent for the rest of the United States and the Western world, even Nazi Germany, for curbing reproductive freedom. The 1927 decision in *Buck v. Bell,* which upheld a Virginia law permitting the government to order the compulsory sterilization of young women it believed were "unfit to continue their kind," received little public attention compared with the implementation by Germany in 1933 of the Law for the Prevention of Hereditarily Diseased Offspring, a sterilization law that led to more than 400,000 forced sterilizations by the end of World War II. *Buck v. Bell* paved the way for other states to implement sterilization laws in the 1930s and 1940s, and the practice continued well into the 1970s. Although *Buck v. Bell* has yet to be repealed, public attitudes have shifted dramatically against its application, and the practice ended in the 1970s. In 2002, the commonwealth of Virginia issued an apology for its part in eugenics.

REPRODUCTIVE RIGHTS AND ABORTION DEBATE CONTINUES

Women have exercised their right to abortion since it became legal in 1973 with the federal Supreme Court decision in *Roe v. Wade*. In 2002, 1.29 million abortions took place, down from an estimated 1.36 million in 1996. From 1973 through 2002, more than 42 million legal abortions occurred. The majority of abortions occurred in the first 12 weeks of pregnancy. With half of American women experiencing unintended pregnancies, an estimated one in three women will have had an abortion by the time she is 45 years old.[48]

In a 2003 TIME/CNN poll, 55 percent of respondents said they support a woman's right to have an abortion in the first three months of pregnancy. However, 60 percent believed abortion had become too easily accessible.

In the constitutional challenge to the statute prohibiting abortion, Henry Wade represented the state of Texas. The original decision of *Roe v. Wade* was based on two cases: that of an unmarried woman from Texas (anonymously named Roe), where abortion was illegal unless the mother's life was at risk, and that of a poor married mother of three from Georgia, where state law required permission for an abortion from a panel of doctors and hospital officials. The Supreme Court ruled on the legality of abortion from these cases and overrode several state laws preventing it. While establishing the right to an abortion in the first trimester, the decision gave states the right to intervene in the second and third trimesters of pregnancy to protect the woman and the "potential" life of the unborn child.

The National Council of Bishops denounced the Supreme Court decision and soon an antiabortion movement was on the move. In 1976, Congress enacted the Hyde Amendment, which undermined *Roe v. Wade* by barring the use of federal funds to reimburse for the medical expenses involved in abortions for the poor under its Medicaid program, except when the woman's life was endangered by a full-term pregnancy or in the case of rape or incest. The amendment made an example of Rosie Jimenez, a 27-year-old single mother who died of an illegal abortion.

The decision caused pressure on the courts. In a 1989 case, *Webster v. Reproductive Health Services,* the Court limited its application, giving states greater latitude in regulating and restricting abortions. A 1992 case, *Planned Parenthood v. Casey,* reaffirmed the right to have an abortion granted in *Roe v. Wade,* while applying further restrictions. In response to violence against abortion clinics, President Bill Clinton signed the Freedom of Access to Clinic Entrances (FACE) Act in 1994, providing a legal defense against anti-abortion terror.

In September 2000, the use of the early abortion pill RU-486, mifepristone, was approved by the U.S. Food and Drug Administration, to be marketed in the United States as an alternative to surgical abortion. About 37,000 medication abortions were performed in the first half of 2001; these proce-dures involved the use of mifepristone or methotrexate. Although the drug was already available to women in 13 other countries, antiabortion activists prepared for their battle in Congress. The Bush administration imposed restrictions on the drug.

Several rulings in 2003 and 2004 are evidence that the right to abortion is not yet secure. President Bush signed a Congress-approved abortion ban in November 2003 that became the first federal law to make a particular form of abortion—partial-birth abortion—illegal. Planned Parenthood Federation of America (PPFA) and the National Abortion Federation both challenged the constitutionality of the ban in court cases, naming the absence of a health exception for women as one of its faults. In *Planned Parenthood Federation v. Ashcroft*, the judge ruled in favor of PPFA in June 2004, citing its uncon-stitutionality. The same ruling occurred in *National Abortion Federation v. Ashcroft* in August 2004.

The 2006 appointment of Judge Samuel Anthony Alito, Jr. (1950–   ), as a new Supreme Court justice to replace the retiring justice Sandra Day O'Connor, the first woman on the high court, who was known for her deci-sive "swing" vote on abortion, has abortion activists concerned. Alito believes the Constitution does not protect abortion rights. About 30 states have a pre-dominantly antiabortion legislature and government that could quickly pass laws restricting abortion access in as little as two years. An ongoing concern of women's organizations in the United States is how the Supreme Court might handle abortion cases in the future.

CONTRACEPTIVE OPTIONS

The decline in the number of abortions in the United States may be due to the increase in contraceptive options available to women: the female condom, foam, cervical cap, Today Sponge, suppository or insert, jelly or cream, and both female and male sterilization. By 2002, 61.5 million women of child-bearing years, representing about 62 percent of all women, used some form of contraception. In that same year, while the most popular method of con-traception among women age 15 to 29 was the Pill, 19 percent of women age 15 to 44 used the Pill, 17 percent used female sterilization, and 11 percent, condoms.[49] As a result, the fertility rate has held steady at 2.04 children per woman in 2005.[50]

The emergency contraceptive Plan B (levonorgestrel)—also known as the "morning after pill"—approved by the FDA in 1999 by prescription only works essentially the same way the Pill works. Advocates believe it will help to reduce unintended pregnancies and lead to fewer abortions; some even envision a future when pharmacies associated with major retail outlets, such as Wal-Mart, can dispense the drug over the counter. In August 2006, the

FDA, after several years' consideration, agreed to permit the sale of Plan B to women over the age of 18. At least 41 other countries currently allow Plan B to be sold over the counter.

ALTERNATIVE GENDER ROLES: LESBIAN RIGHTS

On a national level, the movement for equal rights for lesbians—or women who have sexual orientation toward other women—has been emerging in the political and legal arenas alongside the gay rights movement in the 1970s. The extent of rights runs a broad gamut, from basic legal rights to sexual freedom, employment, family and adoption, political power, cultural and social rights, as well as means by which to respond to violent and employment discrimination.

Homosexuality in the female population varies according to location within the United States, from 1 to 5 percent in rural areas and possibly as high as 12 percent in urban areas.[51]

At the time the U.S. Supreme Court ruled in *Lawrence v. Texas* in 2003 that laws attempting to criminalize homosexual activity between consenting adults are unconstitutional, 14 states in America had sodomy laws on the book.

Since 1994, the Employment Non-Discrimination Act has given gays and lesbians legal recourse in the workplace and the military. President Clinton reaffirmed the government's policy of nondiscrimination in the hiring and promotion of federal employees in Executive Order 13087, by adding sexual orientation to the list of protected parameters. In the U.S. military service, an informal code of conduct of "Don't ask; don't tell" was implemented by the late 1990s.

Federal discrimination laws and sexual harassment under Title XIX as well as state laws are supposed to protect gays and lesbians from harassment. Hate crimes against gays and transgender people were believed to be on the rise in 2001, with 10 percent more incidents than 1999 and one in six attacks nationwide against transgender people in 2001. The Department of Education defined certain physical forms of sexual harassment in schools as hate crimes against gays and lesbians in 1999, but it did not define heckling as harassment.

Today, gay rights activists focus on a wide range of issues, including the recognition of gay marriages and families as legal entities with access to the same tax and social benefits and adoption, parenting, and other legal rights that couples in heterosexual marriages receive. Since 1998, the Defense of Marriage Act (DOMA) passed by Congress has challenged attempts to institute same-sex marriage privileges by defining a married couple as a man and a woman and permitting states the right to reject any other definition.

In 2004, a flurry of same-sex marriages occurred in California, only to be overturned by the state's law disqualifying such marriages. During 2004, 13 states adopted anti–gay marriage amendments—Arkansas, Georgia, Kentucky, Louisiana, Michigan, Mississippi, Missouri, Montana, North Dakota, Ohio, Oklahoma, Oregon, and Utah—10 of which were adopted during the national elections in November. Prior to 2004, Alaska, Hawaii, Nebraska, and Nevada already had amendments. By the end of 2005, a total of 19 states had added amendments and seven more states were scheduled to vote on state constitutional amendments to define marriage in 2006.[52]

In the United States, marriages among same-sex couples have been permitted in Massachusetts since May 2004, but they are not recognized elsewhere in the United States. Since 2000 in Vermont, 2004 in Connecticut, and 2006 in New Jersey, civil unions of same-sex partners have also been allowed, but without the rights automatically conferred on married couples or recognized by the federal government. A landmark decision by the New Jersey Supreme Court on October 25, 2006, gave the state legislature 180 days (April 22, 2007) to provide same-sex couples with equal access to the protection of marriage. The Religious Freedom and Civil Marriage Protection Act, which redefines civil unions to include same-sex couples, was caught in a legislative battle in California in 2004 and 2005. The District of Columbia, Maine, and Hawaii provide rights under domestic partnership laws, which recognize entitlement to various state benefits of gay couples, such as conferring on the partner of a state employee benefits related to entitlements, alimony, divorce, and property division.

Opponents are trying to settle the issue by implementing a constitutional amendment that defines marriage as the union of a man and a woman; to date that idea has not been accepted.

Violence

RAPE AND DOMESTIC VIOLENCE

Domestic violence in the United States is the leading cause of injury to women ages 15 to 44. In the United States, a woman is more likely to experience violence by a family member than by a stranger. Of the 204,307 rapes and sexual assaults reported in 2004, 67 percent were committed by someone close to the victim and 31 percent by a total stranger, and in 2 percent of cases, the relationship was unknown. These numbers are expected to be double in reality, as only about half of violent crimes are reported.[53] About 1,500 women report being beaten every year, and as many as 20 percent of pregnant women are assaulted by their companion.[54] A woman is twice as likely to be murdered by a spouse as by a total stranger.

In the 1990s, a theoretical correlation was made between violence toward women and its portrayal in the media through television, movies, and magazines. Scientific studies conducted on the relation between pornography—or sexually explicit material—and sexual aggression were inconclusive, however, in proving that all men who viewed such material were moved to aggression.[55]

Attempts to turn this tide have been largely legislative. The Violence against Women Act (VAWA) was passed in 1994 to create a means to deal with violence in the home. The landmark legislation set out to improve criminal justice and community-based responses to domestic violence, dating violence, sexual assault, and stalking in the United States. Under the program, government-sponsored STOP (which stands for "Services, training, officers, and prosecutors," or aspects of the criminal justice system) grants are issued to train state agencies and educate young women. In 1996, gender was added as a category to hate crimes legislation, providing ammunition to counter the offense.

In 2000, findings from the National Violence Against Women Survey conducted by the U.S. Justice Department and the Centers for Disease Control and Prevention from 1995 to 1996 were published. Both men and women were surveyed to provide a balanced view of the victimization experience.[56] The high incidence of rape at an early age—over half of the women who have experienced rape in their lifetime said it occurred before they were 17 years of age—suggested measures need to be taken to combat child abuse, which have since attracted much media attention. A pattern of victimization also began to appear when it was discovered that women who reported they were raped, assaulted, or stalked before age 18 were at least twice as likely to report experiencing the same offense as an adult.

PORNOGRAPHY

Pornography (or the "writing about prostitutes") has been a topic of debate in the United States for nearly half a century, but it has been in existence since the invention of the printing press. Women's concerns about pornography stem from the manipulation of the feminine image and the resulting value that is placed on it by society. With the advent of computer technology in the 1980s, pornography in computer and video games and, more recently, on the Internet has been the focus of legislation and concerned women and parents. The development of child pornography has also raised ethical concerns that are difficult for pornography proponents—in the name of free speech—to counter. As have other countries, America has its own form of antipornography laws, but they have been difficult to enforce. As an industry, pornography has also become a pawn in the hands of organized crime in the United States.

The significance of pornography as a representation of the feminine gender in popular media and advertising has led to diverse views. To some it represents sexual emancipation and liberation from inhibition, while others see it as reinforcing the perception of women as sexual objects. A survey of literature and research by the Commission of Obscenity and Pornography in 1970 in the United States could find no proven causality between pornography and violence against women. Yet in 1986, in a final report by the Attorney General's Commission on Pornography, clinical and experimental research showed that exposure to sexually violent material increases the likelihood of aggression toward women, or antisocial, even unlawful, acts of sexual violence.[57] On the other hand, the report concluded that erotic material that is nondegrading and nonviolent did not bear a causal relationship to rape and other acts of sexual violence.

Obscenity—defined as that which appeals to an interest in sex, or depicts sexual conduct in an offensive manner, and lacks serious literary, artistic, political, or scientific merit—is a category of sexual material that the courts hold to be unprotected by the First Amendment and subject to regulation by the state. Its distribution is a federal crime and a crime in most states, along with distribution of child pornography. In the United States, the antiporn activist Catherine MacKinnon drafted the Minneapolis, Minnesota, and Indianapolis, Indiana, antiporn ordinances of 1983 stating that all women who worked in porn and were coerced could bring a civil lawsuit against producers and distributors. Coercion was deemed to be present even if the woman was of age, she fully understood the nature of the performance, she signed a contract and release, there were witnesses, she was under no threat, and she was fully paid. This was supported by the notion that women are not able to provide true consent in a male-dominated society. Another ordinance also permitted a woman to sue the creators and sellers of pornography provided she could prove that she, or women as a class, had been injured by the pornography, an act that was struck down by a Supreme Court decision in 1986, in *American Booksellers v. Hudnut,* when it favored the protection of the First Amendment over the harm done to women.

In the absence of conclusive evidence that pornography leads to violence against women—although there was much evidence that children needed to be protected from being used in pornography—the laws remained in favor of adults' choosing whether to view pornographic material or not. However, the legal struggle to outlaw pornography has had some success in proving that free speech is not necessarily applicable to regulating pornography. Several Supreme Court decisions have determined that pornography may be an exception to free speech in its association with adverse conditions for women.[58]

HUMAN TRAFFICKING

Human trafficking is defined as the ongoing exploitation of victims who are forced to work against their will. Its victims do not consent to their situation, or their consent is invalidated by the coercive, deceptive, or abusive actions of the traffickers. In spite of the United States's signing of multilateral treaties declaring trafficking of women and children a crime in 1905 (International Agreement for the Suppression of the White Slave Traffic) and 1908 (Traffic in Women and Children), the lucrative trade persists. Although precise dollar estimates have been difficult to come by, the conclusion of one two-year investigation by the Federal Bureau of Investigation of a single brothel in Atlanta, Georgia, estimated that up to 1,000 women had been rotated through brothels in 16 states, with some brothels grossing over $1.5 million in a 28-month period.[59]

The Victims of Trafficking and Violence Protection Act of 2000 enforces tougher sentences on traffickers inside and outside the United States and documents international activities in country reports.

On October 2, 2002, President George W. Bush proclaimed, "Trafficking is nothing less than a modern form of slavery, an unspeakable and unforgivable crime against the most vulnerable members of the global society."[60]

The latest attempt to curb trafficking is an international protocol that entered into force in December 2003 and was ratified in November 2005 by the United States along with 116 other signatory countries, the Protocol to Prevent, Suppress and Punish Trafficking in Persons, Especially Women and Children, which will supplement the United Nations Convention against Transnational Organized Crime of September 2003.

Of the estimated 800,000 to 900,000 people trafficked across international borders each year, the U.S. government estimated in 2003 that 18,000 to 20,000 men and women are trafficked annually into the United States. Additionally, 200,000 youths (ages 10 to 17) are believed to be commercially exploited and trafficked within the United States each year.[61]

Sex trafficking operations often masquerade as viable commercial businesses such as modeling agencies, prostitution, pornography, escort services, or labor exploitation in sweatshops, construction sites, and agricultural settings. *Smuggling* is distinct from trafficking in that it involves "the illegal movement of *consenting* people across a national border for financial or material remuneration," in which the relationship between the smuggler and the migrant ends upon arrival at the destination.[62] Additional forms of forced labor and abuse include domestic servitude and forced marriages.

Although sentencing guidelines were issued to produce more effective judgments against offenders, the sentences are still not as strong as they would need to be to deter others from the lucrative business. In one case,

United States v. Quinton Williams, the defendant was the operator of a prostitution business who transported a 16-year-old juvenile and an adult victim cross-country by car to Indiana, Texas, Arizona, and Nevada, where he supervised their prostitution activities and collected and kept all of their earnings. He was convicted of sex trafficking of children, transporting both a minor and an adult for prostitution, money laundering, and interstate travel in aid of racketeering; was sentenced to 125 months in prison; and was ordered to pay a $2,500 fine.

Religion and Spirituality

Citizens in the United States are entitled to the freedom to choose their religion and the way they practice it or do not. More than 75 percent of the U.S. population is Christian, and the balance is made up of all the world religions, including Judaism, Buddhism, and Islam, as well as about 13 percent unaffiliated with any religion.

Societal pressures based on religious beliefs often have a part in women's not taking advantage of legal rights. In the South, for example, a strong Baptist influence often prevents young teenage women from having abortions.

LEADERSHIP ROLES IN RELIGIOUS WORSHIP

Some religious organizations—such as the Quakers (Society of Friends) and the Unitarian Church—have ordained women in the United States since the early 1800s. Even earlier, the 1660 writing of a Friends's founder, Margaret Fell (1614–1702), justified the equal roles of men and women on the premise of God's spirit in every soul. The Church of God began ordaining women in Cleveland, Tennessee, in 1909. The Unitarian Universalist religion, which has been ordaining women in large numbers since 1963, was the first major faith group to establish a majority of female clergy in 1999. The role of women in the clergy did not significantly increase, however, until the 1980s and 1990s, when the Protestant United Methodists, Anglicans, and Episcopalians began ordaining women. This paralleled an atmosphere of more liberal business practices as a result of the 1985 U.S. Supreme Court decision in *Estate of Thornton v. Calder* to uphold separation of church from state and not enforce business closings on the sabbath or Sunday, a practice that dated from the 1600s but did not take into account other religions in America.

Large numbers of women were being ordained by the United Methodist (one-dozen bishops, 5 percent of Protestant senior pastors), Southern Baptist (1,000 ministers), and Anglican and Episcopal Churches (16 bishops) at the start of the 21st century.[63] Churches of various denominations remain biased, however, against women in offering lower pay and demanding more educational requirements of women than of men. Nevertheless, women are making advances: In June 2006, Katherine Jefferts Schori, bishop of Nevada, was elected to be the first female presiding bishop of the Episcopal Church, the U.S. arm of the Anglican Communion.

Meanwhile, the Roman Catholic Church, Eastern Orthodox churches, provinces within the Anglican Communion, the Mormons—also known as the Church of Jesus Christ of Latter-day Saints—and many fundamentalist and evangelical Protestant denominations still do not have female clergy.

The Third Wave

The legislative changes pushed through by women's organizations in the 20th century allowed women to gain access to rights and created equal opportunity of the sexes in the United States in all aspects of life, from property ownership to equal pay and sexual reproduction rights. Social change—such as shared responsibilities within the household and equal compensation at work—has been slower. American women have had the right to vote since 1920, but their political power has increased only minimally. It was not until 1984 that a major party chose a woman, Geraldine Ferraro of New York, to run for vice president. There has not been another female nomination for vice president by a major political party since, although there have been several third-party female candidates.

It has been more than 40 years since the Equal Pay Act was enacted, but the task of convincing employers that women are worth their hire stubbornly persists, although the situation has improved for professional women. Women in their 50s are now going back to school to train for careers as physicians, nurses, and lawyers, prolonging their participation in the labor market to make up for the shortfall that is beginning to occur between available retirement and Social Security funds and the retiring population of baby boomers.

Taking advantage of the opportunities now provided and monitoring the implementation of laws and compliance with them are taking on new measures of effort. With its membership of 50,000 women, NOW is considered one of the major women's rights organization in the United States today. The National Women's Political Caucus, which has chapters in 38 states and advocates leadership training for girls and young women, is also essential to pursuing and tracking legislation that provides gender equality.

The current generation of young women has no personal recall of the struggles their predecessors endured in securing the rights they now have: access to the Pill, abortion, higher education, and workplace equality, among others. Yet problems persist. As the *New York Times* columnist Maureen Dowd writes: "Despite the best efforts of philosophers, politicians, historians, novelists, screenwriters, linguists, therapists, anthropologists and facilitators, men and women are still in a muddle in the boardroom, the bedroom and the Situation Room."[64]

However, whereas the first and second generations of feminists were able to rally around the obvious issues of their time, such as the lack of suffrage and property ownership, problems today are often more subtle and extend to all areas of living, from the right to fair representation in clinical trials to protection against enforced collection of debt, leading to a more diffused movement.[65]

Today, only 34 percent of young women ages 13 to 20 identify themselves as "feminists." However, although many will not use the term *feminist,* the overwhelming majority of them agree with or assume traditional feminist values. One study shows that 97 percent of women in this age bracket believe a woman should receive the same pay for the same work as men, and 92 percent agree that a woman's lifestyle choices should not be limited by her gender. Eighty-nine percent say a woman can be successful without either a man or children.[66]

In a 1998 Time/CNN poll, among those who perceived themselves as feminists, education appears to be the common bond. Fifty-three percent of white college-educated women living in cities embrace the label. Fifty percent of white women who have postgraduate training and no children also do.[67]

Efforts by the movement to monitor the implementation of rights—such as the President's Interagency Council on Women (PICW), which was founded by President Clinton's executive order on the eve of the UN Fourth World Conference on Women in Beijing in 1995—although well intended, are short-lived when dependent on political priorities. The council was developed to "make sure that all the effort and good ideas actually get implemented when we get back home." Chaired by Health and Human Services Secretary Donna Shalala and then–First Lady Hillary Rodham Clinton as honorary chair, activities supporting the Beijing Platform for Action by this agency were discontinued after President Clinton left office in 2001.

On the other hand, the other initiative mentioned by Senator Hillary Clinton during her speech at the 1995 Beijing conference, Vital Voices, has continued its mission to promote the advancement of women as a U.S. foreign policy goal.

WOMEN'S STUDIES PROGRAMS

The events in the 1960s and 1970s helped women's history to become a field of higher educational study, which added to the credibility of the cause. During that time, the term *herstory* was coined to characterize the unrecognized contributions of women to history.

A study conducted in the 1990s to measure the effect of women's studies departments on college students showed that the curriculum in women's programs led to intellectual and personal growth and change. Participation in a women's studies program resulted in "a more progressive gender role orientation and an increased sense of personal control over life outcomes." The latter is associated with *empowerment*, a term often seen in feminist literature today. The other effect measured was improved self-esteem.[68]

In the late 1990s and early 2000s, women's studies programs increasingly evolved into gender studies. In April 2002, Yale University renamed its Women's Studies Department the Women and Gender Studies Department. The National Women's Studies Association (NWSA) hosts an annual conference that fosters national, cultural, and political dialogue about women and their role in race, class, sexuality, and gender developments.

In 2005, the U.S. Senate approved the National Women's History Museum Act by unanimous consent. The museum is to open in Washington, D.C., in the next few years, pending the bill's progress through the House Transportation and Infrastructure Committee, and is expected to draw over 1.5 million visitors a year.

According to Senator Susan Collins (1952–   ), who spearheaded the legislation: "Such a museum would also showcase the many important social, economic, cultural, and political contributions that women have made to our country." [69]

---

[1] Andrew Sum, Neeta Fogg, Paul Harrington, et al. "The Growing Gender Gaps in College Enrollment and Degree Attainment in the U.S. and Their Potential Economic and Social Consequences." Center for Labor Market Studies, Northeastern University, Boston, Massachusetts, May 2003, p. 13.

[2] Christopher J. Tassava. "The American Economy during World War II." EH.Net Encyclopedia. Available online. URL: http://eh.net/encyclopedia/article/tassava.WWII. Accessed May 28, 2006.

[3] Women in Military Service for America Memorial Foundation, Inc. "Woman's Place in War." Poster, 1941–44. Available online. URL: http://www.womensmemorial.org/H&C/History/wwii(wac).html. Accessed May 31, 2006.

[4] Jacqueline Cochran. "Jacqueline Cochran's Final Report." WASP Records. Available online. URL: http://www.wasp-wwii.org/wasp/final_report.htm. Accessed May 22, 2006.

[5] Howard N Fullerton, Jr. "Labor Force Participation: 75 Years of Change, 1950–98 and 1998–2025." *Monthly Labor Review*, Bureau of Labor Statistics, December 1999, p. 4.

[6] Civilrights.org. "Remarks by Coretta Scott King on ENDA" (June 23, 1994). Available online. URL: http://www.civilrights.org/issues/glbt/details.cfm?id=4727. Accessed June 3, 2006.

[7] "Health, United States, 2005." Report, Centers for Disease Control, 2005, p. 150.

[8] "Health, United States, 2005," p. 149.

[9] "Health, United States, 2005," p. 149.

[10] *Women in National Parliaments.* Inter-Parliamentary Union, October 31, 2005.

[11] Nathan Thornburgh. "Dropout Nation." *Time,* April 17, 2006, p. 32.

[12] National Center for Education Statistics. "Digest of Education Statistics Tables and Figures, 2004," chapter 2, Elementary and Secondary Education, table 102—High School Graduates Compared with Population 17 Years of Age, by Sex (April 2005). Available online. URL: http://nces.ed.gov/programs/digest/d04/tables/dt04_102.asp. Accessed March 1, 2006.

[13] National Center for Education Statistics. "Digest of Education Statistics," table 102.

[14] National Center for Education Statistics. "Digest of Education Statistics," table 102.

[15] "On Campus with Women." News release, American Association of Colleges and Universities, spring/summer 2004. Available online. URL: http://www.aacu.org/ocww/volume33_3/inbrief.cfm. Accessed May 29, 2006.

[16] U.S. Department of Labor, Bureau of Labor Statistics. "Quick Stats 2004." Available online. URL: http://www.dol.gov/wb/stats/main.htm. Accessed May 29, 2006.

[17] Howard N. Fullerton, Jr. "Labor Force Participation: 75 Years of Change, 1950–98 and 1998–2025." Bureau of Labor Statistics *Monthly Labor Review* (December 1999), p. 3.

[18] Fullerton. "Labor Force Participation," table 1, p. 4.

[19] Mahshid Jalilvand. "Married Women, Work, and Values." Bureau of Labor Statistics *Monthly Labor Review* (August 2000), p. 26.

[20] Jalilvand. "Married Women, Work, and Values," table 2, p. 6.

[21] Peter Fronczek and Patricia Johnson. *Occupations: 2000—Census 2000 Brief.* Report, U.S. Bureau of Census, August 2003, p. 5.

[22] U.S. Department of Labor, Bureau of Labor Statistics. "Women in the Labor Force: A Databook" (May 13, 2005). Available online. URL: http://www.bls.gov/cps/wlf-databook-2005.pdf. Accessed May 3, 2006.

[23] "Women's Earnings: Work Patterns Partially Explain Difference between Men's and Women's Earnings." Report to Congressional Requesters, United States General Accounting Office, October 2003, p. 2.

[24] Philip N. Cohen and Suzanne M. Bianchi. "Marriage, Children, and Women's Employment: What Do We Know?" Bureau of Labor Statistics *Monthly Labor Review* (December 1999), pp. 26–27.

[25] June Hannan, Mitzi Auchter Ionie, and Katherine Holden, eds. "Child Care." In *International Encyclopedia of Women's Suffrage.* Santa Barbara, Calif.: ABC-CLIO, 2000, p. 159.

[26] National Childcare Information Center. "Child Care and Development Fund Report of State Plans FY 2004–2005." Report, October 2004, p. 1.

[27] Stephen Gaskill. "A Solid Investment: Making Use of the Nation's Human Capital. U.S. Glass Ceiling Commission." U.S. Department of Labor, November 1995.

[28] Gaskill. "A Solid Investment," p. 6.

[29] Gaskill. "A Solid Investment," p. 13.

[30] Federal Glass Ceiling Commission. "Good for Business: Making Full Use of the Nation's Human Capital—the Environmental Scan." Fact-Finding Report, Washington, D.C., March 1995.

[31] Institute for Women's Policy Research Fact Sheet, October 2004.

[32] U.S. Equal Employment Opportunity Commission. "Glass Ceilings: The Status of Women as Officials and Managers in the Private Sector." Office of Research, Information and Planning, Washington, D.C., March 2004.

[33] U.S. General Accounting Office. "A New Look through the Glass Ceiling: Where Are the Women? The Status of Women in Management in Ten Selected Industries" (January 2002), p. 7. Available online. URL: http://www.gao.gov. Accessed May 29, 2006.

[34] Equal Employment Opportunity Commission. "Sexual Harassment Charges: EEOC & FEPAs Combined: FY 1992–FY 2005" (January 27, 2006). Available online. URL: http://www.eeoc.gov/stats/harass.html. Accessed May 29, 2006.

[35] Amy Caiazza, April Shaw, and Misha Werschkul. "Women's Economic Status in the States: Wide Disparities by Race, Ethnicity, and Region." Institute for Women's Policy Research, 2004, p. 1.

[36] U.S. Census Bureau. "S1703. Selected Characteristics of People at Specified Levels of Poverty in the Past 12 Months." 2004 American Community Survey. Available online. URL: http://factfinder.census.gov/servlet/STTable?_bm=y&-geo_id=01000US&-qr_name=ACS_2004_EST_G00_S1703&-ds_name=ACS_2004_EST_G00_. Accessed June 6, 2006.

[37] Elaine Sorensen and Ariel Halpern. "Child Support Enforcement: How Well Is It Doing?" Report, Urban Institute, December 1999, p. 19.

[38] Bendheim-Thoman Center for Research on Child Wellbeing, Princeton University, and Social Indicators Survey Center, Columbia University. "Fragile Families Research Brief: Child Support Enforcement and Fragile Families." April 2003, p. 2.

[39] Thomas N. Bethell. "The Gender Gyp: No Wonder Women Are Worried about Social Security: They Have a Lot More to Lose." *AARP Bulletin*, July–August 2005, p. 8.

[40] U.S. Equal Employment Opportunity Commission. "Workforce Composition of the U.S. Departments of the Army, Navy, Marines, and Air Force" (May 3, 2005). Available online. URL: http://www.eeoc.gov/federal/fsp2004/profiles. Accessed November 29, 2005.

[41] "Department of Defense Selected Manpower Statistics Fiscal Year 2004." Report, Department of Defense, 2005, pp. 35, 73, 75, 76.

[42] Janie Blankenship. "Ever-Changing Roles of Women in the Military: More and More, Women in Uniform Are Thrust into Dangerous Situations Overseas." *VFW Magazine*, March 2005.

[43] Tim McGirk. "Crossing the Line." *Time*, February 27, 2006, p. 38.

[44] McGirk. "Crossing the Line," p. 38.

[45] National Center for Health Statistics. "Women's Health: Leading Causes of Death: Females—United States, 2002" (May 31, 2005). Centers for Disease Control. Available online. URL: http://www.cdc.gov/women/lcod.htm. Accessed February 26, 2006.

[46] Theresa M. Wizemann and Mary-Lou Pardue, eds. "Exploring the Biological Contributions to Human Health: Does Sex Matter?" Report, Institute of Medicine, 2001.

[47] "State Secret: Thousands Secretly Sterilized" (May 15, 2005). ABC News. Available online. URL: http://abcnews.go.com/WNT/Health/story?id=708780. Accessed January 23, 2006.

[48] Guttmacher Institute, Media Kit, "Overview of Abortion in the United States," 2002.

91

[49] William D. Mosher, Gladys M. Martinez, Anjani Chandra, Joyce C. Abma, and Stephanie J. Willson. "Use of Contraception and Use of Family Planning Services in the United States: 1982–2002." Division of Vital Statistics, CDC, December 10, 2004, p. 7.

[50] María José Alcalá. "State of World Population 2005." Report, United Nations Development Fund, p. 110.

[51] James Alm, M. V. Lee Badgett, and Leslie A. Whittington. "Wedding Bell Blues: The Income Tax Consequences of Legalizing Same-Sex Marriage." Center for Economic Analysis, Department of Economics, University of Colorado, Boulder, November 1998, p. 9.

[52] Carolyn Garris. "Research: Marriage in the 50 States." Heritage Foundation. Available online. URL: http://www.heritage.org/Research/Family/Marriage50/Marriage50States.cfm. Accessed June 4, 2006.

[53] Criminal Victimization in the United States, 2003 Statistical Tables. "Percent Distribution of Victimizations, by Type of Crime and Relationship to Offender." U.S. Department of Justice, July 2005, p. 47.

[54] U.S. Department of Justice. "Full Report of the Prevalence, Incidence, and Consequences of Violence against Women." Findings from the National Violence Against Women Survey, 2000, p. 26.

[55] Neil M. Malamuth. "Pornography and Sexual Aggression: Are There Reliable Effects and Can We Understand Them?" *Annual Review of Sex Research* (2000), p. 26.

[56] Patricia Tjaden and Nancy Thoennes. "Full Report of the Prevalence, Incidence, and Consequences of Violence against Women." U.S. Department of Justice, Office of Justice Programs, National Institute of Justice and Centers for Disease Control, November 2000, p. iii.

[57] Mappes and Zembaty. *Social Ethics.* New York: McGraw-Hill, 1997, p. 215.

[58] Gail Dines, Robert Jensen, and Ann Russo. *Pornography: The Production and Consumption of Inequality.* London: Routledge, 1997, p. 4.

[59] Janice G. Raymond and Donna M. Hughes. "Sex Trafficking of Women in the United States: International and Domestic Trends." Coalition against Trafficking in Women, report sponsored by the National Institute of Justice, March 2001, p. 102.

[60] "Assessement of U.S. Activities to Combat Trafficking in Persons." U.S. Department of State, 2003, p. 1. Available online. URL: http://www.state.gov/g/tip/rls/rpt/23495.htm. Accessed December 19, 2005.

[61] "Assessment of U.S. Activities to Combat Trafficking in Persons," p. 1.

[62] International Rescue Committee. "Trafficking in the United States" (November 24, 2003). Available online. URL: http://www.theirc.org/media/www/trafficking_in_the_united_states.html#search. Accessed May 11, 2006.

[63] Ontario Consultants on Religious Tolerance. "When Some Faith Groups Started to Ordain Women." Available online. URL: http://www.religioustolerance.org. Accessed May 30, 2006.

[64] Maureen Dowd. "What's a Modern Girl to Do?" *New York Times Magazine,* October 30, 2005, pp. 50–55.

[65] Jennifer Friedlin. "Second and Third Wave Feminists Clash over the Future" (May 26, 2002). Women's Enews. Available online. URL: http://www.womensenews.org/article.cfm/dyn/aid/920/context/cover. Accessed June 5, 2006.

[66] Rebecca Gardyn. "Granddaughters of Feminism." *American Demographics* (April 2001), p. 42.

[67] Ginia Bellafante. "It's All about Me! Want to Know What Today's Chic Young Feminist Thinkers Care About? Their Bodies! Themselves!" *Time*, June 29, 1998, p. 54.

[68] Karen L. Harris, et al. "The Impact of Women's Studies Courses on College Students of the 1990s." *Sex Roles: A Journal of Research* (June 1999), p. 969.

[69] National Museum of Women's History. "U.S. Senate Approves the National Women's History Museum Act of 2005 (S. 501) by Unanimous Consent" (August 1, 2005). Available online. URL: http://www.nmwh.org/news/museumsite.htm. Accessed November 1, 2005.

3

Global Perspectives

In the following section, the way the women's movement arose and is evolving in the United States is compared with that in four countries that have distinctly different cultural traditions and economic situations: Denmark, China, Afghanistan, and Kenya.

Each country is surveyed for specific characteristics—historical, cultural, religious, national—that make the women's movement in these countries similar to or different from the movement in the United States.

Features of comparison include the following:

1. Issues and events that sparked the women's movement and the timing of the movement
2. The political background of the movement and its challenges
3. The current issues of the movement
4. The connection with the international movement
5. The direction in which the movement is heading

DENMARK

Making Copenhagen, Denmark, the host of the second world conference on women convened by the United Nations in 1980, not only honored Denmark's role as a portal for the women's movement in mainland Europe, but it also launched one of the most powerful instruments created in the 20th century for women's equality, the Convention on the Elimination of All Forms of Discrimination Against Women (CEDAW), in a country where the movement had largely succeeded in reshaping gender roles in society.

The Fermenting of the Women's Rights Movement

Danish women were first moved to action by the early gestures for women's equality during the French Revolution of 1789 and the translation into

Danish of *A Vindication of the Rights of Women* by the British writer Mary Wollstonecraft (1759–97) in 1792.

Another 50 years would pass—after revolts in Europe and events leading up to the American Civil War, a pattern similar to that in the United States—before Denmark saw its own internal wrestling with women's rights emerge. Mathilde Fibiger (1830–72) was a young anonymous novelist who made her living as a seamstress. In her first published novel, *Clara Raphael* (1850), she wrote of female oppression, stirring public sentiment. Her later work, *Twelve Letters,* would cause public debate about women's societal roles.[1] During the next decade, Pauline Worm (1825–83) and Nathalie Zahle (1827–1913) advocated educational opportunities, Worm through her writing and Zahle by establishing girls' schools and teacher colleges for women. Because they confined themselves to education, considered a female profession, they were not yet perceived as a threat to tradition. Similarly, Elisabeth Jerichau Baumann's (1819–81) unique success, as a female painter who eventually exhibited her work at the Great Exhibition in London in 1862, did not stir up resentment because of her well-known antifeminist sentiments.[2]

But in the late 1860s, amid demands by the Danish middle class and farmers for constitutional reform, decreased monarchical powers, and improved civil and labor rights, women's rights and issues appeared in public discussion. John Stuart Mill's *On the Subjection of Women* was translated into Danish in 1869.[3] During the same period, Mathilde (1840–1934) and Fredrik Bajer (1837–1922) established connections with the international women's movement and became spokespersons for the movement in Denmark. In the Danish parliament, Frederik Bajer, an advocate for Nordic unification and peace, represented legislation that supported women's political emancipation and labor rights.

In 1871, a Danish division of the Swiss-based International Association of Women, the Danish Women's League, was founded in the Bajers' home in Copenhagen. Resistance in Danish provinces to the idea of anything "international" during the Franco-Prussian War of 1870–71, however, prompted the organization to cut its ties to the International Association of Women; the Dansk Kvindesamfund, or Danish Women's Society, was formed in its place to focus on moral, economic, and intellectual rights of Danish women.[4]

Around the same time, the first Danish section of the Socialist International was organized, although not until 1901 was the Women Workers' Union (Kvindeligt Arbejderforbund) founded.[5] In 1866, Denmark had adopted a new constitution that restricted suffrage to men. As a result, the Dansk Kvindesamfund initially focused on other benefits to Danish women, such as education and labor, a pattern that also occurred in the United States in the late 1800s. Mathilde Bajer spearheaded the Women's Union for Progress in 1886 to examine military spending and authored *What We Want*, which became the tenet for the Confederation of Women's Unions. To protest low wages, women's labor unions began to stage walkouts.

THE MOVE FOR SUFFRAGE

In the 1880s, Dansk Kvindesamfund was divided over whether to entertain the issue of suffrage. Eventually, Mathilde Bajer and others who supported the move for suffrage formed the United Women's Organizations, chaired by Line Luplau (1823–91) from the organization's chapter in western Jutland, reflecting the broadening of the movement beyond Copenhagen's borders. In 1888, Mathilde Bajer also founded Dansk Kvindelig Valgretsforening (Danish Women's Suffrage Society) to support moral, social, and labor reform issues, particularly for the working class.[6]

In 1897, the Women's Suffrage Organization merged with Dansk Kvindesamfund. In 1898, the Danish Women's Union Suffrage Committee represented an alliance of seven groups to work for the vote. By 1899, these large women's organizations set up together the Danish Women's National Council, which associated them with the Chicago-based International Council of Women (ICW). Copenhagen soon found itself hosting meetings for suffragists from many countries in 1906, including the Alliance of Suffrage for Women founded in 1904 in Berlin. Women associated with the new Radical Party in Denmark—Elna Munch (1871–1945), Johanne Rambusch (1865–1944), and others—took the lead in the struggle for suffrage, creating the National Union for Women's Suffrage in 1907. Women from this group participated in many international meetings, including the International Woman Suffrage Alliance Congress in London in 1909.

During this time, some gains for suffrage had been made by Danish women, similar to the gradual support in America in individual states. For instance, in 1903, all women over 25 received the right to vote for new parish councils. After 1905, women could be appointed to the local boards of guardians, and with a new local election law of 1908, all women of age received the right to vote and be elected to local councils. In 1915, a constitution granted women and servants the right to vote for parliament, five years before the same event would occur in the United States. In the first election in 1918, 10 percent of the candidates of the lower house (Folketing) were women, but only four women, or 3 percent, were elected. To the upper house (Landsting), five women were elected, among them the Social Democrat Nina Bang (1866–1928). In 1924, Bang would go on to become the first female minister in world history, when she was appointed minister of education. (For comparison, in the United States, the first female cabinet minister was Frances Perkins, who became secretary of labor in 1933.)

Still, political opportunities for women emerged gradually and would take another half-century to unfold. Legislation slowly began to favor women and change their lives: The marriage reform acts of 1922 and 1923 put in place equal child custody, property, and divorce rights. A major overhaul in 1953 allowed for a unicameral legislature and a female chief of state. The real growth in the number of women elected to the Folketing, the national parliament, did not occur before the 1970s.

The Redstockings arose in the 1970s among university-educated middle-class women. The group influenced reform in the political, social, and employment sectors and introduced gay and lesbian rights in Denmark. It created public debate about gender issues, including men's and women's roles in the family, workplace, and politics, that soon led to statistical quotas in political parties, domestic violence shelters, women's studies programs, and expanded welfare services. Although the group fragmented in the late 1970s, the women's liberation movement continued. The movement has long focused on women's participation in the decision-making process, starting with the Equal Status Council in 1975. The success of these efforts is reflected in the number of seats in parliament occupied by women, which was 38 percent in 2004, one of the highest rates in the world.[7]

Current Issues

EDUCATION

As within the United States, the movement's focus on access to education in the 19th century, with females achieving the right for a primary education in 1859, led to a high literacy rate over time. With free public education for all children from preschool until the 10th year, a parity in girls' and boys' enrollment in primary schools now exists and has endured.

As in the case of American-educated Elizabeth Blackwell (1821–1910), Nielsine Nielsen's (1850–1916) application to medical school in 1874 opened university education to women who passed physical fitness exams on an equal footing with men. Nielsen graduated from the University of Copenhagen in 1885. Female applicants to higher education increased in the final decade of the 20th century, from a ratio of 114 girls for every 100 boys in 1990 to 141 girls in 2001.[8]

Women's studies programs emerged, as in the United States, in the early 1970s as an outgrowth of the women's movement, gradually making their way into higher education. Awareness of gender issues would also take time to impact women's roles in the labor force.

EMPLOYMENT AND SEXUAL HARASSMENT

Women's access to jobs in the public sector opened up during the first local election in 1909, when 50 percent of registered women voted and 127 women were elected. Their positions in politics were preceded by new national labor unions for women's employment that had also been formed in the previous decade and were ready to act as wage negotiators: the Danish Nurses Council in 1899 and the Copenhagen Municipal Teacheresses Union in 1900.

In spite of gains made in 1915, which included equal property and custody rights, the "housewife" image prevailed well into the 1950s, a trend that also persisted in the United States. In Denmark, however, it was largely encouraged by the country's rural, agricultural economy and structure based on small family holdings. As were their American counterparts, Danish women were mostly able to contribute to the family income through occupations as agricultural and factory workers, schoolteachers, nurses, and clerks. Not until the 1970s was the principle of equal pay for equal work regardless of sex enforced, mirroring the emphasis of the creation of the EEOC in the United States. The difference in women's and men's wages, although small, has resulted in smaller pensions for women. In spite of the Equal Pay Act of 1976, which required equal pay for equal work, female workers in Denmark earned 12–20 percent less than their male counterparts as of 2000, depending on whether the job was in the public or private sector.[9] Danish women have among the highest employment rates in the labor market in the world, at 73.6 percent of women ages 16 to 66 compared with 81.4 percent of men in 2000.[10] Complementing this, the rate of part-time female workers has declined dramatically since the 1970s, from 48 percent in 1978 to 17 percent in 1998.[11]

The Equal Treatment Act of 1978 prohibited job discrimination based on sex and provided recourse to the Equal Status Council, which, much as does America's Title IX of the EEOC, hears complaints of gender discrimination and offers legal council on behalf of victims and authorities. In the 1970s, women began to hold positions of authority throughout society, although they were still underrepresented in senior business positions and on university faculties, a pattern that still holds true in the 21st century. Women's rights groups lobbied the government on matters of wage disparities and parental leave.

A series of legislative measures in 1990 in both the United States and the European Union effectively moderated sexual harassment cases and prevented the subject from being silenced by taboo. The Council of Ministers of the European Community defined sexual harassment for its member states, and the EEOC updated Guidelines on Discrimination Because of Sex, adding regulations on definition and prevention. These guidelines even defined sexual favoritism as a form of sexual harassment.

Although largely underreported, the number of sexual harassment cases in Denmark is comparatively lower than in its European Union and U.S. counterparts. Eleven percent of women reported cases of harassment on the job compared with the average 40 to 50 percent of women in the European Union in 1991.[12] A more recent study stated this pattern had not changed as of 2002.[13]

Denmark's Equal Status Act of 2000 added impetus, allowing women who were opposed to television, film, and print media exploitation to uphold and defend gender balance in the public and private employment sectors.

This was further supported by a European Union Parliamentary directive, known as Directive 2002/73/EC, which required its member nations to implement legislative agencies similar to the American EEOC to deal with sexual harassment at the legislative level by October 2002.[14] It also amended the previously existing directives on the equality of men and women in the workplace with the definitions of *harassment* and *sexual harassment.*

Still, the kinds of occupations women hold are subject to gender stereotype: Women occupy about 65 percent of public sector jobs—mostly low-level and mid-level municipal jobs—while men hold 63 percent of private sector jobs, higher-level public sector jobs, and managerial jobs. As of 2003, 26 percent of administrative and managerial jobs were held by women.[15]

FAMILY RIGHTS

Many fundamental marriage rights were assured comparatively early in the 20th century in Denmark, creating a platform for change as women found their way into the workplace and formed dual-career families. The increase of time spent on the job resulted in a dramatic decline in time spent in housework.

In recent years, women and men have been marrying and starting families later in life, sometimes well into their 30s, a trend that also holds true in the United States. The ratio of 11 annual births per 1,000 people is suggestive of the busier lifestyle women are leading in the West.[16] (For comparison, the rate in the United States is 14 births per 1,000 population.) Maternity benefits in Denmark, along with those in Norway, are superior when compared with the United States—federal law mandates unpaid leave of 12 weeks. Most European countries require 16 paid weeks of maternity leave. In Denmark, since 2002, the law provides a mother with full salary from her employer for the first 18 weeks (four weeks before and 14 weeks after birth, and sometimes the ensuing 28 weeks). Fathers are allowed two weeks of paternal leave. An additional 32 weeks is paid for by the state at a maximum of 3,335 Danish krone per week for either parent to take care of the newborn. As optimal as this sounds, employers may dismiss pregnant employees, an issue that is being countered by the Dansk Kvindesamfund through financial assistance for firms that employ women.

THE GAY MOVEMENT

Gay rights evolved out of the women's movement in 1974 in a similar way to that in the United States. Initially, university-educated middle-class women sought to establish gay and lesbian rights in the political, social, and employment sectors in Denmark. A 1987 law prohibited discrimination on the basis of sexual orientation, in civil service employment, and regarding access to public services and public facilities. Same-sex civil partnerships gained legal privileges similar to those of married couples in 1989 with the Danish Registered Partnership Act.[17]

RELIGION

Because Danish women have been allowed to be in the clergy since 1947, the number of female priests is high compared with that in the United States and other nations. By 2002, 800 of the 2,000 priests in the Lutheran Church, the majority faith of Danes, were female. The first woman bishop, Lise-Lotte Gauger Rebel (1951–   ), from Helsingør (Elsinore), was ordained in 1995. Sofie Bodil Louise Lisbeth Petersen (1955–   ), from Grønland, Denmark, became bishop of Greenland that year.

VIOLENCE

Violence against women has been at the forefront of people's awareness in the new millennium, in Denmark and globally. In 2002, the Danish government initiated a national plan to cope with violence against women. Several measures included a pilot project offering domestic violence family therapy services, an amendment to the Social Services Act that sets minimal living standards for shelters, and an increase in funding for shelters, many of which are run by women's groups and counseling services.

The government also initiated a public media campaign to fight violence against women, issuing brochures about how to get help from doctors' offices, pharmacies, and other public services.

While estimates within Denmark probably underrepresent the real number of incidents—4,250 reports of abuse in a given year—the Institute for Public Health estimated that at least 65,000 women were exposed to domestic violence in a given year, and that domestic violence affected approximately 30,000 children. Rape, spousal abuse, and spousal rape are criminal offenses in Denmark.[18]

Trafficking in women and children for the purpose of sexual exploitation and prostitution has been recognized as a global problem. Denmark, as has the United States, has become a destination country for trafficked women and children, many of whom are from eastern Europe, the Baltic states, the former Soviet Union (particularly Ukraine, Moldova, and Russia), Thailand, and African countries. Victims also transit through Denmark to other European countries.

In Denmark, adult prostitution and pornography are legal, but pimping, coercion into prostitution, solicitation of prostitution from a minor, and trafficking are illegal and are being addressed by the Women's Council.

Prevention efforts by the government included spending $1.7 million for the first three years of a national action plan, "Combat Trafficking in Women," in 2002 and 2003. Under the plan, the government and several nongovernmental organizations (NGOs) published antitrafficking advertisements in major newspapers that provided a hotline telephone number for victims and the public. Speaking with multilingual operators, victims could obtain information on support services, Danish laws, and guidelines on repatriation. In the first seven months of operation, the hotline received 254 calls or inquiries. NGO employees were proactive in finding foreign prostitutes, collecting information, and providing them with information on services.

ACCESS TO HEALTH CARE

In many ways, Denmark is now facing what the United States has already dealt with: the redirecting of women's access and rights to health care to a privatized health care system. This would mean a transition from its public health care programs that make hospital and primary care free to the population to the influence of privatization and international trade agreements. Beginning in fall 2004, an information campaign was carried out by the women's group KULU (Women and Development) in collaboration with the Danish Association of Midwives, the two schools of midwifery in Copenhagen and Ålborg, and the Tanzania Gender Networking Programme (TGNP). Among their concerns was how women's reproductive health and rights will fare in a free market economy, when health services previously funded through taxes are deregulated and subject to price variations based on supply and demand, possibly jeopardizing women's and poor people's access to high-quality health care.[19]

In Denmark, since 1973, abortion has been part of the social health care program and is available to women in their first trimester, although minors under 18 years of age need parental consent.[20] The decline in abortions, from 403 per 1,000 births in 1980 to 234 per 1,000 births in 2000, parallels the increase of use of contraceptive methods, again a pattern that is consistent with what is occurring in the United States. Since 1988, about 71 percent of Danish women in their reproductive years have been using some form of contraception, the same rate as in the United States since 1995.[21]

The Future

Since the 1980s, much attention has been devoted to the disparity between rights secured and their enforcement. As Denmark's population of 5.4 million readjusts its perception to accommodate an expanding European Union, it continues to promote women's rights, nationally and internationally, and develop new strategies. The Women's Council, the Dansk Kvindesamfund, and the Women Workers' Union have training programs for women to run for office. Dansk Kvindesamfund continues its work of making women aware of their rights under CEDAW. They hosted the European Regional Conference on the Implementation of the CEDAW Convention in 2001, when specific strategies were discussed about how to achieve gender mainstreaming, prevent trafficking of women and children, and stop the spread of human immunodeficiency virus/acquired immunodeficiency syndrome (HIV/AIDS).

Meanwhile, the influx of immigrants, including Scandinavian, Inuit, Faroese, German, Turkish, Iranian, and Somali (2 percent of whom follow Muslim traditions), into the country has raised issues that are not unfamiliar to the United States. Employers are dealing with Islamic customs such as women's wearing of head scarves, sometimes resorting to legal action. In 2001, a Muslim woman was fired for wearing a head scarf at work in a large Danish supermarket chain. She lost the ensuing court case in 2003, when the court ruled that her contract contained a dress code banning headgear.[22] Only 41 percent of women of ethnic minority groups are active in the labor market, in contrast to 75 percent of other women.[23] The government continues to take steps to integrate women of minority groups into the labor market and deal with customs such as forced marriages.

CHINA

Women's rights in mainland China emerged as one of many changes in the transition from imperial and military rule in the early 20th century to the Chinese Communist Party (CCP) in 1949. As in the United States and Europe during the 19th-century Industrial Revolution, the People's Republic of China (PRC) under Mao Zedong (1903–76) and his successors, Deng Xiaoping (1904–97) and Jiang Zemin (1925–   ), gradually moved from being a centrally planned, agriculturally based economy to one that promoted trade liberalization, decentralization, and increased autonomy in state enterprises. Economic reforms that began in the late 1970s transformed the country into a modern, industrialized nation with the second most powerful economy in the world by 2005.

Whereas the women's movement was initially driven by politics and social issues in the United States, in China the impetus has been economics. Considered one of the largest countries in the world, China covers an area only slightly smaller than the United States with a population that is four times that of the United States, at 1.3 billion people and 298.4 million people, respectively.[24] On this scale, all issues tend to be magnified, whether about population control, health care, pollution, or the environment. Furthermore, unlike its relatively young American counterpart, China is endowed with one of the oldest civilizations and religions (Confucianism and Taoism) in existence, making it fertile ground for the meeting of ancient ways with global change. The persuasive power of aggressive economic growth between 1985 and 2005—often referred to as the reform years—has driven the country into a deep divide between the poor and the wealthy, although much of the country has seen improved living standards and greater personal choice over the past few decades.

Women and the New Culture Movement

From about 500 B.C.E. until the early 20th century, Chinese society was heavily influenced by Confucianism, a school of thought founded by Confucius (551–479 B.C.E.) that placed the patriarchal family at the center of society. Confucius maintained that when family relationships are in order—when children respect and obey their father and wives obey their husband—there will be order in society. Footbinding, a practice primarily among elite classes that began during the early Sung (Song) dynasty (960–1279), was known as a mark of beauty that lasted well into the 20th century. Women whose feet had been bound could not walk; thus the custom made women highly dependent on their husbands, whom they could not leave. The home was central to a proper women's life, and her sequestered life was the ideal.

In the early 20th century, men and women began to reevaluate the Confucianism-based institutions and beliefs that had defined the Chinese cultural tradition for two millennia. Scholars who were part of this New Culture movement advocated scientific methods to analyze history and literature. Influenced by revolutionary movements in the West, including the women's movement and socialism, they protested Japan's treatment of China, and many joined the Chinese Communist Party when it was founded in 1921.

PARLAY FOR SUFFRAGE

When China formed a new republic with a constitution, Chinese women demanded the right to participate in political decision making and began working for the right to vote in the early 1900s, at the same time as a fresh wave of the suffrage movement was occurring in the United States. A flux of organizations, including the Chinese Women's Franchise Association, the Chinese Women's Cooperative Association, and the Chinese Suffragette Society, were formed. They felt the militant influences of pre–World War I activities by American and international feminist groups and participated in the Wuchang Uprising in 1911, which created a separate Republic of China government under Sun Yat-sen (1866–1925) and ultimately overthrew the Manchu (Qing, Ch'ing) dynasty, the last imperial dynasty of China, in 1912.

Women from 18 provinces rallied for equal rights before the national legislature as the Women's Suffragette Alliance in 1912 in Nanking (today's Nanjing). They used militant and near-violent tactics, imitating their American and British fellow suffragists. This backfired as measures were taken to protect the traditional family model, and as a result, no women were members of the 1913 Permanent Assembly in Canton. A conservative military government took its place under Sun Yat-sen and the women's movement was silenced.

"The women question" resurfaced seven years later, after mass demonstrations by women opposing Japanese persecution of Chinese and expressing their desire to be part of mainstream daily life and the economy. Women were also targeting higher education, professional status, and entrepreneurship, just as their American sisters were honing in on enfranchisement.

Once again Sun Yat-sen's Nationalist Kuomintang (Guomindang) government suppressed activities by the newly formed Women's Suffrage Association and the Women's Rights League in 1921. The National Congress drafted a new constitution that excluded women's voting rights. Meanwhile the newly forming CCP made equality one of its guiding principles, earning the support of many women. By 1923, the Kuomintang and the CCP entered into a short-lived alliance that incorporated the women's movement in a nationalist revolution, although Chiang Kai-shek (1887–1975) led an offensive against women believed to be Communist sympathizers.

Women were not enfranchised at a national level until after the PRC's establishment in 1949, when the Communists had full control of the country. The All-China Democratic Women's Federation was established with representatives from all the provinces and local women's organizations. Renamed the All-China Women's Federation (ACWF), the organization was disbanded briefly during the Cultural Revolution of 1966 to 1976. During the post-Mao reform era in the 1970s, it was reinstated; it continues its work today as an NGO under the close scrutiny of the CCP.

Current Issues

By 1950, the Chinese constitution and other laws recognized equal rights for men and women in many spheres of life, including property ownership, inheritance, land use, and educational opportunities, although their enforcement was modified by custom and reformed laws. Cultural interpretation of the concept of rights differed greatly from its meaning in the United States. Many of the women's issues that arose throughout the 19th and 20th centuries in the United States—inheritance, property ownership, suffrage, and education—as well as the more contemporary ones voiced at the 1995 UN Fourth World Conference on Women in Beijing—equal pay, health care access, and violence—have been under the scrutiny of the ACWF and NGOs in China. When there is a conflict of interest between women's rights and government policy, the latter takes precedence. The CCP limits media coverage of public discussion about unpopular topics: family planning policy, domestic violence and abuse, lesbian rights, and female trafficking.

EDUCATION

Women's ability to receive education and become more skilled is largely perceived as an economic issue and is reflected in government policies that caused the near 90 percent illiteracy rate of 1949 to transmogrify into a 91 percent literacy rate in a little over 50 years. In urban areas, women are encouraged to complete higher education, be independent, and enter fields traditionally dominated by men, such as medicine, law, engineering, science, telecommunications, and even sports. They also play a more active part in the community and society compared with women who live in rural areas.

Despite the 1986 Law on Nine-Year Compulsory Education that made primary school compulsory for both girls and boys, many girls living in rural areas do not attend school since their families do not want to lose the income the child might produce by working in the fields, a pattern that also prevailed in the United States until the late 1800s.

Until recently, the proportion of women to men declined at each educational tier for the general population. However, as in the United States and other countries, the percentage of female undergraduates has grown, from 38 percent in 1998 to 44 percent in 2002, and the number of women in colleges and universities has nearly tripled in that same period. However, institutions of higher education that have a large proportion of female applicants, such as polytechnical schools and foreign language institutes, have been known to require higher entrance exam grades of women.[25]

FAMILY LIFE

In China, the strong patriarchal society still expects women to marry and have children, a pattern that also persists in the United States, but with greater tolerance for other lifestyle choices. As in other Asian nations, arranged marriages are commonplace. Regions still influenced by Chinese traditions expect the new wife to relocate to the husband's community and to handle the domestic and child care chores, but gender roles are starting to modify as couples find themselves needing to be more flexible, with men often traveling to the city for work and women balancing decision-making tasks at home with working in rural industry. The number of divorces increased 67 percent between 2000 and 2005, an increase that may be attributable to revised marriage laws that recognize domestic violence, drug and substance abuse, and extramarital affairs as grounds for divorce.[26]

Although state and village governments own the land, families are given land usage rights. Divorced and widowed women usually lose their usage rights and are forced to relocate to an urban location where rentals are scarce, unless the widow has parents or children who require care. Their land is often then passed into the hands of a son or male relative of the deceased husband.

EMPLOYMENT

According to data collected by the Organization for Economic Cooperation and Development (OECD), Chinese women's salaries average 66.3 percent of men's salaries, a slightly higher rate than the United States's 62.5 percent for women employed in industry in low-skill and low-paying jobs.[27] Open sexual discrimination in hiring practices, which was prevalent well into the 1970s in the United States, still plagues Chinese women, as employers advertise positions for men only and university campus recruiters often state that they will not hire women. Employers justify such discrimination by saying they cannot afford the benefits required for pregnant women, nursing mothers, and infants.

Nevertheless, the government's efforts to curb overt employment discrimination have been documented since 1995, when it stated its intention to "develop energetically vocational education, professional training and practical technical training at all levels and in all categories to raise women's competence in job hunting" in its program for the development of women at the Beijing conference.[28] Women have since been encouraged to enter technical fields to help maintain a competitive edge with other countries. Nearly one-third of teachers at the associate-professor level or above in China's colleges and universities were women in 2001.[29]

In that same year, of the 730.25 million employees in the country, female workers accounted for 37.4 percent in enterprises; 44.1 percent in institutions; 24.8 percent in state organizations, the Communist Party, government departments, and NGOs; 42.7 percent in service trades; and 57.5 percent in the sectors of public health, physical culture, and social welfare service.[30] Women accounted for 49 percent of the 6.81 million registered unemployed people in cities and towns, at an unemployment rate of 3.6 percent in 2001.[31]

This is lower than in the United States, where women's unemployment grew from 4.1 percent in 2000 to 5.4 in 2004.[32]

Use of microcredit funds to help rural women emerge from poverty through self-employment in the past decade is a strategy that has been gradually implemented around the world. From 1998 to 2002, women's federations in China issued a combined 950 million yuan in microcredit, causing more than 2 million rural women to escape poverty.[33] Other microcredit funds have helped urban women become reemployed. At present, the initiative has been launched in 23 provinces, autonomous regions, and municipalities.

FAMILY PLANNING

Unlike in the United States, where family planning is left to individual choice, in China it is a constitutional duty. Since 1979, the one-child policy has been used to control the Chinese population. Although not physically enforced, compliance is achieved through various measures of fines and benefits, from property confiscation and salary cuts to medical, educational, and housing quotas. Residence cards may be denied to "out of plan" children, thus denying them access to education and other state benefits.

Compliance has also been achieved through easy access to contraceptives, abortion for women who already have one child, and sterilization. Until the mid-1990s, forced sterilization was mandatory in certain provinces of China for men (for whom the procedure is referred to as a vasectomy) and for women who had mental illness, retardation, and communicable or hereditary diseases. Even under the 1994 Maternal and Infant Health Care Law and 2002 Population and Family Planning Law, certain categories of people still may be prevented from bearing children, or one member of a couple pressured into sterilization if a couple has more than one child. As of 1997, the World Health Organization (WHO) reported that 87 percent of Chinese women used some form of contraception, the highest rate in the world and higher than the 71 percent rate in the United States.[34]

The one-child policy has taken its toll on the sex ratio of the population, increasing from 111 males in 1989 to 118 males to 100 females in 2000, although there are signs that this ratio had declined to 112 males to 100 females in 2006.[35] This was much higher than the 105 males to 100 females in the United States in 2006.[36] This has also made it difficult for men to find wives. The resulting imbalance of females to males has caused the Chinese government to relax the one-child policy for couples who have only a girl.[37]

Traditional preference for male children has led to the concealment of female births and female infanticide, as well as prenatal sex identification, in spite of a governmental ban on the use of ultrasound machines for this purpose. Unregistered female children cannot attend school or receive medical care or other state services. Female and mentally or physically challenged children populate Chinese orphanages. The Population and Family Planning Law of the PRC went into effect in September 2003 to exert population control yet put an end to coerced abortions and other practices in China: "to bring population into balance with social economic development, resources, and the environment; to promote family planning; to protect citizens' legitimate rights and interests; to enhance family happiness; and to contribute to the nation's prosperity and social progress."[38]

China's high rate of abortion—28 percent of pregnancies were terminated in 2005—was originally thought to be largely due to the one-child policy, but recent research shows that the procedure is mostly performed on young unwed women. Although the country does not have a high rate of maternal mortality or unsafe abortions, with 97 percent of births and abortions attended to by skilled personnel, forced abortions along with female infanticide are influencing the sex ratio.[39]

SEXUAL FREEDOM

The transition to a global economy in which citizens make their own personal decisions—if not political ones—has challenged the Chinese government's control over daily life. American and European music, lifestyle, and fashion are influencing the younger generation through television and the Internet, causing a sort of sexual revolution. The average young woman today has her first sexual experience at 17 in urban areas, much sooner than the 24 years of age reported by women who are now in the 31- to 40-year-old range. In the capital of Beijing, 70 percent of residents claimed they had had sexual relations before marriage in 2005, compared with 15.5 percent in 1989.[40] The rise in requests for abortions by single women in Chinese cities has also risen sharply, from 25 percent in 1999 to 65 percent in 2004.

Although homosexuality is no longer illegal, as it was during the Cultural Revolution of 1966 to 1976, protective laws for lesbians and gays are nonexistent. Same-sex marriages were not included in marriage law revisions. The media minimize coverage of gays, even with advocacy for controlling the burgeoning HIV/AIDs problem. Authorities are quick to close down public events that involve gays or lesbians. The government is dealing with these issues in the same way they were treated for many years in the United States: with nonacknowledgment.

VIOLENCE

China is not denying, however, the global attention to the issue of violence against women and acknowledges infanticide, female trafficking, prostitution, and domestic violence as major problems. In many parts of the country, spousal abuse is common and still socially acceptable, affecting an estimated one-third of marriages. Comprehensive statistics about the extent of domestic violence are unavailable, according to the ACWF and the Women's Federation, since few women report abuse in rural areas. A revised Marriage Law in 2001 provided legislation to protect women but is not regularly enforced.

There appears to be a causal relationship between domestic violence and child abuse, a trend that has also been detected in the United States.[41] The use of harsh physical punishment has been self-reported by parents in China, with a frequency of 461 per 1,000 children.[42] Advocates of the one-child policy claim that the system reduces the number of child abuse cases, but opponents say the system has led to an increase in female infanticide and abandonment.

Another area of violence that is emerging into public light is elder abuse, also a recently noted trend in the United States. Chinese senior citizens were traditionally respected, so mere neglect of an elder can constitute abuse. The higher than average rate of suicide among people over 60 years of age in China, especially among married women and widows, may be due to domestic violence and social isolation.[43]

Because shelters and other resources are not available, it is difficult for battered women to escape abuse. Women are under considerable social pressure to keep families together regardless of the circumstances. Legal action is not taken against batterers unless the victim initiates it, and if she withdraws her testimony, the proceedings end.

Trafficking and sale of women as brides or into prostitution are large-scale problems in China, where women have been sold into brothels in Southeast Asia. Like the United States, China is one of the principal destinations for female trafficking. Until recently, men were not prosecuted for purchasing women as wives. Unless a woman or her family complains, local officials do not follow up on evidence that women are sold into marriage. The PRC government has enacted various laws to combat the sale of women, stating that there were 15,000 cases of kidnapping and trafficking in women and children in 1993, yet as many as 10,000 women may have been abducted and sold in 1992 in Sichuan province alone.

The International Movement

The PRC ratified the UN Convention on the Elimination of All Forms of Discrimination against Women in 1980 and enacted the Law on the Protection of Women's Rights and Interests in 1992. After hosting the 1995 UN-sponsored Global Women's Conference, where the Beijing Platform for Action was created, China formed a five-year plan that established programs for the development of Chinese women, with oversight by the ACWF and the East Asia office of the United Nations Development Fund for Women

(UNIFEM). To marry the ideals of equality, development, and peace with actions, the program has targeted integrating women into legal and political systems so they can play a more active role in the "open-and-reform" modernization efforts. Increasing women's rates and fields of employment were perceived to be part of a social reform and "social productive force." Additionally, improved access to higher education and a decrease in the worldwide illiteracy rate, of which 70 percent was estimated to be women, were goals of this plan, alongside access to medical care, free choice for marriage, limiting of violence against women, and establishment of a system of accountability. Although many female-run NGOs have established themselves in China, the movement continues to identify with organizational efforts rather than those of individuals, underscoring its socialist nature.

The Future

Before the Beijing+10 conference in New York in March 2005, the PRC passed a comprehensive law protecting women's rights and interests on a variety of issues, allocating funds to women's education and health and loans to poor women. They then issued a White Paper that outlined progress made in areas of economic rights and security, political participation, law, health, education, family and marriage, and the environment. An interesting parallel were President Bill Clinton's similar efforts before the World Conference on Women in 1995 in Beijing, when he established the Presidential Interagency Council on Women (PICW) by executive order on the eve of the UN Fourth World Conference on Women to track results of CEDAW-inspired efforts.

Although Chinese women's participation in the economy and political decision making has improved according to the White Paper, the report and the law showed that women are still underrepresented in high-level politics and commerce, where gaps in income between men and women also persist.

In 2005, through UNIFEM, other UN agencies, and NGOs, the China Gender Facility for Research and Advocacy was launched to initiate programs for gender mainstreaming and development. As an initiative inspired by CEDAW, the facility funds proposals that address issues of domestic violence, employment, gender mainstreaming, aging, and disability, highlighting 12 areas as priorities for research and advocacy, including the revision of women's law and the collection and use of data about gender, sex ratios, and girl children.

AFGHANISTAN

Although Afghanistan is considered an Asian country, the role of women in society is more similar to that of countries in the Middle East, which share Afghanistan's Islamic tradition. Unlike those of their American counterparts, women's rights in Afghanistan did not include suffrage until late in the 20th century. Women were conferred rights that were compatible with the Muslim culture when Afghanistan declared national independence of Britain in 1921. The first constitution recognized equal rights of men and women in 1923, but not the right to vote for women.

Since the early 20th century various Afghan rulers have tried to introduce reforms favorable to women's rights, which often provoked anger among religious and tribal leaders. King Amanullah (1919–29) encouraged women to remove their veils and established girls' schools.

In the 1950s, under Prime Minister (1953–63) Muhammad Daoud, and as part of a secularization campaign, attempts were made to institute marriage registration; promote female literacy and women's suffrage; ban the exchange of girls for bride prices; and ban the chadri, or burqa, a head-to-toe garment that women were forced to wear. Under King Mohammad Zahir Shah (1914–   ), the reformed constitution—which women were involved in writing—gave women the right to vote in 1963, to go to school, and to earn the same wages as men, generating in Afghanistan "women's liberation" similar to that in the United States at that time.

Political Potential and Challenges

The 1970s Saur Revolution led to the empowerment of a social democracy under the People's Democratic Party of Afghanistan, which also favored a secular lifestyle. By then, there were three women in the parliament. Women's causes were furthered in the 1980s with the socialist government of Nur Mohammed Taraki (1913–79), who favored women's access to political appointments, employment, equal protection, a minimal age for marriage, a ban on forced marriages, and a growing educational system. The implementation of these rights was subject to regional and tribal influence, however.

The civil war that followed the 1979 invasion of Afghanistan by the Soviet Union and the Taliban rule from 1994 to 2002 dramatically curbed, even eliminated, these gains for women. When the country entered into extremist Islamic rule, even pleasurable aspects of life such as kite flying, bright colors, and women's laughter were forbidden, according to one activist, Zoya (1978–   ), who describes the life of a teenager during this time in her book *Zoya's Story: An Afghan Woman's Battle for Freedom.*[44]

By 2001, unsanitary conditions and lack of shelter, food, and medical care posed a serious risk to pregnant women and their infant children, regardless of economic background. The United Nations Population Fund (UNFPA) mounted an unprecedented humanitarian operation in September 2001 as a response to health emergencies facing thousands of people, including pregnant Afghan women, who were fleeing their homes for the border countries of Pakistan, Iran, Tajikistan, Turkmenistan, and Uzbekistan. UNFPA prepositioned emergency relief supplies and lifesaving reproductive health care services, with a plan to distribute them within Afghanistan.

In November 2001, after the fall of the Taliban, the UN Security Council supported efforts of the Afghan people to establish a new transitional administration leading to the formation of a new government through Resolution 1378. The goal was to establish a government that would be broad-based, multiethnic, and fully representative of all the Afghan people and respectful of human rights, regardless of gender, ethnicity, or religion.

Rebuilding women's rights after nearly 23 years of warfare emerged as an integral part of reconstructing the country under the terms of the 2001 Bonn Agreement. What role Islam should play in the new nation—integrated into the new democratic government or as a belief system guiding a secular state—was still being decided.

Hamid Karzai (1957–), the head of the interim administration, showed support for women's rights by signing the Declaration of the Essential Rights of Afghan Women, which was adopted at a meeting in Dushanbe, Tajikistan, in January 2002. The document conferred the right to equality of men and women.

The *loya jirga* (grand council) convened in June 2002 for the first time since 1964 to discuss the terms of the interim government. Rahima Jami (birthdate unknown) and Nasrine Gross (1945–), two female educators, were invited to attend as consultants to the process, personifying women's issues and the questioning of the role of Islam. Jami wore a head scarf knotted under her chin and a long coat, while Gross wore a black pantsuit and tied her hair in a ponytail. Gross's Paris-based organization, NEGAR, an international NGO that supports Afghan women's rights, was successful in having an equal rights law signed and moved the *loya jirga*'s attention to its implementation.

At the *loya jirga* convention, an Afghan woman, Dr. Massouda Jalal (1962–), became the first female presidential candidate in the country's history. Two women secured seats as ministers: General Suhaila Siddiq (1941–), a female surgeon who practiced in the capital city of Kabul throughout the Taliban regime, became minister of public health; and Dr. Sima Samar (1957–), a physician and founder of the Shuhada Organization network of clinics, hospitals, and schools in Pakistan and central Afghanistan, was elected minister of women's affairs. Alongside them, 220 women took seats in the male-dominated assembly.

Dr. Samar resigned from her post in early 2002 because of bomb threats instigated by her secular views. She took a position within the Human Rights Commission and was replaced in the ministry of women's affairs by an Islamist candidate who offered more moderate views.

A new constitution enacted in January 2004 asserted specific rights for women, including the right to vote in democratic elections and with legal protection. Article 22 guaranteed men and women equal rights and duties before the law. Article 44 provided that the state must promote education for women. Approximately 25 percent of the seats in the Wolesi Jirga (House of the People) was the constitutional quota reserved for women, and the president would be required to appoint additional women to the Meshrano Jirga (House of the Elders).

The presidential election took place in October 2004 and was won by Karzai, and the first free parliamentary and provincial council elections in 30 years were delayed until September 18, 2005, fulfilling the terms of the Bonn Agreement. More than 600 women candidates competed for the 68 (of a total of 249) parliamentary seats guaranteed for women and would have won 27 percent of the seats in the lower house if it were not for the constitutional quota of the Wolesi Jirga.

Of the 10.5 million registered Afghan voters, 43 percent were women, with rates in southern provinces, where conservative Pashtun traditions are particularly strong, significantly lower than the national average, because of many terrorist threats from Taliban and al-Qaeda insurgents. However, news of the registered voter turnout varied from 35 percent to 50 percent. International workers who reported on the election process from the field observed that illiterate voters were confused by the complexity of the ballots. "A lot of voters, especially women in rural areas, were confused about the voting process, did not know how to vote, or did not have any idea of whom to vote for," said one worker.[45]

Several women emerged as leaders during this landmark election: Fauzia Gailani (birthdate unknown) in Herat, Malai Joya (1979–) in Farah, along with Shukria Barekzai (birthdate unknown) of Kabul. Joya became the youngest member of the Afghan parliament and won the second-highest number of votes in the province. Barekzai, editor of *Women Mirror*, a weekly magazine, finished 24 out of the 33 candidates. Their winning showed that, given the chance, women of Afghanistan could be part of the political process.

In December 2005, the first session of the parliament convened with a higher percentage of women representatives, 27.3 percent, than that of many established democracies, including the U.S. Congress (15.2 percent) and British Parliament (19.7 percent).[46]

Current Issues

Since Afghanistan's interim government took power in December 2001, women—who constitute 60 percent of the country's 20 million people—have regained their right to work and go to school. Women have even regained their jobs as television and radio announcers and performers, freedoms that have given them the confidence to speak up.

THE ROLE OF VIOLENCE IN TRIGGERING THE WOMEN'S MOVEMENT

As in the United States, violence has acted as a catalyst for the resurrection of the women's movement in Afghanistan, although rooted in different causes. One of the main causes of violence in Afghanistan is the opium drug trade, which is controlled by warlords. Women in villages are easily victimized in the cross-fire between warlords and used as pawns in their settling of disputes or attempts to increase their market share.[47]

The high level of violence caused by civil and tribal warfare has taken its toll on women in Afghanistan in the form of rape and other sexual violence, with relatively few cases officially reported for fear for the woman's or her family's safety and associated stigma. Violence has caused conditions that put both Afghan women and men at risk for a low life expectancy, 46 years of age, although this has slightly improved since the end of the Taliban era.[48] This life expectancy is among the lowest in the world, along with those of several sub-Saharan African countries.

Repressive customs and 25 years of war have made wife beating commonplace. Only 500 cases a year of abuse of women, usually of wife beating, are reported. Although victims could seek legal support for divorce, such action is taboo and socially detrimental to women, as no one will care for her after divorce. Population surveys prior to 2002 showed that domestic assault by an intimate partner affected 2 percent of women in North America and Australia, compared with 52 percent of Palestinian women in the Gaza Strip.[49] Research suggests that domestic violence in Afghanistan leans to the higher side of this range. In the entire year of 2004, within Kabul, a city of around 4 million people, only 10 to 15 divorces were granted in the family court.[50]

FAMILY LIFE AND SEXUALITY

Suppression of women's femininity during the Taliban years and by extremist Islamic edicts has had consequences upon Afghan society. In Afghanistan, women continue to wear the burqa for various reasons. Many women are only permitted to leave their home wearing a burqa and accompanied by a male. Some women still do not feel safe unless they are wearing one; others wish to respect Muslim custom. Neither wearing the burqa nor seclusion is an edict of the Qur'an—the holy text of Islam—which, if anything, promotes the role of women in public life. These customs were introduced one century after the Prophet Muhammad's death in the seventh century and were symbolic of chastity after puberty and life close to home. The tradition persisted until the 20th century and was respected by Christian, Jewish, and Muslim women. In contemporary times, the custom has been enforced in the name of Islam, however. Foreigners' opinions about the tradition of burqa wearing are often perceived as racist by Muslim women, especially those who are loyal to the tenets of traditional Islam.

FORCED MARRIAGES

In spite of the reemergence of democracy and women's rights in Afghanistan in the post-Taliban era, an estimated 60 to 80 percent of marriages in the country are forced on women, especially in rural areas where tradition is powerful. Girls and women are often married off for economic gain—as much as 352,100 Afghanistan Afghanis (U.S. $7,000, which is significantly more than the estimated 2004 per capita income of $800)[51] can be earned from a marriage—or for settling of scores between feuding families, even though both practices run counter to civil and Islamic law.[52] In 2004, 57 percent of girls were married before the age of 16.[53] While arranged marriages are normal in this conservative Muslim country, they are meant to have the consent of both the bride and groom.

PROPERTY RIGHTS

As in other Asian countries, legal rights in Afghanistan often are not implemented, particularly property rights. Further, inheritance and property rights differ according to the Muslim population: They are passed entirely through the males of the family among the Sunni Pashtuns, while the Shiite Hazaras allow the daughter half and the wife one-fourth of the father's landholdings.

ACCESS TO HEALTH CARE

As are women in sub-Saharan countries, Afghan women are being called to service and trained by national public health programs to make up for a deficient health care system taxed by war, a poor economy, and lack of professional care. About 1,200 NGOs are helping to rebuild the health care system by training women as community health workers and midwives.[54] With the departure of many physicians from the country, the ratio of physicians to patients was about two to 10,000 people. Only 35 percent of the nation had some kind of access to care by 2001. Common preventable diseases such as measles, malaria, and cholera escalated as a result of shortages of clean water, inadequate sanitation, and malnourishment.

War between factional governments and tribal warlords directly affected women's ability to access health care and contraception. Contraceptive use was extremely low, at about 5 percent of women between 1995 and 2002, compared with 76 percent in the United States; this low rate has been attributed to ignorance, illiteracy, and poor access by the general population of women.[55] Of married women under age 50, 72 percent were unaware of contraceptives or methods to delay pregnancy in 2004.[56] The fertility rate was one of the highest in the world, at 7.5 births per woman between 2004 and 2005.[57] Under the Taliban, the rate was 1,900 maternal deaths per 100,000 births. In 2004, the rate decreased but was still considered high: 1,600 maternal deaths per 100,000 births. One province, Badakshan, had a rate of 6,500 maternal deaths per 100,000 live births, the highest recorded rate ever in the world.[58] Currently, midwives are being trained as alternatives to physicians to provide skilled attendance at birth. One in 10 pregnancies results in unsafe abortion, an approximate figure based on that of countries in Asia, Africa, and Latin America, where the maternal mortality rate is the highest.[59]

EDUCATION

Similar to the United States, where education and suffrage were important early targets of the women's rights movement, women in Afghanistan have focused on these issues. Until 1979, even though channels of education existed within urban and rural areas in Afghanistan, Islamic practices determined whether daughters would receive an education. Of the main groupings, Shiite Hazaras and Tajiks in the north usually educated their daughters, while Sunni Pashtuns in the south usually kept their daughters home.

During the Taliban's fundamentalist regime, girls' schools were completely shut down, female teachers dismissed, and girls were either kept home or found their way to secretly established schools. An estimated 3 percent of girls were educated in primary schools during this time.[60] The Taliban policy on female teachers also affected boys' education, as the majority of teachers had formerly been women. By the time the Taliban's extremist rule ended in November 2001, the estimated literacy rate among women had dropped to 7 percent.

Since 2001, schools are reopening, and slowly, girls are making their way back, especially in the north, where 40 percent of girls attend school compared with 20 percent in the south. Conditions are slightly more conducive to girls' education in the capital of Kabul, where over 162 schools have reopened, employing 20,000 teachers, of whom 17,000 are women.

EMPLOYMENT

Afghan women, whether educated career women or day laborers, are facing a similar plight to American women's—earning pay that is equitable for the task and equal to what men earn. Prior to the civil war and Taliban rule, employment opportunities for urban middle-class women were similar to those in the United States. Women had been allowed to work in civil service jobs and in a variety of professions, as teachers, doctors, professors, lawyers, judges, journalists, writers, and artists, and were even provided with 90 days of maternity leave paid by the employer.[61]

What remains different, however, is the trend in rural areas. Even though the seclusion code of the Taliban had been lifted in 2001, tribal customs in the provinces continue to challenge women, considering those who work outside the home as dishonoring the men and the tribe. Mostly, women are expected to serve the family and maintain the land. Data on female agricultural activities remain underreported because women are not considered part of the national labor effort and are often unpaid. Those considered laborers receive about 30 cents a day compared with one dollar per day to soldiers.

The International Movement

In 2001, with the help of international organizations and NGOs, Afghan women participated in a series of high-level negotiations to set up a transitional government for Afghanistan. At the UN talks in Bonn, Germany, on November 27, 2001, four Afghan groups attended: the Rome process; the United Front, also known as the Northern Alliance; the Cyprus Group; and the Peshawar Group. About 40 Afghan women leaders of different ethnic, linguistic, and religious backgrounds also met at the Afghan Women's Summit for Democracy in Brussels, Belgium, on December 4 and 5, 2001. They met with members of the European Parliament, the U.S. Congress, the UN Security Council, UN Secretary-General Kofi Annan, and female ambassadors to the United Nations with requests to increase security in Afghanistan and assist in disarming warring tribal factions. After demands for assistance with education, media and culture, health, human rights, refugees, and internally displaced women were voiced, the Brussels Proclamation was adopted. A UNIFEM-sponsored roundtable drew together Afghan women and UN agencies, the World Bank, and donors, in Brussels December 10–11; their program, Building Women's Leadership in Afghanistan, focused on an action plan of specific strategies to support the role and leadership of Afghan women in shaping the future of their country. At a breakfast meeting on December 19, Afghan women's NGOs shared their vision with the special adviser on gender issues and advancement of women and women ambassadors from the permanent missions to the UN.[62]

Measurable impact of these high-level meetings can be seen in women's and girls' daily lives in parts of Afghanistan: returning to schools and to jobs, traveling abroad to make speeches and raise funds, but they are doing so still in difficult circumstances. Women's advocacy invites intimidation by hard-line Islamic fundamentalists. Zoya, a spokesperson for the Revolutionary Association of the Women of Afghanistan (RAWA), needed the protection of a bodyguard when she spoke at the 2004 Women and Power Conference in New York City. In 2006, even the capital of Kabul still suffered from lack of basic utilities such as clean water and electricity. Taliban forces continue their insurgency, with considerable success in rural areas. The murder of Safia Amajan (1943–2006), the head of the department of women's affairs in Kandahar, on September 25, 2006, is another example of how the Taliban insurgency is creating setbacks for women in Afghanistan. Amajan promoted girls' rights to an education and women's rights to work.

The Future

Reconstruction and development are Afghanistan's focuses, given its status as one of the 50 least-developed countries in the world. A conscious effort to include women in the decision-making process continues, although women still face challenges from Islamic fundamentalists and conservative elements of the population in daily life.

By 2004, Afghanistan was still one of the countries with the lowest ability to report statistics, with war conditions still prevailing in parts of the country, making it difficult to hold programs accountable for progress.[63] UNIFEM has been working to build the skills of women leaders and encourage women voters to involve themselves in the political process.

In Afghanistan, UNIFEM facilitated the first public forum of its kind on women's rights, joining activists, journalists, and presidential candidates, before the national elections. The United Nations Population Fund (UNFPA) trained women leaders, as part of the effort, on gender issues. In addition, other international agencies, such as USAID, funded income-generating training programs—in craftmaking, beekeeping, poultry farming, kitchen gardening, and home-based dairy production—with local NGOs in 2006 for the large population of women widowed during the decades of war in rural areas.

As Nasrine Gross said in a report in 2003, the Afghan people's "ethics of hard work" and "belief in meaning, the quest for a world larger than one's own existence, the attitude that there is more to life than just the daily grind, that ideals exist to die for" are an "omen of what is to come."[64]

KENYA

The end of colonialism in sub-Saharan Africa occurred late in the 20th century, the 1950s and 1960s, in contrast to the rest of the world.[65] In the 50 years since, the 57 African countries would face war, drought, famine, and ethnic diversity to find their new identities. The Republic of Kenya was also challenged by the need for transition from agricultural, social, political, and economic systems embedded under British colonial rule from 1884 until 1963 that segregated land, families, labor, and wealth.

The 1985 Third World Conference on Women, held in Nairobi, Kenya, was a boon to the status of women in African nations, with 15,000 representatives of NGOs and women's organizations marking the "birth of global feminism" that now included Africa in its vision. Largely because of the AIDS epidemic, Kenya was one of many sub-Saharan countries that would then be under the scrutiny of the United Nations's Millennium Development Goals in 2000. This has caused the country's population of nearly 32 million people to receive much attention on issues such as AIDS, poverty, landownership, and gender equality. With different African countries evolving out of diverse cultures, the women of Kenya followed the precedents set by the 150-year struggle in other parts of the world: using women's rights as an economic incentive to develop a nation.

At the grassroots level, an extensive network of women's rights organizations and NGOs grew in the latter part of the 20th century. Over 24,000 groups are registered with Kenya's Ministry of Culture and Social Services. Organizations that have been advocating women's rights at the village level and trying to influence government policy include the Federation of Women Lawyers Kenya (FIDA), the National Council of Women of Kenya, the National Commission on the Status of Women, the Education Center for Women in Democracy, the League of Kenyan Women Voters, and the Women's Political Caucus.

Efforts to ensure women equal rights and access to economic resources have been the major focus of these organizations. By 2005, the National Policy on Gender and Development was adopted and the National Gender Commission established. With a broader target than that of the United States's Equal Employment Opportunity Commission, these commissions are functioning to provide government oversight of the needs and concerns of men and women in all areas of national development.

Suffrage

Although Kenyan women were granted suffrage in 1963, traditional attitudes have curbed the impact of practicing this right, more so than in the United States. In spite of the 1985 World Conference on Women and subsequent follow-up action plans, the number of Kenyan women in politics remained modest at the start of the 21st century. At the December 2002 national elections, there were 15 female members of parliament (seven elected and eight nominated) in the 222-seat National Assembly—a rate that is about half of the percentage of the U.S. equivalent to a parliament—plus three female ministers and three female assistant ministers.[66] Nevertheless, women's roles in politics have grown from 1 percent in 1990 to 7.1 percent in 2005 and are potentially the catalysts for change in public policy.[67] Alice M. W. Kagunda (birthdate unknown), appointed as senior deputy commissioner of police in February 2003, is making her mark with innovative police training programs as well as being the first woman in the country's history to hold the position.[68]

Current Issues

As in Asian countries where cultural practices are deeply ingrained through traditional beliefs and religion, Kenyan women often saw their legal rights overruled by traditional custom, in spite of what was written in the constitution. In November 2005, Kenyans voted against a new and controversial constitution—the first attempt to update it since 1963—in a referendum that split the country. Although the draft constitution improved women's economic rights and introduced local democracy, opponents disagreed on the powers given to President Mwai Kibaki and the government's conservative values. The new constitution outlawed abortion and same-sex marriages and guaranteed women's basic right to inherit property. However, discriminatory practices that affect women's property and inheritance rights and limit their other political and economic rights were condoned in other parts of the constitution through customary and "personal laws" that allow religious courts to rule on a wide range of private and family cases and limit these basic rights.[69]

FAMILY LIFE

Religious custom and family values play an important role in women's lives in Kenya. For marriage, women can choose from five marriage systems: African, civil, Christian, Muslim, and Hindu. The court in Kenya must determine the kind of law to enforce the contract on the basis of the applicable system. Some women's organizations consider customary laws biased in favor of men and have sought to eliminate them. However, the national courts use the customary laws of an ethnic group as a guide in civil matters—marriage, death, and inheritance issues—so long as they do not conflict with statutory law.

In contrast to American women, who assume certain lifelong rights as individuals, regardless of marital status, Kenyan women find themselves governed by a system of consent. To obtain a national identity card or a passport, a married woman must obtain the consent of her husband or father.[70] This restriction is often circumvented by women who claim to be unmarried.

With half of the population Christian and the other half divided between Islam and indigenous religions, women's spiritual or religious roles are empowered by various churches and sects to capitalize on their skills as healers, counselors in initiation rites, and maintainers of sacred shrines.

PROPERTY RIGHTS

A highly controversial topic is property rights as they relate to marriage rights, which is linked to issues that contemporary women do not experience on a significant scale in the United States. Denying equal property rights to Kenyan women has made them vulnerable to poverty, disease (including HIV/AIDS), violence, and homelessness. In precolonial times, the community as a clan decided how property should be handled, and men's and women's rights were fluid. Women owned approximately 20 percent of structures in Kenya as of 1998, but land registration evoked under colonial rule for privatization made it difficult for widows to maintain tenure since the deed was automatically put in the husband's name. Much as in 17th-century colonial America, the influences of British rule and industrialization created an unnatural precedence to appoint ownership and dictate fixed rights under colonial law.

The Law of Succession Act of 1981 proclaimed equal consideration of inheritance rights by male and female children, but most inheritance problems do not appear in court. Under the customary law of most ethnic groups, a woman cannot inherit land and must live on the land as a guest of male blood or marriage relatives. Moreover, a widow cannot be the sole administrator of her husband's estate unless she has her children's consent; she loses her rights to the estate upon remarriage. Having few alternatives for survival beyond a relationship—whether by death, divorce, or separation—women depend on male relatives or lose all their assets with no alternative but to return to their parents.

The HIV/AIDS epidemic has magnified the devastation of women's property violations in multiple ways. HIV/AIDS has increased the population of widowed women in sub-Saharan Africa. Within some parts of the population, tribal customs force widows into risky, traditional practices involving unprotected sex either with a male family member to keep property or with a social outcast. For instance, among the Luo, one of the largest ethnic groups in Kenya, widowed women practice "widow inheritance," an arrangement by which a woman must find another man as an "inheritor."

EDUCATION AND EMPLOYMENT

Since the 1995 Fourth World Conference on Women in Beijing and the 2000 Millennium Development Goals, Kenya has acknowledged the relation of education to an improved literacy rate and a decrease in poverty for both genders. In spite of high costs and poverty, the government has pursued parity in education. Equal numbers of girls and boys are enrolled in primary and secondary education now, consistently with the pattern in the United States and most developed countries.[71]

Recent efforts improved the literacy rate from 60 percent of all women age 15 and older in 1990 to 70 percent by 2004, making Kenya one of 26 developing nations in the running to actualize the Dakar goal of halving adult illiteracy by 2015.[72] The program has also focused on integrating traditional knowledge with current knowledge in its curriculum.

It is hoped that advances made in educating women in the 1990s will improve women's prospects of obtaining salaried positions, although there still is the hurdle of the kinds of jobs that may be open to them. Unlike the United States's industrially based economy, Kenya's economy is market-based—with goods and services subject to a free price system determined by supply and demand—and more than 70 percent of the population is employed within agriculture. About 1.2 percent of employed persons work in professional positions, where there is limited opportunity for women.[73] Few women receive a salary or wage from employment or self-employment, making the population's unemployment rate high. About 56 percent of the population lives below the poverty line, and 25 percent of the population lived on one dollar a day in 2000.[74]

With women constituting 80 percent of the agricultural workforce, they are a primary force in the labor market. In more recent years, some have cultivated entrepreneurial enterprises in small businesses. Women even earned 123 percent of what men earned in manufacturing as of 1997.[75] Nonetheless, the average monthly income of women in other sectors was approximately two-thirds that of men. Women had difficulty moving into nontraditional fields; they were promoted more slowly than men and were laid off more readily. Societal discrimination was most apparent in rural areas.[76] These factors have contributed to a declining level of young women in the workforce over the past 10 years.[77] On the other hand, women are encouraged to pursue entrepreneurship. As in China and India, women are increasingly being provided with access to savings and microcredit through women's banks to run the local farm businesses.

SEXUAL REPRODUCTIVE RIGHTS

Kenya's fertility rate has declined dramatically in recent decades, as a result of the improved educational status of women and the increased use of family planning methods, making its fertility rate among the lowest in sub-Saharan Africa. From its 1970s rate of eight children to the 2003 rate of three to five children (the range depending on urban or rural settings), it is still higher than the U.S. rate of two children.[78] Since the late 1990s, the fertility rate has stalled at four children.[79]

The increased use of family planning methods among an estimated 39 percent of women in the 1995 to 2002 period makes it one of the highest use rates in sub-Saharan countries, although it is still lower than the U.S. rate of 76 percent.[80] The increase in the maternal death rate from an estimated 320 deaths in 1993 to 1,000 per 100,000 live births in 2000, one of the highest in the world, has been attributed to unsafe abortion, a procedure that is considered illegal except to save a woman's life.[81] Nearly half of all births are reported to be unwanted or unplanned, and almost half of Kenyan women give birth before age 20.[82]

The impact of the HIV/AIDS pandemic on the mortality rate has added to the probability of children and infants dying before their fifth birthday, which stood at 247 deaths per 1,000 live births in 2005, an increase of 24 percent from 1993. This is a stark contrast to the eight deaths per 1,000 live births rate in the United States.[83]

Since the discontinuing of U.S. aid to NGO-sponsored family planning services that offer abortion services (known as the Mexico City Policy or the "Global Gag Rule" by its opponents), several organizations have closed their clinics. Agencies such as the United Nations Population Fund are trying to assist with information and educational services but are hindered by religious sectarian beliefs.

Female genital mutilation (FGM), also referred to as female circumcision and female genital cutting (FGC), is customarily practiced on young girls by certain ethnic groups in rural areas of Kenya. Camouflaged as a religious rite, FGM is often used as a way to reduce promiscuity and ensure virginity at marriage and marital fidelity. According to estimates, 38 to 50 percent of females nationwide have suffered from FGM, and this incidence rises to 90 percent in the Eastern, Nyanza, and Rift Valley provinces. The Ministry of Health reported the highest incidence of girls subject to the procedure among the Masai and Kisii, 89 and 90 percent, respectively.[84] Two presidential decrees ban FGM and the practice is prohibited in hospitals and clinics. In 2001, female genital cutting was outlawed for girls under the age of 16.[85] Local woman activists such as Agnes Pareyio (birthdate unknown), who manages the Tasaru Girl's Refuge center, have been educating young girls and their families about the consequences of FGM, which include infection, miscarriage, spontaneous abortion, and other complications. The practice has entered the United States through immigrants who practice native African customs.

ACCESS TO HEALTH CARE AND THE SPREAD OF HIV/AIDS

The challenges of poverty, HIV, and women's rights are intrinsically tied together, as each has repercussions for the others. The private health care system in Kenya has made it difficult for the population to receive basic primary care services, which include giving immunizations, treating communicable diseases, and preventing malnutrition. Malaria is one of the most common diseases, affecting over half of the country's population, about 20 million people. In addition to the 33 percent of the population who are undernourished, the spread of HIV/AIDS is estimated to have infected 15 percent of the population between the ages of 15 and 49, and disproportionately more women than men. This pattern has contributed to reducing the country's average life expectancy to 50 years, thereby reducing the population of wage earners. It is also responsible for the growing number of AIDS orphans living in Kenya, which was 890,000 as of 2001.[86]

Poor economic and social conditions within Kenya have made women more susceptible to contracting HIV/AIDS through inadequate health care, risky tribal customs, partners' high-risk behavior, and overall "disempowerment."[87] Of the 1.2 to 1.4 million infected with HIV/AIDS in Kenya, 65 percent are women, according to estimates by the United Nations Statistics Division. The trend is, however, downward as HIV prevalence declined in antenatal clinics from 13.6 percent in 1997–98 to 9.4 percent in 2002, staying unchanged in 2003.[88] Both international and grassroots efforts to educate Kenyan women and girls about physical abuse, abortion, contraceptives, FGM, and gender relations are largely responsible. In January 2006, Feminenza International sponsored a conference, Gender and Humanity, with UNESCO, inviting over 200 representatives from area NGOs in Kenya and other African nations to confer about all aspects of gender relations, from physical to spiritual.

VIOLENCE

Gender-based violence has exposed a number of women to poverty. Kenya's domestic violence rate—40 percent of women report abuse from domestic violence or rape—is higher than that of the United States, where 22 percent of women report abuse by an intimate partner.[89] In Kenya, a husband's actions against his wife are often seen as a customary method of discipline. Since 2002, the Domestic Violence Family Protection Bill has provided legislation to defend women against such violent treatment, but few women invoke it. Their options are limited by poverty, lack of housing, and unfortunate social customs concerning single women, especially divorced ones, which make them less likely to report incidents.

Some attempt has been made to sensitize local officials, including police, to gender issues. The International Federation of Women Lawyers (FIDA) trained over 500 police officers and developed a curriculum for dealing with gender-based violence. Also, Senior Deputy Commissioner of Police Kagunda has made a point of training female police officers to handle such cases.

HUMAN TRAFFICKING, CHILD ABUSE, AND PROSTITUTION

Data about human trafficking in Africa are lacking; ineffective efforts to combat the problem are the result. There are reports that persons have been trafficked to, from, or within the country, particularly women and children. The law does not specifically prohibit trafficking in persons, but traffickers can be prosecuted under laws that prohibit child labor, the transportation of children for sale, the commercial exploitation of children, and the detention of females against their will for the purposes of prostitution. Women are trafficked to Lebanon and other Middle Eastern countries for labor, and children are often trafficked to Uganda for that purpose. Women from eastern Europe and Asia are trafficked through Kenya to Western countries.

The abuse of children and child prostitution are widespread, particularly in the cities of Nairobi and Mombasa, where a tourist trade thrives. Child prostitution has grown considerably as a result of poverty and the increase in the number of children orphaned by HIV/AIDS. According to the International Labour Organisation (ILO), approximately 30,000 girls under the age of 19 years were engaged in prostitution in the country in 2003.[90] A conservative estimate of 250,000 children live on the streets in urban areas—primarily Nairobi, Mombasa, Kisumu, and Nakuru—where they engage in theft, drug trafficking, assault, trespassing, and property damage to survive.[91]

The Children Act was created in 2001 to assert the rights and promote the welfare of children and guarantee their protection against economic exploitation and any work likely to be hazardous to or interfere with their health or physical, mental, spiritual, moral, or social development. It also addressed parental responsibility and children's need for care and protection. Government programs to shelter and assist street children with education, skills training, counseling, and legal advice are one strategy being adopted to combat the problem.[92]

THE INTERNATIONAL MOVEMENT

In 1985, women's organizations from around the world convened in Nairobi, Kenya, for the third world conference on women. It was here that the Nairobi Forward Looking Strategies for the Advancement of Women set forth specific strategies as concrete measures for the period 1986–2000: sexual equality, women's autonomy and power, recognition of women's unpaid work, and advances in women's paid work. Kenya took steps to meet the commitments at national and district levels at the subsequent 1995 Beijing conference, adopting the Platform for Action for Improving the Welfare of Women in Kenya in October 1997. In 2002, three bills designed to protect women's rights—the Domestic Violence (Family Protection) Bill, the National Policy on Gender and Development Bill, and the Equality Bill—were introduced to Parliament. The National Policy on Gender and Development has helped to implement gender mainstreaming strategy in socioeconomic development and environmental management. Protecting women against domestic violence with equality bills and opening women's self-help groups have also made a difference.

The Future

As in the United States in the early 1970s, grassroots initiatives have intensified local community level partnerships and participation by women's ministries. The establishment of Maendeleo ya Wanawake Organization (MYWO) and the Greenbelt Movement—a network of women planting trees as a way to improve their welfare, organized by the entrepreneur and 2004 Nobel Prize winner Wangari Muta Maathai (1940–   )—is an example.

Although Kenya is working to establish gender equality in development and planning and has made strides in adopting international provisions in national policy, there remains the challenge of interpretation, implementation, and enforcement, a pattern that holds as true for the United States as the rest of the world. Human Rights Watch, a watchdog organization, informed the United Nations in early 2005 of Kenya's violation of women's property rights and noncompliance with the International Covenant on Civil and Political Rights (ICCPR).

Nevertheless, as in Afghanistan, the women's movement has grown into a humanitarian effort. Kenyan women are challenging violations of rights and other societal conditions with the support of international organizations, NGOs, grassroots efforts, and their own ingenuity to reform gender practices in a way that is both natural and progressive for men and women in Kenya.

---

[1] Robin Morgan, ed. *Sisterhood Is Global.* New York: Feminist Press, City University of New York, 1996, p. 180.

[2] Margit Mogensen. "Stays and Suffrage, Women's Liberation in Denmark." Royal Library of Copenhagen. Available online. URL: http://www.kb.dk/kultur/expo/porten/cult96/e06.htm. Accessed November 13, 2005.

[3] June Hannan, Mitzi Auchterlonie, and Katherine Holden, eds. "Denmark." In *International Encyclopedia of Women's Suffrage.* Santa Barbara, Calif: ABC-CLIO, 2000, p. 85.

[4] Mogensen. "Stays and Suffrage."

[5] The Danish State. Official Website of Denmark. "Gender Equality." Available online. URL: http://denmark.dk/portal/page?_pageid=374,520325&_dad=portal&_schema   =PORTAL. Accessed November 15, 2005.

[6] Hannan, Auchterlonie, and Holden, eds. "Denmark." In *International Encyclopedia of Women's Suffrage,* p. 86.

[7] United Nations Statistics Division. Statistics and Indicators on Women and Men, table 6—Women in Parliament (April 22, 2005). Available online. URL: http://unstats.un.org/unsd/demographic/products/indwm/ww2005/tab6.htm. Accessed January 25, 2006.

[8] United Nations Statistics Division. Millennium Indicator: Girls to Boys Ratio, Tertiary Level Enrollment (UNESCO) (February 17, 2005). Available online. URL: http://unstats. un.org/unsd/mi/mi_series_results.asp?rowID=614&fID=r15&cgID=. Accessed February 9, 2006.

[9] Lynn Walter, ed. "Denmark." In *The Greenwood Encyclopedia of Women's Issues Worldwide: Europe.* Westport, Conn.: Greenwood Press, 2003, p. 154.

[10] OECD. The Gender, Institutions and Development Data Base, 2006. Available online. URL: http://www.oecd.org/document/23/0,2340,en_2649_33947_36225815_1_1_1_1,00. html. Accessed April 21, 2006.

[11] Walter, ed. "Denmark." In *The Greenwood Encyclopedia of Women's Issues Worldwide,* p. 154.

[12] Walter, ed. "Denmark." In *The Greenwood Encyclopedia of Women's Issues Worldwide. Europe,* p. 154. Cristien Bajerna. "Denmark." In *Sexual Harassment in the Workplace in the European Union.* Brussels: European Commission, 1998, pp. 63–67.

[13] Ann Moline. "European Union Tells Members to Bar Sex Harassment" (July 22, 2002). Women's E-News. Available online. URL: http://www.womensenews.org/article.cfm/dyn/ aid/980. Accessed June 20, 2006.

[14] "Report on Sexual Harassment in the Workplace in EU Member States." The Irish Presidency of the European Union in Association with Farrell Grant Sparks Consulting and Professor Aileen McGolgan, June 2004, p. xi.

[15] United Nations Statistics Division. Statistics and Indicators on Women and Men, table 5f—Women Administrative and Managerial Workers (April 22, 2005). Available online. URL: http://unstats.un.org/unsd/demographic/products/indwm/ww2005/tab5f.htm. Accessed February 9, 2006.

[16] The World Factbook. Denmark Country Indicators (August 22, 2006). Available online. https://www.cia.gov/cia/publications/factbook/geos/da.html#People. Accessed August 31, 2006.

[17] Paula Snyder, ed. *European Women's Almanac.* New York: Columbia University Press, 1992, p. 83.

[18] U.S. Department of State. "Denmark." Country Reports on Human Rights Practices—2003. (February 25, 2004). Bureau of Democracy, Human Rights, and Labor. Available online. URL: http://www.state.gov/g/drl/rls/hrrpt/2003/27834.htm. Accessed January 7, 2006.

[19] KULU: Women and Development (October 11, 2004). Available online. URL: http://kulu. dk/in_english.htm. Accessed January 7, 2006.

[20] KULU: Women and Development (October 11, 2004). Available online. URL: http://kulu. dk/in_english.htm. Accessed on January 7, 2006.

[21] Wim Van Lerberghe, Annick Manuel, Zoë Matthews, and Cathy Wolfheim. The World Health Report 2005: Make Every Mother and Child Count. Report, Denmark Country Indicators, World Health Organization, p. 212.

[22] "Headscarves in the Headlines." BBC News (February 10, 2004). Available online. URL: http://news.bbc.co.uk/1/hi/world/europe/3476163.stm. Accessed December 12, 2006.

[23] U.S. Department of State. Denmark. Country Reports on Human Rights Practices—2003 (February 25, 2004). Released by the Bureau of Democracy, Human Rights, and Labor. Avail-

able online. URL: http://www.state.gov/g/drl/rls/hrrpt/2003/27834.htm. Accessed January 7, 2006.

[24] CIA. The World Factbook. China Country Indicators (June 13, 2006). Available online. URL: http://www.cia.gov/cia/publications/factbook/geos/ch.html. Accessed June 23, 2006.

[25] ACWF. Chinese Women. "Women and Education." Available online. URL: http://www.women.org.cn/english/duomeiti/english/ssysj/ssysj05.htm. Accessed February 6, 2006.

[26] Hannah Beech. "Breaking up Is Easy to Do." *Time,* November 6, 2006, p. 51.

[27] OECD. The Gender, Institutions and Development Data Base, 2006. Available online. URL: http://www.oecd.org/document/23/0,2340,en_2649_33947_36225815_1_1_1_1,00.html. Accessed April 21, 2006.

[28] UNESCAP. The Program for the Development of Chinese Women (1995–2000). Available online. URL: http://www.unescap.org/esid/psis/population/database/poplaws/law_china/ch_record016.htm. Accessed February 6, 2006.

[29] ACWF. Chinese Women. "Women and Science." Available online. URL: http://www.women.org.cn/english/duomeiti/english/ssysj/ssysj04.htm. Accessed February 6, 2006.

[30] ACWF. Chinese Women. "Women and Economy: Facts and Data." Available online. URL: http://www.women.org.cn/english/duomeiti/english/ssysj/ssysj02.htm. Accessed February 6, 2006.

[31] ACWF. Chinese Women. "Women and Economy: Facts and Data." Accessed February 6, 2006.

[32] Women in the Labor Force: A Databook. U.S. Department of Labor, U.S. Bureau of Labor Statistics, May 2005, p.1.

[33] ACWF. Chinese Women. "Women and Economy: Facts and Data." Accessed February 6, 2006.

[34] Van Lerberghe, Manuel, Matthews, and Wolfheim. "The World Health Report 2005: Make Every Mother and Child Count," pp. 212–218.

[35] The UN Millennium Project. Investing in Development: A Practical Plan to Achieve the Millennium Development Goals. Report, United Nations, 2005, p. 159.

[36] CIA. The World Factbook. China Country Indicators (June 13, 2006). Available online. URL: http://www.cia.gov/cia/publications/factbook/geos/ch.html. Accessed June 23, 2006.

[37] "Serious Birth Gender Imbalance Inflicts 9 Chinese Regions" (August 25, 2004). *People's Daily Online.* Available online. URL: http://english.people.com.cn/200408/25/eng20040825_154752.html. Accessed April 27, 2006.

[38] "Population and Family Planning Law of the People's Republic of China." Beijing: China Population Publishing House, 2002. Available online. URL: http://www.unescap.org/esid/psis/population/database/poplaws/law_china/china%20pop%20and%20family%20planning.pdf. Accessed January 1, 2006.

[39] Van Lerberghe, Manuel, Matthews, and Wolfheim. "The World Health Report 2005: Make Every Mother and Child Count." Report, World Health Organization, 2005, p. 212.

[40] Hannah Beech. "Sex, Please—We're Young and Chinese." *Time,* December 12, 2005, p. 61.

[41] U.S. Department of Justice. Office for Victims of Crime. Report to the Nation 2001. Fiscal Years 1999 and 2000, Report, p. 5.

[42] Etienne G. Krug, Linda L. Dahlberg, James A. Mercy, Anthony B. Zwi, and Rafael Lozano, eds. "World Report on Violence and Health." Report, World Health Organization, 2002, p. 62.

[43] Krug, Dahlberg, Mercy, Zwi, and Lozano, eds. "World Report on Violence and Health," p. 195.

[44] Zoya, James R. Follain, John Follain, and Rita Cristofari. *Zoya's Story: An Afghan Woman's Battle for Freedom.* New York: HarperCollins Publishers, 2002.

[45] Sam Zarifi. "The Road Ahead" (September 19, 2005). Afghan Election Diary. Human Rights Watch Asia. Available online. URL: http://www.hrw.org/campaigns/afghanistan/blog.htm#blog19. Accessed December 18, 2005.

[46] M. Ashraf Haidari. "Civil Society—Afghanistan's Parliamentary Election Results Confirm Stunning Gains for Women" (October 28, 2005). Eurasianet.org. Available online. URL: http://www.eurasianet.org/departments/civilsociety/articles/eav102805b.shtml. Accessed February 3, 2006.

[47] Krug, Dahlberg, Mercy, Zwi, and Lozano, eds. "World Report on Violence and Health," p. 245.

[48] United Nations Department of Economic and Social Affairs. "The World Women's 2005: Progress in Statistics." Report, Statistics Division, 2006, p. 138.

[49] Krug, Dahlberg, Mercy, Zwi, and Lozano, eds. "World Report on Violence and Health," p. 89.

[50] Matthew Pennington. "Forced Marriage Still Rife in Afghanistan." Associated Press, March 14, 2005.

[51] CIA. The World Factbook. Afghanistan Country Indicators (August 22, 2006). Available online. URL: https://www.cia.gov/cia/publications/factbook/geos/af.html. Accessed December 12, 2006.

[52] Pennington. "Forced Marriage." Associated Press, March 14, 2005.

[53] "Status of Women in Afghanistan, October 2004." Study, Afghanistan Ministry of Women's Affairs and Afghan Women's NGOs. Available online. URL: http://www.hawaii.edu/global/projects_activities/Trafficking. Accessed June 15, 2006.

[54] María José Alcalá. State of World Population, 2005. The Promise of Equality: Gender Equity, Reproductive Health and the Millennium Development Goals, Report, UNFPA, 2005, p. 37.

[55] The World Women's 2005: Progress in Statistics. United Nations Department of Economic and Social Affairs, 2006, p. 132.

[56] Human Rights Watch. "Asia: The Status of Women in Afghanistan, October 2004." Available online. URL: http://hrw.org/campaigns/afghanistan/facts.htm. Accessed December 19, 2005.

[57] The World Women's 2005, p. 132.

[58] Van Lerberghe, Manuel, Matthews, and Wolfheim. "The World Health Report 2005: Make Every Mother and Child Count," p. 213.

[59] Alcalá. State of World Population, 2005, p. 35.

[60] United Nations International Women's Day, 2002. "Afghan Women Today: Realities and Opportunities." Available online. URL: http://www.un.org.pk/iwd/index.htm. Accessed June 15, 2006.

[61] The World Women's 2005, p. 150.

[62] The United Nations in Pakistan. "International Women's Day 2002, Afghan Women Today: Realities and Opportunities." Available online. URL: http://www.un.org.pk/iwd/women-situation-afg.htm. Accessed February 3, 2006.

[63] The World Women's 2005, p. 120.

[64] Nasrine Gross. "Afghan Women: March to September 2003 Report of Activities." Kabultec, 2003. Available online. URL: http://www.kabultec.org/mrspt03.html. Accessed August 29, 2006.

[65] The sub-Saharan Africa region is made up of the subregions of central Africa (Angola, Cameroon, Central African Republic, Chad, Congo, Democratic Republic of Congo, Equatorial Guinea, Gabon, São Tomé and Príncipe), eastern Africa (Burundi, Comoros, Eritrea, Ethiopia, Kenya, Madagascar, Malawi, Mauritius, Mozambique, Réunion, Rwanda, Seychelles, Uganda, United Republic of Tanzania, Zambia, Zanzibar, Zimbabwe), southern Africa (Botswana, Lesotho, Namibia, South Africa, Swaziland), and western Africa (Benin, Burkina Faso, Cape Verde, Côte d'Ivoire, Gambia, Ghana, Guinea, Guinea-Bissau, Liberia, Mali, Mauritania, Niger, Nigeria, Senegal, Sierra Leone, St. Helena, Togo).

[66] U.S. Department of State. Kenya—Country Reports on Human Rights Practices—2003 (February 25, 2004). Report. Available online. URL: http://www.state.gov/g/drl/rls/hrrpt/2003/27733.htm. Accessed February 6, 2006.

[67] UNFPA and Population Reference Bureau. *Country Profiles for Population and Reproductive Health, Policy Developments and Indicators 2005.* Report and Database, Population, Health, and Socio-Economic Indicators by Country, pp. 58–59. Available online. URL: http://www.unfpa.org/profile/kenya.cfm. Accessed February 7, 2006.

[68] U.S. Department of State. Kenya—Country Reports on Human Rights Practices—2003 (February 25, 2004). Report. Available online. URL: http://www.state.gov/g/drl/rls/hrrpt/2003/27733.htm. Accessed February 6, 2006.

[69] Lynn Walter and Aili Mari Tripp, eds. "Kenya." In *Greenwood Encyclopedia of Women's Issues Worldwide: Sub-Saharan Africa.* Westport, Conn.: Greenwood Press, 2003, p. 214.

[70] U.S. Department of State. Kenya—Country Reports on Human Rights Practices—2003 (February 25, 2004). Report. Available online. URL: http://www.state.gov/g/drl/rls/hrrpt/2003/27733.htm. Accessed February 6, 2006.

[71] United Nations Statistics Division. Millennium Indicator: Girls to Boys Ratio, Primary Level Enrollment (UNESCO) (February 17, 2005). Available online. URL: http://unstats.un.org/unsd/mi/mi_series_results.asp?rowID=613. Accessed February 14, 2006.

[72] CIA. The World Factbook. Kenya Country Indicators (February 25, 2006). Available online. URL: http://www.cia.gov/cia/publications/factbook/geos/ke.html. Accessed February 6, 2006. UNESCO Institute for Statistics. "Statistics Show Slow Progress towards Universal Literacy" (September 2, 2006). Available online. URL: http://www.uis.unesco.org/ev.php?ID=5063_201&ID2=DO_TOPIC. World Bank Group. GenderStats (Database of Gender Statistics). Available online. URL: http://devdata.worldbank.org/genderstats/genderRpt.asp?rpt=profile&cty=KEN,Kenya&hm=home. Accessed June 27, 2006.

[73] Central Bureau of Statistics, Kenya. Report of 1998/99 Labor Force Survey, Executive Summary, March 2003, p. 4.

[74] Republic of Kenya. National Assessment Report for the Summit on Sustainable Development (RIO + 10), 2002, p. 10.

[75] United Nations Statistics Division. Statistics and Indicators on Women and Men, table 5G—Women's Wages Relative to Men's Wages, Kenya (February 22, 2005). Available online. URL: http://unstats.un.org/unsd/demographic/products/indwm/ww2005/tab5g.htm. Accessed January 25, 2006.

[76] Janet Walsh. "Double Standards: Women's Property Rights Violations in Kenya." Human Rights Watch, 2003, p. 10.

[77] International Labour Office. *Global Employment Trends Brief.* January 2006, p. 3.

[78] Central Bureau of Statistics, Kenya. Kenya Demographic and Health Survey 2003, Preliminary Report, p. 9.

[79] Population Reference Bureau, *2005 World Population Data Sheet,* 2005, p. 7.

[80] UN Department of Economic and Social Affairs. Statistics Division. The World's Women: 2005 Progress in Statistics, Report, 2005, p. 130.

[81] Republic of Kenya. National Assessment Report for the World Summit on Sustainable Development. Johannesburg, South Africa, 2002, p. 22.

[82] Population Action International and Planned Parenthood Federation of America. Country in Focus: Kenya, Report, The Global Gag Rule Impact Project, 2005, p. 1. Available online. URL: http://www.globalgagrule.org. Accessed January 2, 2006.

[83] Alcalá. State of World Population, 2005, pp. 111–114.

[84] U.S. Department of State. Kenya: Report on Female Genital Mutilation (FGM) or Female Genital Cutting (FGC) (June 1, 2001). The Office of the Senior Coordinator for International Women's Issues, Office of the Under Secretary for Global Affairs. Available online. URL: http://www.state.gov/g/wi/rls/rep/crfgm/10103.htm. Accessed February 6, 2006.

[85] UNFPA and Population Reference Bureau. Country Profiles for Population and Reproductive Health, Policy Developments and Indicators 2005. Report and Database, Population, Health, and Socio-Economic Indicators by Country, pp. 58–59. Available online. URL: http://www.unfpa.org/profile/kenya.cfm. Accessed February 7, 2006.

[86] Population Action International and Planned Parenthood Federation of America. Country in Focus: Kenya, Report, The Global Gag Rule Impact Project, 2005, p. 1. Available online. URL: http://www.globalgagrule.org. Accessed January 2, 2006.

[87] UNAIDS/World Health Organization. AIDS Epidemic Update 2004, December 2004, p. 4.

[88] UNAIDS/World Health Organization. AIDS Epidemic Update 2004, p. 26.

[89] Patricia Tjaden, Nancy Thoennes. Full Report of the Prevalence, Incidence, and Consequences of Violence against Women, Research Report, U.S. Department of Justice, 2000, p. iv.

[90] U.S. Department of State. Kenya—Country Reports on Human Rights Practices—2003 (February 25, 2004). Report. Available online. URL: http://www.state.gov/g/drl/rls/hrrpt/2003/27733.htm. Accessed February 6, 2006.

[91] Jim Fisher-Thompson. "U.S. Congress Cites Growing World Problem of 'Street Children'" (September 15, 2005). U.S. Department of State. Available online. URL: http://usinfo.state.gov/gi/Archive/2005/Sep/16-723661.html. Accessed June 27, 2006.

[92] Fisher-Thompson. "U.S. Congress Cites Growing World Problem of 'Street Children.'" Accessed June 27, 2006.

PART II

Primary Sources

4

~

United States Documents

This section draws together excerpts of significant U.S. primary source documents. Please note that all the documents are in their original grammatical style and spelling, with respect to different international and European systems, and any changes to the original text are indicated in brackets. For source notes indicated within documents, consult the original documents. The documents are organized into the following sections:

Historical Documents

Newspaper Articles

Magazine Articles

Scientific Reports

Speeches

Legal Documents

Court Cases

HISTORICAL DOCUMENTS

Declaration of Sentiments (1848)

A landmark document in the women's movement in the United States, written by Elizabeth Cady Stanton on the occasion of the first major conference in Seneca Falls, New York, on July 19, 1848. It was adopted at a meeting of 300 people who focused on the "social, civil, and religious condition and rights of woman," in the Wesleyan Chapel. Modeled on the Declaration of Independence, the declaration spells out the "injuries" sustained by women from men's tyranny over them. It also outlines resolutions to change this condition through efforts of both genders to secure fair and equal participation of both women and men "in the various trades, professions, and commerce."

When, in the course of human events, it becomes necessary for one portion of the family of man to assume among the people of the earth a position different from that which they have hitherto occupied, but one to which the laws of nature and of nature's God entitle them, a decent respect to the opinions of mankind requires that they should declare the causes that impel them to such a course.

We hold these truths to be self-evident: that all men and women are created equal; that they are endowed by their Creator with certain inalienable rights; that among these are life, liberty, and the pursuit of happiness; that to secure these rights governments are instituted, deriving their just powers from the consent of the governed. Whenever any form of government becomes destructive of these ends, it is the right of those who suffer from it to refuse allegiance to it, and to insist upon the institution of a new government, laying its foundation on such principles, and organizing its powers in such form, as to them shall seem most likely to effect their safety and happiness. Prudence, indeed, will dictate that governments long established should not be changed for light and transient causes; and accordingly all experience hath shown that mankind are more disposed to suffer, while evils are sufferable, than to right themselves by abolishing the forms to which they were accustomed. But when a long train of abuses and usurpations, pursuing invariably the same object evinces a design to reduce them under absolute despotism, it is their duty to throw off such government, and to provide new guards for their future security. Such has been the patient sufferance of the women under this government, and such is now the necessity which constrains them to demand the equal station to which they are entitled. . . .

Source: Excerpted from E. C. Stanton, S. B. Anthony, and M. J. Gage, eds., *History of Women's Suffrage,* Vol. 1 (1887), p. 70. Available online. URL: http://usinfo.state.gov/usa/infousa/facts/democrac/17.htm. Accessed May 24, 2006.

Glass Ceiling Commission (1991–1996)

In 1991, the U.S. Department of Labor defined glass ceiling as "those artificial barriers based on attitudinal or organizational bias that prevent qualified individuals from advancing upward in their organization into management-level positions." The department's Glass Ceiling Commission (1991–96) studied these barriers as they apply not only to women but also to minorities.

While minorities and women have made strides in the last 30 years, and employers increasingly recognize the value of workforce diversity, the executive suite is still overwhelmingly a white man's world. Over half of all Master's degrees are now awarded to women, yet 95 percent of senior-level managers of the top Fortune 1000 industrial and 500 service companies are men. Of them, 97 percent are white. African Americans, Hispanics, Asian and Pacific Islander Americans and American Indians also remain woefully under-represented in the upper echelons of American business.

The Commission's recommendations emphasize that government must lead by example, followed by strong commitment and leadership from corporate America. Yet, action by government and business are not enough. For real change to occur, bias and discrimination must be banished from the boardrooms and executive suites of corporate America.

These recommendations build upon strategies that companies and government are already using to end discrimination. The recommendations must be seen as a beginning, not the end. We as a nation, and in particular corporate leaders, must continue to strive to overcome the barriers that keep minorities and women from advancing. We also must encourage the development of business organizations that reflect our population.

The Commission's work clearly shows that breaking the glass ceiling opens avenues to the American Dream, and gives all Americans the opportunity to benefit from and contribute to economic growth. Economic gains must, and can, be shared by all.

Source: Excerpted from "Glass Ceiling Commission—A Solid Investment: Making Full Use of the Nation's Human Capital," by the Glass Ceiling Commission, November 1995, p. 6. Available online. URL: http://digitalcommons.ilr. cornell.edu/glassceiling.

NEWSPAPER ARTICLES

EEOC Issues New Guide on Workplace Bias (April 19, 2006)

WASHINGTON—The U.S. Equal Employment Opportunity Commission issued new guidelines Wednesday aimed at combating subtle forms of race discrimination, a persistent problem in the workplace. . . .

The manual also addresses harassment and retaliation, "glass ceilings" for groups based on stereotypes, as well as cases in which discrimination may involve a multiple set of categories—such as race, gender and disability—and thus involve bias laws with varying standards to win in court.

"Issuing this chapter reaffirms the EEOC's commitment to the vigorous enforcement of Title VII's prohibitions against race and color discrimination in the workplace," EEOC commissioner Stuart J. Ishimaru said at the agency's meeting Wednesday.

"We want to educate people so they know to complain, go to the EEOC and vindicate their rights," he said.

EEOC staff said at the meeting that the guidelines also encourage people to look beyond an employer's explanation for a job decision to see if bias is actually at work, as well as to determine whether there is a pattern of behavior that might point to systemic discrimination.

The guidelines come as workplace bias suits have been in the forefront.

Source: Excerpted from "EEOC Issues New Guide on Workplace Bias," by Hope Yen, *The Associated Press (The D.C. Examiner),* April 19, 2006.

State Secret: Thousands Secretly Sterilized: N.C. Woman among 65,000 Sterilized by Gov't., Often Without Their Knowledge, in 20th Century (May 15, 2005)

WINDFALL, N.C.,—Beneath the surface of this Southern town, with its lush evergreens and winding riverbanks, is a largely forgotten legacy of pain, secrecy and human indignity.

"My heart still bleeds, and it will forever bleed, because of what had happened to me," local resident Elaine Riddick said.

Riddick was one of thousands of people secretly sterilized by the state between 1929 and 1974.

From the early 1900s to the 1970s, some 65,000 men and women were sterilized in this country, many without their knowledge, as part of a government eugenics program to keep so-called undesirables from reproducing.

Source: Excerpted from "State Secret: Thousands Secretly Sterilized: N.C. Woman among 65,000 Sterilized by Gov't., Often Without Their Knowledge, in 20th Century," by *ABC News,* May 15, 2005. Available online. URL: http://abcnews.go.com/WNT/Health/story?id=708780. Accessed January 23, 2006.

Second and Third Wave Feminists Clash over the Future (May 26, 2002)

A growing conflict between two generations of feminists comes to light at a recent Veteran Feminists of America conference. Do women in their 20s appreciate what was done 30 years ago? Do women in their 50s understand what women young now still cope with?

NEW YORK (WOMEN'S E-NEWS)—Feminists have never been known for their uniformity of opinions, so it should come as no surprise that the transition from the second to the third wave of feminists has left a clear rift between the generations.

Feminist revolutionaries from the 1960s and 1970s gathered at a recent conference at Barnard College in New York to share their thoughts on the effects their words and actions have had on the history of the United States. Although the conference, sponsored by the Veteran Feminists of America, was designed as a celebration of feminist nonfiction and fiction literature and not as a forum to discuss the problems with the women's movement today, the theme of "us versus them" emerged time and again.

Source: Excerpted from "Second and Third Wave Feminists Clash over the Future," by Jennifer Friedlin, *Women's E-News,* May 26, 2002. Available online. URL: http://www.womensenews.org/article.cfm/dyn/aid/920/context/cover. Accessed June 5, 2006.

A Chorus of Amens as More Women Take over Pulpits (July 25, 1998)

Encouraged by her male pastor at Zion Baptist Church, (Mary) Fowler finally decided to go for her dream, and it quickly fell into place: ordination in 1996; graduation from Howard University's School of Divinity in 1997; and last year, founder and pastor of Mary's Missionary Baptist Church in Northeast, which ministers to unwed mothers and boasts an all-male choir.

Comments such as Fowler's are arousing a chorus of amens as a growing number of women across Washington and the rest of the country are occupying Christian pulpits and church leadership posts. In the process, many female clergy in the area say, they are offering young women new role models, helping to "democratize" their congregations and perhaps even altering worshipers' traditional view of God as male.

Locally, despite some barriers, there are many examples of women's growing role in the church. In Frederick, Md., the Rev. Muriel Heichler, another late-bloomer, is the pastor at Bethel Evangelical Lutheran Church at age 72. At Manassas Presbyterian Church, the Rev. Mary Boyd Click supervises an all-female clergy staff as senior pastor. The Rev. Jane Holmes Dixon has been an Episcopal bishop here since 1992. And Prince George's

County's $35 million 10,000-seat Jericho City of Praise is led by the Rev. Betty P. Peebles, an independent Baptist.

Source: Excerpted from "A Chorus of Amens as More Women Take over Pulpits," by Caryle Murphy, *The Washington Post,* July 25, 1998.

Suffrage Wins in Senate; Now Goes to States (June 5, 1919)

Constitutional Amendment Is Passed, 56 to 25, or Two More Than Two-Thirds Women May Vote In 1920 Leaders Start Fight to Get Ratification by Three-Fourths of States in Time Debate Precedes Vote Wadsworth Explains His Attitude In Opposition—Resolution Signed with Ceremony

WASHINGTON, June 4—After a long and persistent fight advocates of woman suffrage won a victory in the Senate today when that body, by a vote of 56 to 25, adopted the Susan Anthony amendment to the Constitution. The suffrage supporters had two more than the necessary two-thirds vote of Senators present. Had all the Senators known to be in favor of suffrage been present the amendment would have had 66 votes, or two more than a two-thirds vote of the entire Senate.

The amendment, having already been passed by the House, where the vote was 304 to 89, now goes to the States for ratification, where it will be passed upon in the form in which it has been adopted by Congress, as follows:

"Article—, Section 1.—The right of citizens of the United States to vote shall not be denied or abridged by the United States or by any State on account of sex.

"Section 2.—Congress shall have power, by appropriate legislation, to enforce the provisions of this article."

Leaders of the National Woman's Party announced tonight that they would at once embark upon a campaign to obtain ratification of the amendment by the necessary three-fourths of the States so that women might have the vote in the next Presidential election. To achieve this ratification it will be necessary to hold special sessions of some Legislatures which otherwise would not convene until after the Presidential election in 1920. Miss Alice Paul, Chairman of the Woman's Party, predicted that the campaign for ratification would succeed and that women would vote for the next President.

Source: Excerpted from "Suffrage Wins in Senate; Now Goes to States," by *The New York Times,* June 5, 1919.

MAGAZINE ARTICLES

Why Your Boss May Start Sweating the Small Stuff: New sensitivity training at the office focuses on all the little ways a tone-deaf manager can demoralize a staff (March 15, 2006)

As corporate America struggles to promote more women and minorities up the ladder, a new workplace buzzword is moving from executive suite to lowly cubicle. Part pop psychology, part human-resources jargon, the term microinequities puts a name on all the indirect offenses that can demoralize a talented employee. Equipped with this handy label, scores of companies, including IBM and Wells Fargo, are starting to hold training seminars that don't so much teach office etiquette as hold up a mirror showing how such minor, often nonverbal unpleasantries affect everyone.

This growing awareness is due largely to the efforts of globetrotting consultant Stephen Young, a former chief diversity officer at JP Morgan Chase who has addressed audiences as varied as rocket scientists at Raytheon and readers of *Seventeen Magazine* on the power of small signals. "It's not so much what I say, but what you hear," he says. One of his most effective demonstrations—the one that has left even mighty CEOs stammering—has him role-playing a guy who is less and less interested in what a speaker is saying. "When you do this," Young says of the exercise, "you see performance change right on the spot."

Here's why: many of the companies that already spend big bucks to recruit and train talented employees are bracing for even stiffer competition as baby boomers start to retire amid a shortage of skilled labor. Teaching execs to be on the lookout for microinequities—a term that has bounced around academia since a professor at M.I.T. coined it in 1973—is a cheap way to hold on to hard-won recruits. After all, says Andrea Bernstein, diversity chair at the New York City–based white-shoe law firm Weil Gotshal, "you never know, when somebody leaves, if she would have been the next rainmaker." And no company wants even a single good idea to fall through the cracks because a manager has subconsciously written off the employee making the suggestion.

Source: Excerpted from "Why Your Boss May Start Sweating the Small Stuff," by Julie Rawe, *Time*, March 15, 2006.

Crossing the Lines:
Though barred from combat, female troops in Iraq often find themselves in full-fledged battle. An intimate look at the lives of the real G.I. Janes (February 19, 2006)

For Captain Shonnel Makwakwa, it was a rare assignment "outside the wire": a chance to break the monotony of life on the base and get out onto the streets of Baghdad. But it didn't take long to realize that this was no routine mission. Minutes after Makwakwa's humvee pulled out of Camp Liberty last December, bad news crackled over the radio: a supply convoy of six 18-wheel trucks was ambushed at Checkpoint 50, a freeway cloverleaf that is a notorious shooting alley for insurgents. Makwakwa, a bright, fit New Orleans native, handles medical logistics for the U.S. 10th Mountain Division—the kind of deskbound job often assigned to women G.I.s. Now she found herself wearing a first-aid kit on her belt, gripping an M-4 rifle and crawling on her stomach as enemy fire rained down. "I could hear the rounds pinging all around me," she says. "It was surreal." The scene was horrific. Flies were everywhere, and so was blood. "I'd dealt with people dying in the hospital, but it was nothing like this," she says. Makwakwa and another soldier kicked in the bullet-shattered windshield of the lead vehicle, but the driver was already dead. The driver of the second vehicle was screaming in agony from his wounds; he later died. Makwakwa and the patrol were able to save three other wounded drivers, but the memories of Checkpoint 50 are hard to erase—a constant reminder that while the military officially bars women from combat, the insurgency makes no such distinctions. "In Iraq, female soldiers are in combat," she says. "We're out there.". . .

It is also the first time they are suffering substantial casualties. Women troops make up nearly 15% of active-duty service members. Since 2003, 48 women have died in Iraq—just 2% of the total number of U.S. troops killed but far more than the 8 nurses killed out of 7,500 servicewomen in the Vietnam War. Three hundred have been wounded in Iraq. Few female troops are out of the line of fire. While military police patrol Baghdad with Iraqi cops who skirmish almost daily with insurgents, women clerks and cooks inside U.S. camps are vulnerable to rocket and mortar attacks by militants. Such hazards underscore the threats to life and limb that still confront all U.S. troops in Iraq, even as the military attempts to turn over more combat responsibility to Iraqi forces. First Sergeant Michelle Collins, 38, who waits anxiously every day for "her kids" to come back to Camp Liberty from patrol, says, "An IED [improvised explosive device] or a bullet doesn't have the gender marked on it."

Source: Excerpted from "Crossing the Lines: Though barred from combat, female troops in Iraq often find themselves in full-fledged battle. An intimate look at the lives of the real G.I. Janes," by Tim McGirk, *Time,* February 19, 2006.

Rising above the Stained-Glass Ceiling: Women preachers are still rare in the pulpits of "tall-steeple churches." Here's how a few got in (June 28, 2004)

Joanna Adams almost pulled it off. In 2001, John Buchanan, the pastor of Chicago's Fourth Presbyterian Church, announced that the congregation had chosen the Rev. Adams as co-pastor, with the understanding that she would eventually succeed him. The news raised hopes, and eyebrows. The Presbyterian Church (U.S.A.), like most of the old mainline Protestant communions, has ordained women for decades. But none had yet achieved any of the denomination's flagship pulpits, the senior pastorships in what are sometimes called "tall-steeple churches." Fourth Presbyterian, with its hefty 5,300-member-and-still-growing congregation, certainly fit that bill, and Adams appeared poised to ascend. At the same time, observers were bemused by what seemed her unusual acclimation period. "Fourth Presbee is one of the great beauty-pageant churches of American Christianity," noted the Rev. Eileen Lindner, deputy secretary of the National Council of Churches, last fall. "But prospective pastors at tall-steeple churches don't usually get training wheels."

And then last December, the wheels fell off, with a vengeance. Adams suddenly left the job and moved back home to Atlanta. "Co-leadership is difficult," Adams, 59, told *TIME.* "There are genuine issues of power and authority." And whereas the congregation regarded Buchanan as a great man, "a Moses," she says, she "had no credibility or right to respect of the sort I had earned in Atlanta . . . Men newly introduced are given that respect. But it's harder for women."

Adams' high-profile disappointment mirrors a larger-scale feminist frustration. The percentage of female seminary students has exploded in the past 35 years, from 4.7% in 1972 to 31% (or roughly 10,470 women) in 2003, and it continues to accelerate 1 to 2 percentage points a year. Yet women make up only about 11% of the nation's clergy. This is not totally unexpected, since more conservative denominations do not ordain women and are exempt on First Amendment grounds from equal-opportunity laws. More startling, however, was a set of data on 15 Protestant denominations in a 1998 study called Clergy Women: An Uphill Calling. It showed that even in more liberal fellowships, female clergy tended to be relegated to specialized ministries like music, youth or Bible studies. Those who did achieve pastorhood found it difficult to rise above associate positions, and the lucky few who achieved their own churches frequently had to make do with smaller or financially iffy congregations. Regardless of title, women clergy earned on average 9% less than identically trained men in the same positions.

Source: Excerpted from "Rising above the Stained-Glass Ceiling: Women preachers are still rare in the pulpits of 'tall-steeple churches,'" by David Van Biema, *Time,* June 28, 2004.

For Women at the Top, Pay Lags
(June 24, 2002)

When Carly Fiorina declared earlier this month she wouldn't get a raise until everybody in Hewlett-Packard did, the edict was hailed as a sly preemptive strike. At the height of her bitter merger battle, critics had lambasted her $1 million salary and $1.7 million bonus. Despite the brickbats, Fiorina's pay package was a pittance compared with that of most male Fortune 500 CEOs. Even Andrea Jung's $7.7 million plum from Avon—making her the highest-paid female chief executive last year—seems paltry beside Douglas Daft's $55 million bonanza from Coca-Cola. Amid outcries against overcompensated CEOs, it's clear that the biggest female names in corporate America aren't making the biggest bucks. One reason: They haven't demanded—or cashed in—as many stock options. Another is that as the economy slid last year, the leading female-run companies, including HP, felt the gravitational pull. But a congressional study released in January found that even during the economic boom, the top women in many private sector jobs were falling behind. Between 1995 and 2000, when the nation was awash in stock profits, female managers in seven of the 10 leading industries that employ 71 percent of women not only made less than an equivalent man; they actually saw that wage gap widen. In 1995, a woman in communications management made 86 cents for every dollar earned by a man. By 2000, she made only 73 cents on that scale. "When our nation was most prosperous, women slipped," says Rep. Carolyn Maloney, a Democrat from New York who cocommissioned the report. "What's going to happen during a downturn?"

Source: Excerpted from "For Women at the Top, Pay Lags," by Marci McDonald, *U.S. News & World Report,* June 24, 2002, p. 32.

It's All about Me!
Want to know what today's chic young feminist
thinkers care about? Their bodies! Themselves!
(June 29, 1998)

If women were able to make their case in the '60s and '70s, it was largely because, as the slogan went, they turned the personal into the political. They used their daily experience as the basis for a critique, often a scholarly one, of larger institutions and social arrangements. From Simone de Beauvoir's *Second Sex* to Betty Friedan's *Feminine Mystique* to Kate Millett's *Sexual Politics*—a doctoral dissertation that became a national best seller—feminists made big, unambiguous demands of the world. They sought absolute equal rights and opportunities for women, a constitutional amendment to make it so, a chance to be compensated equally and to share the task of raising a family. But if feminism of the '60s and '70s was steeped in research and obsessed with social change, feminism today is wed to the culture of celebrity and self-obsession. . . .

If feminism has come to seem divorced from matters of public purpose, it is thanks in part to shifts in the academy. "Women's studies, a big chunk of it at least, has focused increasingly on the symbols of the body and less on social action and social change," explains Leslie Calman, a political-science professor and director of the Center for Research on Women at Barnard College. Moreover, gender studies, the theoretical analysis of how gender identities are constructed, have become increasingly incorporated into women's studies or turned into rival departments of their own. In April, Yale University renamed its Women's Studies Department the Women and Gender Studies Department.

Source: Excerpted from "It's All about Me! Want to know what today's chic young feminist thinkers care about? Their bodies! Themselves!" by Ginia Bellafante, *Time,* June 29, 1998.

SCIENTIFIC REPORTS

Biobehavioral Responses to Stress in Females:
Tend-and-Befriend, Not Fight-or-Flight
(July 2000)

The human stress response has been characterized, both physiologically and behaviorally, as "fight-or-flight." Although fight-or-flight may characterize the primary physiological responses to stress for both males and females, study findings propose that, behaviorally, females' responses are more marked by a pattern of "tend-and-befriend." Tending involves nurturing activities designed to protect the self and offspring that promote safety and reduce distress; befriending is the creation and maintenance of social networks that may aid in this process. The biobehavioral mechanism that underlies the tend-and-befriend pattern appears to draw on the attachment-caregiving system, and neuroendocrine evidence from animal and human studies suggests that oxytocin, in conjunction with female reproductive hormones and endogenous opioid peptide mechanisms, may be at its core. This previously unexplored stress regulatory system has manifold implications for the study of stress.

Source: Excerpted from "Biobehavioral Responses to Stress in Females: Tend-and-Befriend, Not Fight-or-Flight," by Shelley E. Taylor, Laura Cousino Klein, Brian P. Lewis, Tara L. Gruenewald, Regan A. R. Gurung, and John A. Updegraff, *Psychological Review,* July 2000, Volume 107(3), pp. 411–429.

The Impact of Women's Studies Courses on College Students of the 1990s—Statistical Data Included (June 1999)

In response to many of the challenges facing women, women's studies courses emerged among universities in the 1970s (Berkovitz, 1993). Over 600 programs exist today offering a major or minor in women's studies (Sandler, Silverberg, & Hall, 1996). A flurry of research activity examining the usefulness of women's studies courses was conducted in the mid- to late-1970s and in the early 1980s. Interest in the topic has recently experienced a resurgence. The current study, representative of this trend, assesses the impact of women's studies courses on college students of the 1990s. . . . Participants

The sample consisted of 124 women and 41 men enrolled in courses at a medium-sized Midwestern university, during the fall semester of 1995. Of a sample totaling 165 participants, 138 reported that they were white caucasians, while 27 self-classified as members of an ethnic minority. . . .

Eighty-four students (65 women and 19 men) were enrolled in either of two women's studies courses. The first was a Women's Studies course titled "Women's Studies: An Overview," which was a course required of women's studies minors at this particular institution. The second was a psychology course titled "Women and Work," an elective for women's studies minors and a multicultural general education course. Each of the two courses was taught by different women instructors. We judged these two courses to be adequate representatives of women's studies courses because the content highlighted systematic oppression of women and other marginalized groups. Moreover, these courses were pedagogically similar, in that they introduced a forum in which all participants, instructor and students alike, were actively encouraged to critically analyze the material, to express alternative viewpoints, and to draw on personal experience. Both faculty members were individuals committed to premises underlying the women's studies curriculum as a change agent and a means of conveying the feminist perspective. . . .

Eighty-one students (59 women and 22 men) were enrolled in traditional content courses that did not emphasize diversity ("Human Social Behavior" and "Abnormal Psychology"); these participants comprised the control group. Our course selection strategy was aimed at one goal: to minimize potentially confounding effects stemming from nonrandom assignment to groups by constructing a control group as similar as possible to the experimental group, with regard to size, instruction quality and style, and pedagogical format. We tried to accomplish this goal, in part, by including the "Human Social Behavior" course because it was taught by the same psychology instructor as the one teaching the "Women and Work" class. To increase the sample size of the control group, we were compelled to include a second psychology course—"Abnormal Psychology"—taught by a different instructor possessing an ideological orientation similar to those of the other instructors included in both the experimental and control groups. . . .

Discussion

Results of this study confirmed that, aside from educational benefits deriving from the content of a women's studies course, students further experience change on a more personal level. This conclusion is consistent with the broader literature on college impact, which indicates that the college experience offers great potential for change on both intellectual and personal levels (Pascarella & Terenzini, 1996). It also supports the position of proponents that women's studies courses offer a forum to induce personal development in the student (Musil, 1992). Changes detected in this research were a more progressive gender role orientation and an increased sense of personal control over life outcomes. These changes were similarly experienced by both men and women enrolled in women's studies courses, an encouraging result in itself.

Particularly noteworthy is the observed improvement in locus of control among women's studies students, which has heretofore met with mixed results. Those enrolled in women's studies displayed a more internalized locus of control subsequent to taking courses, indicating that they gained a confidence that their behavior directly impacted the life outcomes they achieved. This sense of personal control over one's destiny is also known in feminist literature as "empowerment." Empowering students, women in particular, is an important goal in any women's studies curriculum since empowerment prompts the individual to more vigorously pursue future opportunities—a key ingredient to personal success (Chamberlain, 1988).

Another form of personal growth presumed to be the byproduct of a women's studies education is an increased self-esteem. Past research (Shueman & Sedlacek, 1977; Stake & Gerner, 1987; Zuckerman, 1983) has been mixed on the issue of self-esteem. The present study, like others before it (Brush et al., 1978; Shueman & Sedlacek, 1977), failed to detect a significant increase in self-esteem among individuals completing a women's studies course. We attribute this to the nature of the self-esteem concept. Global self-esteem tends to be a stable trait, and thus behavioral changes are difficult to detect. Stake and colleagues (Stake, 1979; Stake & Gerner, 1987) recommended a more specific dimension, performance self-esteem, as a more appropriate target for examining effects of an intervention like women's studies. Indeed, Stake and Gerner reported gains in performance self-esteem among students taking women's studies courses. Future research should draw upon more specific self-esteem measures for investigations into the women's studies experience.

Source: Excerpted from "The Impact of Women's Studies Courses on College Students of the 1990s—Statistical Data Included," by Karen L. Harris, *Sex Roles: A Journal of Research,* June 1999.

SPEECHES

The Solitude of Self (January 18, 1892)

Elizabeth Cady Stanton considered "The Solitude of Self" as "the best thing I have ever written." She gave this speech three times, first on January 18, 1892, when she resigned as president of the National American Woman Suffrage Association. The United States House Committee on the Judiciary heard the speech on January 18, and the United States Senate Committee on Woman Suffrage heard it on January 20.

The point I wish plainly to bring before you on this occasion is the individuality of each human soul; our Protestant idea, the right of individual conscience and judgment; our republican idea, individual citizenship. In discussing the rights of woman, we are to consider, first, what belongs to her as an individual, in a world of her own, the arbiter of her own destiny, an imaginary Robinson Crusoe, with her woman Friday on a solitary island. Her rights under such circumstances are to use all her faculties for her own safety and happiness.

Secondly, if we consider her as a citizen, as a member of a great nation, she must have the same rights as all other members, according to the fundamental principles of our government.

Thirdly, viewed as a woman, an equal factor in civilization, her rights and duties are still the same; individual happiness and development.

Fourthly, it is only the incidental relations of life, such as mother, wife, sister, daughter, that may involve some special duties and training. In the usual discussion in regard to woman's sphere, such men as Herbert Spencer, Frederic Harrison and Grant Allen, uniformly subordinate her rights and duties as an individual, as a citizen, as a woman, to the necessities of these incidental relations, neither of which a large class of women may ever assume. In discussing the sphere of man, we do not decide his rights as an individual, as a citizen, as a man, by his duties as a father, a husband, a brother or a son, relations he may never fill. Moreover, he would be better fitted for these very relations, and whatever special work he might choose to do to earn his bread, by the complete development of all his faculties as an individual.

Just so with woman. The education that will fit her to discharge the duties in the largest sphere of human usefulness will best fit her for whatever special work she may be compelled to do.

The isolation of every human soul, and the necessity of self-dependence, must give each individual the right to choose his own surroundings.

The strongest reason for giving woman all the opportunities for higher education, for the full development of her faculties, forces of mind and body; for giving her the most enlarged freedom of thought and action; a complete emancipation from all forms of bondage, of custom, dependence, superstition; from all the crippling influences of fear—is the solitude and personal responsibility of her own individual life. The strongest reason why we ask for woman a voice in the government under which she lives; in the religion she is asked to believe; equality in social life, where she is the chief factor; a place in the trades and professions, where she may earn her bread, is because of her birthright to self-sovereignty; because, as an individual, she must rely on herself. No matter how much women prefer to lean, to be protected and supported, nor how much men desire to have them to do so, they must make the voyage of life alone, and for safety in an emergency, they must know something of the laws of navigation. To guide our own craft, we must be captain, pilot, engineer; with chart and compass to stand at the wheel; to watch the winds and waves, and know when to take in the sail, and to read the signs in the firmament over all. It matters not whether the solitary voyager is man or woman; nature, having endowed them equally, leaves them to their own skill and judgment in the hour of danger, and, if not equal to the occasion, alike they perish.

To appreciate the importance of fitting every human soul for independent action, think for a moment of the immeasurable solitude of self. We come into the world alone, unlike all who have gone before us; we leave it alone, under circumstances peculiar to ourselves. No mortal ever has been, no mortal ever will be like the soul just launched on the sea of life. There can never again be just such a combination of prenatal influences; never again just such environments as make up the infancy, youth and manhood of this one. Nature never repeats herself, and the possibilities of one human soul will never be found in another. No one has ever found two blades of ribbon grass alike, and no one will ever find two human beings alike. Seeing, then, what must be the infinite diversity in human character, we can in a measure appreciate the loss to a nation when any large class of the people is uneducated and unrepresented in the government.

We ask for the complete development of every individual, first, for his own benefit and happiness. In fitting out an army, we give each soldier his own knapsack, arms, powder, his blanket, cup, knife, fork and spoon. We provide alike for all their individual necessities; then each man bears his own burden.

Again, we ask complete individual development for the general good; for the consensus of the competent on the whole round of human interests, on all questions of national life; and here each man must bear his share of the general burden. It is sad to see how soon friendless children are left to bear their own burdens, before they can analyze their feelings; before they can even tell their joys and sorrows, they are thrown on their own resources. The great lesson that nature seems to teach us at all ages is self-dependence, self-protection, self-support. What a touching instance of a child's solitude, of that hunger of the heart for love and recognition, in the case of the little girl who helped to dress a Christmas tree for the children of the family in which she served. On finding there was no present for herself, she slipped away in the darkness and spent the night in an open field sitting on a stone, and when found in the morning was weeping as if her heart would break. No mortal will ever know the thoughts that passed through the mind of that friendless child in the long hours of that cold night, with only the silent stars to keep her company. The mention of her case in the daily papers moved many generous hearts to send her presents, but in the hours of her keenest suffering she was thrown wholly on herself for consolation.

In youth our most bitter disappointments, our brightest hopes and ambitions, are known only to ourselves. Even our friendship and love we never fully share with another; there is something of every passion, in every situation, we conceal. Even so in our triumphs and our defeats. The successful candidate for the presidency, and his opponent, each has a solitude peculiarly his own, and good form forbids either to speak of his pleasure or regret. The solitude of the king on his throne and the prisoner in his cell differs in character and degree, but it is solitude nevertheless.

We ask no sympathy from others in the anxiety and agony of a broken friendship or shattered love. When death sunders our nearest ties, alone we sit in the shadow of our affliction. Alike amid the greatest triumphs and darkest tragedies of life, we walk alone. On the divine heights of human attainment, eulogized and worshipped as a hero or saint, we stand alone. In ignorance, poverty and vice, as a pauper or criminal, alone we starve or steal; alone we suffer the sneers and rebuffs of our fellows; alone we are hunted and hounded through dark courts and alleys, in by-ways and highways; alone we stand in the judgment seat; alone in the prison cell we lament our crimes and misfortunes; alone we expiate them on the gallows. In hours like these we realize the awful solitude of individual life, its pains, its penalties, its responsibilities; hours in which the youngest and most helpless are thrown on their own resources for guidance and consolation. Seeing, then, that life must ever be a march and a battle, that each soldier must be equipped for his own protection, it is the height of cruelty to rob the individual of a single natural right.

Source: Excerpted from "The Solitude of Self," by Elizabeth Cady Stanton, *The Woman's Journal,* January 23, 1892. Available online. URL: http://www.lclark.edu/~ria/stanton.solitude.html. Accessed December 26, 2005.

Shirley Chisholm's Speech to the House of Representatives (May 21, 1969)

The Honorable Shirley Chisholm of New York presented this speech on May 21, 1969, to the House of Representatives.

Mr. Speaker, when a young woman graduates from college and starts looking for a job, she is likely to have a frustrating and even demeaning experience ahead of her. If she walks into an office for an interview, the first question she will be asked is, "Do you type?"

There is a calculated system of prejudice that lies unspoken behind that question. Why is it acceptable for women to be secretaries, librarians, and teachers, but totally unacceptable for them to be managers, administrators, doctors, lawyers, and Members of Congress.

The unspoken assumption is that women are different. They do not have executive ability orderly minds, stability, leadership skills, and they are too emotional.

It has been observed before, that society for a long time, discriminated against another minority, the blacks, on the same basis—that they were different and inferior. The happy little homemaker and the contented "old darkey" on the plantation were both produced by prejudice.

As a black person, I am no stranger to race prejudice. But the truth is that in the political world I have been far oftener discriminated against because I am a woman than because I am black.

Prejudice against blacks is becoming unacceptable although it will take years to eliminate it. But it is doomed because, slowly, white America is beginning to admit that it exists. Prejudice against women is still acceptable. There is very little understanding yet of the immorality involved in double pay scales and the classification of most of the better jobs as "for men only."

More than half of the population of the United States is female. But women occupy only 2 percent of the managerial positions. They have not even reached the level of tokenism yet no women sit on the AFL-CIO council or Supreme Court. There have been only two women who have held Cabinet rank, and at present there are none. Only two women now hold ambassadorial rank in the diplomatic corps. In Congress, we are down to one Senator and 10 Representatives.

Considering that there are about 3 1/2 million more women in the United States than men, this situation is outrageous.

It is true that part of the problem has been that women have not been aggressive in demanding their rights. This was also true of the black population for many years. They submitted to oppression and even cooperated with it. Women have done the same thing. But now there is an awareness of this situation particularly among the younger segment of the population.

As in the field of equal rights for blacks, Spanish-Americans, the Indians, and other groups, laws will not change such deep-seated problems overnight. But they can be used to provide protection for those who are most abused, and to begin the process of evolutionary change by compelling the insensitive majority to reexamine it's unconscious attitudes.

It is for this reason that I wish to introduce today a proposal that has been before every Congress for the last 40 years and that sooner or later must become part of the basic law of the land—the equal rights amendment.

Let me note and try to refute two of the commonest arguments that are offered against this amendment. One is that women are already protected under the law and do not need legislation. Existing laws are not adequate to secure equal rights for women. Sufficient proof of this is the concentration of women in lower paying, menial, unrewarding jobs and their incredible scarcity in the upper level jobs. If women are already equal, why is it such an event whenever one happens to be elected to Congress?

It is obvious that discrimination exists. Women do not have the opportunities that men do. And women that do not conform to the system, who try to break with the accepted patterns, are stigmatized as 'odd' and "unfeminine." The fact is that a woman who aspires to be chairman of the board, or a Member of the House, does so for exactly the same reasons as any man. Basically, these are that she thinks she can do the job and she wants to try.

A second argument often heard against the equal rights amendment is that is would eliminate legislation that many States and the Federal Government have enacted giving special protection to women and that it would throw the marriage and divorce laws into chaos.

As for the marriage laws, they are due for a sweeping reform, and an excellent beginning would be to wipe the existing ones off the books. Regarding special protection for working women, I cannot understand why it should be needed. Women need no protection that men do not need. What we need are laws to protect working people, to guarantee them fair pay, safe working conditions, protection against sickness and layoffs, and provision for dignified, comfortable retirement. Men and women need these things equally. That one sex needs protection more than the other is a male supremacist myth as ridiculous and unworthy of respect as the white supremacist myths that society is trying to cure itself of at this time.

Source: Excerpted from "Equal Rights for Women," by Shirley Chisholm, "Documents from the Women's Liberation Movement. An On-line Archival Collection," Special Collections Library, Duke University. Available online. URL: http://scriptorium.lib.duke.edu/wlm/equal. Accessed February 27, 2006.

Gloria Steinem's Speech at the Third Annual Women & Power Conference (September 2004)

The following excerpt is from a transcript of the keynote speech delivered by Gloria Steinem at the Third Annual Women & Power Conference organized by Omega Institute and V-Day in September 2004 in New York City.

But a friend asked me—a friend who had been going to some women's meetings and the subject of those meetings was what is the future? What's next? What is new? What are the leaps of consciousness? And she said to me what would you say? And in that way the questions are precious because they help us to understand what we ourselves have been thinking and not said.

I said well, I guess in a very general way I would say first we had dependence. And that was women's classical role. And then we understood and celebrated and are still exploring independence. Absolutely crucial. It cannot be—we can't do, we can't progress without that. But probably when we're ready the next step is interdependence.

Bella Abzug always used to say about nations and this country especially, we've had our Declaration of Independence. Now this country needs a declaration of interdependence.

Source: Excerpted from "Leaps of Consciousness," by Gloria Steinem. Available online. URL: http://www.feminist.com/resources/artspeech/genwom/leaps.html. Accessed November 3, 2005.

LEGAL DOCUMENTS

New York Married Women's Property Act (1848)

During the 19th century, states began enacting laws affecting the property rights of married women, which otherwise automatically moved into the hands of their husbands. Connecticut was one of the first states to pass a law (1809) that would permit women to write wills. New York's 1848 Married Women's Property Act was used by other states as a model, as they began to pass similar statutes in the 1850s. Paulina Wright Davis, Ernestine Rose, and Elizabeth Cady Stanton were among the women who worked for the passage of the New York law.

AN ACT for the effectual protection of the property of married women.

Passed April 7, 1848.

The People of the State of New York, represented in Senate and Assembly do enact as follows:

Sec. 1. The real and personal property of any female who may hereafter marry, and which she shall own at the time of marriage, and the rents issues and profits thereof shall not be subject to the disposal of her husband, nor be liable for his debts, and shall continue her sole and separate property, as if she were a single female.

Sec. 2. The real and personal property, and the rents issues and profits thereof of any female now married shall not be subject to the disposal of her husband; but shall be her sole and separate property as if she were a single female except so far as the same may be liable for the debts of her husband heretofore contracted.

Sec. 3. It shall be lawful for any married female to receive, by gift, grant devise or bequest, from any person other than her husband and hold to her sole and separate use, as if she were a single female, real and personal property, and the rents, issues and profits thereof, and the same shall not be subject to the disposal of her husband, nor be liable for his debts.

Source: Excerpted from the "New York Married Women's Property Act." Available online. URL: http://memory.loc. gov/ammem/awhhtml/awlaw3/property_law.html. Accessed July 5, 2006.

The Fourteenth Amendment to the U.S. Constitution (1868)

The Fourteenth Amendment, ratified on July 9, 1868, gave all males age 21 and over who were residents of the United States the right to vote. Susan B. Anthony, testing the interpretation of this amendment as a citizen of the United States, voted in the 1872 presidential elections and was arrested.

1. All persons born or naturalized in the United States, and subject to the jurisdiction thereof, are citizens of the United States and of the State wherein they reside. No State shall make or enforce any law which shall abridge the privileges or immunities of citizens of the United States; nor shall any State deprive any person of life, liberty, or property, without due process of law; nor deny to any person within its jurisdiction the equal protection of the laws.

2. Representatives shall be apportioned among the several States according to their respective numbers, counting the whole number of persons in each State, excluding Indians not taxed. But when the right to vote at any election for the choice of electors for President and Vice-President of the United States, Representatives in Congress, the Executive and Judicial officers of a State, or the members of the Legislature thereof, is denied to any of the male inhabitants of such State, being twenty-one years of age, and citizens of the United States, or in any way abridged, except for participation in rebellion, or other crime, the basis of representation therein shall be reduced in the proportion which the number of such male citizens shall bear to the whole number of male citizens twenty-one years of age in such State.

3. No person shall be a Senator or Representative in Congress, or elector of President and Vice-President, or hold any office, civil or military, under the United States, or under any State, who, having previously taken an oath, as a member of Congress, or as an officer of the United States, or as a member of any State legislature, or as an executive or judicial officer of any State, to support the Constitution of the United States, shall have engaged in insurrection or rebellion against the same, or given aid or comfort to the enemies thereof. But Congress may by a vote of two-thirds of each House, remove such disability.

4. The validity of the public debt of the United States, authorized by law, including debts incurred for payment of pensions and bounties for services in suppressing insurrection or rebellion, shall not be questioned. But neither the United States nor any State shall assume or pay any debt

or obligation incurred in aid of insurrection or rebellion against the United States, or any claim for the loss or emancipation of any slave; but all such debts, obligations and claims shall be held illegal and void.

5. The Congress shall have power to enforce, by appropriate legislation, the provisions of this article.

Source: Excerpted from the U.S. Constitution. Available online. URL: http://www.usconstitution.net/const.htmlAm14. Accessed December 16, 2006.

The Nineteenth Amendment to the U.S. Constitution (1920)

The Nineteenth Amendment guaranteed all American women the right to vote and was considered a radical change of the Constitution. After being passed by Congress on June 4, 1919, the amendment needed three-fourths of the 48 states to be ratified. The momentous event occurred on August 18, 1920, when Harry T. Burn, from Niota, Tennessee, after receiving a persuasive note from his mother, cast the deciding vote that made Tennessee the 36th state required for the amendment to pass, changing the way Americans voted from that point forward.

Sixty-sixth Congress of the United States of America; At the First Session, Begun and held at the City of Washington on Monday, the nineteenth day of May, one thousand nine hundred and nineteen.

JOINT RESOLUTION

Proposing an amendment to the Constitution extending the right of suffrage to women.

Resolved by the Senate and House of Representatives of the United States of America in Congress assembled (two-thirds of each House concurring therein), That the following article is proposed as an amendment to the Constitution, which shall be valid to all intents and purposes as part of the Constitution when ratified by the legislature of three-fourths of the several States.

"ARTICLE ——.

"The right of citizens of the United States to vote shall not be denied or abridged by the United States or by any State on account of sex.

Congress shall have power to enforce this article by appropriate legislation."

[endorsements]

Source: Excerpted from "The 19th Amendment to the U.S. Constitution," from the U.S. Constitution. Available online. URL: http://ourdocuments.gov/doc.php?flash=true&doc=63. Accessed November 7, 2005.

Equal Rights Amendment (1929)

The ERA was first drafted in 1923 by Alice Paul, suffragist leader and founder of the National Woman's Party, who considered it the next step after enacting the Nineteenth Amendment (woman suffrage) to guarantee "equal justice under law" to all citizens. The ERA asserted the equal application of the U.S. Constitution to both females and males. It was introduced into every session of Congress between 1923 and 1972, when it was passed and sent to the states for ratification. The seven-year time limit in the ERA's proposing clause was extended by Congress to June 30, 1982, but at the deadline, the ERA had been ratified by 35 states, leaving it three states short of the 38 required for ratification. It has been reintroduced into every Congress since that time.

Section 1. Equality of rights under the law shall not be denied or abridged by the United States or by any state on account of sex.

Section 2. The Congress shall have the power to enforce, by appropriate legislation, the provisions of this article.

Section 3. This amendment shall take effect two years after the date of ratification.

Source: Excerpted from the "Equal Rights Amendment," by Alice Paul, 1923. Available online. URL: http://www.equalrightsamendment.org. Accessed December 26, 2006.

Title VII of the 1964 Civil Rights Act

This act signed into law by President Lyndon Johnson on July 2, 1964, prohibited discrimination on the basis of sex as well as race, religion, and national origin in public places and employment. It also provided for the integration of schools and other public facilities. The specifics of Title VII applied to employers with 15 or more employees and included state and local governments, employment agencies, labor organizations, and the federal government.

DISCRIMINATION BECAUSE OF RACE, COLOR, RELIGION, SEX, OR NATIONAL ORIGIN

SEC. 703. (a) It shall be an unlawful employment practice for an employer—

(1) to fail or refuse to hire or to discharge any individual, or otherwise to discriminate against any individual with respect to his compensation, terms, conditions, or privileges of employment, because of such individual's race, color, religion, sex, or national origin; or

(2) to limit, segregate, or classify his employees in any way which would deprive or tend to deprive any individual of employment opportunities

or otherwise adversely affect his status as an employee, because of such individual's race, color, religion, sex, or national origin.

(b) It shall be an unlawful employment practice for an employment agency to fail or refuse to refer for employment, or otherwise to discriminate against, any individual because of his race, color, religion, sex, or national origin, or to classify or refer for employment any individual on the basis of his race, color, religion, sex, or national origin.

(c) It shall be an unlawful employment practice for a labor organization—

(1) to exclude or to expel from its membership, or otherwise to discriminate against, any individual because of his race, color, religion, sex, or national origin;

(2) to limit, segregate, or classify its membership, or to classify or fail or refuse to refer for employment any individual, in any way which would deprive or tend to deprive any individual of employment opportunities, or would limit such employment opportunities or otherwise adversely affect his status as an employee or as an applicant for employment, because of such individual's race, color, religion, sex, or national origin; or

(3) to cause or attempt to cause an employer to discriminate against an individual in violation of this section.

(d) It shall be an unlawful employment practice for any employer, labor organization, or joint labor-management committee controlling apprenticeship or other training or retraining, including on-the-job training programs to discriminate against any individual because of his race, color, religion, sex, or national origin in admission to, or employment in, any program established to provide apprenticeship or other training.

(e) Notwithstanding any other provision of this title, (1) it shall not be an unlawful employment practice for an employer to hire and employ employees, for an employment agency to classify, or refer for employment any individual, for a labor organization to classify its membership or to classify or refer for employment any individual, or for an employer, labor organization, or joint labor-management committee controlling apprenticeship or other training or retraining programs to admit or employ any individual in any such program, on the basis of his religion, sex, or national origin in those certain instances where religion, sex, or national origin is a bona fide occupational qualification reasonably necessary to the normal operation of that particular business or enterprise, and (2) it shall not be an unlawful employment practice for a school, college, university, or other educational institution or institution of learning to hire and employ employees of a particular religion if such school, college, university, or other educational institution or institution of learning is, in whole or in substantial part, owned, supported, controlled, or managed by a particular religion or by a particular religious corporation, association, or society, or if the curriculum of such school, college, university, or other educational institution or institution of learning is directed toward the propagation of a particular religion.

(f) As used in this title, the phrase "unlawful employment practice" shall not be deemed to include any action or measure taken by an employer, labor organization, joint labor-management committee, or employment agency with respect to an individual who is a member of the Communist Party of the United States or of any other organization required to register as a Communist-action or Communist-front organization by final order of the Subversive Activities Control Board pursuant to the Subversive Activities Control Act of 1950.

(g) Notwithstanding any other provision of this title, it shall not be an unlawful employment practice for an employer to fail or refuse to hire and employ any individual for any position, for an employer to discharge any individual from any position, or for an employment agency to fail or refuse to refer any individual for employment in any position, or for a labor organization to fail or refuse to refer any individual for employment in any position, if—

(1) the occupancy of such position, or access to the premises in or upon which any part of the duties of such position is performed or is to be performed, is subject to any requirement imposed in the interest of the national security of the United States under any security program in effect pursuant to or administered under any statute of the United States or any Executive order of the President; and

(2) such individual has not fulfilled or has ceased to fulfill that requirement.

(h) Notwithstanding any other provision of this title, it shall not be an unlawful employment practice for an employer to apply different standards of compensation, or different terms, conditions, or privileges of employment pursuant to a bona fide seniority or merit system, or a system which measures earnings by quantity or quality of production or to employees who work in different locations, provided that such differences are not the result of an intention to discriminate because of race, color, religion, sex, or national origin, nor shall it be an unlawful employment practice for an employer to give and to act upon the results of any professionally developed ability test provided that such test, its administration or action upon the results is not designed, intended or used to discriminate because of race, color, religion, sex or national origin. It shall not be an unlawful employment practice under this title for any employer to differentiate upon the basis of sex in determining the amount of the wages or compensation paid or to be paid to employees of such employer if such differentiation is authorized by the provisions of section 6(d) of the Fair Labor Standards Act of 1938, as amended (29 U.S.C. 206(d)).

(i) Nothing contained in this title shall apply to any business or enterprise on or near an Indian reservation with respect to any publicly announced employment practice of such business or enterprise under which a preferential treatment is given to any individual because he is an Indian living on or near a reservation.

(j) Nothing contained in this title shall be interpreted to require any employer, employment agency, labor organization, or joint labor-management committee subject to this title to grant preferential treatment to any individual or to any group because of the race, color, religion, sex, or national origin of such individual or group on account of an imbalance which may exist with respect to the total number or percentage of persons of any race, color, religion, sex, or national origin employed by any employer, referred or classified for employment by any employment agency or labor organization, admitted to membership or classified by any labor organization, or admitted to, or employed in, any apprenticeship or other training program, in comparison with the total number or percentage of persons of such race, color, religion, sex, or national origin in any community, State, section, or other area, or in the available work force in any community, State, section, or other area.

Source: Excerpted from "Title VII of the 1964 Civil Rights Act," by the U.S. Government, July 2, 1964. Available online. URL: http://ourdocuments.gov/doc.php?doc=97. Accessed December 2, 2005.

Title IX in the Education Codes of 1972

The purpose of Title IX of the Education Amendments of 1972 was to eliminate discrimination on the basis of sex in any education program or activity receiving federal financial assistance. In addition, the Women's Educational Equity Act of 1974, which provided for federal financing and technical support to local efforts to remove barriers for females in all areas of education, and Title IV of the Civil Rights Act of 1964, which ensured funding for regional Desegregation Assistance Centers and grants to state education departments, helped make higher education more available to women.

Sec. 1681. Sex
(a) Prohibition against discrimination; exceptions

No person in the United States shall, on the basis of sex, be excluded from participation in, be denied the benefits of, or be subjected to discrimination under any education program or activity receiving Federal financial assistance, except that:

(1) Classes of educational institutions subject to prohibition

in regard to admissions to educational institutions, this section shall apply only to institutions of vocational education, professional education, and graduate higher education, and to public institutions of undergraduate higher education;

(2) Educational institutions commencing planned change in admissions

in regard to admissions to educational institutions, this section shall not apply

(A) for one year from June 23, 1972, nor for six years after June 23, 1972, in the case of an educational institution which has begun the process of changing from being an institution which admits only students of one sex to being an institution which admits students of both sexes, but only if it is carrying out a plan for such a change which is approved by the Secretary of Education or

(B) for seven years from the date an educational institution begins the process of changing from being an institution which admits only students of only one sex to being an institution which admits students of both sexes, but only if it is carrying out a plan for such a change which is approved by the Secretary of Education, whichever is the later;

(3) Educational institutions of religious organizations with contrary religious tenets

this section shall not apply to an educational institution which is controlled by a religious organization if the application of this subsection would not be consistent with the religious tenets of such organization;

(4) Educational institutions training individuals for military services or merchant marine

this section shall not apply to an educational institution whose primary purpose is the training of individuals for the military services of the United States, or the merchant marine;

(5) Public educational institutions with traditional and continuing admissions policy

in regard to admissions this section shall not apply to any public institution of undergraduate higher education which is an institution that traditionally and continually from its establishment has had a policy of admitting only students of one sex;

(6) Social fraternities or sororities; voluntary youth service organizations

this section shall not apply to membership practices—

(A) of a social fraternity or social sorority which is exempt from taxation under section 501 (a) of title 26, the active membership of which consists primarily of students in attendance at an institution of higher education, or

(B) of the Young Men's Christian Association, Young Women's Christian Association, Girl Scouts, Boy Scouts, Camp Fire Girls, and voluntary youth service organizations which are so exempt, the membership of which has traditionally been limited to persons of one sex and principally to persons of less than nineteen years of age;

(7) Boy or Girl conferences

this section shall not apply to—

(A) any program or activity of the American Legion undertaken in connection with the organization or operation of any Boys State conference, Boys Nation conference, Girls State conference, or Girls Nation conference; or

(B) any program or activity of any secondary school or educational institution specifically for—

(i) the promotion of any Boys State conference, Boys Nation conference, Girls State conference, or Girls Nation conference; or

(ii) the selection of students to attend any such conference;

(8) Father-son or mother-daughter activities at educational institutions

this section shall not preclude father-son or mother-daughter activities at an educational institution, but if such activities are provided for students of one sex, opportunities for reasonably comparable activities shall be provided for students of the other sex; and

(9) Institution of higher education scholarship awards in "beauty" pageants

this section shall not apply with respect to any scholarship or other financial assistance awarded by an institution of higher education to any individual because such individual has received such award in any pageant in which the attainment of such award is based upon a combination of factors related to the personal appearance, poise, and talent of such individual and in which participation is limited to individuals of one sex only, so long as such pageant is in compliance with other nondiscrimination provisions of Federal law.

(b) Preferential or disparate treatment because of imbalance in participation or receipt of Federal benefits; statistical evidence of imbalance

Nothing contained in subsection (a) of this section shall be interpreted to require any educational institution to grant preferential or disparate treatment to the members of one sex on account of an imbalance which may exist with respect to the total number or percentage of persons of that sex participating in or receiving the benefits of any federally supported program or activity, in comparison with the total number or percentage of persons of that sex in any community, State, section, or other area: Provided, That this subsection shall not be construed to prevent the consideration in any hearing or proceeding under this chapter of statistical evidence tending to show that such an imbalance exists with respect to the participation in, or receipt of the benefits of, any such program or activity by the members of one sex.

(c) "Educational institution" defined

For purposes of this chapter an educational institution means any public or private preschool, elementary, or secondary school, or any institution of vocational, professional, or higher education, except that in the case of an educational institution composed of more than one school, college, or department which are administratively separate units, such term means each such school, college, or department.

Source: Excerpted from "Title IX of the Education Amendments of 1972, 20 U.S.C., 1681–1688," by the U.S. Government. Available online. URL: http://www.usdoj.gov/crt/cor/coord/titleixstat.htm. Accessed November 13, 2005.

The Family and Medical Leave Act of 1993

The Family and Medical Leave Act of 1993 took effect in the United States as a result of finding an equitable arrangement for employers and employees to accommodate these needs. In addition, President George W. Bush signed an order in 2002 to preserve reservists' and armed forces members' rights to accrued time during their leave of absence from the workplace.

(a) The Family and Medical Leave Act of 1993 (FMLA or Act) allows "eligible" employees of a covered employer to take job-protected, unpaid leave, or to substitute appropriate paid leave if the employee has earned or accrued it, for up to a total of 12 workweeks in any 12 months because of the birth of a child and to care for the newborn child, because of the placement of a child with the employee for adoption or foster care, because the employee is needed to care for a family member (child, spouse, or parent) with a serious health condition, or because the employee's own serious health condition makes the employee unable to perform the functions of his or her job (see Sec. 825.306(b)(4)). In certain cases, this leave may be taken on an intermittent basis rather than all at once, or the employee may work a part-time schedule.

(b) An employee on FMLA leave is also entitled to have health benefits maintained while on leave as if the employee had continued to work instead of taking the leave. If an employee was paying all or part of the premium payments prior to leave, the employee would continue to pay his or her share during the leave period. The employer may recover its share only if the employee does not return to work for a reason other than the serious health condition of the employee or the employee's immediate family member, or another reason beyond the employee's control.

(c) An employee generally has a right to return to the same position or an equivalent position with equivalent pay, benefits and working conditions at the conclusion of the leave. The taking of FMLA leave cannot result in the loss of any benefit that accrued prior to the start of the leave.

Sec. 825.101 What is the purpose of the Act?

(a) FMLA is intended to allow employees to balance their work and family life by taking reasonable unpaid leave for medical reasons, for the birth or adoption of a child, and for the care of a child, spouse, or parent who has a serious health condition. The Act is intended to balance the demands of the workplace with the needs of families, to promote the stability and economic security of families, and to promote national interests in preserving family integrity. It was intended that the Act accomplish these purposes in a manner that accommodates the legitimate interests of employers, and in a manner consistent with the Equal Protection Clause of the Fourteenth Amendment in minimizing the potential for employment discrimination on the basis of sex, while promoting equal employment opportunity for men and women.

(b) The enactment of FMLA was predicated on two fundamental concerns—the needs of the American workforce, and the development of high-performance organizations. Increasingly, America's children and elderly are dependent upon family members who must spend long hours at work. When a family emergency arises, requiring workers to attend to seriously-ill children or parents, or to newly-born or adopted infants, or even to their own serious illness, workers need reassurance that they will not be asked to choose between continuing their employment, and meeting their personal and family obligations or tending to vital needs at home.

(c) The FMLA is both intended and expected to benefit employers as well as their employees. A direct correlation exists between stability in the family and productivity in the workplace. FMLA will encourage the development of high-performance organizations. When workers can count on durable links to their workplace they are able to make their own full commitments to their jobs. The record of hearings on family and medical leave indicate the powerful productive advantages of stable workplace relationships, and the comparatively small costs of guaranteeing that those relationships will not be dissolved while workers attend to pressing family health obligations or their own serious illness.

Source: Excerpted from "The Family and Medical Leave Act of 1993," by the U.S. Government. Available online. URL: http://www.dol.gov/esa/regs/statutes/whd/fmla.htm. Accessed December 1, 2005.

Victims of Trafficking and Violence Protection Act of 2000

In October 2000, Congress passed the Victims of Trafficking and Violence Protection Act of 2000 (VTVPA) to extend to victims of trafficking the ability to remain in the United States (temporarily and in some cases longer) and receive federal and state assistance. The law offers specific protections to victims of certain crimes such as those specific to women. The law also offers law enforcement agencies a comprehensive law that will enable them to pursue the prosecution and conviction of traffickers.

SEC. 102. PURPOSES AND FINDINGS.

(a) PURPOSES.—The purposes of this division are to combat trafficking in persons, a contemporary manifestation of slavery whose victims are predominantly women and children, to ensure just and effective punishment of traffickers, and to protect their victims.

(b) FINDINGS.—Congress finds that:

(1) As the 21st century begins, the degrading institution of slavery continues throughout the world. Trafficking in persons is a modern form of slavery, and it is the largest manifestation of slavery today. At least 700,000 persons annually, primarily women and children, are trafficked within or across international borders. Approximately 50,000 women and children are trafficked into the United States each year.

(2) Many of these persons are trafficked into the international sex trade, often by force, fraud, or coercion. The sex industry has rapidly expanded over the past several decades. It involves sexual exploitation of persons, predominantly women and girls, involving activities related to prostitution, pornography, sex tourism, and other commercial sexual services. The low status of women in many parts of the world has contributed to a burgeoning of the trafficking industry.

(3) Trafficking in persons is not limited to the sex industry. This growing transnational crime also includes forced labor and involves significant violations of labor, public health, and human rights standards worldwide.

(4) Traffickers primarily target women and girls, who are disproportionately affected by poverty, the lack of access to education, chronic unemployment, discrimination, and the lack of economic opportunities in countries of origin. Traffickers lure women and girls into their networks through false promises of decent working conditions at relatively good pay as nannies, maids, dancers, factory workers, restaurant workers, sales clerks, or models. Traffickers also buy children from poor families and sell them into prostitution or into various types of forced or bonded labor.

(5) Traffickers often transport victims from their home communities to unfamiliar destinations, including foreign countries away from family and friends, religious institutions, and other sources of protection and support, leaving the victims defenseless and vulnerable.

(6) Victims are often forced through physical violence to engage in sex acts or perform slaverylike labor. Such force
includes rape and other forms of sexual abuse, torture, starvation, imprisonment, threats, psychological abuse, and coercion.

(7) Traffickers often make representations to their victims that physical harm may occur to them or others should the victim escape or attempt to escape. Such representations can have the same coercive effects on victims as direct threats to inflict such harm.

(8) Trafficking in persons is increasingly perpetrated by organized, sophisticated criminal enterprises. Such trafficking is the fastest growing source of profits for organized criminal enterprises worldwide. Profits from the trafficking industry contribute to the expansion of organized crime in the United States and worldwide. Trafficking in persons is often aided by official corruption in countries of origin, transit, and destination, thereby threatening the rule of law.

(9) Trafficking includes all the elements of the crime of forcible rape when it involves the involuntary participation of another person in sex acts by means of fraud, force, or coercion.

(10) Trafficking also involves violations of other laws, including labor and immigration codes and laws against kidnapping, slavery, false imprisonment, assault, battery, pandering, fraud, and extortion.

(11) Trafficking exposes victims to serious health risks. Women and children trafficked in the sex industry are exposed to deadly diseases, including HIV and AIDS. Trafficking victims are sometimes worked or physically brutalized to death.

(12) Trafficking in persons substantially affects interstate and foreign commerce. Trafficking for such purposes as involuntary servitude, peonage, and other forms of forced labor has an impact on the nationwide

employment network and labor market. Within the context of slavery, servitude, and labor or services which are obtained or maintained through coercive conduct that amounts to a condition of servitude, victims are subjected to a range of violations.

(13) Involuntary servitude statutes are intended to reach cases in which persons are held in a condition of servitude through nonviolent coercion. In United States v. Kozminski, 487 U.S. 931 (1988), the Supreme Court found that section 1584 of title 18, United States Code, should be narrowly interpreted, absent a definition of involuntary servitude by Congress. As a result, that section was interpreted to criminalize only servitude that is brought about through use or threatened use of physical or legal coercion, and to exclude other conduct that can have the same purpose and effect.

(14) Existing legislation and law enforcement in the United States and other countries are inadequate to deter trafficking and bring traffickers to justice, failing to reflect the gravity of the offenses involved. No comprehensive law exists in the United States that penalizes the range of offenses involved in the trafficking scheme. Instead, even the most brutal instances of trafficking in the sex industry are often punished under laws that also apply to lesser offenses, so that traffickers typically escape deserved punishment.

(15) In the United States, the seriousness of this crime and its components is not reflected in current sentencing guidelines, resulting in weak penalties for convicted traffickers.

(16) In some countries, enforcement against traffickers is also hindered by official indifference, by corruption, and sometimes even by official participation in trafficking.

Source: Excerpted from "Trafficking Victims Protection Act of 2000," by the U.S. Government. October 28, 2000. Available online. URL: http://www.uscis.gov/graphics/services/PL106_386.pdf. Accessed July 1, 2006.

COURT CASES

Buck v. Bell (1927)
274 U.S. 200

Carrie Buck was a weak-minded (meaning not very smart) daughter of a mother who was institutionalized by the state of Virginia. Her condition had been present in her family for the last three generations. A Virginia law allowed for the sexual sterilization of inmates of institutions to promote the "health of the patient and the welfare of society." Before the procedure could be performed, however, a hearing was required to determine whether or not performing the operation would be wise. This 1927 Virginia Supreme Court case decision legalized forced sterilization in the United States. After Buck's sterilization, she was freed from the State Colony for Epileptics and Feeble-minded, and later married. A formal apology from the State of Virginia was extended to Ms. Buck in 2002.

ERROR TO THE SUPREME COURT OF APPEALS
OF THE STATE OF VIRGINIA
No. 292 Argued: April 22, 1927—Decided: May 2, 1927
Mr. JUSTICE HOLMES delivered the opinion of the Court.

Carrie Buck is a feeble minded white woman who was committed to the State Colony above mentioned in due form. She is the daughter of a feeble minded mother in the same institution, and the mother of an illegitimate feeble minded child. She was eighteen years old at the time of the trial of her case in the Circuit Court, in the latter part of 1924. An Act of Virginia, approved March 20, 1924, recites that the health of the patient and the welfare of society may be promoted in certain cases by the sterilization of mental defectives, under careful safeguard, &c.; that the sterilization may be effected in males by vasectomy and in females by salpingectomy, without serious pain or substantial danger to life; that the Commonwealth is supporting in various institutions many defective persons who, if now discharged, would become a menace, but, if incapable of procreating, might be discharged with safety and become self-supporting with benefit to themselves and to society, and that experience has shown that heredity plays an important part in the transmission of insanity, imbecility, &c. The statute then enacts that, whenever the superintendent of certain institutions, including the above-named State Colony, shall be of opinion that it is for the best interests of the patients and of society that an inmate under his care should be sexually sterilized, he may have the operation performed upon any patient afflicted with hereditary forms of insanity, imbecility, &c., on complying with the very careful provisions by which the act protects the patients from possible abuse.

The superintendent first presents a petition to the special board of directors of his hospital or colony, stating the facts and the grounds for his opinion, verified by affidavit. Notice of the petition and of the time and place of the hearing in the institution is to be served upon the inmate, and also upon his guardian, and if there is no guardian, the superintendent is to apply to the Circuit Court of the County to appoint one. If the inmate is a minor, notice also is to be given to his parents, if any, with a copy of the petition. The board is to see to it that the inmate may attend the hearings if desired by him or his guardian. The evidence is all to be reduced to writing, and, after the board has made its order for or against the operation, the superintendent, or the inmate, or his guardian, may appeal to the Circuit Court of the County. The Circuit Court may consider the record of the board and the evidence before it and such other admissible evidence as may be offered, and may affirm, revise, or reverse the order of the board and enter such order as it deems just. Finally any party may apply to the Supreme Court of Appeals, which, if it grants the appeal, is to hear the case upon the record of the trial in the Circuit Court, and may enter such order as it thinks the Circuit Court should have entered. There can be no doubt that, so far as procedure is concerned, the rights of the patient are most carefully considered, and, as every step in this case was taken in scrupulous compliance with the statute and after months of observation, there is no doubt that, in that respect, the plaintiff in error has had due process of law.

The attack is not upon the procedure, but upon the substantive law. It seems to be contended that in no circumstances could such an order be justified. It certainly is contended that the order cannot be justified upon the existing grounds. The judgment finds the facts that have been recited, and that Carrie Buck is the probable potential parent of socially inadequate offspring, likewise afflicted, that she may be sexually sterilized without detriment to her general health, and that her welfare and that of society will be promoted by her sterilization, and thereupon makes the order. In view of the general declarations of the legislature and the specific findings of the Court, obviously we cannot say as matter of law that the grounds do not exist, and, if they exist, they justify the result. We have seen more than once that the public welfare may call upon the best citizens for their lives. It would be strange if it could not call upon those who already sap the strength of the State for these lesser sacrifices, often not felt to be such by those concerned, in order to prevent our being swamped with incompetence. It is better for all the world if, instead of waiting to execute degenerate offspring for crime or to let them starve for their imbecility, society can prevent those who are manifestly unfit from continuing their kind. The principle that sustains compulsory vaccination is broad enough to cover cutting the Fallopian tubes. Jacobson v. Massachusetts, 197 U.S. 11. Three generations of imbeciles are enough.

But, it is said, however it might be if this reasoning were applied generally, it fails when it is confined to the small number who are in the institutions named and is not applied to the multitudes outside. It is the usual last resort of constitutional arguments to point out shortcomings of this sort. But the answer is that the law does all that is needed when it does all that it can, indicates a policy, applies it to all within the lines, and seeks to bring within the lines all similarly situated so far and so fast as its means allow. Of course, so far as the operations enable those who otherwise must be kept confined to be returned to the world, and thus open the asylum to others, the equality aimed at will be more nearly reached.

Judgment affirmed.

MR. JUSTICE BUTLER dissents.

Source: Excerpted from "U.S. Supreme Court—*Buck v. Bell,* 274 U.S. 200 (1927)." Available online. URL: http://laws.findlaw.com/us/274/200.html. Accessed January 7, 2006.

2002 SESSION
ENGROSSED
028229964
HOUSE JOINT RESOLUTION NO. 299
Offered January 25, 2002
Honoring the memory of Carrie Buck.

WHEREAS, in 1924 Virginia passed two eugenics-related laws, the second of which permitted involuntary sterilization, the most egregious outcome of the lamentable eugenics movement in the Commonwealth; and WHEREAS, under this act, those labeled "feebleminded," including the "insane, idiotic, imbecile, feebleminded or epileptic" could be involuntarily sterilized, so that they would not produce similarly disabled offspring; and

WHEREAS, May 2, 2002, is the 75th anniversary of the United States Supreme Court decision in the case of *Buck v. Bell,* in which Virginia's 1924 Eugenical Sterilization Act was allowed to stand; and

WHEREAS, following the *Buck* decision, an estimated 60,000 Americans, including about 8,000 in Virginia, were sterilized under similar state laws, and the decision was applauded by German eugenicists who supported comparable legislation early in the Nazi regime; and

WHEREAS, in 1927 Carrie Buck, a poor and unwed teenage mother from Charlottesville, was the first person sterilized under the provision of the 1924 law; and

WHEREAS, subsequent scholarship has demonstrated that the Sterilization Act was based on the now-discredited and false science of eugenics; and

WHEREAS, legal and historical scholarship analyzing the *Buck* decision has condemned it as an embodiment of bigotry against the disabled and an example of the use of faulty science in support of public policy; and

WHEREAS, that scholarship has also pointed out the fallacies contained in the *Buck* opinion, noting, among other points, that Carrie Buck's daughter, Vivian, the supposed third-generation "imbecile," later won a place on her school's honor roll; and

WHEREAS, the General Assembly in 2001 expressed its "profound regret" over the Commonwealth's role in the eugenics movement in this country and over the damage done in the name of eugenics; now, therefore, be it

RESOLVED by the House of Delegates, the Senate concurring, That the General Assembly honor the memory of Carrie Buck on the occasion of the 75th anniversary of the *Buck v. Bell* Supreme Court decision.

Source: Excerpted from "2002 Session" by University of Virginia Center for Biomedical Ethics. Available online. URL: https://www.med.virginia.edu/internet/bio-ethics/hjr299.pdf. Accessed January 7, 2006.

Griswold v. Connecticut (1965)

In 1965, the Supreme Court decision in Griswold v. Connecticut *allowed married couples in all states to obtain contraceptives legally. In 1972, in* Eisenstadt v. Baird, *the United States Supreme Court found that the right of privacy recognized for married couples in* Griswold v. Connecticut *should extend to unmarried couples and their procreative decisions. These two decisions finally overturned the Comstock Law of 1873, which had ruled information about birth control "obscene."*

MR. JUSTICE DOUGLAS delivered the opinion of the Court.

Appellant Griswold is Executive Director of the Planned Parenthood League of Connecticut. Appellant Buxton is a licensed physician and a professor at the Yale Medical School who served as Medical Director for the League at its Center in New Haven—a center open and operating from November 1 to November 10, 1961, when appellants were arrested.

They gave information, instruction, and medical advice to married persons as to the means of preventing conception. They examined the wife and prescribed the best contraceptive device or material for her use. Fees were usually charged, although some couples were serviced free.

The statutes whose constitutionality is involved in this appeal are 53-32 and 54-196 of the General Statutes of Connecticut (1958 rev.). The former provides:

"Any person who uses any drug, medicinal article or instrument for the purpose of preventing conception shall be fined not less than fifty dollars or imprisoned not less than sixty days nor more than one year or be both fined and imprisoned."

Section 54-196 provides:

"Any person who assists, abets, counsels, causes, hires or commands another to commit any offense may be prosecuted and punished as if he were the principal offender."

The appellants were found guilty as accessories and fined $100 each, against the claim that the accessory statute as so applied violated the Fourteenth Amendment. The Appellate Division of the Circuit Court affirmed. The Supreme Court of Errors affirmed that judgment. 151 Conn. 544, 200 A. 2d 479. We noted probable jurisdiction. 379 U.S. 926.

Page 381 U.S. 479, 481

We think that appellants have standing to raise the constitutional rights of the married people with whom they had a professional relationship. Tileston v. Ullman, 318 U.S. 44, is different, for there the plaintiff seeking to represent others asked for a declaratory judgment. In that situation we thought that the requirements of standing should be strict, lest the standards of "case or controversy" in Article III of the Constitution become blurred. Here those doubts are removed by reason of a criminal conviction for serving married couples in violation of an aiding-and-abetting statute. Certainly the accessory should have standing to assert that the offense which he is charged with assisting is not, or cannot constitutionally be, a crime.

Source: Excerpted from "U.S. Supreme Court, *Griswold v. Connecticut*, 381 U.S. 479 (1965)." Available online. URL: http://supreme.justia.com/us/381/479/case.html. Accessed April 29, 2006.

Reed v. Reed (1971)
404 U.S. 71

Argued on October 19, 1971, and decided on November 22, 1971, this U.S. Supreme Court decision found a mandatory provision of the Idaho probate code that gave preference to men over women for appointment as estate administrators to be a violation of the Equal Protection Clause of the Fourteenth Amendment.

Allen R. Derr argued the cause for appellant. With him on the briefs were Melvin L. Wulf, Ruth Bader Ginsburg, Pauli Murray, and Dorothy Kenyon.

Charles S. Stout argued the cause for appellee. With him on the brief was Myron E. Anderson.

Briefs of amici curiae urging reversal were filed by J. Lee Rankin and Norman Redlich for the City of New York; by Martha W. Griffiths, Phineas Indritz, Leo Kanowitz, Marguerite Rawalt, Sylvia Roberts, and Faith Seidenberg for American Veterans Committee, Inc., et al.; and by Birch Bayh for the National Federation of Business and Professional Women's Clubs, Inc.

MR. CHIEF JUSTICE BURGER delivered the opinion of the Court.

Richard Lynn Reed, a minor, died intestate in Ada County, Idaho, on March 29, 1967. His adoptive parents, who had separated sometime prior to his death, are the parties to this appeal. Approximately seven months after Richard's death, his mother, appellant Sally Reed, filed a petition in the Probate Court of Ada County, [404 U.S. 71, 72] seeking appointment as administratrix of her son's estate. Prior to the date set for a hearing on the mother's petition, appellee Cecil Reed, the father of the decedent, filed a competing petition seeking to have himself appointed administrator of the son's estate. The probate court held a joint hearing on the two petitions and thereafter ordered that letters of administration be issued to appellee Cecil Reed upon his taking the oath and filing the bond required by law. The court treated 15-312 and 15-314 of the Idaho Code as the controlling statutes and read those sections as compelling a preference for Cecil Reed because he was a male.

Section 15-312 designates the persons who are entitled to administer the estate of one who dies intestate. In making these designations, that section lists 11 classes of persons who are so entitled and provides, in substance, [404 U.S. 71, 73] that the order in which those classes are listed in the section shall be determinative of the relative rights of competing applicants for letters of administration. One of the 11 classes so enumerated is "[t]he father or mother" of the person dying intestate. Under this section, then, appellant and appellee, being members of the same entitlement class, would seem to have been equally entitled to administer their son's estate. Section 15-314 provides, however, that

> "[o]f several persons claiming and equally entitled [under 15-3121 to administer, males must be preferred to females, and relatives of the whole to those of the half blood."

In issuing its order, the probate court implicitly recognized the equality of entitlement of the two applicants under 15-312 and noted that neither of the applicants was under any legal disability; the court ruled, however, that appellee, being a male, was to be preferred to the female appellant "by reason of Section 15-314 of the Idaho Code." In stating this conclusion, the probate judge gave no indication that he had attempted to determine the relative capabilities of the competing applicants to perform the functions incident to the administration of an estate. It seems clear the probate judge considered himself bound by statute to give preference to the male candidate over the female, each being otherwise "equally entitled."

Sally Reed appealed from the probate court order, and her appeal was treated by the District Court of the Fourth Judicial District of Idaho as a constitutional attack on 15-314. In dealing with the attack, that court held that the challenged section violated the Equal Protection Clause of the Fourteenth Amendment and was, therefore, [404 U.S. 71, 74] void; the matter was ordered "returned to the Probate Court for its determination of which of the two parties" was better qualified to administer the estate.

This order was never carried out, however, for Cecil Reed took a further appeal to the Idaho Supreme Court, which reversed the District Court and reinstated the original order naming the father administrator of the estate. In reaching this result, the Idaho Supreme Court first dealt with the governing statutory law and held that under 15-312 "a father and mother are 'equally entitled' to letters of administration," but the preference given to males by 15-314 is "mandatory" and leaves no room for the exercise of a probate court's discretion in the appointment of administrators. Having thus definitively and authoritatively interpreted the statutory provisions involved, the Idaho Supreme Court then proceeded to examine, and reject, Sally Reed's contention that 15-314 violates the Equal Protection Clause by giving a mandatory preference to males over females, without regard to their individual qualifications as potential estate administrators. 93 Idaho 511, 465 P.2d 635.

. . .

Sally Reed thereupon appealed for review by this Court pursuant to 28 U.S.C. 1257 (2), and we noted probable jurisdiction. 401 U.S. 934. Having examined the record and considered the briefs and oral arguments of the parties, we have concluded that the arbitrary preference established in favor of males by 15-314 of the Idaho Code cannot stand in the face of the Fourteenth Amendment's command that no State deny the equal protection of the laws to any person within its jurisdiction. [404 U.S. 71, 75]

Idaho does not, of course, deny letters of administration to women altogether. Indeed, under 15-312, a woman whose spouse dies intestate has a preference over a son, father, brother, or any other male relative of the decedent. Moreover, we can judicially notice that in this country, presumably due to the greater longevity of women, a large proportion of estates, both intestate and under wills of decedents, are administered by surviving widows.

Section 15-314 is restricted in its operation to those situations where competing applications for letters of administration have been filed by both male and female members of the same entitlement class established by 15-312. In such situations, 15-314 provides that different treatment be accorded to the applicants on the basis of their sex; it thus establishes a classification subject to scrutiny under the Equal Protection Clause.

In applying that clause, this Court has consistently recognized that the Fourteenth Amendment does not deny to States the power to treat different classes of persons in different ways. Barbier v. Connolly, 113 U.S. 27 (1885); Lindsley v. Natural Carbonic Gas Co., 220 U.S. 61 (1911); Railway Express Agency v. New York, 336 U.S. 106 (1949); McDonald v. Board of Election Commissioners, 394 U.S. 802 (1969). The Equal Protection Clause of that amendment does, however, deny to States the power to legislate that different treatment be accorded to persons placed by a statute into [404 U.S. 71, 76] different classes on the basis of criteria wholly unrelated to the objective of that statute. A classification "must be reasonable, not arbitrary, and must rest upon some ground of difference having a fair and substantial relation to the object of the legislation, so that all persons similarly circumstanced shall be treated alike." Royster Guano Co. v. Virginia, 253 U.S. 412, 415 (1920). The question presented by this case, then, is whether a difference in the sex of competing applicants for letters of administration bears a rational relationship to a state objective that is sought to be advanced by the operation of 15-312 and 15-314.

In upholding the latter section, the Idaho Supreme Court concluded that its objective was to eliminate one area of controversy when two or more persons, equally entitled under 15-312, seek letters of administration and thereby present the probate court "with the issue of which one should be named." The court also concluded that where such persons are not of the same sex, the elimination of females from consideration "is neither an illogical nor arbitrary method devised by the legislature to resolve an issue that would otherwise require a hearing as to the relative merits . . . of the two or more petitioning relatives. . . ." 93 Idaho, at 514, 465 P.2d, at 638.

Clearly the objective of reducing the workload on probate courts by eliminating one class of contests is not without some legitimacy. The crucial question, however, is whether 15-314 advances that objective in a manner consistent with the command of the Equal Protection Clause. We hold that it does not. To give a mandatory preference to members of either sex over members of the other, merely to accomplish the elimination of hearings on the merits, is to make the very kind of arbitrary legislative choice forbidden by the Equal Protection Clause of the Fourteenth Amendment; and whatever may be [404 U.S. 71, 77] said as to the positive values of avoiding intrafamily controversy, the choice in this context may not lawfully be mandated solely on the basis of sex.

We note finally that if 15-314 is viewed merely as a modifying appendage to 15-312 and as aimed at the same objective, its constitutionality is not thereby saved. The objective of 15-312 clearly is to establish degrees of entitlement of various classes of persons in accordance with their varying degrees and kinds of relationship to the intestate. Regardless of their sex, persons within any one of the enumerated classes of that section are similarly situated with respect to that objective. By providing dissimilar treatment for men and women who are thus similarly situated, the challenged section violates the Equal Protection Clause. Royster Guano Co. v. Virginia, supra.

The judgment of the Idaho Supreme Court is reversed and the case remanded for further proceedings not inconsistent with this opinion.

Reversed and remanded.

Source: Excerpted from "U.S. Supreme Court, *Reed v. Reed*, 404 U.S. 71 (1971)." Available online. URL: http://laws. findlaw.comlus/404/71.html. Accessed December 16, 2006.

Eisenstadt v. Baird (1972)

Appellee attacks his conviction of violating Massachusetts law for giving a woman a contraceptive foam at the close of his lecture to students on contraception. That law makes it a felony for anyone to give away a drug, medicine, instrument, or article for the prevention of conception except in the case of (1) a registered physician administering or prescribing it for a married person or (2) an active registered pharmacist furnishing it to a married person presenting a registered physician's prescription. The District Court dismissed appellee's petition for a writ of habeas corpus. The Court of Appeals vacated the dismissal, holding that the statute is a prohibition on contraception per se and conflicts "with fundamental human rights" under Griswold v. Connecticut, 381 U.S. 479. Appellant, inter alia, argues that appellee lacks standing to assert the rights of unmarried persons denied access to contraceptives because he was neither an authorized distributor under the statute nor a single person unable to obtain contraceptives. Held:

1. If, as the Court of Appeals held, the statute under which appellee was convicted is not a health measure, appellee may not be prevented, because he was not an authorized distributor, from attacking the statute in its alleged discriminatory application to potential distributees. Appellee, furthermore, has standing to assert the rights of unmarried persons denied access to contraceptives because their ability to obtain them will be materially impaired by enforcement of the statute. Cf. Griswold, supra; Barrows v. Jackson, 346 U.S. 249. Pp. 443–446.

2. By providing dissimilar treatment for married and unmarried persons who are similarly situated, the statute violates the Equal Protection Clause of the Fourteenth Amendment. Pp. 446–455.

(a) The deterrence of fornication, a 90-day misdemeanor under Massachusetts law, cannot reasonably be regarded as the purpose of the statute, since the statute is riddled with exceptions making contraceptives freely available for use in premarital sexual relations and its scope and penalty structure are inconsistent with that purpose. Pp. 447–450.

(b) Similarly, the protection of public health through the regulation of the distribution of potentially harmful articles cannot reasonably be regarded as the purpose of the law, since, if health were the rationale, the statute would be both discriminatory and overbroad, and federal and state laws already regulate the distribution of drugs unsafe for use except under the supervision of a licensed physician. Pp. 450–452.

(c) Nor can the statute be sustained simply as a prohibition on contraception per se, for whatever the rights of the individual to access to contraceptives may be, the rights must be the same for the unmarried and the married alike. If under Griswold, supra, the distribution of contraceptives to married persons cannot be prohibited, a ban on distribution to unmarried persons would be equally impermissible, since the constitutionally protected right of privacy inheres in the individual, not the marital couple. If, on the other hand, Griswold is no bar to a prohibition on the distribution of contraceptives, a prohibition limited to unmarried persons would be underinclusive and invidiously discriminatory. Pp. 452–455.

Source: Excerpted from "U.S. Supreme Court, *Eisenstadt v. Baird*, 405 U.S. 438 (1972)," by the U.S. Government. Available online. URL: http://supreme.justia.com/us/405/438/case.html. Accessed April 29, 2006.

Roe v. Wade (1973)
410 U.S. 113

The original 1973 decision of Roe v. Wade *(410 U.S. 113) from which the Supreme Court then ruled on the legality of abortions, overriding several state laws preventing them, was based on two cases, that of an unmarried woman from Texas, where abortion was illegal unless the mother's life was at risk, and that of a poor married mother of three from Georgia, where state law required permission for an abortion from a panel of doctors and hospital officials. While establishing the right to an abortion in the first trimester, the decision gave states the right to intervene in the second and third trimesters of pregnancy to protect the woman and the "potential" life of the unborn child.*

U.S. Supreme Court
ROE ET AL. v. WADE, DISTRICT ATTORNEY OF DALLAS COUNTY APPEAL FROM THE UNITED STATES DISTRICT COURT FOR THE NORTHERN DISTRICT OF TEXAS No. 70-18.
Argued December 13, 1971. Reargued October 11, 1972. Decided January 22, 1973

A pregnant single woman (Roe) brought a class action challenging the constitutionality of the Texas criminal abortion laws, which proscribe procuring or attempting an abortion except on medical advice for the purpose of saving the mother's life. A licensed physician (Hallford), who had two state abortion prosecutions pending against him, was permitted to intervene. A childless married couple (the Does), the wife not being pregnant, separately attacked the laws, basing alleged injury on the future possibilities of contraceptive failure, pregnancy, unpreparedness for parenthood, and impairment of the wife's health. A three-judge District Court, which consolidated the actions, held that Roe and Hallford, and members of their classes, had standing to sue and presented justiciable controversies. Ruling that declaratory, though not injunctive, relief was warranted, the court declared the abortion statutes void as vague and overbroadly infringing those plaintiffs' Ninth and Fourteenth Amendment rights. The court ruled the Does' complaint not justiciable. Appellants directly appealed to this Court on the injunctive rulings, and appellee cross-appealed from the District Court's grant of declaratory relief to Roe and Hallford.

Source: Excerpted from "U.S. Supreme Court, *Roe et al. v. Wade*," by the U.S. Government. Available online. URL: http://supreme.justia.com/us/410/113/case.html. Accessed April 18, 2006.

Rostker v. Goldberg (1981)

Opponents of the proposed Equal Rights Amendment are concerned that its exact interpretation could lead to a requirement that women register for military service. In spite of the National Organization for Women's (NOW's) lobbying efforts for women's equal access to the military, this 1981 Supreme Court decision only required male 18-year-olds to register with the draft board. The Selective Service law still does not require women to register for the draft because of the Department of Defense's policy of restricting women from direct ground combat.

453 U.S. 57 (1981)
ROSTKER, DIRECTOR OF SELECTIVE SERVICE v. GOLDBERG ET AL.

APPEAL FROM THE UNITED STATES DISTRICT COURT FOR THE EASTERN DISTRICT OF PENNSYLVANIA.

No. 80-251.

Argued March 24, 1981. Decided June 25, 1981.

The Military Selective Service Act (Act) authorizes the President to require the registration for possible military service of males but not females, the purpose of registration being to facilitate any eventual conscription under the Act. Registration for the draft was discontinued by Presidential Proclamation in 1975 (the Act was amended in 1973 to preclude conscription), but as the result of a crisis in Southwestern Asia, President Carter decided in 1980 that it was necessary to reactivate the registration process, and sought Congress' allocation of funds for that purpose. He also recommended that Congress amend the Act to permit the registration and conscription of women as well as men. Although agreeing that it was necessary to reactivate the registration process, Congress allocated only those funds necessary to register males and declined to amend the Act to permit the registration of women. Thereafter, the President ordered the registration of specified groups of young men. In a lawsuit brought by several men challenging the Act's constitutionality, a three-judge District Court ultimately held that the Act's gender-based discrimination violated the Due Process Clause of the Fifth Amendment and enjoined registration under the Act.

Held:

The Act's registration provisions do not violate the Fifth Amendment. Congress acted well within its constitutional authority to raise and regulate armies and navies when it authorized the registration of men and not women. Pp. 64–83.

(a) The customary deference accorded Congress' judgments is particularly appropriate when, as here, Congress specifically considered the question of the Act's constitutionality, and perhaps in no area has the Court accorded Congress greater deference than in the area of national defense and military affairs. While Congress is not free to disregard the Constitution when it acts in the area of military affairs, this Court must be particularly careful not to substitute its judgment of what is desirable for that of Congress, or its own evaluation of evidence for a reasonable evaluation by the Legislative Branch. Congress carefully considered whether to register only males for potential conscription or whether to register both sexes, and its broad constitutional authority

Page 453 U.S. 57, 58

cannot be ignored in considering the constitutionality of its studied choice of one alternative in preference to the other. Pp. 64–72.

(b) The question of registering women was extensively considered by Congress in hearings held in response to the President's request for authorization to register women, and its decision to exempt women was not the accidental byproduct of a traditional way of thinking about women. Since Congress thoroughly reconsidered the question of exempting women from the Act in 1980, the Act's constitutionality need not be considered solely on the basis of the views expressed by Congress in 1948, when the Act was first enacted in its modern form. Congress' determination that any future draft would be characterized by a need for combat troops was sufficiently supported by testimony adduced at the hearings so that the courts are not free to make their own judgment on the question. And since women are excluded from combat service by statute or military policy, men and women are simply not similarly situated for purposes of a draft or registration for a draft, and Congress' decision to authorize the registration of only men, therefore, does not violate the Due Process Clause. The testimony of executive and military officials before Congress showed that the argument for registering women was based on considerations of equity, but Congress was entitled, in the exercise of its constitutional powers, to focus on the question of military need rather than "equity." The District Court, undertaking an independent evaluation of the evidence, exceeded its authority in ignoring Congress' conclusions that whatever the need for women for noncombat roles during mobilization, it could be met by volunteers, and that staffing noncombat positions with women during a mobilization would be positively detrimental to the important goal of military flexibility. Pp. 72–83.

Source: Excerpted from *"Rostker, Director of Selective Service v. Goldberg et al.,"* by the U.S. Government. Available online. URL: http://supreme.justia.com/us/448/1306/case.html. Accessed April 29, 2006.

Baby M (1988)

First Surrogacy Case—In re Baby M, 537 A.2d 1227, 109 N.J. 396 (N.J. 02/03/1988)

New Jersey Supreme Court
Decided: February 3, 1988.
IN THE MATTER OF BABY M, A PSEUDONYM FOR AN ACTUAL PERSON

In this matter the Court is asked to determine the validity of a contract that purports to provide a new way of bringing children into a family. For a fee of $10,000, a woman agrees to be artificially inseminated with the semen of another woman's husband; she is to conceive a child, carry it to term, and after its birth surrender it to the natural father and his wife. The intent of the contract is that the child's natural mother will thereafter be forever separated from her child. The wife is to adopt the child, and she and the natural father are to be regarded as its parents for all purposes. The contract providing for this is called a "surrogacy contract," the natural mother inappropriately called the "surrogate mother."

We invalidate the surrogacy contract because it conflicts with the law and public policy of this State. While we recognize the depth of the yearning of infertile couples to have their own children, we find the payment of money to a "surrogate" mother illegal, perhaps criminal, and potentially degrading to women. Although in this case we grant custody to the natural father, the evidence having clearly proved such custody to be in the best interests of the infant, we void both the termination of the surrogate mother's parental rights and the adoption of the child by the wife/stepparent. We thus restore the "surrogate" as the mother of the child. We remand the issue of the natural mother's visitation rights to the trial court, since that issue was not reached below and the record before us is not sufficient to permit us to decide it de novo. . . .

We find no offense to our present laws where a woman voluntarily and without payment agrees to act as a "surrogate" mother, provided that she is not subject to a binding agreement to surrender her child. Moreover, our holding today does not preclude the Legislature from altering the current statutory scheme, within constitutional limits, so as to permit surrogacy contracts. Under current law, however, the surrogacy agreement before us is illegal and invalid.

Source: Excerpted from "First Surrogacy Case—*In re Baby M*, 537 A.2d 1227, 109 N.J. 396 (N.J. 02/03/1988)," by the New Jersey Supreme Court. Available online. URL: http://biotech.law.lsu.edu/cases/cloning/baby_m.htm. Accessed April 29, 2006.

Partial-Birth Abortion Ban Act of 2003

In November 2003, the United States president signed a partial-birth abortion ban, legislation that was first introduced in 1995 and subsequently passed by Congress. Partial-birth abortions are performed in the second and third trimesters, when babies are in their 20th to 24th week. The bill proposed to ban "partial-birth abortion," legally defined as any abortion in which the baby is delivered "past the [baby's] navel . . . outside the body of the mother," or "in the case of head-first presentation, the entire fetal head is outside the body of the mother," before being killed. The bill would allow the method if it was necessary to save a mother's life. The following are excerpts from the ban (as agreed to by the House and Senate), as well as the subsequent trace of the legal proceedings from Planned Parenthood of America, and Carhart v. Gonzales.

The Congress finds and declares the following:

(1) A moral, medical, and ethical consensus exists that the practice of performing a partial-birth abortion—an abortion in which a physician deliberately and intentionally vaginally delivers a living, unborn child's body until either the entire baby's head is outside the body of the mother, or any

part of the baby's trunk past the navel is outside the body of the mother and only the head remains inside the womb, for the purpose of performing an overt act (usually the puncturing of the back of the child's skull and removing the baby's brains) that the person knows will kill the partially delivered infant, performs this act, and then completes delivery of the dead infant—is a gruesome and inhumane procedure that is never medically necessary and should be prohibited.

(2) Rather than being an abortion procedure that is embraced by the medical community, particularly among physicians who routinely perform other abortion procedures, partial-birth abortion remains a disfavored procedure that is not only unnecessary to preserve the health of the mother, but in fact poses serious risks to the long-term health of women and in some circumstances, their lives. As a result, at least 27 States banned the procedure as did the United States Congress which voted to ban the procedure during the 104th, 105th, and 106th Congresses.

Planned Parenthood Federation of America challenged the constitutionality of the ban, which among other things lacked a health exception for the mother. PPFA filed Planned Parenthood Federation of America v. Ashcroft *in the U.S. District Court for the Northern District of California. Ashcroft was the attorney general at the time.*

In addition, the National Abortion Federation, represented by the ACLU, filed National Abortion Federation v. Ashcroft *in the U.S. District Court for the Southern District of New York, and the Center for Reproductive Rights represented four doctors licensed to practice in several states in* Carhart v. Ashcroft.

On June 1, 2004, Federal District Court Judge Phyllis Hamilton ruled in favor of PPFA in Planned Parenthood Federation v. Ashcroft, *concluding that the ban is unconstitutional and cannot be enforced (*Planned Parenthood Federation of America v. Ashcroft, 2004).

On August 26, 2004, Federal District Court Judge Richard Conway Casey ruled in favor of the National Abortion Federation (NAF), in National Abortion Federation v. Ashcroft, *echoing the ruling in the Planned Parenthood suit (*National Abortion Federation v. Ashcroft, 2004). *This ruling was appealed by the Bush administration in September 2004. On January 31, 2006, the U.S. Court of Appeals for the Second Circuit affirmed that the ban was unconstitutional because it lacked a health exception and asked for further legal briefing to determine how to remedy the violation (ACLU, 2006;* National Abortion Federation v. Gonzales, 2006).

On September 8, 2004, Federal District Court Judge Richard G. Kopf ruled in favor of Dr. LeRoy Carhart and three other physicians in Carhart v.

Ashcroft, *echoing the rulings in both* Planned Parenthood v. Ashcroft *and* National Abortion Federation v. Ashcroft *(*Carhart v. Ashcroft, *2004). This ruling was appealed by the Bush administration in November 2004. On July 8, 2005, the U.S. Court of Appeals for the Eighth Circuit declared the Federal Abortion Ban unconstitutional (*Carhart v. Gonzales, *2005). This ruling has since been petitioned to the U.S. Supreme Court, and on February 21, 2006, the Court agreed to review the case.* Gonzales v. Carhart *was argued before the Court on November 8, 2006, and a decision is expected before July 2007.*

The procedures in question in this case are used during late-term abortions and we therefore must, for context, present some basic information regarding these procedures. There are three primary methods of late-term abortions: medical induction; dilation and evacuation (D&E); and dilation and extraction (D&X). In a medical induction, formerly the most common method of second-trimester abortion, a physician uses medication to induce premature labor. Stenberg, 530 U.S. at 924.

In a D&E, now the most common procedure, the physician causes dilation of the woman's cervix and then "the physician reaches into the woman's uterus with an instrument, grasps an extremity of the fetus, and pulls." Women's Med. Prof'l Corp. v. Taft, 353 F.3d 436, 439 (6th Cir. 2003). "When the fetus lodges in the cervix, the traction between the grasping instrument and the cervix causes dismemberment and eventual death, although death may occur prior to dismemberment." Id. This process is repeated until the entire fetus has been removed. D&X and a process called intact D&E are what are "now widely known as partial birth abortion." Id. In these procedures, the fetus is removed "intact" in a single pass. If the fetus presents head first, the physician collapses the skull of the fetus and then removes the "intact" fetus. Stenberg, 530 U.S. at 927. This is what is known as an intact D&E. If the fetus presents feet first, the physician "pulls the fetal body through the cervix, collapses the skull, and extracts the fetus through the cervix." Id. This is the D&X procedure. "Despite the technical differences" between an intact D&E and a D&X, they are "sufficiently similar for us to use the terms interchangeably." Id. at 928. . . .

Stenberg identified what some refer to as "evidentiary circumstances" upon which the Court purportedly relied in determining whether "substantial medical authority" supported the need for a health exception. The Stenberg Court noted (1) the district court's conclusion that D&X significantly obviates health risks in certain circumstances and a highly plausible record-based explanation of why that might be so; (2) a division of opinion among medical experts regarding the procedure; and (3) an absence of controlled medical studies that address the safety and medical necessity of the banned procedures. 530 U.S. at 936–37. In evaluating the government's case, we take Stenberg as the baseline and then determine if the government has proffered evidence sufficient to distinguish the present situation from Stenberg's "evidentiary circumstances." If the government marshals such evidence, we must then determine whether the evidence on the other side remains "substantial medical authority." Because we conclude the government has not adduced evidence distinguishing this case from Stenberg, we need not attempt to define the precise contours of "substantial medical authority.". . .

We know from Stenberg that "substantial medical authority" supports the conclusion that the banned procedures obviate health risks in certain situations. For example, there is "substantial medical authority" (in the form of expert testimony and amici submissions) that these procedures reduce the risk of uterine perforation and cervical laceration because they avoid significant instrumentation and the presence of sharp fetal bone fragments. Stenberg, 530 U.S. at 930–34. There is also evidence the procedure takes less time and thus reduces blood loss and prolonged exposure to anesthesia. Id. The banned procedure may also eliminate the risk posed by retained fetal tissue and embolism of cerebral tissue into the woman's bloodstream. Id. Moreover, there is evidence regarding the health advantages the banned procedures provide when the woman has prior uterine scarring or when the fetus is nonviable due to hydrocephaly. Id.

There is some evidence in the present record indicating each of the advantages discussed in Stenberg are incorrect and the banned procedures are never medically necessary. See Carhart, 331 F. Supp. 2d at 822–51. There were, however, such assertions in Stenberg as well. See Stenberg, 530 U.S. at 933–34; id. at 964–66 (Kennedy, J., dissenting). Though the contrary evidence now comes from (some) different doctors, the substance of this evidence does not distinguish this case from Stenberg in any meaningful way. . . .

We need not belabor the point. The record in this case and the record in Stenberg are similar in all significant respects. See Nat'l Abortion Fed'n, 330 F. Supp. 2d at 492 (explaining that the government's arguments "all fail to meaningfully distinguish the evidentiary circumstances present here from those that Stenberg held required a health exception to a ban on partial-birth abortion"). There remains no consensus in the medical community as to the safety and medical necessity of the banned procedures. There is a dearth of studies on the medical necessity of the banned procedures. In the absence of new evidence which would serve to distinguish this record from the record reviewed by the Supreme Court in Stenberg, we are bound by the Supreme Court's conclusion that "substantial medical authority" supports the medical necessity of a health exception. "As a court of law, [our responsibility] is neither to devise ways in which to circumvent the opinion of the Supreme Court nor to indulge delay in the full implementation of the Court's opinions. Rather, our responsibility is to faithfully follow its opinions, because that court is, by constitutional design, vested with the ultimate authority to interpret the Constitution." Richmond Med. Ctr. for Women v. Gilmore, 219 F.3d 376, 378 (4th Cir. 2000) (Luttig, J., concurring). Because the Act does not contain a health exception exception, it is unconstitutional. We therefore do not reach the district court's conclusion of the Act imposing an undue burden on a woman's right to have an abortion.

Source: Excerpted from "Partial-Birth Abortion Ban Act of 2003," by the U.S. Government. Available online. URL: http://thomas.loc.gov. Accessed April 29, 2006.

5

International Documents

This section draws together excerpts of significant international primary source documents. The documents are organized into the following sections:

International Women's Movement

International Treaties

Denmark

China

Afghanistan

Kenya

INTERNATIONAL WOMEN'S MOVEMENT

A Vindication of the Rights of Woman (1792)

In 1792, Mary Wollstonecraft responded critically with "A Vindication of the Rights of Woman" to M. Talleyrand-Perigord, the late bishop of Autun in France, after she read a pamphlet he had authored. Her treaties stirred the hearts of the public with her cry for women "to acquire strength, both of mind and body." She introduced the novel concept of education for women and ventured "to predict that virtue will never prevail in society till the virtues of both sexes are founded on reason; and, till the affections common to both are allowed to gain their due strength by the discharge of mutual duties." She emphasized her principle, that if women were not prepared by education to become the companions of men, they had the power to "stop the progress of knowledge and virtue" in the world.

PART I.

    Chap. I. The Rights and Involved Duties of Mankind Considered.

    In the present state of society it appears necessary to go back to first principles in search of the most simple truths, and to dispute with some prevailing prejudice every inch of ground. To clear my way, I must be allowed to ask some plain questions, and the answers will probably appear as unequivocal as the axioms on which reasoning is built; though, when entangled with various motives of action, they are formally contradicted, either by the words or conduct of men.

In what does man's pre-eminence over the brute creation consist? The answer is as clear as that a half is less than the whole; in Reason.

What acquirement exalts one being above another? Virtue; we spontaneously reply.

For what purpose were the passions implanted? That man by struggling with them might attain a degree of knowledge denied to the brutes; whispers Experience.

Consequently the perfection of our nature and capability of happiness, must be estimated by the degree of reason, virtue, and knowledge, that distinguish the individual, and direct the laws which bind society: and that from the exercise of reason, knowledge and virtue naturally flow, is equally undeniable, if mankind be viewed collectively.

The rights and duties of man thus simplified, it seems almost impertinent to attempt to illustrate truths that appear so incontrovertible; yet such deeply rooted prejudices have clouded reason, and such spurious qualities have assumed the name of virtues, that it is necessary to pursue the course of reason as it has been perplexed and involved in error, by various adventitious circumstances, comparing the simple axiom with casual deviations.

Men, in general, seem to employ their reason to justify prejudices, which they have imbibed, they cannot trace how, rather than to root them out. The mind must be strong that resolutely forms its own principles; for a kind of intellectual cowardice prevails which makes many men shrink from the task, or only do it by halves. Yet the imperfect conclusions thus drawn, are frequently very plausible, because they are built on partial experience, on just, though narrow, views.

Going back to first principles, vice skulks, with all its native deformity, from close investigation; but a set of shallow reasoners are always exclaiming that these arguments prove too much, and that a measure rotten at the core may be expedient. Thus expediency is continually contrasted with simple principles, till truth is lost in a mist of words, virtue, in forms, and knowledge rendered a sounding nothing, by the specious prejudices that assume its name.

That the society is formed in the wisest manner, whose constitution is founded on the nature of man, strikes, in the abstract, every thinking being so forcibly, that it looks like presumption to endeavour to bring forward proofs; though proof must be brought, or the strong hold of prescription will never be forced by reason; yet to urge prescription as an argument to justify the depriving men (or women) of their natural rights, is one of the absurd sophisms which daily insult common sense. . . .

Consequently, the most perfect education, in my opinion, is such an exercise of the understanding as is best calculated to strengthen the body and form the heart. Or, in other words, to enable the individual to attain such habits of virtue as will render it independent. In fact, it is a farce to call any being virtuous whose virtues do not result from the exercise of its own reason. This was Rousseau's opinion respecting men: I extend it to women, and confidently assert that they have been drawn out of their sphere by false refinement, and not by an endeavour to acquire masculine qualities. Still the regal homage which they receive is so intoxicating, that till the manners of the times are changed, and formed on more reasonable principles, it may be impossible to convince them that the illegitimate power, which they obtain, by degrading themselves, is a curse, and that they must return to nature and equality, if they wish to secure the placid satisfaction that unsophisticated affections impart. But for this epoch we must wait- wait, perhaps, till kings and nobles, enlightened by reason, and, preferring the real dignity of man to childish state, throw off their gaudy hereditary trappings: and if then women do not resign the arbitrary power of beauty- they will prove that they have less mind than man.

I may be accused of arrogance; still I must declare what I firmly believe, that all the writers who have written on the subject of female education and manners from Rousseau to Dr. Gregory, have contributed to render women more artificial, weak characters, than they would otherwise have been; and, consequently, more useless members of society. I might have expressed this conviction in a lower key; but I am afraid it would have been the whine of affectation, and not the faithful expression of my feelings, of the clear result, which experience and reflection have led me to draw. When I come to that division of the subject, I shall advert to the passages that I more particularly disapprove of, in the works of the authors I have just alluded to; but it is first necessary to observe, that my objection extends to the whole purport of those books, which tend, in my opinion, to degrade one half of the human species, and render women pleasing at the expense of every solid virtue. . . .

Chap. II. The Prevailing Opinion of a Sexual Character Discussed.

Women ought to endeavour to purify their heart; but can they do so when their uncultivated understandings make them entirely dependent on their senses for employment and amusement, when no noble pursuit sets them above the little vanities of the day, or enables them to curb the wild emotions that agitate a reed over which every passing breeze has power? To gain the affections of a virtuous man is affectation necessary? Nature has given woman a weaker frame than man; but, to ensure her husband's affections, must a wife, who by the exercise of her mind and body whilst she was discharging the duties of a daughter, wife, and mother, has allowed her constitution to retain its natural strength, and her nerves a healthy tone, is she, I say, to condescend to use art and feign a sickly delicacy in order to secure her husband's affection? Weakness may excite tenderness, and gratify the arrogant pride of man; but the lordly caresses of a protector will not gratify a noble mind that pants for, and deserves to be respected. Fondness is a poor substitute for friendship!

In a seraglio, I grant, that all these arts are necessary; the epicure must have his palate tickled, or he will sink into apathy; but have women so little ambition as to be satisfied with such a condition? Can they supinely dream life away in the lap of pleasure, or the languor of weariness, rather than assert their claim to pursue reasonable pleasures and render themselves conspicuous by practising the virtues which dignify mankind? Surely she has not an immortal soul who can loiter life away merely employed to adorn her person, that she may amuse the languid hours, and soften the cares of a fellow-creature who is willing to be enlivened by her smiles and tricks, when the serious business of life is over.

Besides, the woman who strengthens her body and exercises her mind will, by managing her family and practising various virtues, become the friend, and not the humble dependent of her husband, and if she deserves his regard by possessing such substantial qualities, she will not find it necessary to conceal her affection, nor to pretend to an unnatural coldness of constitution to excite her husband's passions. In fact, if we revert to history, we shall find that the women who have distinguished themselves have neither been the most beautiful nor the most gentle of their sex.

Nature, or, to speak with strict propriety, God, has made all things right; but man has sought him out many inventions to mar the work. I now allude to that part of Dr. Gregory's treatise, where he advises a wife never to let her husband know the extent of her sensibility or affection. Voluptuous precaution, and as ineffectual as absurd.—Love, from its very nature, must be transitory. To seek for a secret that would render it constant, would be as wild a search as for the philosopher's stone, or the grand panacea; and the discovery would be equally useless, or rather pernicious, to mankind. The most holy band of society is friendship. It has been well said, by a shrewd satirist, "that rare as true love is, true friendship is still rarer."

Source: Excerpted from "A Vindication of the Rights of Woman," by Mary Wollstonecraft, 1792. Available online. URL: http://www.sacred-texts.com/wmn/vind.txt. Accessed December 9, 2005.

First Lady Hillary Rodham Clinton
Remarks at Women 2000—Beijing + Five,
the United Nations (June 5, 2000)

Five years after the Beijing Conference, the then–first lady Hillary Clinton delivered these remarks, commending the recent efforts of international agencies but recognizing what still needed to be achieved.

Beijing was important—because women broke centuries of silence and spoke out on issues that matter most to us, to our families to our societies. Women put our hopes and fears, our concerns and challenges on the world's agenda.

Beijing was important because countries agreed to a Platform for Action to meet goals in 12 different areas. The platform provided a blueprint for achieving economic, social and political equality and progress for women. So that, in the future, inaction and regression on women's rights would be viewed, not simply as the way things are and always have been, but rather as a violation of promises agreed to.

After the delegates went home, we used the Platform as a roadmap for elected officials and as a rallying cry for NGOs and citizens who began forming partnerships to fulfill the commitments that were entered into.

And since we spoke out in Beijing, look what has happened. Countries have passed laws raising the legal age for marriage, banning female genital mutilation, and criminalizing domestic violence.

Since we spoke out in Beijing, rape is now recognized as a crime by international war tribunals. More women are getting microcredit, running their own businesses, and owning property in their own names. . . .

These women and countless others like them who started in Beijing are now part of a movement. Where before women too often worked in isolation, now we are increasingly working together, blending our voices in a chorus for change. . . .

We come here to honor those voices and to speak for all those women who still do not have a voice.

We come here today because, for all our progress we can point to, our work is far from done.

When girls are doused with gasoline, set on fire, and burned to death because their marriage dowries are deemed too small—and when honor killings continue to be tolerated—our work is far from done. When millions of girls are still kept out of school, often by their own families, our work is far from done.

When babies are still denied food, drowned, suffocated, and abandoned simply because they are born girls, our work is far from done.

When women are still denied the right to plan their families, when they are still forced to have abortions, or are circumcised or sterilized against their will, our work is far from done.

When women and girls are increasingly victims of war, and turned into refugees by the millions, our work is far from done.

When girls are abducted, and used as child soldiers, human shields, and sexual slaves, our work is far from done.

When UNICEF tells us, as they did this week, that violence against women and girls is a global epidemic that kills, tortures and maims—and yet still it is viewed in too many places as acceptable, cultural or trivial, our work is far from done.

When women in some countries are still denied the right to vote, our work is far from done.

And when women's work is still not valued, by economists, by governments, and by employers who pay them less and treat them worse, our work is far from done.

So we must continue to stand up and speak out and keep working—not only to eliminate the inequities that have confronted women for millennia, but also to confront the new dangers that threaten to derail the progress we have already made.

We must speak out for the women who are still dying in childbirth or from unsafe abortions, for the women who cannot get health care, for the women suffering from cancer, malaria, TB and HIV/AIDS.

You know, the face of AIDS today is increasingly female in the world today. And it is tragically cutting short young women's lives, leaving behind AIDS orphans, who too often are left on dangerous streets to fend for themselves.

Source: Excerpted from "First Lady Hillary Rodham Clinton Remarks at Women 2000—Beijing + Five the United Nations June 5, 2000," unofficial transcript by the U.S. Mission at the United Nations. Available online. URL: http://www.un.int/usa/00_072.htm. Accessed December 26, 2005.

United Nations Secretary-General Kofi Annan's Message (March 2002)

The secretary-general was in Islamabad on the occasion of International Women's Day, to be observed on March 8, 2002.

The Millennium Declaration has given us an overriding mission for the twenty-first century. As we pursue that agenda and work for freedom from fear, freedom from want, and protection of the resources of this planet, our guiding motto is clear: putting people at the centre of everything we do. Thus, we are resolved to work for gender equality and the empowerment of women as vital tools to combat poverty and disease, and to achieve development that is truly sustainable; equally, we are determined to build on the contribution of women in managing conflict and building peace.

We can and should draw strength from the progress that has taken place in the past year. In Afghanistan, after years of conflict, hardship and human rights violations, hope has returned to women and girls who are yet again exercising their rights to education, work and an active role in society. At the United Nations, Security Council resolution 1325 of 2000 continues to inspire Member States to address women, peace and security on several fronts: to protect women from the impact of armed conflict, but also to strengthen their role in peace-building and reconstruction. In a growing number of countries, ratification of the Optional Protocol to the Convention on the Elimination of All Forms of Discrimination against Women is ensuring the right of women to petition an international body when their rights are violated. And in the international community as a whole, there has been growing recognition of the importance of the advancement of women in the fight against the AIDS epidemic, as reflected in the outcome of the General Assembly's Special Session on HIV/AIDS.

There will be several important opportunities for further progress in the weeks and months ahead. The International Conference on Finance for Development and the World Summit on Sustainable Development offer important opportunities to recognize the central role of women in achieving sustainable development in a globalizing world. The Second World Assembly on Ageing will address the dramatic impact on women of global population ageing, and the need to ensure that all women can age with security and dignity. And the General Assembly's Special Session on Children is expected to set specific, time-bound targets for protecting and fulfilling the rights of all children and women.

On this International Women's Day, as we prepare for the vital challenges before us, let us all be mindful that the achievement of women's rights is not the responsibility of women alone—it is the responsibility of us all. Let us step up our efforts to create an environment where progress towards gender equality is not a daily struggle, but a natural part of all our actions. Let that resolve underpin all our work to translate the Millennium Declaration into reality.

Source: Excerpted from "U.N. Secretary-General Kofi Annan's Message," in recognition of International Women's Day 2002, February 28, 2002. Available online. URL: http://www.un.org.pk/iwd/sg-msg.htm. Accessed March 3, 2006.

Whatever Happened to Family Planning and, for That Matter, Reproductive Health? (March 2004)

In 1994, the nations of the world gathered in Cairo for the International Conference on Population and Development (ICPD) and hammered out the comprehensive Programme of Action to improve women's sexual and reproductive health.

Just six years later, the nations of the world agreed on eight Millennium Development Goals (MDGs), and reproductive health was excluded.

This exclusion is emblematic of the declining priority placed on reproductive health and is a needed wake-up call. The time has come to reflect on the poor standing of reproductive health as a development issue and to mount efforts to get it back on the agenda. Like reproductive health more generally, family planning has received declining attention as a development priority and is at a disadvantage in the competition for scarce resources. Steps that would sharpen its competitive edge would also result in significant health benefits. . . .

A Tumultuous History

Family planning has always been a contentious issue. In the early 1900s, the debate about "birth control" encompassed a volatile mixture of religion, feminism, eugenics, social reform, and neo-Malthusian and pronatalist philosophies. In the United States, debate over abortion has always been a feature of discussion about family planning.

The legalization of abortion in the 1973 Roe v. Wade decision intensified that debate. In 1984, the Reagan administration unveiled its Mexico City policy, which exported the domestic debate to the rest of the world. The policy prohibits the U.S. Agency for International Development (USAID) from funding foreign nongovernmental organizations that provide abortion services, legal or illegal, or that promote the legalization of abortion, even if those organizations use their own funds for these activities.

The U.S. contribution represents 53% of all donor funds for reproductive health; additionally, the United States devotes 8% of its official development assistance to reproductive health, while the average for all donor countries (including the United States) is 3%.

The ascendancy of the United States over international and reproductive health resources helps explain the policy's success, and also suggests that we must look elsewhere to understand fully the de-emphasis on family planning in the donor community. It is unproductive to unduly focus on the U.S. government as the major cause of family planning's decline when the U.S. government is the sector's paramount donor. Other factors worth examining take us back to the 1990s, when two forces converged to lower the priority of family planning: its marginalization at Cairo and the wide acceptance of the view that family planning was unnecessary because of the drop in the global rate of population growth.

Family Planning at Cairo

Women's groups—many of which have long been uncomfortable with organized family planning—were a powerful force at Cairo. They called for a more complete range of health services for women, correctly pointing out that family planning programs did not serve all of women's reproductive needs. They also proposed major political, social and economic changes to improve women's general wellbeing. Their efforts paid off, and reproductive health became the core of the Programme of Action.

Unfortunately, the new approach not only developed an expanded agenda, it also downgraded and, in the eyes of some, demonized family planning programs. An undercurrent at Cairo was that family planning programs were an instrument of demographic imperialism used by the rich North to control the behavior of women in the developing world as a means of stemming population growth. This criticism was not directed at family planning per se, but at programs that were considered ill conceived and poorly implemented. For many, the message coming out of Cairo was not that we needed to do more than provide family planning, but that we needed to provide less family planning.

Source: Excerpted from "Whatever Happened to Family Planning and, for That Matter, Reproductive Health?" by Duff G. Gillespie, The Guttmacher Institute, *International Family Planning Perspectives,* March 2004; Volume 30, Number 1: pp. 35–38.

UN Links Poverty, Violence against Women (October 2005)

LONDON (AP)—The world will never eliminate poverty until it confronts social, economic and physical discrimination against women, the United Nations said Wednesday.

"Gender apartheid" could scuttle the global body's goal of halving extreme poverty by 2015, the U.N. Population Fund's annual State of World Population report said.

"We cannot make poverty history until we stop violence against women and girls," the fund's executive director, Thoraya Ahmed Obaid, said at the report's launch in London. "We cannot make poverty history until women enjoy their full social, cultural, economic and political rights."

The report said gender equality and better reproductive health could save the lives of 2 million women and 30 million children over the next decade—and help lift millions around the world out of poverty.

In 2000, the U.N. agreed to eight Millennium Development Goals, which include halving extreme poverty, achieving universal primary education and stemming the AIDS pandemic, all by 2015.

The report said one of the targets—promoting gender equality and empowering women—is "critical to the success of the other seven."

Improving women's political, economic and educational opportunities would lead to "improved economic prospects, smaller families, healthier and more literate children, lower HIV prevalence rates and reduced incidence of harmful traditional practices."

"Inequality is economically inefficient, it is a violation of human rights and it is a hazard to health," Obaid said.

But for many women around the world, the U.N. agency said, the picture remains grim.

It said 250 million years of productive life are lost annually because of reproductive health problems including HIV/AIDS, the leading cause of death among women between 15 and 44. Half the 40 million people infected with HIV around the world are women, and in sub-Saharan Africa, women make up a majority of those infected.

Lack of contraception leads to 76 million unintended pregnancies in the developing world and 19 million unsafe abortions worldwide each year, the agency said. More than half a million women die annually from preventable pregnancy-related causes—a figure that has changed little in a decade.

One woman in three around the world is likely to experience physical, psychological or sexual abuse in her lifetime. Many still lack the educational opportunities available to men: 600 million women around the world are illiterate, compared with 320 million men. . . .

"I think since the world summit, it's the first time world leaders have committed themselves to universal access to reproductive health by 2015. The issue has gone up the scale of importance. I am much more hopeful this time than before."

Source: Excerpted from "U.N. Links Poverty, Violence against Women," *Associated Press,* October 12, 2005. Available online. URL: http://abcnews.go.com/International/wireStory?id=1205776. Accessed January 2, 2006.

Women Taking Charge of Retirement Purse Strings, Sort of (July 2005)

After decades of feminist rhetoric about the need for women to take charge of their money, they are doing it, sort of. Today, most women no longer have a choice about whether to manage their money. They have money, and almost all of them will have to handle that money without a man at some point in their lives.

Women have long worked on a grassroots level to help their peers become financially competent, but lately global aging and the frailty of social safety nets have given the issue of women's financial security a new—some say dire—gravitas. In addition to ongoing activism by women for women, financial services companies have awakened to the fact that women, who control an increasing share of the world's wealth, are an appealing emerging market. Nonetheless, so far, there seems mostly to have been a revolution of ideas, not of action.

"Women are aware of the need to secure a comfortable retirement, invest properly, look at their finances and take responsibility," said Maria Umbach, vice president for life product marketing at Prudential Financial, "but their actions are not matching where they think they need to be. There's a gap."

Globally, the means to ensure a secure retirement and health care are shifting, which is one reason women—and men—around the world report with alarming consistency that they feel ill-equipped to manage their financial futures.

It is not clear that people have been able to adjust adequately to the changing circumstances, whether it is the shift in U.S. and British pension benefit programs, the strain on public retirement plans wrought by aging populations in Europe and Japan, or the declining percentage of children who care for their elderly parents in Asia.

While such insecurity is gender neutral, the failure to prepare for the changing future hits women harder than men. Women have fewer retirement resources than men because they tend to move in and out of the work force more often. This trend is not about to disappear, as evidenced by the rising number of young, professional stay-at-home moms who have "opted out" of the very game their mothers once scrambled to join. In addition, despite rising levels of education and professional attainment, women as a group still have lower wages and lower-level jobs than men have.

At the same time, women live longer than men, which means they have a longer retirement to prepare for with fewer resources.

"While women have entered the labor force in record numbers, their ability to retire is simply not based on access to a pension," said Teresa Heinz Kerry, chairwoman of the Heinz Family Philanthropies and founder of the Women's Institute for a Secure Retirement. "For too many women today, the costs of caring for aging parents, as well as grandparents, adult children and grandchildren, are making retirement a myth, not a reality."

The signs are not good: 83 percent of U.S. women postponed retirement to save more money, compared with 48 percent of men. And women, more than two to one over men, postponed retirement to maximize Social Security benefits, according to a new survey on retirement by Prudential.

At the same time, women control a growing share of the world's wealth—a fact that financial services companies have begun to exploit.

Source: Excerpted from "Women Taking Charge of Retirement Purse Strings, Sort of," by Erika Kinetz, *International Herald Tribune,* July 2, 2005. Available online. URL: http://www.womenandco.com/womenandco/homepage/iht0705.htm. Accessed January 6, 2006.

Presentation to the Third Committee of the Secretary-General's In-depth Study on Violence Against Women (October 9, 2006).

The then-secretary-general Kofi Annan addressed all forms of violence against women at the United Nations.

The first point I wish to underscore is that violence against women is both a cause and a consequence of **discrimination against women.** In many countries, discriminatory customs and traditions that perpetuate or condone violence against women are allowed to persist, sometimes despite legislation outlawing such practices. And discriminatory attitudes and stereotypes that view violence against women, particularly domestic violence, as a private matter that is acceptable, remain common.

Efforts to prevent and ultimately end violence against women must therefore be systematically grounded in the work of all States and other actors to eliminate discrimination against women and promote women's enjoyment of all their human rights and fundamental freedoms. Let me stress here the particularly important role of local communities—and families—in awareness-raising and education. Men have a role, especially in preventing violence, and this role needs to be further explored and strengthened. And our youth need to learn from their elders—from what we say and especially from what we do; from men as well as women; at home, at school, through our communications networks, and in the wider public domain—that women and men are equal and that violence against women is fundamentally wrong.

The most common of the **forms of violence** against women is intimate partner violence, sometimes leading to death. Certain harmful traditional practices are also widespread, including early and forced marriage and female genital mutilation. Gender-based murder of women, sexual violence, sexual harassment, and trafficking in women are receiving increasing attention. Violence perpetrated by States, through their agents, through omission or through the implications of public policies, spans physical, sexual, and psychological violence. And the high incidence of violence against women in armed conflict, particularly sexual violence including rape, has been clearly documented in several cases.

It is one of the great successes of grass-roots women's organizations and movements around the world that the challenge of violence against women was drawn out of the private domain into public attention and the arena of State accountability. And these advocates continue to push for more "visibility" of the effects of policies and socio-economic practices on women.

The study shows that international attention to violence against women has grown significantly in the last twenty years—and particularly since 1995, when the Beijing Platform for Action called for improved **research and data collection** on different forms of violence against women. In some areas, notable progress has been made in this regard. Intimate partner violence is an example. We now have 71 countries in which at least one survey has been conducted on the subject. And a national survey has been conducted in at least 41 countries. These are complemented by research studies on specific issues or aspects that provide evidence on the scope of particular forms of violence, as well as its consequences and costs, for women, their families, communities, and countries. In general, occurrences of acts of violence against women are well documented, including by advocacy organizations and service providers.

Nonetheless, the available evidence remains uneven and, in many cases, non-existent. As also underscored by our report, The World's Women 2005: Progress in Statistics, we continue to face serious research and data gaps, particularly on forms other than intimate partner violence, including trafficking in women and girls and violence against women by agents of the State. As the Secretary-General's study before you shows, information to assess and evaluate what policies and practices are most effective in addressing violence against women is particularly scarce. The study presents a range of information on specific countries, but this is not to suggest that countries going unmentioned are free from violence against women. It simply means that the information is not available, which should itself be seen as a major cause for concern. Ensuring adequate data collection is part of every State's obligation to address violence against women, yet inadequate data does not diminish that responsibility.

Now is the time to strengthen the knowledge base about the scope and extent of violence against women, as well as the impact of policies and practices that are in place so that resources to address this scourge can be used most effectively. This must include efforts to collect data systematically on the most common forms of violence. We also need to strengthen data collection and knowledge on forms that affect relatively few women overall but have a devastating effect on those concerned, or on new or emerging forms of violence, including economic violence and abuse, stalking, and violence through use of the Internet or cell phones.

The study makes a number of recommendations for action in this area, including developing a set of international indicators for assessing the prevalence of violence against women and the impact of different interventions. As in many other areas of work, this will not be possible unless the international community seriously steps up its support—technical, material, and financial—for strengthening national statistical systems in developing countries, as part of their broader capacity to monitor and evaluate progress in meeting their development goals.

The global attention to violence against women has also resulted in a comprehensive **international legal and policy framework** for addressing violence against women. Yet, States are failing in their responsibility to implement this framework fully at the national level. An example is the field of legislation. Only about half of Member States have some legislative provisions that specifically address domestic violence. Fewer than half have legislation on sexual harassment or on trafficking. And even where such legislation exists, there are often inadequacies in scope and coverage, such as definitions of domestic violence limited to physical violence or penal laws that discriminate against women. Or there are serious gaps in implementation, shown, for example, in the lack of regulations to implement legislation, the lack of clear procedures for law enforcement and health-care professionals, or the lack of legal aid, especially for indigent women.

Source: Excerpted from "Presentation to the Third Committee of the Secretary-General's In-depth Study on Violence Against Women." Available online. URL: http://www.un.org/esa/desa/ousg/statements/2006/20061009_ ga61_3rd.html. Accessed December 16, 2006.

INTERNATIONAL TREATIES

International Agreement for the Suppression of the "White Slave Traffic" (May 18, 1904)

The following international agreement signed on May 18, 1904, in Paris, France, and entered into force July 18, 1905, with oversight by the French Republic, is one of the first documented attempts by an international body to deal with human trafficking, specifically of women and children. A protocol later amended the agreement at Lake Success, New York, in May 1949, when responsibilities were shifted to the newly founded United Nations and its attorney-general.

Being desirous of securing to women of full age who have suffered abuse or compulsion, as also to women and girls under age, effective protection against the criminal traffic known as the "White Slave Traffic," have decided to conclude an Agreement with a view to concerting measures calculated to attain this object, and have appointed as their Plenipotentiaries, that is to say:

Who, having exchanged their full powers, found in good and due form, have agreed upon the following provisions:

Article 1

Each of the Contracting Governments undertakes to establish or name some authority charged with the coordination of all information relative to the procuring of women or girls for immoral purposes abroad; this authority shall be empowered to correspond direct with the similar department established in each of the other Contracting States.

Article 2

Each of the Governments undertakes to have a watch kept, especially in railway stations, ports of embarkation, and en route, for persons in charge of women and girls destined for an immoral life. With this object instructions shall be given to the officials, and all other qualified persons, to obtain, within legal limits, all information likely to lead to the detection of criminal traffic.

The arrival of persons who clearly appear to be the principals, accomplices in, or victims of, such traffic shall be notified, when it occurs, either to the authorities of the place of destination, or to the diplomatic or consular agents interested, or to any other competent authorities.

Article 3

The Governments undertake, when the case arises, and within legal limits, to have the declarations taken of women or girls of foreign nationality who are prostitutes, in order to establish their identity and civil status, and to discover who has caused them to leave their country. The information obtained shall be communicated to the authorities of the country of origin of the said women and girls, with a view to their eventual repatriation.

The Governments undertake, within legal limits, and as far as can be done, to entrust temporarily, and with a view to their eventual repatriation, the victims of a criminal traffic when destitute to public or private charitable institutions, or to private individuals offering the necessary security.

The Governments also undertake, within legal limits, and as far as possible, to send back to their country of origin those women and girls who desire it, or who may be claimed by persons exercising authority over them. Repatriation shall only take place after agreement as to identity and nationality, as well as place and date of arrival at the frontiers. Each of the Contracting Countries shall facilitate transit through its territory.

Correspondence relative to repatriation shall be direct as far as possible.

Article 4

Where the woman or girl to be repatriated cannot herself repay the cost of transfer, and has neither husband, relations, nor guardian to pay for her, the cost of repatriation shall be borne by the country where she is in residence as far as the nearest frontier or port of embarkation in the direction of the country of origin, and by the country of origin as regards the rest.

Source: Excerpted from "International Agreement for the Suppression of the White Slave Traffic," by the United Nations. Available online. URL: http://www1.umn.edu/humanrts/instree/whiteslavetraffic1904.html. Accessed April 29, 2006.

The Universal Declaration of Human Rights (1948)

After World War II and the founding of the United Nations as a mediator for world peace, the U.S. delegate, Eleanor Roosevelt, chaired the newly formed UN Commission on Human Rights in June 1946. The horrors of the Nuremberg trials of Nazi war criminals and recent war experiences fueled the involvement of several countries and international nongovernmental organizations in the process of defining human rights and championing human dignity. Adopted by the General Assembly on December 10, 1948, without dissent upon presentation by Eleanor Roosevelt, the declaration established human rights standards and norms. Although the declaration was intended to be nonbinding, through time its various provisions have become so respected by states that it can now be said to be customary international law. Eleanor Roosevelt's words resounded: "The destiny of human rights is in the hands of all our citizens in all our communities."

Whereas the peoples of the United Nations have in the Charter reaffirmed their faith in fundamental human rights, in the dignity and worth of the human person and in the equal rights of men and women and have determined to promote social progress and better standards of life in larger freedom,

Whereas Member States have pledged themselves to achieve, in cooperation with the United Nations, the promotion of universal respect for and observance of human rights and fundamental freedoms,

200

Whereas a common understanding of these rights and freedoms is of the greatest importance for the full realization of this pledge,

Now, therefore,

The General Assembly proclaims

This Universal Declaration of Human Rights

as a common standard of achievement for all peoples and all nations, to the end that every individual and every organ of society, keeping this Declaration constantly in mind, shall strive by teaching and education to promote respect for these rights and freedoms and by progressive measures, national and international, to secure their universal and effective recognition and observance, both among the peoples of Member States themselves and among the peoples of territories under their jurisdiction.

Article 2

Everyone is entitled to all the rights and freedoms set forth in this Declaration, without distinction of any kind, such as race, colour, sex, language, religion, political or other opinion, national or social origin, property, birth or other status.

Furthermore, no distinction shall be made on the basis of the political, jurisdictional or international status of the country or territory to which a person belongs, whether it be independent, trust, non-self-governing or under any other limitation of sovereignty.

Article 3

Everyone has the right to life, liberty and security of person.

Article 4

No one shall be held in slavery or servitude; slavery and the slave trade shall be prohibited in all their forms.

Article 5

No one shall be subjected to torture or to cruel, inhuman or degrading treatment or punishment.

Article 6

Everyone has the right to recognition everywhere as a person before the law.

Article 7

All are equal before the law and are entitled without any discrimination to equal protection of the law. All are entitled to equal protection against any discrimination in violation of this Declaration and against any incitement to such discrimination. . . .

Article 16

(1) Men and women of full age, without any limitation due to race, nationality or religion, have the right to marry and to found a family.

They are entitled to equal rights as to marriage, during marriage and at its dissolution.

(2) Marriage shall be entered into only with the free and full consent of the intending spouses.

(3) The family is the natural and fundamental group unit of society and is entitled to protection by society and the State.

Article 17

(1) Everyone has the right to own property alone as well as in association with others.

(2) No one shall be arbitrarily deprived of his property.

Source: Excerpted from "The Universal Declaration of Human Rights," by the United Nations. Available online. URL: http://www.udhr.org/UDHR/default.htm. Accessed December 22, 2005.

Inter-American Convention on the Granting of Civil Rights to Women (1948)

Established in 1928, the Inter-American Commission of Women (CIM) was the first intergovernmental agency to defend civil and political rights of women in the Americas. This convention was signed at the Ninth International Conference of American States in Bogotá, Colombia, March 30–May 2, 1948.

That the majority of the American Republics, inspired by lofty principles of justice, have granted civil rights to women;

That it has been a constant aspiration of the American community of nations to equalize the status for men and women in the enjoyment and exercise of civil rights;

That Resolution XX of the Eighth International Conference of American States expressly declares:

"That women have the right to the enjoyment of equality as to civil status";

That long before the women of America demanded their rights they were able to carry out nobly all their responsibilities side by side with men;

That the principle of equality of human rights for men and women is contained in the Charter of the United Nations,

Have Resolved:

To authorize their respective Representatives, whose Full Powers have been found to be in good and due form, to sign the following articles:

Article 1. The American States agree to grant to women the same civil rights that men enjoy.

Article 2. The present Convention shall be open for signature by the American States and shall be ratified in accordance with their respective constitutional procedures. The original instrument, the Spanish, English, Portuguese and French texts of which are equally authentic, shall be deposited with the General Secretariat of the Organization of American States, which shall transmit certified copies to the Governments for the purpose of ratification. The instruments of ratification shall be deposited with the General Secretariat of the Organization of American States, which shall notify the signatory governments of the said deposit. Such notification shall serve as an exchange of ratifications.

Source: Excerpted from "Inter-American Convention on the Granting of Civil Rights to Women," by the Organization for American States. Available online. URL: http://www.oas.org/CIM/english/Convention%20Civil%20Rights.htm. Accessed July 5, 2006.

The International Convention on the Elimination of All Forms of Racial Discrimination (1969)

This convention is considered to be one of the oldest and most widely ratified United Nations human rights instruments. The convention was adopted and opened for signature and ratification by General Assembly resolution 2106 (XX) of December 21, 1965, and entered into force January 4, 1969. In addition to identifying the obligations of state parties, the convention established the Committee on the Elimination of Racial Discrimination, which became the first body created by the United Nations to monitor and review actions by states to fulfill their obligations under a specific human rights agreement.

The States Parties to this Convention,

Considering that the Charter of the United Nations is based on the principles of the dignity and equality inherent in all human beings, and that all Member States have pledged themselves to take joint and separate action, in co-operation with the Organization, for the achievement of one of the purposes of the United Nations which is to promote and encourage universal respect for and observance of human rights and fundamental freedoms for all, without distinction as to race, sex, language or religion,

Considering that the Universal Declaration of Human Rights proclaims that all human beings are born free and equal in dignity and rights and that everyone is entitled to all the rights and freedoms set out therein, without distinction of any kind, in particular as to race, colour or national origin,

Considering that all human beings are equal before the law and are entitled to equal protection of the law against any discrimination and against any incitement to discrimination,

Considering that the United Nations has condemned colonialism and all practices of segregation and discrimination associated therewith, in whatever form and wherever they exist, and that the Declaration on the Granting of Independence to Colonial Countries and Peoples of 14 December 1960 (General Assembly resolution 1514 (XV)) has affirmed and solemnly proclaimed the necessity of bringing them to a speedy and unconditional end,

Considering that the United Nations Declaration on the Elimination of All Forms of Racial Discrimination of 20 November 1963 (General Assembly resolution 1904 (XVIII)) solemnly affirms the necessity of speedily eliminating racial discrimination throughout the world in all its forms and manifestations and of securing understanding of and respect for the dignity of the human person,

Convinced that any doctrine of superiority based on racial differentiation is scientifically false, morally condemnable, socially unjust and dangerous, and that there is no justification for racial discrimination, in theory or in practice, anywhere,

Reaffirming that discrimination between human beings on the grounds of race, colour or ethnic origin is an obstacle to friendly and peaceful relations among nations and is capable of disturbing peace and security among peoples and the harmony of persons living side by side even within one and the same State,

Convinced that the existence of racial barriers is repugnant to the ideals of any human society,

Alarmed by manifestations of racial discrimination still in evidence in some areas of the world and by governmental policies based on racial superiority or hatred, such as policies of apartheid, segregation or separation,

Resolved to adopt all necessary measures for speedily eliminating racial discrimination in all its forms and manifestations, and to prevent and combat racist doctrines and practices in order to promote understanding between races and to build an international community free from all forms of racial segregation and racial discrimination,

Bearing in mind the Convention concerning Discrimination in respect of Employment and Occupation adopted by the International Labour Organisation in 1958, and the Convention against Discrimination in Education adopted by the United Nations Educational, Scientific and Cultural Organization in 1960,

Desiring to implement the principles embodied in the United Nations Declaration on the Elimination of All Forms of Racial Discrimination and to secure the earliest adoption of practical measures to that end.

Source: Excerpted from "The International Convention on the Elimination of All Forms of Racial Discrimination," by the United Nations. Available online. URL: http://www.unhchr.ch/html/menu3/b/d_icerd.htm. Accessed July 5, 2006.

UN Convention on the Elimination of All Forms of Discrimination against Women (CEDAW) (1981)

CEDAW was adopted in 1979 and entered into force September 3, 1981. It became the first legally binding international document prohibiting discrimination against women and obligating governments to take affirmative steps to advance the equality of women. A group of over 190 national nongovernmental organizations engaged in outreach and education in December 1979 to eliminate discrimination against women. Often referred to as "The Treaty for the Rights of Women" or as an international "Bill of Rights" for women, the treaty in its preamble and 30 articles defines what constitutes discrimination against women in the form of sex trafficking, illiteracy, maternal mortality, HIV/AIDS exposure, domestic violence, political and legal rights, and FGM. It also includes in it provisions that set up an agenda for national action to end such discrimination. The treaty required regular progress reports from ratifying countries, but it did not impose any changes in existing laws or require new laws of countries ratifying the treaty. It laid out models for achieving equality but contained no enforcement authority. The treaty still awaits ratification by the United States, although it has been ratified by 179 other nations, including Afghanistan, Denmark, China, and Kenya. The treaty is awaiting approval by a two-thirds vote in the U.S. Senate (67 votes of 100 senators). Ratification does not require consideration by the House of Representatives. The treaty is in the Senate Foreign Relations Committee, where it has been awaiting the Bush administration's and Justice Department's review, having received endorsement from the State Department stating that it is "generally desirable and should be ratified." Over 190 U.S. religious, civic, and community organizations have shown support, including the American Association of Retired Persons (AARP), American Nurses Association, National Education Association, National Coalition of Catholic Nuns, American Bar Association, United Methodist Church, Young Women's Christian Association (YWCA), and Amnesty International.

The States Parties to the present Convention,

Noting that the Charter of the United Nations reaffirms faith in fundamental human rights, in the dignity and worth of the human person and in the equal rights of men and women,

Noting that the Universal Declaration of Human Rights affirms the principle of the inadmissibility of discrimination and proclaims that all human beings are born free and equal in dignity and rights and that everyone is entitled to all the rights and freedoms set forth therein, without distinction of any kind, including distinction based on sex,

Noting that the States Parties to the International Covenants on Human Rights have the obligation to ensure the equal rights of men and women to enjoy all economic, social, cultural, civil and political rights,

Considering the international conventions concluded under the auspices of the United Nations and the specialized agencies promoting equality of rights of men and women,

Noting also the resolutions, declarations and recommendations adopted by the United Nations and the specialized agencies promoting equality of rights of men and women,

Concerned, however, that despite these various instruments extensive discrimination against women continues to exist,

Recalling that discrimination against women violates the principles of equality of rights and respect for human dignity, is an obstacle to the participation of women, on equal terms with men, in the political, social, economic and cultural life of their countries, hampers the growth of the prosperity of society and the family and makes more difficult the full development of the potentialities of women in the service of their countries and of humanity,

Concerned that in situations of poverty women have the least access to food, health, education, training and opportunities for employment and other needs,

Convinced that the establishment of the new international economic order based on equity and justice will contribute significantly towards the promotion of equality between men and women,

Emphasizing that the eradication of apartheid, all forms of racism, racial discrimination, colonialism, neo-colonialism, aggression, foreign occupation and domination and interference in the internal affairs of States is essential to the full enjoyment of the rights of men and women,

Affirming that the strengthening of international peace and security, the relaxation of international tension, mutual co-operation among all States irrespective of their social and economic systems, general and complete disarmament, in particular nuclear disarmament under strict and effective international control, the affirmation of the principles of justice, equality and mutual benefit in relations among countries and the realization of the right of peoples under alien and colonial domination and foreign occupation to self-determination and independence, as well as respect for national sovereignty and territorial integrity, will promote social progress and development and as a consequence will contribute to the attainment of full equality between men and women,

Convinced that the full and complete development of a country, the welfare of the world and the cause of peace require the maximum participation of women on equal terms with men in all fields,

Bearing in mind the great contribution of women to the welfare of the family and to the development of society, so far not fully recognized, the social significance of maternity and the role of both parents in the family and in the upbringing of children, and aware that the role of women in procreation should not be a basis for discrimination but that the upbringing of children requires a sharing of responsibility between men and women and society as a whole,

Aware that a change in the traditional role of men as well as the role of women in society and in the family is needed to achieve full equality between men and women,

Determined to implement the principles set forth in the Declaration on the Elimination of Discrimination against Women and, for that purpose, to adopt the measures required for the elimination of such discrimination in all its forms and manifestations, . . .

Source: Excerpted from "Convention on the Elimination of All Forms of Discrimination against Women," by the United Nations. Available online. URL: http://www.un.org/womenwatch/daw/cedaw. Accessed May 4, 2006.

Beijing Declaration and Platform for Action (1995)

Presented and agreed to at the United Nations's fourth world conference on women in Beijing, China, in 1995, the Beijing Declaration and Platform for Action symbolized an international plan for the 189 participating governments who adopted the statement for achieving women's rights and empowerment and served as an agenda for the next 20 years. The declaration identified 12 specific directives for international organizations, national organizations and institutions, and governments to achieve the commitments of the Beijing Declaration, with poverty, education and training, health, and violence against women top priorities. The countries acknowledged that dealing with the issues of violence against women, reproductive control, and poverty was key to progress. The Platform for Action made the public aware of the important economic role that women workers play, including domestic workers, who contribute their remittance to the economy of their countries of origin and participate in the labor force of the country of destination. The participating governments are now held accountable for their follow-up actions by submitting yearly reports to the United Nations and providing international cooperation among agencies.

1. We, the Governments, participating in the Fourth World Conference on Women,

2. Gathered here in Beijing, in September 1995, the year of the fiftieth anniversary of the founding of the United Nations,

3. Determined to advance the goals of equality, development and peace for all women everywhere in the interest of all humanity,

4. Acknowledging the voices of all women everywhere and taking note of the diversity of women and their roles and circumstances, honouring the women who paved the way and inspired by the hope present in the world's youth,

5. Recognize that the status of women has advanced in some important respects in the past decade but that progress has been uneven, inequalities between women and men have persisted and major obstacles remain, with serious consequences for the well-being of all people,

6. Also recognize that this situation is exacerbated by the increasing poverty that is affecting the lives of the majority of the world's people, in particular women and children, with origins in both the national and international domains,

7. Dedicate ourselves unreservedly to addressing these constraints and obstacles and thus enhancing further the advancement and empowerment of women all over the world, and agree that this requires urgent action in the spirit of determination, hope, cooperation and solidarity, now and to carry us forward into the next century. . . .

Chapter III

CRITICAL AREAS OF CONCERN

43. The advancement of women and the achievement of equality between women and men are a matter of human rights and a condition for social justice and should not be seen in isolation as a women's issue. They are the only way to build a sustainable, just and developed society. Empowerment of women and equality between women and men are prerequisites for achieving political, social, economic, cultural and environmental security among all peoples.

44. Most of the goals set out in the Nairobi Forward-looking Strategies for the Advancement of Women have not been achieved. Barriers to

women's empowerment remain, despite the efforts of Governments, as well as non-governmental organizations and women and men everywhere. Vast political, economic and ecological crises persist in many parts of the world. Among them are wars of aggression, armed conflicts, colonial or other forms of alien domination or foreign occupation, civil wars and terrorism. These situations, combined with systematic or de facto discrimination, violations of and failure to protect all human rights and fundamental freedoms of all women, and their civil, cultural, economic, political and social rights, including the right to development and ingrained prejudicial attitudes towards women and girls are but a few of the impediments encountered since the World Conference to Review and Appraise the Achievements of the United Nations Decade for Women: Equality, Development and Peace, in 1985.

45. A review of progress since the Nairobi Conference highlights special concerns—areas of particular urgency that stand out as priorities for action. All actors should focus action and resources on the strategic objectives relating to the critical areas of concern which are, necessarily, interrelated, interdependent and of high priority. There is a need for these actors to develop and implement mechanisms of accountability for all the areas of concern.

46. To this end, Governments, the international community and civil society, including non-governmental organizations and the private sector, are called upon to take strategic action in the following critical areas of concern:

—The persistent and increasing burden of poverty on women

—Inequalities and inadequacies in and unequal access to education and training

—Inequalities and inadequacies in and unequal access to health care and related services

—Violence against women

—The effects of armed or other kinds of conflict on women, including those living under foreign occupation

—Inequality in economic structures and policies, in all forms of productive activities and in access to resources

—Inequality between men and women in the sharing of power and decision-making at all levels

—Insufficient mechanisms at all levels to promote the advancement of women

—Lack of respect for and inadequate promotion and protection of the human rights of women

—Stereotyping of women and inequality in women's access to and participation in all communication systems, especially in the media

—Gender inequalities in the management of natural resources and in the safeguarding of the environment

—Persistent discrimination against and violation of the rights of the girl child

Source: Excerpted from "Beijing Declaration and Platform for Action," by the United Nations. Available online. URL: http://www.un.org/geninfo/bp/women.html. Accessed March 27, 2006.

The October 2000 UN Resolution 1325 on Women, Peace and Security

On October 31, 2000, the United Nations Security Council unanimously adopted Resolution 1325 on women, peace, and security. Resolution 1325 represented the first time the Security Council addressed the disproportionate and unique impact of armed conflict on women; recognized the undervalued and underutilized contributions women make to conflict prevention, peace-keeping, conflict resolution, and peace building; and stressed the importance of their equal and full participation as active agents in peace and security.

The Security Council,

Recalling its resolutions 1261 (1999) of 25 August 1999, 1265 (1999) of 17 September 1999, 1296 (2000) of 19 April 2000 and 1314 (2000) of 11 August 2000,

as well as relevant statements of its President, and recalling also the statement of its President to the press on the occasion of the United Nations Day for Women's Rights and International Peace (International Women's Day) of 8 March 2000 (SC/6816),

Recalling also the commitments of the Beijing Declaration and Platform for Action (A/52/231) as well as those contained in the outcome document of the twenty-third Special Session of the United Nations General Assembly entitled "Women 2000: Gender Equality, Development and Peace for the Twenty-First Century" (A/S-23/10/Rev.1), in particular those concerning women and armed conflict,

Bearing in mind the purposes and principles of the Charter of the United Nations and the primary responsibility of the Security Council under the Charter for the maintenance of international peace and security,

Expressing concern that civilians, particularly women and children, account for the vast majority of those adversely affected by armed conflict, including as refugees and internally displaced persons, and increasingly are targeted by combatants and armed elements, and recognizing the consequent impact this has on durable peace and reconciliation,

Reaffirming the important role of women in the prevention and resolution of conflicts and in peace-building, and stressing the importance of their equal participation and full involvement in all efforts for the maintenance and promotion of peace and security, and the need to increase their role in decision-making with regard to conflict prevention and resolution,

Reaffirming also the need to implement fully international humanitarian and human rights law that protects the rights of women and girls during and after conflicts,

Emphasizing the need for all parties to ensure that mine clearance and mine awareness programmes take into account the special needs of women and girls,

Recognizing the urgent need to mainstream a gender perspective into peacekeeping operations, and in this regard noting the Windhoek Declaration and the Namibia Plan of Action on Mainstreaming a Gender Perspective in Multidimensional Peace Support Operations

Recognizing also the importance of the recommendation contained in the statement of its President to the press of 8 March 2000 for specialized training for all peacekeeping personnel on the protection, special needs and human rights of women and children in conflict situations,

Recognizing that an understanding of the impact of armed conflict on women and girls, effective institutional arrangements to guarantee their protection and full participation in the peace process can significantly contribute to the maintenance and promotion of international peace and security,

Noting the need to consolidate data on the impact of armed conflict on women and girls,

1. Urges Member States to ensure increased representation of women at all decision-making levels in national, regional and international institutions and mechanisms for the prevention, management, and resolution of conflict;

2. Encourages the Secretary-General to implement his strategic plan of action (A/49/587) calling for an increase in the participation of women at decision making levels in conflict resolution and peace processes;

3. Urges the Secretary-General to appoint more women as special representatives and envoys to pursue good offices on his behalf, and in this regard calls on Member States to provide candidates to the Secretary-General, for inclusion in a regularly updated centralized roster;

4. Further urges the Secretary-General to seek to expand the role and contribution of women in United Nations field-based operations, and

especially among military observers, civilian police, human rights and humanitarian personnel;

5. Expresses its willingness to incorporate a gender perspective into peacekeeping operations, and urges the Secretary-General to ensure that, where appropriate, field operations include a gender component;

6. Requests the Secretary-General to provide to Member States training guidelines and materials on the protection, rights and the particular needs of women, as well as on the importance of involving women in all peacekeeping and peacebuilding measures, invites Member States to incorporate these elements as well as HIV/AIDS awareness training into their national training programmes for military and civilian police personnel in preparation for deployment, and further requests the Secretary-General to ensure that civilian personnel of peacekeeping operations receive similar training;

7. Urges Member States to increase their voluntary financial, technical and logistical support for gender-sensitive training efforts, including those undertaken by relevant funds and programmes, inter alia, the United Nations Fund for Women and United Nations Children's Fund, and by the Office of the United Nations High Commissioner for Refugees and other relevant bodies;

8. Calls on all actors involved, when negotiating and implementing peace agreements, to adopt a gender perspective, including, inter alia:

(a) The special needs of women and girls during repatriation and resettlement and for rehabilitation, reintegration and post-conflict reconstruction;

(b) Measures that support local women's peace initiatives and indigenous processes for conflict resolution, and that involve women in all of the implementation mechanisms of the peace agreements;

(c) Measures that ensure the protection of and respect for human rights of women and girls, particularly as they relate to the constitution, the electoral system, the police and the judiciary;

9. Calls upon all parties to armed conflict to respect fully international law applicable to the rights and protection of women and girls, especially as civilians, in particular the obligations applicable to them under the Geneva Conventions of 1949 and the Additional Protocols thereto of 1977, the Refugee Convention of 1951 and the Protocol thereto of 1967, the Convention on the Elimination of All Forms of Discrimination against Women of 1979 and the Optional Protocol thereto of 1999 and the United Nations Convention on the Rights of the Child of 1989 and the two Optional Protocols thereto of 25 May 2000, and to bear in mind the relevant provisions of the Rome Statute of the International Criminal Court;

10. Calls on all parties to armed conflict to take special measures to protect women and girls from gender-based violence, particularly rape and other forms of sexual abuse, and all other forms of violence in situations of armed conflict;

11. Emphasizes the responsibility of all States to put an end to impunity and to prosecute those responsible for genocide, crimes against humanity, and war crimes including those relating to sexual and other violence against women and girls, and in this regard stresses the need to exclude these crimes, where feasible from amnesty provisions;

12. Calls upon all parties to armed conflict to respect the civilian and humanitarian character of refugee camps and settlements, and to take into account the particular needs of women and girls, including in their design, and recalls its resolutions 1208 (1998) of 19 November 1998 and 1296 (2000) of 19 April 2000;

13. Encourages all those involved in the planning for disarmament, demobilization and reintegration to consider the different needs of female and male ex-combatants and to take into account the needs of their dependants;

14. Reaffirms its readiness, whenever measures are adopted under Article 41 of the Charter of the United Nations, to give consideration to their potential impact on the civilian population, bearing in mind the special needs of women and girls, in order to consider appropriate humanitarian exemptions;

15. Expresses its willingness to ensure that Security Council missions take into account gender considerations and the rights of women, including through consultation with local and international women's groups;

16. Invites the Secretary-General to carry out a study on the impact of armed conflict on women and girls, the role of women in peace-building and the gender dimensions of peace processes and conflict resolution, and further invites him to submit a report to the Security Council on the results of this study and to make this available to all Member States of the United Nations;

17. Requests the Secretary-General, where appropriate, to include in his reporting to the Security Council progress on gender mainstreaming throughout peacekeeping missions and all other aspects relating to women and girls;

18. Decides to remain actively seized of the matter.

Source: Excerpted from "United Nations Security Council Resolution 1325 On Women, Peace and Security," by the United Nations. Available online. URL: http://www.peacewomen.org/un/sc/1325.html. Accessed December 28, 2005.

2005 World Summit Outcome

The Millennium Declaration adopted by the General Assembly in 2000 was proof that world leaders recognized the link between poverty and gender inequality and acknowledged the central role of gender equality to combating poverty and hunger and stimulating sustainable development. By 2005, it had become clear that unless women's economic security is strengthened, progress toward the Millennium Development Goals would be limited. The following was presented in September 2005 at the convening of the General Assembly's 60th session.

Gender equality and empowerment of women

58. We remain convinced that progress for women is progress for all. We reaffirm that the full and effective implementation of the goals and objectives of the Beijing Declaration and Platform for Action and the outcome of the twenty-third special session of the General Assembly is an essential contribution to achieving the internationally agreed development goals, including those contained in the Millennium Declaration, and we resolve to promote gender equality and eliminate pervasive gender discrimination by:

Eliminating gender inequalities in primary and secondary education by the earliest possible date and at all educational levels by 2015;

Guaranteeing the free and equal right of women to own and inherit property and ensuring secure tenure of property and housing by women;

Ensuring equal access to reproductive health;

Promoting women's equal access to labour markets, sustainable employment and adequate labour protection;

Ensuring equal access of women to productive assets and resources, including land, credit and technology;

Eliminating all forms of discrimination and violence against women and the girl child, including by ending impunity and by ensuring the protection of civilians, in particular women and the girl child, during and after armed conflicts in accordance with the obligations of States under international humanitarian law and international human rights law;

Promoting increased representation of women in Government decisionmaking bodies, including through ensuring their equal opportunity to participate fully in the political process.

59. We recognize the importance of gender mainstreaming as a tool for achieving gender equality. To that end, we undertake to actively promote the mainstreaming of a gender perspective in the design, implementation, monitoring and evaluation of policies and programmes in all political, eco-

nomic and social spheres, and further undertake to strengthen the capabilities of the United Nations system in the area of gender. . . .

Rule of law

134. Recognizing the need for universal adherence to and implementation of the rule of law at both the national and international levels, we:

Reaffirm our commitment to the purposes and principles of the Charter and international law and to an international order based on the rule of law and international law, which is essential for peaceful coexistence and cooperation among States;

Support the annual treaty event;

Encourage States that have not yet done so to consider becoming parties to all treaties that relate to the protection of civilians;

Call upon States to continue their efforts to eradicate policies and practices that discriminate against women and to adopt laws and promote practices that protect the rights of women and promote gender equality.

Source: Excerpted from "2005 World Summit Outcome," by the United Nations. Available online. URL: http://www.un.org/summit2005/documents.html. Accessed November 14, 2005.

DENMARK

Denmark's Equal Status Act (1998)

This act consolidated the provisions of the Act on Equal Treatment of Men and Women as It Regards the Access to Employment and Maternity Leave (see Consolidation Act No. 875 of October 17, 1994) with the amendments following from Section 2 of Act No. 1111 of December 29, 1997. Act No. 213 was entered into force on April 3, 1998.

Part 1

1.—(1) For the purpose of this Act equal treatment of men and women means that no discrimination may take place on the ground of sex. This applies to both direct discrimination and indirect discrimination, in particular by reference to pregnancy or to marital or family status.

(2) The Act shall be without prejudice to provisions on protection of women, especially in connection with pregnancy or maternity, cf. part 3 of the Act.

(3) The provisions of this Act shall not apply to the extent that a similar obligation to equal treatment follows from a collective agreement, cf., however section 18 (2).

Part 2

Equal treatment of men and women

2. Any employer shall observe the principle of equal treatment of men and women in connection with recruitment, transfers and promotions.

3.—(1) Any employer who employs men and women shall treat them equally as regards access to vocational guidance, vocational training, vocational continued training and retraining.

(2) The obligation to observe the principle of equal treatment shall also apply to any person who undertakes guidance and training activities as mentioned in subsection (1).

4. Any employer who employs men and women shall treat them equally as regards working conditions. This shall also apply in connection with dismissal.

5.—(1) The obligation to observe the principle of equal treatment also applies to any person who lays down provisions and makes decisions concerning access to exercise activities on the basis of self-employment. This shall also apply to the establishment, organisation or extension of an enterprise and the taking-up or extension of any other form of self-employment, including the financing hereof.

(2) The obligation to observe the principle of equal treatment also applies to any person who lays down provisions and makes decisions concerning vocational training etc. and concerning the terms governing the performance of such activities.

6. No advertisement may state that persons of a specific sex are wanted or preferred in connection with recruitment or vocational training etc.

Part 3

Pregnancy, maternity and adoption

7.—(1) A female employee shall be entitled to absence from work due to pregnancy and maternity from the date estimated to be 4 weeks before the birth. After the birth the parents are entitled to absence from the work for a total period of 26 weeks. Up to 10 weeks of this total period can be taken by the father after the 14th week after the birth. The right to absence may only be used by one parent at a time. For a further period of up to 2 weeks after the 24th week after the birth the right to absence can only be used by the father.

(2) The mother of the child has a duty to absence for 2 weeks after the birth.

(3) The father of the child shall be entitled to absence for up to 2 weeks after the birth or reception of the child in the home or—as agreed with the employer—within the first 14 weeks after the birth. This right is independent of the right to absence under subsection (1) above.

(4) If the child is hospitalised, the right to absence under subsection (3) may be postponed, cf. section 10 (6).

(5) Furthermore, an employee has the right to absence from work in connection with pregnancy, maternity, and adoption in periods where the employee is entitled to daily cash benefits according to Part 7 of the Act on daily cash benefits in connection with sickness or birth.

(6) A female employee has the right to absence from work in connection with pregnancy examinations when these are to take place during working hours.

7a.—Periods during which the right to daily cash benefits is reduced or lapses under section 16a (1), (2), and (4) of the Act on daily cash benefits during sickness or birth because the employee has resumed work, are included in the calculation of the periods where the employee has the right to absence according to section 7.

8. The time during which the employee has been absent under section 7 shall be included in connection with calculation of seniority in the employment relationship. This provision shall not apply to pension questions.

9. An employer may not dismiss an employee for having put forward a claim to use the right to absence or for having been absent under section 7 or for any other reason related to pregnancy, maternity or adoption.

10.—(1) A female employee who uses her right to absence under section 7(1) shall within 8 weeks after the birth inform her employer of the date on which she intends to resume work.

(2) A male employee who uses his right to absence in connection with the birth or reception of the child in the home under section 7 (3) shall with a notice of 4 weeks inform his employer of the date on which he expects the absence to start and of the duration of the absence.

(3) A male employee who uses his right to absence under section 7(1) shall not later than 8 weeks after the birth inform the employer of the date of the start of the absence and its duration. A male employee who uses his right to absence under section 7(1) clause 5 shall not later than 14 weeks after the birth inform the employer of the date of the start of the absence and its duration.

(4) If the right to absence after the 14th week after the birth is shared between the parents so that the absence of the female employee falls in several periods, she shall in connection with the notice to the employer under section (1) above inform the employer of the date of commencement and the duration of later absences.

(5) In connection with absence by virtue of section 7 (5) adoptive parents shall, if the duration and time of the leave has not been fixed when the child is received, observe the time limits laid down in subsections (1) to (4).

(6) A female employee who uses the right to absence under section 7 (5) because the child is hospitalised within the first 26 weeks after the birth or reception in the home shall, without undue delay, inform her employer about the hospitalisation. At the same time, the male employee shall inform his employer hereof. The parents shall, without undue delay, inform their employers about the date on which the child is received in the home after the hospitalisation. If the child is received before notice has been given under subsections (1) to (4), the time limits shall be extended with the time during which the child has been hospitalised. If not, the notices given shall lapse and new notices shall be given within 2 weeks after the reception.

(7) An employee who uses the right to absence under section 7 (5) because the employee is subrogated to the other parent's entitlement to daily cash benefits shall, without undue delay, inform the employer hereof and of the duration of the absence.

Source: Excerpted from "Denmark's Equal Status Act," by NATLEX database, the International Labour Organization. Available online. URL: http://www.ilo.org/dyn/natlex/docs/WEBTEXT/51713/65154/E98DNK01.htm. Accessed December 23, 2005.

Gender Equality (Consolidation) Act (2002)

Mainstreaming gender equality into government practice and forums had become an important strategy in Denmark by the 21st century. The Consolidation Act No. 553 of July 2, 2002, was implemented to consolidate various laws from the past several years about gender equality.

Part 1

Purpose of the Act

1 The purpose of this Act is to promote gender equality, including equal integration, equal influence and equal opportunities in all functions in society on the basis of women's and men's equal status. The purpose of the Act is also to counteract direct and indirect discrimination on the ground of gender and to counteract sexual harassment.

Part 2

Prohibition against unequal treatment on the ground of gender (gender discrimination)

2(1) Women and men shall receive equal treatment by employers, authorities or organisations within the public administration and in connection with business and general activities. Any person whose rights under the first sentence are violated may be awarded compensation.

(2) The Minister for Gender Equality is authorised to lay down rules to the effect that certain specified business and general activities shall not be subject to subsection (1) above.

(3) Persons who have been exposed to sexual harassment within the scope of subsection (1) may be awarded compensation. In this connection, special importance shall be attached to whether a relationship of dependence existed between the person harassed and the harasser.

(4) The Act on Equal Treatment of Men and Women in respect of Employment and Maternity Leave etc., the Act on Equal Pay to Men and Women and the Act on Equal Treatment of Men and Women in relation to the Occupational Social Security Schemes shall apply to the areas covered by the said acts.

2 a(1) Where a person who considers that his or her rights have been violated, cf. section 2 hereof, establishes matters of fact indicating that such person has been discriminated against, directly or indirectly, the opposing party shall prove that the equal treatment principle has not been violated.

(2) Indirect discrimination means that a provision, a criterion or a practice, which seems to be neutral, places a considerably larger number of persons of one gender in an inferior position compared with the other gender, unless such provision, criterion or practice is appropriate and necessary and may be justified by objective non-gender related factors.

Measures to promote gender equality

3(1) Notwithstanding the provision of section 2 hereof, the responsible minister may within his area of responsibility permit measures for the promotion of gender equality aiming at preventing or compensating for unequal treatment on the ground of gender.

(2) The Minister for Gender Equality is authorised to lay down rules specifying the cases in which measures to promote gender equality may be taken without authorisation under subsection (1) above.

(3) Section 13 of the Act on Equal Treatment of Men and Women in respect of Employment and Maternity Leave etc. shall apply to the areas covered by the Act.

Part 3

Obligations of public authorities

4 Public authorities shall within their respective areas of responsibility seek to promote gender equality and incorporate gender equality in all planning and administration.

Reports on gender equality

5(1) Prior to 1 September of every second year, ministries, state institutions and state-owned undertakings shall prepare a report on gender equality. State institutions and state-owned undertakings shall prepare reports only if their number of employees exceeds 50.

(2) Such reports shall include information on:

(i) whether the ministry, the institution or the undertaking has formulated a policy on gender equality and if so, the detailed contents of such policy;

(ii) the gender distribution across job categories; and

(iii) any other matter deemed to be of importance for an evaluation of the efforts made by the ministry, the institution or the undertaking in respect of gender equality.

(3) The reports from the institutions and undertakings specified in subsection (1) above shall be submitted to the responsible minister.

(4) The responsible minister shall edit the said reports and submit an overall report accompanied by the individual reports to the Minister for Gender Equality not later than 1 November of the years in which such reports are prepared.

5 a(1) At least every second year, the local council and the county council shall submit a report on gender equality among local and county authority employees to their citizens. Such reports shall be subject to adoption by the local council and the county council.

(2) Such reports shall include information on:

(i) whether the local authority or the county authority has formulated a policy on gender equality and if so, the detailed contents of such policy;

(ii) the gender distribution across job categories; and

(iii) any other matter deemed to be of importance for the efforts made by the local authority or the county authority in respect of gender equality.

(3) The said reports shall be submitted to the Minister for Gender Equality not later than 1 September of the years in which such reports are prepared.

6 The Minister for Gender Equality is authorised to lay down rules in respect of the contents of the reports set out in section 5(1) and section 5 a hereof.

7(1) Prior to 1 March of each year, the Minister for Gender Equality shall submit a report and a perspective and action plan for gender equality to Folketinget (the Danish Parliament).

(2) Public authorities, undertakings and organisations shall upon request submit to the Minister for Gender Equality the information on gender equality which is necessary for the preparation of the annual report and the perspective and action plan.

Source: Excerpted from "Gender Equality (Consolidation) Act," by the Ministry of Social Affairs in Denmark, Social. dk. Available online. URL: http://eng.social.dk/index.aspx?id=6b4eeb6e-37a7-42a5-96e5-1e10b43c0771. Accessed August 29, 2006.

Comments of the Danish Women's Society on the Sixth Periodic Report by the Government of Denmark on the Implementation of the CEDAW Convention (2004)

Because accountability is a vital aspect of implementing strategies and causing reform, the Danish Women's Society (DWS) has taken to publishing its observations of how effectively the international CEDAW treaty is being implemented in their own country.

The Danish Women's Society (DWS) appreciates the opportunity to comment on the Danish Government's Report on the Implementation of the CEDAW Convention. As we find the National Report in general a fair and comprehensive description of the position of women in Denmark and the policies and measures implemented to ensure gender equality, our comments will be limited to the following points.

Article 2: Constitution and Legislation

Since 1991 DWS has worked to make the CEDAW Convention known to the general public as an important tool for equality work. We are therefore pleased that the Government has published a manual on how to use the UN complaint procedures, including the Optional Protocol. Women cannot gain their rights if they have no knowledge of their existence.

Article 3: National Policy

Likewise, DWS would like to commend the Government on its establishment of a new website where reports on the work of local and national institutions for gender equality can be found. This visible and easy access will facilitate the monitoring work of NGOs.

We are also happy to see that the fears we expressed in our comments to the fifth periodic report that women's core issues of concern might be lost in the process of mainstreaming gender equality have been addressed. The Government's two-pronged approach, i.e. gender mainstreaming supplemented by a focus on key action areas requiring specific government attention, is essential.

Article 4: Equality Bodies and Temporary Measures

NGOs

The report acknowledges that the official Danish gender equality work benefits from the fact that these activities are widely realised in close cooperation and dialogue with NGOs and experts in the fields. The Government is to be commended for these efforts to involve NGOs in its work for the advancement of women.

However, as we did in the fifth periodic report, DWS would like to call attention to the fact that the work done by most NGOs in Denmark is done on a volunteer basis. This is work that, although voluntary, must be as professional as possible to have impact. This is becoming increasingly difficult for women's organisations today. Most Danish women are working full-time or more in a combination of labour market and family obligations. They have little time for volunteer work.

In addition, the costs of operating a women's organisation today are increasing. The Government has recently removed support to NGOs for postage costs, for example, and it is nearly impossible to raise funds for international networking such as participation in international conferences. These considerations are particularly important in light of the fact that many people mistakenly think that women's rights at home and abroad are now won—forever. Experience tells us that continual monitoring of rights won is necessary if we are to maintain them—and not all rights are as yet guaranteed for all women. Therefore this situation must be acknowledged and appropriate financial assistance provided to women's organisations, not only for specific activities but also for daily administrative costs if we are to continue our efforts to ensure further advancements for women both in Denmark and internationally.

Article 5: Priorities

DWS finds the priorities of the Government for 2000–2004 relevant and important. We have the following comments.

Gender mainstreaming

DWS finds that the work regarding gender mainstreaming at ministerial level is excellent. In particular, we would like to commend the efforts of the Department of Gender Equality to train other ministries and the electronic toolbox of methodologies, good practice examples and relevant literature which will be made available at the Ministry's website.

No mention is made of similar special efforts to train local and regional institutions, but DWS hopes that they will make good use of the electronic toolbox and that the Ministry will keep a watchful eye on developments locally and regionally.

International cooperation

While we agree with the Danish government strategy to promote gender equality in rights, access to and control over resources and access to political and economic influence as fundamental starting points for the advancement of women in Danish development cooperation, we would like to stress the importance of consulting with women's organisations in the countries concerned. The overall sector program support approach used by most donor agencies today, including Danish development assistance, tends to place the development dialogue in the ministerial arena. Unfortunately not all ministries/governments represent the true interests of their women populace. Other viewpoints are essential if women's real concerns are to be addressed.

Youth and gender

DWS is well aware of young people's lack of knowledge regarding the long and difficult process to gain the rights they now enjoy and their lack of awareness of the importance of these rights for their lives. Therefore we are particularly pleased with the work the Government is doing in the area of youth and gender.

Targeted integration

Gender equality as a theme in Danish language teaching for ethnic minorities is a good step forward and the issues used for teaching material mentioned in the report are relevant. DWS would like to suggest that the CEDAW Convention and women's rights should also be a topic for such teaching material. In 1999 DWS held a seminar for teachers of Danish language for immigrant women in Copenhagen on the CEDAW Convention and how it could be used not only as teaching material but also as a tool to improve the situation of immigrant women in Denmark. The teachers found our information kit on the Convention useful and agreed with us that knowing their internationally agreed rights could empower these women.

Men and gender equality

DWS agrees that it is necessary to involve men in gender equality work. Until gender equality is seen as a common issue and a win-win situation for both women and men, the final goal will never be achieved.

Source: Excerpted from "Comments of the Danish Women's Society on the Sixth Periodic Report by the Government of Denmark on the Implementation of the CEDAW Convention," by the Danish Women's Society. Available online. URL: http://kvindesamfund.dk/internationalt/comments_on_6th_cedaw_report.pdf#search=%22Leslie%20Larsen%20Danish%20Women's%20Society%22. Accessed August 26, 2006.

CHINA

China's Population and Family Planning Law (2002)

This law was adopted at the 25th Session of the Standing Committee of the Ninth National People's Congress on December 29, 2001.

Chapter I. General provisions

Article 1. This law is enacted, in accordance with the Constitution, so as to bring population into balance with social economic development, resources, and the environment: to promote family planning; to protect citizens' legitimate rights and interests; to enhance family happiness, and to contribute to the nation's prosperity and social progress.

Article 2. China is a populous country. Family planning is a fundamental state policy.

The State shall adopt a comprehensive approach to controlling population size and improving socio-economical and public health characteristics of population.

The State shall rely on publicity and education, advances in science and technology, comprehensive services and the establishment and improvement of the incentive and social security systems to carry out the family planning program.

Article 3. Population and family planning programs shall act in concert with programs that expand women's educational and employment opportunities, enhance their health, and elevate their status.

Article 4. The People's Governments and staff at all levels implementing the family planning program shall act strictly within the law, enforcing it in a civil manner, and must not infringe on citizens' legitimate rights and interest.

The family planning administrative departments and their staff acting within the law are protected by law.

Article 5. The State Council shall exercise authority over the national population and family planning program. Local people's governments at all levels shall exercise authority over the population and family planning programs in their respective jurisdictions.

Article 6. The family planning administrative department of the State Council shall be in charge of the national family planning program and population programs related to family planning.

Family planning administrative departments of people's governments at county level and above shall be in charge of family planning programs and population programs related to family planning in their respective jurisdictions.

Other government administrative departments at county level and above shall be in charge of aspects of the population and family planning programs falling within their mandates.

Article 7. Social organizations such as Trade Unions, Communist Youth Leagues, Women's Federations, and Family Planning Associations; enterprises; institutions; and individual citizens shall assist the people's government in carrying out population and family planning programs.

Article 8. Organizations and individuals making outstanding achievements in the population and family planning programs shall be recognized and rewarded by the State.

Source: Excerpted from "Population and Family Planning Law of the People's Republic of China," China Population Publishing House, 2002. Available online. URL: http://www.unescap.org/esid/psis/population/database/poplaws/ law_china/china%20pop%20and%20family%20planning.pdf. Accessed January 1, 2006.

Chinese Women and Their Contraceptive Choices (January 18, 2005)

In recent decades, a better global understanding of birth control techniques has contributed to women's development and gender equality.

Research by the United Nations Population Fund published in 2003 indicates that the use of contraception in China is almost universal—at 83 percent.

China, in fact, leads the world in the use of contraception. However, that does not reflect the whole picture.

China's family planning policy is aimed mainly at married women, and it emphasizes long-term or permanent methods of contraception.

A study conducted in 2004 by the Medical Center of Fudan University in Shanghai and the International Health Research Group found premarital sex among China's urban youth was becoming more common.

It also found that the abortion rate among unmarried women was alarmingly high. The use of contraception such as condoms or the contraceptive pill remains low, which accounts in part for the high abortion rate among China's young women.

The Fudan University report concluded "there is a large unmet need for temporary methods of contraception in urban areas of China." . . .

A Sexual Revolution?

China is experiencing a social revolution. Chinese society is changing, opening up, and developing. Not only are ideas and perceptions changing, but so is behavior.

Several decades ago, a Chinese woman would not see her husband before her wedding day; now, some young people in the cities are choosing to live with their partners before they decide to wed. The topic of sex is becoming more open, and sex before marriage is not the taboo it once was.

Mu Zimei has become a symbol of the sexual revolution. She has a website that details her 70-plus one-night stands and offers sex tips, such as how to have intercourse in a car. Sex and the City, the US comedy-drama about the sex lives of four party-goers in New York, can be found in even the smallest DVD shops in China.

According to the research conducted by Fudan University, of the five urban studies which reported sexual activity, the majority of women—from

54 percent in one study to 82 percent in another—said they had sex before marriage.

Source: Excerpted from "Chinese Women and Their Contraceptive Choices," by Kristina Sivelle. Available online. URL: http://www.chinadaily.com.cn/english/doc/2005-01/18/content_410003.htm. Accessed February 6, 2006.

AFGHANISTAN

Afghan Women Debate the Terms of Their Future (June 2002)

KABUL, Afghanistan (WOMEN'S E-NEWS)—When at last she was welcomed under the tent of the loya jirga, the grand council convened to determine the future of Afghanistan's government, Rahima Jami decided to wear a headscarf knotted under her chin. A long coat hid the curves of her body.

Nasrine Gross had waited a long time to help determine the next two years of her country's government, too. She wore a black pants suit and tied her soft black hair in a ponytail.

"If you're wearing this because you really believe in it, I respect you, but if you feel you have to wear it, you should take it off," Gross told Jami. "I've chosen to keep my hair visible and I'm sure you respect that too."

The veiled Jami nodded but said, "If you just put on a small headscarf, it would be much better."

This significant discussion took place during the nine-day loya jirga that ended June 19. It was the first meeting of its kind since 1964, when then-king Mohammad Zahir Shah reformed the constitution to give women the right to vote, go to school and earn the same wages as men.

Source: Excerpted from "Afghan Women Debate the Terms of Their Future," by Fariba Nawa, Women's E-News, June 30, 2002. Available online. URL: http://www.womensenews.org/article.cfm/dyn/aid/956. Accessed October 30, 2005.

"No One Listens to Us and No One Treats Us as Human Beings: Justice Denied to Women" (October 2003)

Amnesty International established a field presence in Afghanistan in June 2002 to facilitate reporting and campaigning on human rights. This report is based on research that includes interviews with women detainees and with law enforcement professionals on issues of women's rights conducted in April and May 2003. These report excerpts are in the last of four reports resulting from a year-long investigation of the reconstruction of the Afghan criminal justice system.

The rights and status of women in Afghanistan became an issue of global concern prior to the military intervention by a US-led coalition that led to the end of the Taleban regime in November 2001. The international community, including members of the coalition, made repeated undertakings that their intervention would support women in realising their rights. Colin Powell, US Secretary of State, declared that, "The recovery of Afghanistan must entail the restoration of the rights of Afghan women. Indeed, it will not be possible without them. The rights of the women of Afghanistan will not be negotiable."

During the rule of the Taleban, the women's movement, Amnesty International and other human rights organizations repeatedly highlighted serious concerns regarding the situation of women in Afghanistan. The rigid social, moral and behavioural codes imposed by the Taleban included severe restrictions on women's freedom of movement, expression and association. Widespread human rights abuses committed during the same period by regional commanders of the Northern Alliance were little publicized outside Afghanistan. Many of those commanders today hold powerful positions in the regions and in central government.

Two years after the ending of the Taleban regime, the international community and the Afghan Transitional Administration (ATA), led by President Hamid Karzai, have proved unable to protect women. Amnesty International is gravely concerned by the extent of violence faced by women and girls in Afghanistan. The risk of rape and sexual violence by members of armed factions and former combatants is still high. Forced marriage, particularly of girl children, and violence against women in the family are widespread in many areas of the country. These crimes of violence continue with the active support or passive complicity of state agents, armed groups, families and communities. This continuing violence against women in Afghanistan causes untold suffering and denies women their fundamental human rights.

The criminal justice system is too weak to offer effective protection of women's right to life and physical security, and itself subjects them to discrimination and abuse. Prosecution for violence against women, and protection for women at acute risk of violence is virtually absent. . . .

The UN Security Council has expressed its commitment to giving gender equality a central place in post-conflict reconstruction and peace operations through the adoption of UN Security Council Resolution 1325 on "Women Peace and Security." Resolution 1325 and the Namibia Plan of Action on "Mainstreaming a Gender Perspective in Multidimensional

Peace Operations" (Namibia Plan of Action) outline measures to protect the rights of women that should be integrated in such operations. The particular need for law enforcement activities and judicial and legal reform to ensure protection of women's rights is detailed in the UN study on implementation of Resolution 1325. The international community's involvement in Afghanistan is an important test case for seeing whether the will and resources to ensure such commitments are in fact implemented.

In early 2003, the ATA made a legally binding commitment to respect and ensure respect for women's rights through ratifying the Convention on the Elimination of All Forms of Discrimination against Women (CEDAW). Afghanistan is a party to other important human rights treaties and has thus undertaken to guarantee that the rights contained in these instruments are afforded to all Afghans without discrimination.

The ratification of CEDAW was a major development. Afghanistan has made a specific commitment to address women's rights in law and practice; in public, political, social and cultural life; as well as in personal status laws, education, health and work. The ATA has also ratified the Rome Statute for the International Criminal Court (ICC), which contains gender sensitive definitions of crimes and procedures to protect vulnerable victims and witnesses. This constitutes a model for domestic legal reform.

Amnesty International recognizes the difficulties facing Afghanistan as it seeks to recover from over 23 years of conflict. However, it is vital that measures to protect the rights of women are built into legal and constitutional reform, and integrated into policing and criminal justice processes. . . .

Women seeking to realize their rights do so in a context of continuing insecurity and threat of violence. The ATA has been unable to establish control outside Kabul, where insecurity results from the existence of private armed groups under the leadership of powerful regional commanders and factional fighting between some of these armed groups. A number of reports have highlighted the specific effects on women of the lack of security and effective law enforcement in many parts of Afghanistan, and the failure to curtail abuses by powerful regional commanders.

Women and girls are vulnerable to rape, sexual violence and abduction. The burning of a number of girls' schools has demonstrated the threat to provision for the realization of the rights of women. Many organizations have drawn attention to the insufficient international security provision, and the problems surrounding the response by ATA law enforcement. . . .

The prevailing insecurity has directly impacted on attempts by women to engage in political activities and ensure integration of women's rights in the process of reconstruction. Women delegates at the Emergency Loya Jirga were subject to intimidation, and activists have articulated a deep concern that their participation at the Constitutional Loya Jirga will be similarly threatened.

The question of the rights of women is central to the nature of Afghanistan's future government and society. Progress and emancipation have been characterized by some political forces as unIslamic and contrary to Shari'a (Islamic law). The history of Afghanistan demonstrates resistance to central government attempts to change traditions relating to women's status in the family and community. Women in civil society and government in Afghanistan however strongly assert that progressive formulations of law must be created and implemented to protect the rights of women.

Source: Excerpted from "No One Listens to Us and No One Treats Us as Human Beings: Justice Denied to Women," by Amnesty International, a report about Afghanistan women, October 6, 2003. Available online. URL: http://www.web.amnesty.org/library/index/engasa110232003. Accessed December 23, 2005.

New Rights, but Afghan Women Still May Face Forced Marriages (March 2005)

KABUL—Fourteen-year-old Bibi has never seen the father who wants to sell her into marriage with a stranger.

She hid when he sent the police to her village home in northern Afghanistan a month ago. Her elder brother Kareem refused to hand her over and was dragged off to jail.

But Bibi found sanctuary with a sympathetic relative in Kabul, where she now lives in fear her father, divorced from her mother, will one day catch up with her.

The relative, Shahnoz, said the girl's father was not interested in finding a suitable mate for his daughter and only wanted to get his hands on the dowry she could command.

"She's like a check," said Shahnoz, whose husband is a first cousin of Bibi's mother. "She's beautiful and he wants to sell the girl for marriage,"

Bibi's story is far from unique. Despite the re-emergence of democracy and women's rights in Afghanistan, human rights officials say that between 60 percent and 80 percent of marriages in the country are forced on women.

In rural areas, "tradition is so powerful women feel they really are the property of male relatives. Whatever they are told, they obey," said Sima Samar, chairwoman of the Afghan Independent Human Rights Commission, the country's leading rights watchdog.

Girls and women are often wedded off for economic gain or to settle scores between feuding families, even though both practices run counter to civil and Islamic law.

While arranged marriages are normal in this conservative Muslim country, they are meant to have the consent of the bride and groom.

In Bibi's case the groom is a wealthy, older man looking for a second wife. Her relatives reckon he is willing to pay about $7,000 for her—a small fortune in one of the world's poorest countries. . . .

Fawzia Amini, deputy director of the law and rights department at the Ministry of Women's Affairs, said the department investigated about 500 cases a year of abuse against women, usually of husbands beating their wives.

She said victims could seek legal support for divorce, but such a step is so socially detrimental to the woman that it is usually better to try to force the husband to cooperate with the authorities and rescue the marriage. She said there were only 10 to 15 divorces last year in the family court in Kabul, a city of around 4 million people. "Our culture does not tolerate divorce. Divorced women will have a painful life. No one will care for them," Amini said. "There's no legal support for divorced women. Mostly they can't get a share of their dowry and they lose their children."

Source: Excerpted from "New Rights, but Afghan Women Still May Face Forced Marriages," *The International Herald Tribune/Associated Press,* March 15, 2005.

KENYA

Wangari Maathai—Nobel Lecture (December 2004)

Following are Dr. Maathai's remarks upon receiving the 2004 Nobel Prize in peace on December 10, 2004, in the Oslo City Hall, Norway, for her contribution to sustainable development, democracy, and peace.

I stand before you and the world humbled by this recognition and uplifted by the honour of being the 2004 Nobel Peace Laureate.

As the first African woman to receive this prize, I accept it on behalf of the people of Kenya and Africa, and indeed the world. I am especially mindful of women and the girl child. I hope it will encourage them to raise their voices and take more space for leadership. I know the honour also gives a deep sense of pride to our men, both old and young. As a mother, I appreciate the inspiration this brings to the youth and urge them to use it to pursue their dreams. . . .

I am immensely privileged to join my fellow African Peace laureates, Presidents Nelson Mandela and F. W. de Klerk, Archbishop Desmond Tutu, the late Chief Albert Luthuli, the late Anwar el-Sadat and the UN Secretary General, Kofi Annan.

I know that African people everywhere are encouraged by this news. My fellow Africans, as we embrace this recognition, let us use it to intensify our commitment to our people, to reduce conflicts and poverty and thereby improve their quality of life. Let us embrace democratic governance, protect human rights and protect our environment. I am confident that we shall rise to the occasion. I have always believed that solutions to most of our problems must come from us.

In this year's prize, the Norwegian Nobel Committee has placed the critical issue of environment and its linkage to democracy and peace before the world. For their visionary action, I am profoundly grateful. Recognizing that sustainable development, democracy and peace are indivisible is an idea whose time has come. Our work over the past 30 years has always appreciated and engaged these linkages.

My inspiration partly comes from my childhood experiences and observations of Nature in rural Kenya. It has been influenced and nurtured by the formal education I was privileged to receive in Kenya, the United States and Germany. As I was growing up, I witnessed forests being cleared and replaced by commercial plantations, which destroyed local biodiversity and the capacity of the forests to conserve water. . . .

In 1977, when we started the Green Belt Movement, I was partly responding to needs identified by rural women, namely lack of firewood, clean drinking water, balanced diets, shelter and income.

Throughout Africa, women are the primary caretakers, holding significant responsibility for tilling the land and feeding their families. As a result, they are often the first to become aware of environmental damage as resources become scarce and incapable of sustaining their families.

The women we worked with recounted that unlike in the past, they were unable to meet their basic needs. This was due to the degradation of their immediate environment as well as the introduction of commercial farming, which replaced the growing of household food crops. But international trade controlled the price of the exports from these small-scale farmers and a reasonable and just income could not be guaranteed. I came to understand that when the environment is destroyed, plundered or mismanaged, we undermine our quality of life and that of future generations.

Tree planting became a natural choice to address some of the initial basic needs identified by women. Also, tree planting is simple, attainable and guarantees quick, successful results within a reasonable amount of time. This sustains interest and commitment.

So, together, we have planted over 30 million trees that provide fuel, food, shelter, and income to support their children's education and household needs. The activity also creates employment and improves soils and watersheds. Through their involvement, women gain some degree of power over their lives, especially their social and economic position and relevance in the family. This work continues. . . .

Today, over 50 years later, the stream has dried up, women walk long distances for water, which is not always clean, and children will never know what they have lost. The challenge is to restore the home of the tadpoles and give back to our children a world of beauty and wonder.

Source: Excerpted from "Wangari Maathai's Nobel Lecture," Oslo, Norway, December 10, 2004. Available online. URL: http://nobelprize.org/nobel_prizes/peace/laureates/2004/maathai-lecture-text.html. Accessed January 3, 2006.

Kenya's Draft Constitution (2005)

The first attempt to update Kenya's constitution since 1963 met with great resistance in November 2005. The draft constitution favored women's economic and property rights and introduced local democracy, but its empowerment of the president and conservative values stirred opposition. The new constitution outlawed abortion and same-sex marriages and allowed religious courts to rule on a wide range of private and family cases.

Gender

38. (1) Women and men have the right to equal treatment, including the right to equal opportunities in political, economic, cultural and social activities.

(2) Women and men have an equal right to inherit, have access to and manage property.

(3) Any law, culture, custom or tradition that undermines the dignity, welfare, interest or status of women or men is prohibited.

(4) Despite clause (1), the State shall—

(a) protect women and their rights, taking into account their unique status and natural maternal role in society; and

(b) provide reasonable facilities and opportunities to enhance the welfare of women to enable them to realize their full potential and advancement. . . .

Part III—Human Rights Commissions

Gender Commission

76. (1) For the purposes of Article 38, there is established the Gender Commission.

(2) The functions of the Commission are to—

(a) promote gender equality and equity generally and to coordinate and facilitate gender mainstreaming in national development; and

(b) perform such other functions as may be prescribed by legislation and generally carry out the objectives of this Article.

(3) Parliament shall, by legislation, make comprehensive provision for all matters necessary to give effect to this Article.

CHAPTER TEN

REPRESENTATION OF THE PEOPLE

Part I—The Electoral System and Process

General principles

101. The electoral system shall satisfy the following principles—

(a) the freedom of citizens to exercise their political rights under Article 54;

(b) gender equity in elected bodies as provided for in Article 13(1)(j);

(c) representation of persons with disabilities as provided for in Article 13(1)(k);

(d) fair representation of the people generally, including the workers and the youth;

(e) fair elections which are—

(i) free from violence, intimidation, improper influence and corruption;

(ii) conducted by an independent body; and

(iii) administered in an impartial, neutral, transparent, accurate, efficient and accountable manner.

Membership of Parliament

116. (1) Parliament shall consist of—

(a) one member elected from each constituency as may be prescribed by law;

(b) one woman member elected from each special constituency created for women as may be prescribed by law;

(c) a number of members nominated by political parties in proportion to the votes received by each party at the election, based on lists submitted by political parties contesting the election;

(d) the Attorney-General, who shall be an ex officio member;

(e) the Speaker, who shall be an ex officio member; and

(f) the Ministers appointed under Article 168(5), who shall be ex officio members.

(2) The members referred to under clause (1)(c) shall consist of—

(a) a number of members equal to five per cent of the total membership of Parliament who shall be persons with disabilities, of whom one-third shall be women;

(b) a number of members equal to five per cent of the total membership of Parliament who shall be nominated by political parties to represent special interests, including the youth and workers; and

(c) such number of members as may be required to ensure that not more than two-thirds of all the members of Parliament are of the same gender.

(3) A member referred to under clause (1)(c) and clause (2) shall serve as such a member for only one term.

(4) Parliament shall enact legislation to give effect to this Article.

Source: Excerpted from the Republic of Kenya Web site, in a supplement to the *Kenya Gazette,* August 22, 2005. Available online. URL: http://www.kenyaconstitution.org. Accessed December 23, 2005.

Kenyans Reject New Constitution (November 2005)

Voters in Kenya have emphatically rejected a proposed new constitution, incomplete results show.

With fewer than 500,000 ballots to count, the "No" campaign has an unassailable lead of almost 1m votes. The BBC's Adam Mynott says the result is a huge setback for President Mwai Kibaki who led the "Yes" campaign. His spokesman has conceded defeat. Crowds of people have been celebrating the result on the streets of the capital, Nairobi.

"No, no, no," they shouted, some wearing orange—the colour of the "No" campaign.

The president is due to address the nation shortly.

Government spokesman Alfred Mutua told the AP news agency that the "No" campaign has an unassailable lead.

Many Kenyans treated the referendum as a protest vote against Mr. Kibaki ahead of general elections due in 2007.

The latest figures released by the Electoral Commission of Kenya (ECK) show 58% (3,480,642) voted "No" while 42% (2,492,229) backed the draft. . . .

DRAFT CONSTITUTION

Prime minister—works to the president

Bans foreign land ownership

Land commission formed—individuals can no longer distribute land

Christian and other religious courts set up; Muslim courts already exist

Regional parties banned

Elections for local officials

Same-sex marriages banned

Women get equal rights to inherit property

Abortion outlawed—unless permitted by parliament. . . .

Mr. Kibaki's cabinet was split, with seven ministers, including charismatic Roads Minister Raila Odinga, joining with the opposition, urging voters to reject the constitution.

If the president had won the referendum, it is likely he would have sacked the rebel ministers but his authority is now diminished and theirs is enhanced.

Our correspondent says the returns have shown Kenyans voting according to tribal affiliations—evidence of how the referendum campaign has split the nation along ethnic lines. . . .

The new constitution would have introduced the role of a prime minister and provided greater rights for women, devolution and land reform.

Kenya's basic law has not been re-written since independence from the UK in 1963.

The president has promised a new constitution since 2002 but the drafting process has seen many delays.

His opponents say his final draft reneged on previous promises to share out power and so reduce corruption.

Source: Excerpted from "Kenyans Reject New Constitution," *BBC News,* November 22, 2005. Available online. URL: http://news.bbc.co.uk/2/hi/africa/4455538.stm. Accessed December 23, 2005.

Finance-Kenya: Small Loans for Men Will Keep Violence against Women Down (December 27, 2005)

Micro-credit facilities for men could emerge as a powerful tool to check the alarming increase in cases of violence against women in Kenya.

Experts say that with easy access to small loans for income generating activities, men would have less time on their hands to be abusive.

Violence against women has been on the increase in this East African nation. An estimated 2,800 rape cases were reported in 2004, according to the police. This was 500 times more than the figure reported in 2003.

Jennifer Riria, chief executive of the internationally-known Kenya Women Finance Trust (KWFT), is pushing to expand micro-credit services to include men.

She says: "There needs to be micro-credit services (for men), to make them engage in development projects. This will also address the question of violence and irresponsibility on the part of men."

According to findings by KWFT, men have become even more indifferent, abandoning their duties when their spouses became financially independent.

"By empowering women financially, their gender roles have increased," she laments. "They are the ones taking children to school, caring for the cows, the household budget, paying bills—everything."

Source: Excerpted from "Finance-Kenya: Small Loans for Men Will Keep Violence against Women Down," by Joyce Mulama, *All Africa.com (Inter Press Service–Johannesburg).* Available online. URL: http://www.ipsnews.org/news. asp?idnews=31578. Accessed December 27, 2005.

PART III

Research Tools

6

How to Research the
Women's Rights Movement

TO BEGIN

Whether you are a student or professional researcher, a similar approach to investigating the U.S. and global women's movement can be used.

Start by consulting a variety of resources, using the following techniques and research suggestions:

- Get a general feeling for the topic by reading part I of this book, then review part II for primary documents and research resources referred to in part I.
- The chronology and glossary can make sense of events and issues encountered in part I.
- Browse through the many Web sites provided by organizations involved in women's issues, including both neutral ones and advocacy groups that support or criticize particular women's legislation. Their pages have current news, articles, and related links to other organizations that describe particular cases and discuss the pros and cons of various aspects.
- Use the relevant sections of the annotated bibliography to find more books, articles, online publications, and multimedia sources about specific topics.
- Find more current materials by using the Internet and bibliographic tools, such as the library, online catalogs, and periodical indexes.

WEB SITES AND ONLINE RESOURCES

The World Wide Web, or the Internet as it is commonly called, provides a vast network of resources at the fingertips of the researcher, where some basic keywords can gain access to significant, historical documents. On the other hand, anyone can publish on the Internet now, especially with the development of blogs, which are online diaries in which one can speak with authority on any subject. The one caution about the Web is always to check sources for validity and accuracy. Good questions to ask include the following:

- Who is responsible for this Web site?
- What is the background or reputation of the person or group?
- Does the person or group have a stated objective or agenda?
- What biases might this person or group have?
- Do a number of high-quality sites link to this one?
- What is the source given for a particular fact?
- Does that source actually say what is quoted?
- Where did they get their information?
- What is the date of the information?

WEB SITES

The following Web sites are recommended as good starting places for research. They offer well-organized overviews of issues, provide numerous resources and links, and answer frequently asked questions. Most are educational institution sites, government sites, or large intergovernmental organizations sites.

- U.S. Census Bureau http://factfinder.census.gov/home/saff/main.html?_lang=en
- U.S. government information through about.com http://usgovinfo.about.com/od/censusandstatistics/index_a.htm
- The National Archives and Records Administration http://ourdocuments.gov
- International Labor Organization database of conventions http://www.ilo.org/ilolex
- Organization for Economic Cooperation and Development (OECD) http://www.oecd.org
- Nongovernmental organizations at the United Nations http://habitat.igc.org/ngo-rev/index.html
- United Nations Dag Hammarskjöld Library http://www.un.org/Depts/dhl/resguide/r53.htm

Educational Web sites host document archives and professional studies that are a useful source of statistical information on women's status in various domains:

- Center for American Woman and Politics: http://www.cawp.rutgers. edu/index.html
- The School of Industrial and Labor Relations (ILR) at Cornell University has an extensive collection of key workplace federal documents: http:// digitalcommons.ilr.cornell.edu/key_workplace
- Michigan State University Documentary Library: http://www.lib.msu. edu/publ_ser/docs/igos/unconfs.htm#nair

The following advocacy Web sites deal with and take positions on specific issues:

- PeaceWomen.org: http://www.peacewomen.org
- ReligiousTolerance.org: http://www.religioustolerance.org/fem_newf.htm
- Amnesty International's extensive online document archive on human rights: http://web.amnesty.org/library/engindex

Media Web sites of national magazines, special-interest journals, and metropolitan newspapers can provide the most current information on activities, events, and legislation in the women's movement. Some may require a print subscription—or a less expensive online subscription—to access their archives:

- *U.S. News & World Report:* http://www.usnews.com/usnews/home.htm
- *Time:* http://www.time.com/time
- *Wall Street Journal:* http://online.wsj.com/public/us
- *Washington Post:* http://www.washingtonpost.com
- *New York Times:* http://www.nytimes.com
- *International Herald Tribune:* http://www.iht.com/pages/index.php
- *CNN:* http://www.cnn.com
- *USA TODAY:* http://www.usatoday.com
- *BBC NEWS:* http://www.bbc.com

SEARCH ENGINES

A search engine index offers a different type of searching, usually scanning through Web documents and indexing them by relevance to the keywords used. There are many search engines; the following are among the most widely used:

- AltaVista: http://www.altavista.com
- Excite: http://www.excite.com
- Google: http://www.google.com
- Hotbot: http://www.hotbot.com
- Lycos: http://www.lycos.com
- WebCrawler: http://www.webcrawler.com

When looking for a general topic that might be expressed with several different words or phrases, try using several descriptive words. The following search techniques may help:

- Use AND to narrow a search.
- Use OR to broaden a search.
- Use NOT to exclude unwanted results.
- Use quotes to search for a specific set of words.

Metasearch engines automate the process of submitting a keyword query to many search engines at the same time. There are new engines added frequently; the following are some of the well-known engines:

- A9: http://www.generic.A9.com from Amazon.com includes media columns, images, and blogs in the results.
- Answer: http://www.answers.com searches authoritative sites such as Columbia University Press and Merriam-Webster.
- Clusty: http://www.clusty.com sorts by topic and also searches news sources including Reuters.
- Grokker: http://www.grokker.com is a visual-based tool.
- Info: http://www.info.com searches 14 different search engines and directories and integrates news feeds from Topix.net.

- Librarian Index to the Internet: http://www.lii.org rounds up librarian-selected Internet resources serving California, the nation, and the world.
- Teoma: http://www.teoma.com focuses on relevance and filters the topic findings.
- Metacrawler: http://www.metacrawler.com.
- SurfWax: http://www.surfwax.com.
- Copernic: http://www.copernic.com is a search utility that is downloaded and operated from the user's personal computer (PC) to gather Web references from the Internet.

The one drawback is that the many results can be overwhelming and generate an enormous list of unrelated references.

There are also utilities, such as www.furl.net, that allow the researcher to archive addresses of potentially useful Web pages found while browsing that can be referred to later for use or elimination.

KEYWORDS

To search with a search engine, use keywords that include specific phrases, names, dates, and proper nouns. For example:

- Women's movement
- Women's history
- Women
- Working women
- Feminists
- Women clergy
- Feminism today
- Women voter statistics U.S. Census Bureau
- 1972 ERA
- Affirmative action China
- Denmark Equal Pay Act
- Afghanistan women
- Kenya women
- Female cutting
- ICCPR

These words should be accompanied by qualifiers such as *in the United States* or the name of the country to which the search pertains.

ORGANIZATIONS AND PEOPLE

Although much of what an organization has to offer can now be found on its Web site, it may also be useful to follow up with an in-person visit or phone call for further information.

Chapter 9 provides a list of organizations and agencies, and chapter 8 lists key players involved with research or advocacy concerning women's issues. News organizations also supply up-to-date information. The resource sites and Web portals mentioned earlier are good places to look for information and links to organizations or individuals.

When reading materials by an unfamiliar author, it is often useful to learn about that person's affiliation, credentials, and other achievements. There are several ways to find a person on the Internet:

- Try typing *contact information* and the person's name in a search engine, which may lead you to a paper he or she authored, his or her home page, or a biographical sketch put out by the institution for which the person works.
- Contact the person's employer (such as a university for an academic, or a corporation for a technical professional). Most such organizations have Web pages that include a searchable faculty or employee directory.
- A people-finder service, such as Yahoo! People Search (http://people.yahoo.com) or BigFoot (www.bigfoot.com) may yield contact information, including an e-mail address, mail address, and/or phone number.

ONLINE DATABASES AND PERIODICAL INDEXES

Likewise, you may also be able to access abstracts and bibliographies through a library where you hold a card. IngentaConnect (http://www.ingentaconnect.com) is an index that contains brief descriptions about documents from journals in all disciplines. The complete documents can then be ordered with a credit card or obtained free at a local library.

Most public libraries subscribe to database services such as InfoTrac or EBSCO Host, which index articles from thousands of general-interest and specialized periodicals. This kind of database can be searched by author or by words in the title, subject headings, and sometimes words found anywhere in the article text. Depending on the database used, *hits* can produce a bibliographical citation (author, title, pages, periodical name, issue date, etc.), a citation and abstract, or the full text of the article. With InfoTrac, it is useful to view the list of newspapers and magazines covered, decide whether the search will cover all or a selection of them, and determine which years to include in the search.

Libraries often provide password-protected Internet or telnet access to their periodical databases from their public Web pages with the user's library card bar code number as the password. Ask your public or school librarian about databases and electronic resources with which they are affiliated.

PRINT SOURCES

Although the Web sites are useful for quickly becoming acquainted with a topic, in-depth research can still require trips to the library or bookstore. Getting the most out of the library, in turn, requires the use of reference tools.

Magazines

Many articles can now be retrieved via online databases, such as findarticle. com, or in a library online consortium subscribing to InfoTrac or other online catalogs.

Articles about women's issues can be found in many kinds of publications, not just political or feminist sources. *Marie Claire,* a women's magazine known mostly for its fashion and grooming tips, published several articles on female genital mutilation that helped to draw attention to the dilemma in 2003. The November 2005 issue of *Elle* has a lengthy interview about women and the U.S. Army.

Library Catalogs

Most libraries maintain their holdings on computer. Many have adapted their systems to the Internet, making it possible for people who are not card holders to survey their system from any location. The Library of Congress, the largest library in the United States, has a catalog that can be accessed at http://catalog.loc.gov. Yahoo! offers a categorized listing of libraries at http://dir.yahoo.com/Reference/Libraries. Searches often depend on the system and whether it offers word searches that are "fuzzy" (editing words you may have entered and providing alternate findings) or exact.

A typical way to search catalogs is by category:

- Author—Try cross-referencing the first and last name, or just the last name.

- Title—Generally you need only use the first few words of the title, excluding initial articles (*a, an, the*).
- Keyword—Although it is more flexible than a title search, the search may fail if all keywords are not present.
- Subject—Search by subject headings assigned by the library with words that are not necessarily in the book's title.

Often systems list additional subject, title, and author headings that might be of interest to someone searching that item. If not, consider using some of the keywords or subject headings assigned to that book in a subsequent search.

Newspapers

Major metropolitan area newspapers, such as the *Washington Post, New York Times, Boston Globe,* and *Los Angeles Times,* often are a ready resource for articles with current perspectives on the topic. Most newspapers have Web sites with current news and features, offering recent articles from the past 15 to 30 days free, with earlier material found in the archives. It is common to have to pay for older articles, but it is worth checking with your local library about free online access to nationwide databases for card holders. Also, if you know the e-mail address of the author, a request for the article might encourage him or her to send you a PDF file of the article.

If your library does not provide you access to one of the databases in which such articles can be obtained free, you can pay a fee of a few dollars to the publisher of the information for the complete article, or even buy access to articles at a discount within a specified time limit on the Web. Of course, back issues of newspapers and magazines can also be found in hard copy, bound, or on microfilm in local libraries.

Textbooks

Certain texts used in secondary education can be useful. Check with a reference librarian and consult the annotated bibliography in chapter 10.

Books

Library catalogs and online directories will direct you to books that complement your research into the subject.

For instance, *Desert Flower,* by Waris Dirie, although an autobiography, holds a tremendous amount of information about trafficking and prostitution of women as well as a detailed description of female genital mutilation.

Digital books are a relatively recent development in technology that can put books at the fingertips of readers. The search engine Google now has a partnership with a consortium of universities to make some of their holdings available in digital format at http://www.googlebooks.com. Also, ask your librarian about other digital book projects within your state.

Many people have discovered that online bookstores such as Amazon (www.amazon.com) and Barnes & Noble (www.barnesandnoble.com) provide convenient ways to shop for books. A less-known benefit of online bookstore catalogs is that they often include publishers' information, book reviews, and readers' comments about a given title. They can thus serve as a form of annotated bibliography.

Highly specialized materials and out-of-print books may also be checked in other online bookstores such as Alibris (www.alibris.com).

FILMS AND TELEVISION PROGRAMS

News discussion programs and movies are another way to perceive issues, with the facts conveyed through dramatizations or documentaries.

A 2005 Lifetime for Women movie, *Human Trafficking*, dramatized the issue of human trafficking that heavily depends on the United States. An eloquent dramatization about a Zulu woman coping with HIV/AIDS in her rural South African village was the topic of an award-winning film made by HBO, *Yesterday*, in 2004, followed by a panel of experts who discussed the future of HIV as a national security threat.

Films and television documentaries that portray women's rights issues can be found in the annotated bibliography in chapter 10.

LEGAL RESEARCH

Legislation, or the making of laws, occurs at both the federal and state levels of government in the United States. News coverage of important cases in the general media may alert researchers about a case, but the specific court opinions or the text of decision or pending legislation is more reliable.

Federal legislation is compiled in the massive U.S. Code. The Government Printing Office (http://www.gpoaccess.gov) has links to the Code of Federal Regulations (which contains federal regulations that have been finalized), the Federal Register (which contains announcements of new federal agency regulations), the Congressional Record, the U.S. Code, congressional bills, a catalog of U.S. government publications, and other databases. It also provides links to individual agencies, grouped by government branch (legislative, executive, judicial) and regulatory agencies. Administrative decisions, core documents of U.S. history such as the U.S. Constitution, and federal Web sites are also listed.

The Internet provides ways to search laws and court cases easily by entering the name of the law, bill, or court case into a search engine. Cornell Law School at http://www.law.cornell.edu/uscode provides a fast way to retrieve a law by its title and section citation and keywords.

U.S. treaties are equivalent in status to federal legislation, forming part of what the Constitution calls "the supreme Law of the Land." Treaties can be referred to by a number of different names: *international conventions, international agreements, covenants, final acts, charters, protocols, pacts, accords,* and *constitutions for international organizations.* Usually these different names have no legal significance in international law. Treaties may be bilateral (between two parties) or multilateral (among several parties), and a treaty is usually only binding on the parties to the agreement. Bilateral treaties usually enter into force when both parties agree to be bound as of a certain date. Treaties in force in the United States can be found online (http://www. state.gov/s/l/treaties/c15824.htm) or through research indexes.

A uniform act is an act proposed by the Uniform Law. The National Conference of Commissioners on Uniform State Laws (NCCUSL) consists of lawyers and other professionals who work for the standardization of U.S. state laws but does not have any legislative power. A uniform act requires the approval of state legislatures to become legal.

The existence of uniform acts results in large part from the nature of the American federal system. The United States Congress does not have authority under the Constitution to legislate many issues, leaving many powers to state governments. At the same time, there is a desire to have consistent laws across the states.

Many state agencies have home pages that can be accessed through the Washburn University School of Law Library (http://www.washlaw.edu) or the Findlaw state resources Web site (http://findlaw.com/11). This site also has links to state law codes. These links may not provide access to the text of specific regulations, however.

To keep up with legislative changes, consult state and local advocacy groups for pending legislation. Chapter 9, "Organizations and Agencies," contains their contact information. International organizations such as UNI-FEM will provide an international perspective on treaties and conventions, while groups such as the National Organization for Women or the Women's Political Caucus for legislation in the United States or the All-Women China Organization in China offer details on current national issues.

The Library of Congress Thomas Web site (http://thomas.loc.gov/home/ abt_thom.html) includes files summarizing legislation by the number of the

Congress (each two-year session of Congress has a consecutive number; for example, the 109th Congress was in session in 2005 and 2006). Legislation can be searched for by the name of its sponsor(s), the bill number, or topical keywords.

FINDING COURT DECISIONS

The way laws are interpreted is decided by the Supreme Court and state courts. As are laws, legal decisions are organized using a system of citations. The general form is as follows: *Party 1 v. Party 2* volume reporter [optional start page] (court, year).

Here is an example of a Supreme Court decision: *Roe v. Wade,* 410 U.S. 113(1973). The parties are Roe and Wade (the first listed is the plaintiff or appellant, the second the defendant). The plaintiff is a person who brings an action in a court of law, and the appellant is the party who challenges and appeals a decision from a lower court. The case is in volume 410 (the U.S. Supreme Court Reports), beginning on page 113, and the case was decided in 1973. (For the U.S. Supreme Court, the name of the court is omitted.)

A state court decision is identified by the state's name appearing in the title. In this example of a state court decision, 87 N.Y.2d 130, 637 N.Y.S.2d 964 (1995), two different books need to be consulted to find the case: on page 130 of volume 87 of the New York Reports, second series, and on page 964 of volume 637 of New York Supplement, second series. The case was decided in 1995.

The states call their books different names, so you may have to find out what the letters stand for in your state's case. For example, in *Aguinda et al. v. Texaco,* 142 F Supp. 2d 53 (SDNY 2001), the 142 F Supp. 2nd is the federal district court from which the case was transferred, but SDNY refers to the New York state court where it was first heard.

After the jurisdiction of a case has been decided, the researcher can then find cases by citation, names of the parties, or subject keywords on the Internet. Useful Web sites include the following:

- Justia U.S. Supreme Court Center (http://www.justia.us/index.html) offers updates of the latest Supreme Court decisions.
- The Legal Information Institute (http://www.law.cornell.edu/co.html) has all Supreme Court decisions since 1990, plus 610 of the most important historic decisions.
- Washlaw Web (http://www.washlaw.edu) has a variety of court decisions (including states' decisions) and legal topics listed, making it a good starting place for many types of legal research.

- Visit http://www.landmarkcases.org for landmark Supreme Court case decisions.
- The OYEZ Project (http://www.oyez.org) of Northwestern University's Learning Technologies Group provides access to over 2,000 hours of Supreme Court audio since 1995, with selective recordings from the period October 1955 to 1995.

Researchers who have access to a university or corporate library may be able to access two commercial legal databases, Lexis and Westlaw, which have extensive information and use detailed relational methods. A certain amount of training is required to use legal databases.

7

Facts and Figures

GLOBAL STATISTICS

1.1 Worldwide Women's Earnings as Percentage of Men's Earnings, 2005, by Region

	FEMALE INCOME AS % OF MALE INCOME
East Asia and Pacific	58.7
Latin America and Caribbean	42.4
Europe and central Asia	60.4
Middle East and North Africa	31.0
South Asia	45.7
Sub-Saharan Africa	56.2
OECD countries*	57.7

*OECD countries = 30 countries (Australia, Austria, Belgium, Canada, Czech Republic, Denmark, Finland, France, Germany, Greece, Hungary, Iceland, Ireland, Italy, Japan, Korea, Luxembourg, Mexico, Netherlands, New Zealand, Norway, Poland, Portugal, Slovak Republic, Spain, Sweden, Switzerland, Turkey, United Kingdom, and the United States).

Source: Organization for Economic Cooperation and Development, 2006. Available online. URL: http://www.oecd.org/dataoecd/19/28/36223936.xls. Accessed April 21, 2006.

1.2 Worldwide Economic Activity of Women in Major Labor Sectors, 2005, by Region

REGION	RATIO OF SELF-EMPLOYED WOMEN TO SELF-EMPLOYED MEN	FEMALE LEGIS-LATORS, SENIOR OFFICIALS, AND MANAGERS (% OF TOTAL)	FEMALE PROFES-SIONAL AND TECHNICAL WORKERS (% OF TOTAL)	WOMEN IN PAID LABOR (% OF TOTAL)	WOMEN IN NON-AGRICULTURAL PAID LABOR (% OF TOTAL)
East Asia and Pacific	0.5	21.8	45.0	37.5	41.8
Latin America and Caribbean	0.9	32.2	47.3	38.6	41.3
Europe and central Asia	0.7	31.3	59.1	44.4	46.8
Middle East and North Africa	0.4	10.8	31.3	19.2	20.3
South Asia	1.0	6.6	30.3	16.9	19.3
Sub-Saharan Africa	1.1	13.7	29.9	28.1	27.6
OECD countries	0.6	26.5	48.8	44.0	45.4

Source: Organization for Economic Cooperation and Development, 2006. Available online. URL: http://www.oecd.org/dataoecd/19/28/36223936.xls. Accessed April 21, 2006.

UNITED STATES STATISTICS

2.1 United States Civilian Labor Force Participation, Past, Present, and Future, 1950–2025

GROUP	1950	1960	1970	1980	1990	1998	2015	2025
(IN PERCENTAGES)								
Total population, 16 and older	59.2	59.4	60.4	63.8	66.4	67.1	66.9	63.2
Men, 16 years and older	86.4	83.3	79.7	77.4	76.1	74.9	72.2	68.8
Women, 16 years and older	33.9	37.7	43.3	51.5	57.5	59.8	61.9	58.1

Source: Bureau of Labor Statistics (BLS), *Monthly Labor Review,* December 1999. Available online. URL: http://www.bls.gov/opub/mlr/1999/12/part1full.pdf, p. 4, table 1, "Civilian Labor Force Participation Rates by Sex and Age, 1950 to 1998 and Projected, 2015 to 2025." Accessed December 2, 2005.

2.2 United States Women's Earnings as Percentage of Men's Wages, 1951–2004

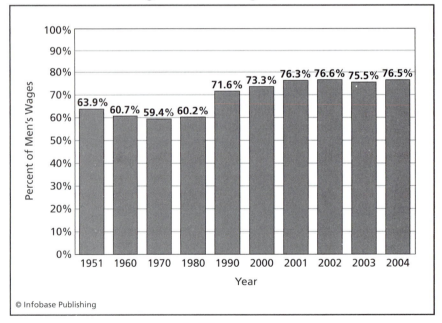

© Infobase Publishing

Source: U.S. Census Bureau, Current Population Survey, *Annual Social and Economic Supplements,* 2005.

2.3 United States Average Number of Hours and Weeks of Paid Employment for All Women, Married Women, and Women with Children, 1978 and 1998

ALL WOMEN	ALL WOMEN			MARRIED WOMEN			MARRIED WITH CHILDREN UNDER 6 YEARS OLD		
	1978	1998	CHANGE	1978	1998	CHANGE	1978	1998	CHANGE
Average no. hours/wk	19.6	26.6	7.0	17.4	25.1	7.7	11.8	19.6	7.8
Percentage (%) employed full time	38.1	51.2	13.1	32.5	47.2	14.7	21.1	34.5	13.4
Average no. of weeks	27.5	36.8	9.3	25.2	35.8	10.6	17.5	30.9	13.4

Source: U.S. Bureau of Labor Statistics, March Current Population Surveys. Available online. URL: http://www.bls.gov/opub/mlr/1999/12/part3full.pdf, p. 27, table 2. "Hours and Weeks of Paid Work for All Women Aged 25–54, Married Women Aged 25–54, and Married Women Aged 25–54 with Young Children, 197[8]–98." Accessed November 29, 2006.

2.4 United States Leading Causes of Death by Sex, 2002

CAUSE OF DEATH	WOMEN	MEN
	PERCENTAGE (%) OF TOTAL DEATHS	
Disease of the heart	28.6	28.4
Malignant neoplasms (cancer)	21.6	24.1
Cerebrovascular conditions (stroke)	8.0	5.2
Chronic lower respiratory conditions	5.2	5.1
Alzheimer's disease	3.4	1.4
Diabetes	3.1	2.9
Accidents (unintentional)	3.0	5.8
Influenza and pneumonia	3.0	2.4
Kidney diseases	1.7	1.6
Septicernia	1.5	1.2
Liver diseases	0.8	1.5
Suicide	0.5	2.1

Source: Centers for Disease Control. *National Vital Statistics Report,* March 7, 2005, Vol. 53, No. 4, p. 8.

8

Key Players A to Z

BELLA SAVITSKY ABZUG (1920–1998)   U.S. politician from New York City and one of the leaders of the women's liberation movement in the 1970s, who helped found Women Strike for Peace in 1961 and the New Democratic Coalition in 1968. She was a high-profile activist, along with Gloria Steinem and Betty Friedan, known for her New York chutzpah and wide-brimmed hat. She became the first Jewish congresswoman.

ABIGAIL ADAMS (1744–1818)   Wife of John Adams; she rallied for a woman's right to education. An avid letter writer, she expressed women's demand to be included in the government when writing to her husband at the time the Founding Fathers were drafting the Declaration of Independence in 1776: "If women are not represented in this new republic there will be another revolution."

JANE ADDAMS (1860–1935)   American activist and spokeswomen for peace during World War I. She founded the Women's Peace Party in 1915 and later the International League for Peace and Freedom (WILPF), in Geneva, Switzerland, in 1919. She was awarded the Nobel Prize in peace in 1931.

AMENA AFZALI (1958–   )   Afghan, minister for youth affairs since December 2004. After the Soviet invasion of Afghanistan, she helped Afghan refugees settle in Iran. She held senior positions on the Norwegian Afghanistan Committee and the United Nations High Commission for Refugees. In 2002, she was appointed commissioner on the Afghan Independent Human Rights Commission.

MADELEINE ALBRIGHT (1937–   )   First female U.S. Secretary of State, from 1997 to 2001. Recognized for her talents in foreign policy, she was the highest-ranking woman in the history of the U.S. government. She also had served as U.S. ambassador to the United Nations from 1993 to 1997.

SAFIA AMAJAN (1943–2006)   Head of the department of women's affairs in Kandahar, Afghanistan; she was assassinated by the Taliban on September 25, 2006. A dynamic teacher and public servant, she promoted the emancipation of Pashtun women to work and the right for girls to go to school.

MATHILDA ANNEKE (1817–1884)   German writer, feminist, Social Democrat, antislavery campaigner, and editor of the *Neue Kölinische Zeitung (New Cologne Times),* which she renamed the *Frauen-Zeitung* (The Woman's Journal). Anneke took her family to America after her husband's arrest and the unsuccessful 1848 revolution; there she met Susan B. Anthony and Elizabeth Cady Stanton and joined the women's movement.

SUSAN B. ANTHONY (1820–1906)   American reformer and one of the organizers of the 1846 Seneca Falls Conference in New York. A Quaker, Anthony in her early advocacy work focused on equal pay for female teachers, coeducation, and college training for girls in New York State. In 1851, she met Elizabeth Cady Stanton, who became a lifelong friend. They formed the National Women Suffrage Association (NWSA) in 1869 with the purpose of making changes to the U.S. Constitution that would allow women the vote. She authored volumes I to III of the *History of Woman Suffrage* with Elizabeth Cady Stanton and Matilda Joslyn Gage.

MARY ASTELL (1668–1731)   British author and feminist, who promoted opportunities for women, in her *Serious Proposal to the Ladies,* written in two parts, between 1694 and 1697. The work offered a scheme for a women's college, an idea that was well before its time and subjected to ridicule in the British tabloids.

RUTH BADER GINSBURG (1933–   )   Lawyer, who advocated the application of the equal protections afforded under the Fourteenth Amendment to gender as well as race. She successfully argued *Reed v. Reed* before the Supreme Court in 1971 and, thereafter, continued to argue more cases involving sex-role stereotyping. She joined the Supreme Court in 1993 as an Associate Justice.

FREDRIK BAJER (1837–1922)   Danish pacifist who was the son of a clergyman. He became an active spokesperson for women's rights and, with the help of his wife, Mathilde (1840–1934), helped found the Dansk Kvindesamfund (Danish Women's Society), in 1871. He supported legislation in the Folketing for women's equal rights in economic matters.

SEDIQA BALKHI (1946–   )   Afghan educator, manager, and minister of martyrs and disabled. She was raised in a religious and educated family. She earned a bachelor's degree in Islamic studies and studied religion in Iran. She wrote and held public seminars about the anti–Soviet invasion movement. She educated young Afghan refugees and taught business skills to women and girls.

NINA BANG (1866–1928) A Danish politician, historian, and journalist, who became the world's first female minister for education in 1924. She was a member of the Executive Committee of the Social Democrats from 1903 to 1928, and of the City Council of Copenhagen from 1913 to 1917, and the first of three women in the Landstinget (upper chamber), from 1918 to 1928. Bang resigned as minister in 1926 and died in 1928.

SHUKRIA BAREKZAI (UNKNOWN BIRTHDATE) Afghan founder and editor in chief of *Aina-e Zan* (Women's Mirror Weekly), which is dedicated to women's issues, and one of 68 women elected to the Afghan Parliament in September 2005. During the Taliban rule, she coordinated underground schools for women. She was named International Editor of the Year in 2005 by WorldPress.org.

ELISABETH JERICHAU BAUMANN (1819–1881) Polish painter, who rejected the women's movement per se but whose life illustrated independence. She became a Dane when she married the sculptor J. A. Jerichau and moved to Denmark in the late 1840s. She left her family to focus on her art and to win financial independence through it. She was the first female member of the Art Academy in Copenhagen in 1861 and the first woman painter to exhibit for Denmark at a World's Fair outside Denmark.

MARY BECKENHAM (UNKNOWN BIRTHDATE) Kenyan activist who won the She Woman Award in 2005 for her work of caring for HIV-positive babies. In 1994, she opened New Life Home Trust's first home in the Loresho suburb of Nairobi. There are five homes and centers now: two in Nairobi, one in Kisumu (in western Kenya, on the shores of Lake Victoria), and two on the Indian Ocean island of Lamu (off the Kenyan northern coast, near Somalia).

MARY MCLEOD BETHUNE (1875–1955) African-American missionary and educator, who founded the secondary school in 1904 that later became a four-year accredited college, Bethune-Cookman College. She also established the National Council of Negro Women in 1935 by uniting several major national black women's associations. She remained its president until 1949 and was its representative at the founding conference of the United Nations in San Francisco, California, in 1945.

ANTOINETTE L. BROWN BLACKWELL (1825–1921) The first U.S. woman to be ordained to the ministry, in the 1850s. As a writer and women's rights activist, she advocated abolition, temperance, prison reform, antipoverty measures, and tried to reconcile Christianity with women's rights. She authored books on religious and philosophical issues, and even novels. She married the brother of Elizabeth Blackwell.

ELIZABETH BLACKWELL (1821–1910)   Physician, the first woman awarded the M.D. degree in the United States. Originally from Britain, she submitted applications to major medical schools that were rejected in the United States because of her sex, except to Geneva Medical School (now Hobart & William Smith Colleges in Geneva, New York). In spite of hostility from professors, students, and townspeople, she earned her medical degree in 1849 and completed her medical education in Europe. Eventually she founded the Women's Medical College.

BOADICEA (ALSO "BOUDICCA") (61 c.e.)   Queen of the Iceni, led a revolt against the Roman invaders of England. After her husband, Prasutagus's, death, the Roman invaders plundered his territory, whipped Boadicea, and forced her to watch Roman soldiers rape her daughters. She raised an army against the invaders, defeating the Roman troops at Camulodonum. In time, Boadicea was defeated but not captured. Her family avoided execution in Rome, it is believed, by taking poison.

GERTRUDE BONNIN (1876–1938)   Native American author and educator, who founded the reform group the National Council of American Indians in 1926 and became its first president.

HALLIE QUINN BROWN (1849–1949)   African-American educator. She earned her B.S. degree in 1873 from Wilberforce University in Ohio, where she eventually became teacher, principal, dean, and professor. In 1893, she cofounded and presided over the Colored Woman's League of Washington, D.C., which was the forerunner to the National Association of Colored Women.

CARRIE CHAPMAN CATT (1859–1947)   American suffragist and peace advocate, who was educated in Iowa, where she became superintendent of schools in the early 1880s. Her two marriages—in 1885 to the journalist Lee Chapman and in 1890 to George Catt—left her as a widow. From 1890 to 1900, she organized the National Alliance of Women's Suffrage Association (NAWSA). Catt organized the League of Women Voters to educate women in political decision making. At the Berlin meeting of the International Council of Women, she organized the International Woman Suffrage Alliance (IWSA), over which she presided from 1904 to 1923.

SHIRLEY CHISHOLM (1924–2005) The first African-American woman to be elected to the House of Representatives in 1968. From Brooklyn, New York, she was an advocate for women and minorities during her seven terms, and she became the first woman to run for president in 1972. She founded the National Political Congress of Black Women to address social, economic, educational, and political issues impacting black women. She received over 100 honorary doctorate degrees from universities throughout the world. Chisholm authored two books, *Unbought and Unbossed* and *The Good Fight*.

SISTER JOAN CHITTISTER (1936–   ) A Benedictine nun, lecturer, and writer, she is the executive director of Benetvision, a resource center for contemporary spirituality in Erie, Pennsylvania. She cochaired the Global Peace Initiative of Women Religious and Spiritual Leaders, which originated at the Millennium World Peace Summit of Religions and Spiritual Leaders at the United Nations in August 2000. She helped found the International Committee for the Peace Council and is past president of the Leadership Conference of Women Religious, a national organization.

JOHNNETTA COLE (1936–) An advocate for African Americans and women and professor of anthropology, women's studies, and African-American studies. In 1987, she became the first African-American woman president of Spelman College. She also served as cluster coordinator for education, labor, and the arts and humanities on President Clinton's transition team. Cole currently serves as the 14th president of Bennett College for Women. Her publications include *Conversations: Straight Talk with America's Sister President* and *Dream the Boldest Dreams: And Other Lessons in Life*.

PAULINA WRIGHT DAVIS (1813–1876) Women's rights advocate, social reformer, educator, and author. She collaborated with Ernestine Rose and Elizabeth Cady Stanton to secure the Married Women's Property Act in 1848. An independently wealthy woman by marriage, she invested her time in studying the anatomy and physiology of women and then conducted a lecture series about the topics, which are believed to have inspired the first generation of women physicians.

JEANNE DEROIN (1805–1894) French feminist, who joined the Saint Simonianist movement because of its positions on feminism and became one of several women who formed an unofficial, international feminist network in the early and mid-19th century. At the start of the French Revolution in 1848, she helped found the Society for the Emancipation of Women, joined Eugénie Niboyet's Society of the Voice of Women, and wrote articles for its journal, *La Voix des femmes*. In addition to lobbying government ministers for women's suffrage, she operated an adult women's education program.

ABIGAIL SCOTT DUNIWAY (1834–1915) American women's rights advocate in Oregon and Washington in the early 1900s. She became Oregon's first woman to speak before the state legislature and the state's first female publisher, of *New Northwest.* She addressed the legislature and published legislators' replies in her newspaper. She finally cast her vote in the 1916 election after more than 40 years of advocacy.

GERALDINE FERRARO (1935–) The first woman on a major party's national presidential election ticket as vice president. Daughter of Italian immigrants, Ferraro became assistant district attorney in the Investigations Bureau in Queens, New York, and went on to handle cases of domestic violence and rape. In 1978, she was elected to the U.S. House of Representatives from New York's Ninth Congressional District. She was appointed chair of the 1984 Democratic platform committee, the first woman to hold the post, and the Democratic Party presidential candidate Walter Mondale selected Ferraro as his running mate for vice president.

MATHILDE FIBIGER (1830–1872) Danish writer, author of the novel *Clara Raphael.* Her 12 letters, published in Copenhagen in 1850 with a foreword written by J. L. Heiberg, a prestigious author, led to a literary controversy that made it part of the history of Danish women's liberation.

ABIGAIL KELLEY FOSTER (1810–1887) 19th-century American teacher, abolitionist, and lecturer on women's rights from Massachusetts. After teaching in Quaker schools, Abby Kelley fought against slavery in 1837 and married a radical abolitionist and reformer. She often experienced hostility from audiences when she lectured on abolition. She turned her attention to women's rights, becoming a prominent suffragist for the rest of her life.

BETTY FRIEDAN (1921–2006) Author who published in 1963 *The Feminine Mystique,* which evolved out of a survey of 20-year college reunion colleagues. In it, she documented the emotional and intellectual oppression that middle-class educated women were experiencing because of limited lifestyles. The best seller inspired thousands of women to seek a life beyond homemaking.

FATANA GAILANI (UNKNOWN BIRTHDATE) Founder of the Afghanistan Women Council, who began her humanitarian work for human, children, and women's rights in 1980 after fleeing the Communist regime in her native Kabul for shelter in Pakistan. She represented Afghan women at the Beijing Conference on Women in 1995 and at the 1997 Post-Beijing Follow-up Conference in Thailand. She lived 20 years in Pakistan and three years in Switzerland as an Afghan refugee. After she received death threats from the Taliban, Amnesty International issued an urgent action bulletin in 1999 calling for her enhanced protection.

FAUZIA GAILANI (UNKNOWN BIRTHDATE) An Afghan women's rights campaigner and professional fitness instructor, was a female candidate in the 2005 parliamentary elections. Popular among young Afghans, she was elected to Afghanistan's parliament in an upset victory. Gailani topped the ballot with nearly 17,000 votes and eclipsed powerful allies of the province's former ruler, the warlord Ismail Khan. One of Gailani's pledges is to form Afghanistan's first women's party. She opposes child marriage, an experience she had herself, which is common in Afghanistan.

MARY GOEGG (1826–1899) Founder of the International Association of Women in Geneva, Switzerland, in 1868. She published articles advocating that women make their case known as part of the universal right of suffrage. She also contributed to *La Solidarité* in France. In 1872, she became the first woman to petition the government about women's right to higher education, an act that was followed by women's admission in the winter semester of 1872 and 1873. At 68 years old, she became vice president of l'Union des femmes de Genève, founded by a new generation of feminists in 1891.

EMMA GOLDMAN (1869–1940) American radical and feminist, who advocated free speech, birth control, women's equality and independence, and union organization. Her criticism of mandatory conscription of young men into the military during World War I led to her two-year imprisonment, followed by deportation in 1919. For the rest of her life until her death in 1940, she participated in social and political movements of her era, from the Russian Revolution to the Spanish civil war.

OLYMPIA DE GOUGES (1745–1793) A French feminist, writer, and revolutionary. In her famous 1791 work "Rights of Woman," she argued for applying the new "Rights of Man" to women during the French Revolution of 1789–99. In her many pamphlets written during the revolution, she criticized bloodshed and was outspoken against revolutionary figures such as Robespierre; she was beheaded as a traitor in 1793.

KATHARINE MEYER GRAHAM (1917–2001) Publisher, who assumed leadership of the *Washington Post* after the suicide of her husband, its president, in 1963. She also became the first female member of the board of the Associated Press in 1974. She was known as one of the most powerful women in America through her role with the *Washington Post* and the disclosures of the Watergate scandal involving President Richard Nixon.

ANGELINA EMILY GRIMKÉ (1805–1879)   American abolitionist and advocate of women's rights in the 19th century. Converted to the Quaker faith by her elder sister, Sarah Moore Grimké (1792–1873), she became an abolitionist in 1835 and wrote *An Appeal to the Christian Women of the South* as a testimony of her conversion. She began speaking to the public around New York City with her sister and developed powerful oratory skills, which led to her addresses to the Massachusetts legislative committee on antislavery petitions in 1838 on three occasions.

NASRINE GROSS (1945–)   Afghan founder and president of the Roqia Center for Women's Rights, Studies and Education, Afghanistan, which provides women's rights seminars, academic information, and adult literacy classes. Its literacy program for couples is modeled to shape democratic behavior and experience by requiring that both husbands and wives attend classes.

FANNY LOU HAMER (1917–1977)   Civil rights worker and member of the Mississippi Freedom Democratic Party who called black voting discrimination and physical abuse to public attention at the 1964 Democratic Party presidential convention. One of 11 children of a Mississippi sharecropping family, Fanny Lou Hamer, who had little formal education, spoke from her heart: "I'm sick and tired of being sick and tired." A year later, President Lyndon B. Johnson signed the Voting Rights Act.

HATSHEPSUT   Egyptian pharaoh, who became known for her military campaigns and building projects during her 15-year reign (ca. 1473–1458 B.C.E.). Upon the death of her husband, Thutmose II, she became regent for Thutmose III and within two years became pharaoh. Her reign is characterized by growing commerce on the Red Sea and extensive building of temples. After her death, Thutmose III discredited her rule and her memory, by leaving her tomb at Deir el-Bahari, in the Valley of the Kings, unfinished.

ANITA HILL (1956–)   African-American lawyer whose 1991 landmark testimony raised public awareness of sexual harassment. Hill received her degree from Yale University, and after working at the Equal Employment Opportunity Commission (EEOC), taught law at the University of Oklahoma. She brought allegations of sexual harassment against Supreme Court nominee Clarence Thomas during his Senate confirmation hearings. Although Thomas's appointment was subsequently confirmed, Hill's testimony called the issue of sexual harassment to public attention.

MASSOUDA JALAL (1962–)   Physician and politician, a member of the ethnic Tajik minority in Afghanistan. She earned her degree from Kabul

Medical Institute in 1988. From 1993 to 1995, she was the women's right director in a women's organization and was a member of the Children's Department of Kabul Medical Institute. In 1996, she worked for the United Nations High Commissioner for Refugees (UNHCR); afterward she was the health adviser and a national program officer for the World Food Program in Afghanistan. In June 2002, she became a candidate during the first post-Taliban *loya jirga* in Kabul to discuss the future of Afghanistan and its constitution. She was minister of women's affairs from 2004 to 2006 under the Afghanistan transitional administration.

RAHIMA JAMI (UNKNOWN BIRTHDATE)   Afghan educator and politician, who participated in the 2005 elections in Afghanistan. As the principal of a girl's school in western Afghanistan, she represents the more moderate view of feminism in Afghanistan, believing women need to work within the Islamic framework, covering themselves and obeying the laws of the Qur'an.

BARBARA JORDAN (1936–1996)   Political science educator and congresswoman. She held an unprecedented reign as a black woman in the Texas state senate in 1966 and became the first black state senator to chair a committee (Labor and Management Relations), in 1967. She was the first African-American woman to give a keynote speech at the Democratic National Convention, 1976.

MALAI JOYA (1978–   )   Prominent young activist elected from the province of Farah for the Afghan *loya jirga* in September 2005. Joya presented grassroots opposition through her experience working in a refugee camp and as an underground teacher during the Taliban rule. Her speech in Kabul denounced the warlords in power as criminals who should be brought to justice as well as the discrimination against women that has required her to employ an armed bodyguard.

TANG JUNYING (UNKNOWN BIRTHDATE)   Chinese suffragist of the Chinese Suffragette Society in 1912, who modeled the organization on those of the militant British suffragists and translated and published articles from the West into Chinese.

JEAN KAGGIA (UNKNOWN BIRTHDATE)   Antiabortionist activist from Kenya. She is the chairperson of the Christian Medical Fellowship of Kenya and the leader of the Protecting Life Movement of Kenya.

ALICE KAGUNDA (UNKNOWN BIRTHDATE)   Kenya's first female senior deputy commissioner of police, appointed in 2004. She grew up in the early 1960s in Nyeri, where there were no policewomen; seeing one while visiting a relative in Nairobi inspired her to enter the field of police work.

CORETTA SCOTT KING (1927–2006)   Activist and founder of the Martin Luther King, Jr. Center for Nonviolent Social Change and wife of Dr. Martin Luther King, Jr., who was assassinated in 1968. In 1983, an act of Congress instituted the Martin Luther King, Jr. Federal Holiday Commission, which she chaired until January 1986, when she oversaw the first legal holiday in honor of her husband, one now celebrated in over 100 countries.

LINE LUPLAU (1823–1891)   Danish founder of the Association of Women's Right to Vote in 1889.

MARY LYON (1797–1849)   Founder of Mount Holyoke College in South Hadley, Massachusetts. Educated at a female academy in Byfield, Massachusetts, Lyon cofounded Ipswich Female Seminary in Massachusetts. Perceiving the limitations of the seminary, which based its criteria on personal conduct and discipline, she conceived the idea of an educational institution for women.

WANGARI MUTA MAATHAI (1940–   )   The first African woman to win the 2004 Nobel Prize in peace. Maathai was active in the National Council of Women of Kenya and became its chair from 1981 to 1987. She introduced the idea of planting trees and developed the Green Belt Movement as a grassroots organization that focused on conserving the environment and improving the quality of life through women's groups. Green Belt coordinated the planting of over 20 million trees on farms and school and church property. In December 2002, Professor Maathai was elected to parliament by a majority vote and was subsequently appointed by the president as assistant minister for environment, natural resources and wildlife in Kenya's ninth parliament.

MALALAI (UNKNOWN BIRTHDATE)   Afghan female leader, who inspired Afghan troops to fight the British in the Second Anglo-Afghan War of 1880. The image of her waving a veil over her head and her life serve as a model for many girls today, and schools are named in her honor.

RONA MANSURI (UNKNOWN BIRTHDATE)   Activist for Afghan refugees and daughter of a former prime minister, who moved in the 1960s to Germany, where her father was Afghanistan's ambassador. She was one of three women who took part as delegates in the United Nations talks in Bonn, Germany, to form the provisional government for post-Taliban Afghanistan.

DIANA K. MAYER (1947–   )   Citicorp's first female vice president in 1974 when she was 27 years old. She went on to become vice president in the money management division of the Marine Midland Bank of New York, and then was appointed a senior vice president in 1981.

MARGARET MEAD (1901–1978)   Activist and inspiration to the American women's movement, who spoke the famous words "'Never doubt that a small group of thoughtful committed citizens can change the world. Indeed it is the only thing that ever has.'"

JOHN STUART MILL (1806–1873)   An English philosopher and economist, who addressed the rights of women in his 1869 book *The Subjection of Women*, which was immediately translated into Danish. He coauthored works with Mary Wollstonecraft Shelley, the daughter of Mary Wollstonecaft and author of *Frankenstein.*

JUTTA BOJSEN MØLLER (1837–1927)   Nineteenth- and 20th-century Danish pioneer for women's rights. An estimated 12,000 women participated in the march led by her and other pioneers to the Rigsdag and Amalienborg Castle on Constitution Day, June 5, 1915.

ESTHER MORRIS (1814–1902)   First woman to hold a judicial position, who led the first successful state campaign for woman suffrage, in Wyoming in 1869.

JAMES MOTT (1788–1868)   Lucretia Mott's husband, who also worked for the antislavery and woman suffrage causes. He was a delegate to the World Anti-Slavery Convention in London and Seneca Falls. With other members of the Religious Society of Friends, a Quaker organization, he helped found Swarthmore College in 1864 as a coeducational institution.

LUCRETIA MOTT (1793–1880)   Nineteenth-century American reformer, international and national figure in the women's movement, from Massachusetts. She was first known after 1818 as a lecturer for temperance, peace, the rights of labor, and the abolition of slavery. After her intervention to aid slaves and a meeting of the American Anti-Slavery Society, she organized the Philadelphia Female Anti-Slavery Society in 1833. Refusal by the 1840 World Anti-Slavery Convention in London to recognize women delegates led to her championship of the cause of women's rights. She organized the first women's rights convention in the United States with Elizabeth Cady Stanton at Seneca Falls, New York, in 1848.

ELNA MUNCH (1871–1945)   Danish chairperson of the National League for Voting Rights and radical politician at the turn of the 20th century. She was inspired by the 1909 International Woman Suffrage Alliance Congress in London when some women were imprisoned in the fight for the right to vote.

NIELSINE NIELSEN (1850–1916) The first Danish woman academic, a medical school graduate of the University of Copenhagen in 1885. Her application in 1874 to medical school influenced women's gaining access to the gymnasial entrance exam and university degrees in various disciplines, except theology.

ANTONIA C. NOVELLO (1944–) First woman and Hispanic to be appointed surgeon general of the United States Public Health Service, in 1990. Born, raised, and educated in Puerto Rico, Novello completed her master's degree in public health at Johns Hopkins University and earned an M.D. in 1970. She worked for 12 years in the U.S. Public Health Service at the National Institutes of Health. She became the first female president of the Pan American Medical Society.

SANDRA DAY O'CONNOR (1933–) The Supreme Court's 102nd justice and first female member. She grew up on a cattle ranch in El Paso, Texas, then attended Stanford University, where she received her B.A. in economics and her law degree two years later. O'Connor served as an Arizona assistant attorney general from 1965 to 1969, when she was appointed to the Arizona Senate. In 1974, she ran successfully for trial judge, a position she held until her appointment to the Arizona Court of Appeals in 1979. President Ronald Reagan nominated her 18 months later, in September 1981, to the Supreme Court. She announced her retirement from the Supreme Court on July 1, 2005.

MILLIE AKOTH ODHIAMBO (UNKNOWN BIRTHDATE) Lawyer and protector of women's rights in Kenya. She graduated from the University of Nairobi in 1990 and passed the bar exam in 1991. She worked as a state attorney until 1996, when she joined the International Federation of Women Lawyers, Kenya Chapter (FIDA (K)), a public education and advocacy organization that offers legal aid to indigent women. While there, Millie represented a Masai woman in a landmark domestic violence case that received local and international attention and became a milestone in the protection of the rights of women in Kenya.

EMMELINE PANKHURST (1858–1928) Radical British feminist, who along with her two daughters, Christabel (1880–1958), and Sylvia (1882–1960), founded the Women's Social and Political Union (WSPU) in 1903. They used extreme measures to promote women's suffrage, including chaining themselves to fences of Parliament and having prison hunger strikes. They inspired the radical faction of the women's movement in the United States, represented by Alice Paul, and in other countries.

AGNES PAREYIO (UNKNOWN BIRTHDATE) Anti–female genital mutilation activist. First known as a protector of Masai girls in the Narok District of Kenya from female genital cutting and early marriages, Pareyio founded the Tasaru Girl's Refuge as a safe house and was later made deputy mayor of Narok. In 2005, she was recognized as Kenya's United Nations Person of the Year. Masai men accepted the practice of circumcising women as part of the culture and never questioned it until Pareyio began educating them about its devastating effects.

ROSA PARKS (1913–2005) The African-American woman who spurred the Civil Rights movement by refusing to give up her seat at the front of a bus in Montgomery, Alabama. Her arrest in December 1955 in Montgomery, sparked a 13-month civil rights protest and the formation of the Montgomery Improvement Association, led by the young pastor Dr. Martin Luther King, Jr. In 1957, Mrs. Parks and her husband moved to Detroit, Michigan, where she served on the staff of U.S. Representative John Conyers. After the death of her husband in 1977, she founded the Rosa and Raymond Parks Institute for Self-Development. She was presented with the Presidential Medal of Freedom in 1996 and the Congressional Gold Medal in 1999. Rosa Parks died in 2005, and her casket was placed in the rotunda of the United States Capitol; she was the first woman in American history to lie in state at the Capitol.

ALICE PAUL (1885–1977) Radical suffragist, who, in 1916, broke off from NAWSA to form the National Women's Party with Lucy Burns. Her infamous prison hunger strikes attracted national and international attention, causing President Woodrow Wilson to acknowledge the role of women in the war effort in 1919 and to prompt the states to consider a constitutional amendment.

NANCY PELOSI (1940–) The first woman to be nominated Speaker of the House when the Democratic Party won control of the House of Representatives during midterm national elections in November 2006. She was the first woman to lead a political party in the history of the U.S. Congress when she was named Minority Leader in November 2002.

ESTHER PETERSON (1906–1997) Director of the Women's Bureau of the Department of Labor in 1961. She encouraged President John F. Kennedy to convene the Commission on the Status of Women, naming Eleanor Roosevelt as its chair. The report issued by that commission in 1963 documented discrimination against women in virtually every area of American life. State and local governments quickly followed suit and established their own commissions for women, to research conditions and recommend changes.

CONDOLEEZA RICE (1954–   )   Secretary of state of the United States from January 2005 (the first African-American woman to hold that position), Dr. Rice was formerly the national security advisor to President George W. Bush. Prior to that, she was a professor of political science on the Stanford University faculty, where she received distinguished awards for teaching. She received the third annual Woman of Valor Award in May 2006 from the Independent Women's Forum (IWF).

SALLY RIDE (1951–   )   Nominated in 2005 by the National Women's History Museum for the "35 Who Made a Difference," Dr. Ride was the first U.S. female astronaut in the 1983 flight on the *Challenger*. Her current work encourages girls to participate in the field of science with the Sally Ride Science Club. She is among the few women to be inducted into the Women's Hall of Fame at a young age and while still alive.

ELEANOR ROOSEVELT (1884–1962)   Wife of President Franklin D. Roosevelt; she was active in political and reform work, redefining the role of first lady by advocating rights for women, blacks, and union workers. She was among the first to join the League of Women Voters in 1920. After her husband's death in 1945, she was named the U.S. delegate to the newly established United Nations; she presented the *Universal Declaration of Human Rights* to the General Assembly for adoption in 1948.

ERNESTINE ROSE (1810–1892)   One of the first women to speak publicly for women's rights in America. A rabbi's daughter, born in Poland, she arrived in New York in May 1836, with a petition for married women's property rights. After 12 years of activism, New York became the first state to pass a married women's property law and was followed by other states. The campaign led to lifelong association with Elizabeth Cady Stanton and Paulina Wright Davis. Susan B. Anthony, who joined the movement in 1852, and Stanton credited Rose's pioneering role.

SIMA SAMAR (1957–   )   Chairwoman of the Independent Human Rights Commission from Aghanistan. Dr. Samar was selected as the John Humphrey Freedom Award recipient for her efforts to strengthen the human rights of women and girls in Afghanistan and in refugee camps on the northern border of Pakistan in 2001.

MARGARET SANGER (1879–1966)   Nurse and advocate for *birth control*, she is credited with coining the term. In her work as a public health nurse in New York City, she was aware of the effects of unplanned pregnancies. In 1912, Sanger gave up nursing work to distribute birth control information; she was challenged by the Comstock Act of 1873, which forbade distribution of birth control devices and information, and she was arrested numerous times. In 1914, she founded the National Birth Control League and set up the first clinic in the United States. In 1942, after several organizational mergers and name changes, Planned Parenthood Federation emerged. In 1927, Sanger helped organize the first World Population Conference in Geneva.

ANNA HOWARD SHAW (1847–1919)   American ordained Methodist minister, physician, temperance lecturer, woman's suffrage orator, and peace advocate. The second woman to graduate from Boston University School of Theology, in 1878, Shaw was a friend and colleague of Susan B. Anthony. She also became the first woman to receive the highest civilian presidential citation, the Distinguished Service Medal, for her work as chair of the Women's Committee of the National Council of Defense during World War I.

SUHAILA SIDDIQ (1941–   )   Afghanistan's woman general and surgeon, who became the minister of health in 2002. She spent two decades working in Kabul's 400-bed military hospital, and her abdominal surgery is credited with saving hundreds of lives. She played a pivotal role in keeping hospitals functioning in the 1990s during rocket attacks.

MARY SIMALO SIMAT (UNKNOWN BIRTHDATE)   The first girl in her Masai village in Kenya to flee an arranged marriage. At 35, she refused to circumcise her daughter, and at 38, she ran for tribal chief, the first woman ever to do so.

ELIZABETH CADY STANTON (1815–1902)   A pioneer of women's rights in the United States, organizer of the Seneca Falls Conference, and founder of the National Women Suffrage Association (NWSA), with Susan B. Anthony. With her husband, Henry Brewster Stanton, a journalist and abolitionist, she tried to attend the international slavery convention in London. Women delegates were excluded from the floor of the convention, arousing indignation in both Stanton and Lucretia Mott and moving them to organize women and win greater equality with men.

GLORIA STEINEM (1934–   )   Writer, activist, and leader in the women's rights movement in the early 1960s. Steinem began her career as a freelance writer with an interest in politics, which was considered novel at the time. She founded *Ms.* magazine, the National Women's Political Caucus, the Women's Action Alliance, and the Ms. Foundation for Women. Then, in the 1980s and 1990s, Steinem became a best-selling author with books that such as *Outrageous Acts and Everyday Rebellions, Revolution from Within: A Book of Self-Esteem, Doing Sixty, and Moving beyond Words.*

LUCY STONE (1818–1893)   American reformer and leader in the women's rights movement. In 1847, she gave her first lecture on women's rights, and the following year, she was engaged by the Anti-Slavery Society as one of their regular lecturers. Her eloquent speaking often captivated even difficult audiences. She married Henry Brown Blackwell in 1855 but continued, as a matter of principle, to use her own name and was known as "Mrs. Stone." In 1870, she founded the *Woman's Journal,* which represented AWSA and NAWSA for 50 years.

DORA JEAN DOUGHERTY STROTHER (1921–) U.S. military pilot. Her military flying career began in 1942, when she entered the Women's Air Force Service Pilots (WASP). Her piloting jobs included flight training, target towing for antiaircraft gunnery, ferrying, and radio control piloting. Established primarily to relieve male pilots who were needed in combat roles, the WASPs flew almost every type of plane used by the Army Air Forces, including liaison, training, cargo, fighters, attack bombers, dive bombers, and very heavy bombers.

MARIA W. STUART (1803–1879) An 1830s black orator who spoke about women's rights in the United States. She spoke against African colonization and stirred public sentiment with her speeches about self-determination. She published two collections of essays and speeches: *Religion and the Pure Principles of Morality* (1831) and *Meditations from the Pen of Mrs. Maria W. Stuart* (1832).

HELEN BROOKE TAUSSIG (1898–1986) Physician whose groundwork changed the face of cardiac surgery when she teamed with the surgeon Dr. Alfred Blalock in 1945 to perform the first "blue baby" operation in the United States. Blue babies were often left to die because they lacked oxygen exchange as a result of arterial constriction between the heart and lungs until Taussig proposed a novel technique, creating a new vessel.

MARY CHURCH TERRELL (1863–1954) African-American women's and civil rights activist from Tennessee. Educated at Oberlin College in Ohio and well traveled, she received multiple honorary doctorates during her life. In Washington, D.C., she founded in 1892 the Colored Women's League, which merged four years later with the National Federation of Afro-American Women to become the National Federation of Colored Women. Church Terrell became its first president. She was appointed to the District of Columbia Board of Education in 1895. A lecturer and writer on equal rights for women and blacks and related social issues, she served as an American delegate to international women's rights conferences.

TZ'U-HSI (CIXI) (1835–1908) Concubine to Emperor Hs'en Feng, who ruled China in 1861 after his death. She held the reins of power until 1889.

She ruled against foot binding and legitimized intermarriage of Chinese and Manchu. She also gave girls access to state educational facilities.

SIMA WALI (UNKNOWN BIRTHDATE)   Activist for Afghan women's rights, who settled in the United States after the Russians invaded Afghanistan in 1979. She worked to improve the lives of Afghan women and was one of three women who took part as delegates in the United Nations talks on a provisional government for post-Taliban Afghanistan. Wali is head of the Washington, D.C.–based agency Refugee Women in Development.

BISHOP MARGARET WANJIRU (UNKNOWN BIRTHDATE)   Respected church leader in Kenya. In 1990, Bishop Wanjiru founded the Jesus Is Alive Ministries, now based in Nairobi. Her rapidly growing church has a membership of 22,000 and branches in Uganda, Tanzania, South Africa, the United Kingdom, and the United States. She is the first woman to be ordained as bishop in Kenya, but not without such difficulties as being a young single mother and having the option to live by practicing witchcraft for income.

MARY WOLLSTONECRAFT (1759–1797)   Author of *A Vindication of the Rights of Men*, with which she established her reputation as a writer in 1790. Two years later, she wrote *A Vindication of the Rights of Woman*, which inspired the international women's movement. Her second daughter. Mary Wollstonecraft Shelley, authored *Frankenstein*.

FRANCES "FANNY" WRIGHT (1795–1852)   Socialist and freethought advocate in 1830s America. The first American woman to speak publicly against slavery and for the equality of women, she also advocated birth control and liberalized divorce laws among other rights. As a rebel, she inspired Susan B. Anthony and Elizabeth Cady Stanton. She joined a utopian community, New Harmony, in Indiana created by Robert Owen. In 1825, she published a plan for the gradual emancipation of American slaves and created a settlement, Nashoba, in Memphis, Tennessee, to train slaves for freedom, which was not successful financially.

NATHALIE ZAHLE (1827–1913)   Danish educator, who for nearly 50 years influenced the educational system in Copenhagen. In 1852, she started a girls' school, in which girls had the same curriculum as boys, learning geography, history, and natural history. She advocated instruction in the native tongue. Her curriculum had parallels in both Norway and Sweden, but otherwise she was a woman who worked out her own systems. She established a teachers' college in 1851 for private women teachers, and, after 1859, when women were accepted as primary school teachers, she started a teacher's training college.

ZOYA (1981–) Afghan activist. The daughter of activists in Kabul, Zoya was raised by her grandmother after her parents disappeared. She was a child during the 1979 Russian invasion and a teen when the Taliban took power in 1994. She is now a member of the Revolutionary Association of the Women of Afghanistan (RAWA) and lives and works in a refugee camp near the Afghan-Pakistani border. She also travels abroad to raise funds for the organization.

9

Organizations and Agencies

Afghan Independent Human Rights Commission
URL: http://www.aihrc.org.af
Pul-i-Surkh, Karti 3
Kabul, Afghanistan
Phone: (93) (20) 2500676, (93) (20) 2500677, (93) (20) 2500197
E-mail: aihrc@aihrc.org.af

The women's rights unit of the commission monitors the situation of women in Afghanistan. It also attempts to eliminate and reduce the discriminatory attitudes toward women in Afghan society.

Afghan Women's Council (AWC)
URL: http://www.afghanistanwomencouncil.org
House # 117, Str. 6, Sector H-4, Phase II, Hayatabad
P.O. Box 1215 GPO
Peshawar, Pakistan
Phone: (92) (91) 811261
Fax: (92) (91) 812138

Founded in 1986, AWC started its activities for human rights, women's rights, children's rights, and peace building in 1993. As a nongovernmental, nonprofit, nonsectarian organization, it runs the Ariana School, the Mother and Child Health Clinic, in Peshawar, where it provides education and medical care to refugee families. Its 20-bed Nazo Ana Clinic in Kabul stayed open during the five years of the Taliban regime. AWC also manages humanitarian relief efforts for newly arrived refugees and publishes the monthly journal *Zan-e-Afghan* (Afghan women) to encourage women to act as a resource for peace and stability in the country.

Afghan Women's Network (AWN)
URL: http://www.afghanwomensnetwork.org
H#193, Street-3 Qalai Fathullah
Kabul, Afghanistan
Phone: (93) 2200691
E-mail: awnkabul@hotmail.com

Established in 1995, this nonpartisan network of women and women's NGOs is committed to empowering Afghan women and ensuring their equal participation in society. Currently, there are 70 NGO members and over 3,000 individual members in Afghanistan and in Pakistan. The Web site provides current reports on legislation and elections in Afghanistan and announcements for women's training programs.

African Women's Development Fund (AWDF)
URL: http://www.awdf.org
25 Yiyiwa Street
Abelenkpe
Accra, Ghana
Phone: (233) (21) 780477
Fax: (233) (21) 782502
E-mail: awdf@awdf.org

AWDF supports work in women's human rights, political participation, peace building, health, reproductive rights, HIV/AIDS, and economic empowerment. It offers grants that range from $1,000 to a maximum of $25,000.

The Alice Paul Institute (API)
URL: http://www.alicepaul.org
128 Hooton Road
Mt. Laurel, NJ 08054
Phone: (856) 231-1885
Fax: (856) 231-4223
E-mail: info@alicepaul.org

A not-for-profit corporation established in 1984 with the goal to enhance public awareness of the life and work of Alice Paul as author of the Equal Rights Amendment. The organization also develops and presents educational programs to empower women and girls to accept leadership in their communities and workplaces.

All-China Women's Federation (ACWF)
URL: http://www.women.org.cn/english/index.htm

The Chinese Women's Delegation on Africa
Phone: (010) 65211639
Fax: (010) 65211156

Founded on April 3, 1949, the All-China Women's Federation (ACWF) has as its main task helping women out of poverty and illiteracy. It works closely with the Chinese government to create approved means for advancing Chinese women of different ethnic groups in all professions through a variety of training programs.

American Civil Liberties Union (ACLU)
URL: http://www.aclu.org
125 Broad Street, 18th Floor
New York, NY 10004-2400
Phone: (800) 775-2258

Founded in 1920, this nonprofit and nonpartisan organization has grown from a roomful of civil liberties activists to an organization of more than 500,000 members and supporters. The ACLU handles nearly 6,000 court cases annually through offices in almost every state in America. Its mission is to preserve all of the protections and guarantees stated in the Constitution's Bill of Rights. The ACLU's Women's Rights Project, founded in 1972 by Ruth Bader Ginsburg, also focuses on low-wage Latina workers' rights in the New York area, tackling the issues of sexual harassment, gender discrimination, pregnancy discrimination, and full and fair wages for working Latina women's labor. The project conducts know-your-rights workshops for working women at these organizations and work related to translating rights legislation and literature into Spanish.

Amnesty International
URL: http://www.amnesty.org
322 8th Avenue
New York, NY 10001
Phone: (212) 807-8400

This NGO is a worldwide movement of 1.8 million members, supporters, and subscribers in over 150 countries and territories in every region of the world, who campaign for internationally recognized human rights. AI upholds the *Universal Declaration of Human Rights* and other international human rights standards and undertakes research and action focused on preventing and ending grave abuses of the rights to physical and mental integrity, freedom of conscience and expression, and freedom from discrimination, within the context of its work to promote all human rights.

Asia-Japan Women's Resource Center (AJWRC)
URL: http://www.jca.apc.org/ajwrc and http://www.aworc.org/org/
   ajwrc/ajwrc.html
14-10-311 Sakuragaoka
Shibuya-ku
Tokyo 150-0031, Japan
Phone: (81) (0)3 3780 5245
Fax: (81) (0)3 3463 9752
E-mail: ajwrc@jca.apc.org

The Asia-Japan Women's Resource Center (AJWRC) was formed in 1995; its foundations are in the Asian Women's Association (AWA), which pioneered from the 1970s the development of a strong gender, a North-South perspective within the Japanese progressive mass movements in general, and the women's movement. The founding of AJWRC is a response to the challenge of creating an alternative society for the 21st century: a society that is based on gender justice, ecological sustainability, as well as local and global democracy.

Asian Centre for Women's Human Rights (ASCENT)
URL: http://www.achrweb.org
P.O. Box AC 662 Cubao 1135
Quezon City, Philippines
Phone: (632) 928-4973; (632) 410-1512
Fax: (632) 533-0452; (632) 928-4973
E-mail: ascent@csi.com.ph

ASCENT was set up to respond to the training needs of women's organizations in Asia on human rights standards. ASCENT uses the human rights system to monitor, investigate, document, report, and enforce women's human rights. It has developed a women's human rights defenders program that gives women's rights training including understanding of and access to UN systems and international human rights standards and mechanisms.

Center for Health and Human Rights
URL: http://www.hsph.harvard.edu/fxbcenter
Harvard School of Public Health
8 Story Street
Cambridge, MA 02138
Phone: (617) 496-4370
Fax: (617) 496-4380

The François-Xavier Bagnoud Center for Health and Human Rights is the first academic center to focus exclusively on health and human rights. The center combines research and teaching with a strong commitment to service and policy development, with its faculty working at international and national levels through collaboration and partnerships with health and human rights practitioners, governmental and nongovernmental organizations, academic institutions, and international agencies.

The Center for Reproductive Rights
URL: http://www.crlp.org
120 Wall Street
New York, NY 10005
Phone: (917) 637-3600
Fax: (917) 637-3666
E-mail: info@reprorights.org

The Center for Reproductive Rights provides national and international reports on reproductive law.

The Center for Women's Global Leadership (CWGL)
URL: http://www.cwgl.rutgers.edu
Douglass College
Rutgers, The State University of New Jersey
160 Ryders Lane
New Brunswick, NJ 08901-8555
Phone: (732) 932-8782
Fax: (732) 932-1180
E-mail: cwgl@igc.org

The CWGL develops and facilitates women's leadership for human rights and social justice worldwide. Founded as a project of Douglass College in 1989, it is a unit of the Institute for Women's Leadership (IWL)—a consortium of six women's programs at Rutgers University—created to study and promote how and why women lead, and to develop programs that prepare women of all ages to lead effectively.

The Center for Women Veterans
URL: http://www1.va.gov/womenvet
Department of Veterans Affairs
810 Vermont Avenue NW
Washington, DC 20420
Phone: (202) 273-6193

In fulfillment of Congress's Public Law 103-446, the center assesses women veterans' services within and outside the department to assure that Veterans

Administration (VA) policy and planning practices address the needs of women veterans and foster VA participation in general federal initiatives focusing on women's issues. It identifies policies, practices, programs, and related activities that are unresponsive or insensitive to the needs of women veterans. It also recommends changes and initiatives designed to address these deficiencies.

Chinese Academy of Social Science (CASS)
URL: http://bic.cass.cn/english
Bureau of International Cooperation
Hongkong Maco and Taiwan Academic Affairs Office

The National Academy of the People's Republic of China for the Social Sciences, CASS is an institution of the State Council of China, founded in 1977. It develops scholarship in the fields of social sciences and the humanities and carries out theoretical exploration and policy studies, which include women's rights.

Committee on the Elimination of Discrimination against Women
  (CEDAW)
URL: http://www.unhchr.ch/html/menu2/6/cedw.htm
c/o Division for the Advancement of Women, Department of Economic
  and Social Affairs
United Nations Secretariat
2 United Nations Plaza, DC-2/12th Floor
New York, NY 10017

The committee acts as a monitoring system to oversee the implementation of the convention of the same name by those states that have acceded to the convention through reports submitted by those states' parties. The committee considers these reports and makes suggestions and recommendations based on their consideration. It may also invite United Nations specialized agencies to submit reports for consideration and may receive information from nongovernmental organizations. The committee reports annually on its activities to the General Assembly through the Economic and Social Council, and the council transmits these reports to the Commission on the Status of Women.

The Committee on Women in the NATO Forces (CWINF)
URL: http://www.nato.int/issues/women_nato/index.html
NATO Headquarters
Blvd Leopold III

1110 Brussels, Belgium
E-mail: natodoc@hq.nato.int

CWINF is a mission to advise NATO leadership and member nations on critical issues affecting women in the Alliance's Armed Forces that has been in effect since 1961.

The Danish Institute for Human Rights (DIHR)
URL: http://www.humanrights.dk/frontpage
56 Strandgade
1401 Copenhagen, Denmark
Phone: (45) 32698888
Fax: (45) 32698800
E-mail: center@humanrights.dk

DIHR is a national human rights institution in accordance with the UN Paris Principles. It became part of the Danish Centre for International Studies and Human Rights on January 1, 2003. The work of DIHR includes research, analysis, information, education, documentation, and complaints handling, as well as a large number of national and international programs. DIHR takes a multidisciplinary approach to human rights and employs staff versed in law, political science, and economics.

Danish Women's Society (Dansk Kvindesamfund)
URL: http://www.kvindesamfund.dk
Niels Hemmingsensgade 10, 3
1153 Copenhagen, Denmark
Phone: (45) 33157837
E-mail: kontor@kvindesamfund.dk

The first women's suffrage organization in Denmark, formed in 1871, the Danish Women's Society works for establishing real equality of liberties, responsibilities, and opportunities of women and men. It is a nonpartisan organization affiliated with the International Alliance of Women (IAW).

Equal Employment Opportunity Commission (EEOC)
URL: http://www.eeoc.gov
1801 L Street NW
Washington, DC 20507
Phone: (202) 663-4900

The EEOC has five commissioners and a General Counsel appointed by the president and confirmed by the Senate. The commission makes equal employment opportunity policy and approves most litigation. The General Counsel is responsible for conducting EEOC enforcement litigation under Title VII of the Civil Rights Act of 1964 (Title VII), the Equal Pay Act (EPA), the Age Discrimination in Employment Act (ADEA), and the Americans with Disabilities Act (ADA).

EMILY's List
URL: http://www.emilyslist.org
1120 Connecticut Avenue NW, Suite 1100
Washington, DC 20036
Phone: (202) 326-1400
Fax: (202) 326-1415

Founded in 1985, EMILY's List is a financial resource for women seeking federal office. Before it existed, no Democratic Party woman had ever been elected to the U.S. Senate in her own right, no woman had ever been elected governor of a large state, and the number of Democratic women in the U.S. House had declined to 12—less than 3 percent of the chamber's 435 members. Since then, the grassroots network has helped elect 61 Democratic members of Congress, 11 senators, and eight governors.

The Federation of Women Lawyers Kenya (FIDA)
URL: http://www.fidakenya.org
P.O. Box 46324
Nairobi, Kenya
Phone: (254) (20) 570444, (20) 573511

A nonprofit, nonpartisan, and nongovernmental membership organization, committed to the creation of a society that is free of all forms of discrimination against women through provision of legal aid, women's rights monitoring, advocacy, education, and referral. Membership to FIDA Kenya is open to Kenyan women lawyers and law students.

FemAid
URL: http://www.femaid.org
33, rue Guy Moquet
92240 Malakoff, France
E-mail: info@femaid.org

FemAid is an unaffiliated, independent nonprofit organization based in Paris, run by a team that has worked in humanitarian aid in war zones. They were active in Bosnia with the Enfants de Bosnie, an NGO that helped women and children in the suburb of Sarajevo, culminating in the reconstruction of a major primary school in Dobrinja. Since late 1999, they have been working mainly but not exclusively with the Revolutionary Association of Women of Afghanistan (RAWA), the only secular feminist group in Afghanistan. FemAid also aided victims of the earthquake in Kashmir, both Pakistani and Indian, at the end of 2005.

Feminenza International
URL: http://www.feminenza.org
P.O. Box 271
Welwyn Garden City, Herts AL7 1WJ, United Kingdom
Phone: (44) 1707 335420
E-mail: PressOffice@Feminenza.org

An international women's network that holds self-development workshops, courses, talks, seminars, and retreats for personal and spiritual growth for women. Teachings are based on original research concerning the three inner lives of the woman—referred to as female, woman, and lady—and how understanding these three aspects can enrich and improve women's lives, relationships, and choices.

Feminist Majority Foundation
URL: http://www.feminist.org
1600 Wilson Boulevard, Suite 801
Arlington, VA 22209
Phone: (703) 522-2214
Fax: (703) 522-2219

Advocacy group that provides news feeds about the latest legislation that may impact women's rights in the United States and abroad. Areas of particular concern to the organization are human trafficking, Afghanistan women's rights, domestic violence, and reproductive rights.

FEMNET
URL: http://www.femnet.or.ke
The African Women's Development and Communication Network
P.O. Box 54562
00200 Nairobi, Kenya
Fax: (254) (20) 3742927
E-mail: admin@femnet.or.ke

The African Women's Development and Communications Network (FEMNET) is a pan-African network addressing African women's development, equality, and other human rights. Set up in 1988 and based in Nairobi, Kenya,

FEMNET works on advocacy at the regional and international levels and training on gender analysis, mainstreaming, and communications.

The Foundation for Women's Health, Research and Development (FORWARD)
URL: http://www.forwarduk.org.uk
Unit 4, 765–767 Harrow Road
London, United Kingdom NW10 5NY
Phone: (44) (0)20 8960 4000
Fax: (44) (0)20 8960 4014

An international nongovernmental organization, FORWARD is pursuing the elimination of human trafficking, especially of women and girls, and unsafe traditional practices such as female genital mutilation.

Global Peace Initiative of Women
URL: http://www.gpiw.org
301 East 57 Street, 3rd Floor
New York, NY 10022
Phone: (212) 593-5877
Fax: (646) 792-3871
E-mail: info@gpiw.org

This global network includes women and men in all walks of life.

Green Belt Movement (GBM Kenya)
URL: http://greenbeltmovement.org/index.php
P.O. Box 67545
Kilimani Lane (off Elgeyo Marakwet Road)
Adams Arcade
Nairobi, Kenya
Phone: (254) (20) 3873057, (254) (20) 3871523
E-mail: gbm@wananchi.com

The Nobel Prize laureate Professor Wangari Muta Maathai oversees the Green Belt Movement, which she established in 1977, under the auspices of the National Council of Women of Kenya. A grassroots nongovernmental organization, Green Belt focuses on environmental conservation, community development, and capacity building through women's efforts.

The Guttmacher Institute
URL: http://www.guttmacher.org

1301 Connecticut Avenue NW, Suite 700
Washington, DC 20036
Phone: (202) 296-4012, (877) 823-0262
Fax: (202) 223-5756
E-mail: info@guttmacher.org

A nonprofit organization that focuses on sexual and reproductive health research, policy analysis, and public education. The institute's mission is to protect the reproductive choices of all women and men in the United States and throughout the world. It supports people's ability to obtain the information and services needed to achieve their full human rights, safeguard their health, and exercise their individual responsibilities in regard to sexual behavior and relationships, reproduction, and family formation.

Heritage Foundation
URL: http://www.heritage.org
214 Massachusetts Avenue NE
Washington, DC 20002
Phone: (202) 546-4400

A research and educational think tank whose mission is to formulate and promote conservative public policies based on the principles of free enterprise, limited government, individual freedom, traditional American values, and a strong national defense.

Human Rights Watch
URL: http://hrw.org/women
485 Fifth Avenue
New York, NY 10017
Phone: (212) 972-8400
Fax: (212) 972-0905

Human Rights Watch has portals specific to different regions of the globe, including Afghanistan, China, and Tibet. Originally founded in 1978, as Helsinki Watch, the Human Rights Watch Asia office was opened in 1985 and the Watch Committees became Human Rights Watch in 1988. A special division devoted to women now surveys their rights across all regions.

Institute for Women's Policy Research (IWPR)
URL: http://www.iwpr.org
1707 L Street NW, Suite 750
Washington, DC 20036

Phone: (202) 785-5100
Fax: (202) 833-4362
E-mail: iwpr@iwpr.org

A research organization founded in 1987 to meet the needs for women-centered policy-oriented scientific research, IWPR focuses on issues of poverty and welfare, employment and earnings, work and family issues, health and safety, and women's civic and political participation.

International Labour Organisation's Bureau for Gender Equality
URL: http://www.ilo.org
4, route des Morillons
CH-1211, Geneva 22, Switzerland
Phone: (41) (22) 799 6090
Fax: (41) (22) 799 7657
E-mail: genprom@ilo.org

The role of the Bureau for Gender Equality, part of the Geneva-based Secretariat of the International Labour Organisation, is to advocate gender equality throughout the organization. It produces a yearly document, monitoring global employment trends.

Inter-Parliamentary Union (IPU)
URL: http://www.ipu.org
5, chemin du Pommier
Case postale 330, CH-1218
Le Grand-Saconnex
Geneva, Switzerland
Phone: (41) (22) 919 4150
Fax: (41) (22) 919 4160

The IPU is the international organization of parliaments of sovereign states (Article 1 of the Statutes of the Inter-Parliamenary Union). Established in 1889, the union is the focal point for worldwide parliamentary dialogue and works for peace and cooperation among peoples and for the firm establishment of representative democracy.

KULU—Women and Development
URL: http://www.kulu.dk/in_english.htm
Rosenoerns Allé 12, st. 1634
Copenhagen V, Denmark
Phone: (45) 3315 7870

Fax: (45) 3332 5330
E-mail: kulu@kulu.dk

KULU is an umbrella NGO for 25 women's organizations, with three local organizations and an individual membership base. It is also part of the Network on Indigenous Peoples, Gender and Natural Resource Management (IGNARM), a Danish NGO network collaboration that is active in African nations and China.

League of Kenyan Women Voters (LKWV)
URL: http://www.leaguekenya.org
Muchai Drive, off Ngong Road
P.O. Box 8332
00300 Nairobi, Kenya
Phone: (254) (20) 2712713, (254) (20) 2720605
Fax: (254) (20) 2711287
E-mail: info@leaguekenya.org

The League of Kenyan Women Voters (LKWV) is a nonpartisan political women's membership organization, which was founded in 1992 by a voluntary group of like-minded Kenyan women to advance the rights of women in elective political leadership and other positions of decision making.

League of Women Voters
URL: http://www.lwv.org
1730 M Street NW, Suite 1000
Washington, DC 20036-4508
Phone: (202) 429-1965
Fax: (202) 429-0854

The voluntary nonpartisan public service organization was organized in 1920 in Chicago as an outgrowth of Carrie Chapman Catt's National American Woman Suffrage Association. The league was organized to educate American women in the intelligent use of their newly won suffrage. Formerly limited to female membership, the league voted in 1974 to accept men as full members and now has over 110,000 members.

Maasai Girls Education Fund (MGEF)
URL: http://www.maasaigirlseducation.org
5800 MacArthur Boulevard NW
Washington, DC 20016-2512
Contact: Barbara Lee Shaw

Executive Director
Phone: (202) 237-0535
Fax: (202) 237-2536
E-mail: bshaw@maasaigirlseducation.org

Kenya Office
P.O. Box 299,
001100 Kajiado, Kenya

MGEF's mission is to educate a generation of Masai women and girls in Kenya through their complete reeducation, hand in hand with the education of the community in which they live, which includes local area chiefs. It addresses social and cultural issues such as early marriage, female circumcision, illiteracy among women, and the spread of HIV/AIDS and poverty.

Maasai Women for Education and Economic Development (MAWEED)
URL: http://www.unpo.org/member.php?arg=64

A community-based organization whose main objective is to fight for the rights of the Masai women and the educational rights of the Masai youth. The nongovernmental organization was founded in 2001 and is based in the Narok district of Kenya. With the backing of the Mainyoito Pastoralist Integrated Development Organization and the Kitengela Ilparakuo Land Owners Association, MAWEED joined the Unrepresented Nations and Peoples Organization (UNPO) in December 2004.

Muslim Women's League (MWL)
URL: http://www.mwlusa.org
3010 Wilshire Boulevard, Suite #519
Los Angeles, CA 90010
Phone: (626) 358-0335
E-mail: mwl@mwlusa.org

MWL is a nonprofit American Muslim organization working to implement the values of Islam and thereby reclaim the status of women as free, equal, and vital contributors to society.

National Abortion Federation (NAF)
URL: http://www.prochoice.org
1755 Massachusetts Avenue NW, Suite 600
Washington, DC 20036
Phone: (202) 667-5881

Fax: (202) 667-5890
E-mail: naf@prochoice.org

A professional association of abortion providers in the United States and Canada that believes women should be trusted to make private medical decisions in consultation with their health care providers. NAF offers training and services to abortion providers and information and referral services to women.

National Coalition against Domestic Violence (NCADV)
URL: http://www.ncadv.org
1120 Lincoln Street, Suite 1603
Denver, CO 80203
Phone: (303) 839-1852
Fax: (303) 831-9251
E-mail: sbaca@ncadv.org

NCADV was formally organized in January 1978 when over 100 battered women's advocates from all parts of the nation attended the U.S. Commission on Civil Rights hearing on battered women in Washington, D.C., to address common problems these programs usually faced in isolation. NCADV is the only national organization with grassroots shelter and service programs for battered women.

National Commission on the Status of Women (NCSW)
URL: http://www.ncsw.gov.pk
House # 39, Street 56, F-6/4
Islamabad, Pakistan
Phone: (51) 922 4875
Fax: (51) 922 4877

Founded in 2000 by the president of Pakistan, under the Ordinance of July 17, 2000, the commission has as its main objectives the emancipation of women, equalization of opportunities and socioeconomic conditions of women and men, and elimination of all types of discrimination against women. Functions of the commission include the examination of the policy, programs, and other measures taken by the government for women's development and the review of all policies, laws, rules, and regulations affecting the status and rights of women and gender equality in accordance with the country's constitution.

National Council of Negro Women, Inc. (NCNW)
URL: http://www.ncnw.org

633 Pennsylvania Avenue NW
Washington, DC 20004
Phone: (202) 737-0120
Fax: (202) 737-0476

Mary McLeod Bethune founded NCNW in 1935, forming it out of several major national black women's associations. She remained its president until 1949 and was its representative at the founding conference of the United Nations in San Francisco, California, in 1945. NCNW helps women of African descent to improve the quality of life for themselves, their families, and their communities with an outreach to 4 million women and has consultative status at the United Nations.

National Council of Women's Organizations (NCWO)
URL: http://www.womensorganizations.org, http://www.equalrights
  amendment.org
1050 17th Street NW, Suite 250
Washington, DC 20036
Phone: (202) 293-4505
Fax: (202) 293-4507
E-mail: ncwo@ncwo-online.org

NCWO is a nonpartisan, nonprofit umbrella organization of about 200 groups, which collectively represent over 10 million women across the country. The national coalition grew out of an informal group of women's organizational leaders after defeat of the Equal Rights Amendment in 1983. Capitalizing on the energy and inspiration that followed the 1995 Beijing Conference, NCWO has taken an active role in the policy arena, uniting women's groups across the country to work together to advance the progressive women's agenda and the Equal Rights Amendment.

National Organization for Women
URL: http://www.now.org
1100 H Street NW, 3rd Floor
Washington, DC 20005
Phone: (202) 628-8669
Fax: (202) 785-8576

The National Organization for Women (NOW) is the largest organization of feminist activists in the United States. NOW has 500,000 contributing members and 550 chapters in all 50 states and the District of Columbia. Since its founding in 1966, NOW has had the goal of taking action to bring about equality for all women. NOW works to eliminate discrimination and harassment in the workplace, schools, the justice system, and all other sectors of society; secure abortion, birth control, and reproductive rights for all women; end all forms of violence against women; and eradicate racism, sexism, and homophobia.

The National Women's History Project (NWHP)
URL: http://www.nwhp.org, http://www.legacy98.org
3343 Industrial Drive, Suite 4
Santa Rosa, CA 95403
Phone: (707) 636-2888
Fax: (707) 639-2909

A nonpartisan, nonprofit educational organization dedicated to promoting the historic contributions and the rich, diverse experiences of women to mainstream culture and society. Founded in 1996, the National Women's History Museum is scheduled to open in Washington, D.C., in 2007.

National Women's Law Center (NWLC)
URL: http://www.nwlc.org
11 Dupont Circle NW, Suite 800
Washington, DC 20036
Phone: (202) 588-5180
Fax: (202) 588-5185
E-mail: info@nwlc.org

NWLC is a nonprofit organization that has been working since 1972 to expand the possibilities for women and their families at work, in school, and in virtually every aspect of their lives. NWLC focuses on major concerns to women and girls, including family economic security, education, employment opportunities, and health, with special attention given to low-income women.

National Women's Political Caucus
URL: http://www.nwpc.org
1712 Eye Street NW, Suite 503
Washington, DC 20006
Phone: (202) 785-1100
Fax: (202) 370-6306
E-mail: info@nwpc.org

The National Women's Political Caucus is a multicultural, intergenerational, and multiissue grassroots organization dedicated to increasing women's participation in the political process and creating a true women's political power base to achieve equality for all women. NWPC recruits, trains, and supports pro-choice women candidates for elected and appointed offices at all levels of government regardless of party affiliation.

Office on Violence against Women, U.S. Department of Justice
URL: http://www.usdoj.gov/ovw
800 K Street NW, Suite 920
Washington, DC 20530
Phone: (202) 307-6026
Fax: (202) 307-3911

Since its inception in 1995, the Violence against Women Office, now the Office on Violence against Women, has worked closely with components of the Office of Justice Programs, the Office of Legal Policy, the Office of Legislative Affairs, the Office of Intergovernmental Affairs, the Immigration and Naturalization Office, the Executive Office for United States Attorneys, U.S. Attorneys' Offices, and state, tribal, and local jurisdictions to implement the mandates of the Violence against Women Act and subsequent legislation.

PeaceWomen Project
URL: http://www.peacewomen.org
WILPF, UN Office
777 United Nations Plaza, 6th Floor
New York, NY 10017
Phone: (212) 682-1265
Fax: (212) 286-8211
E-mail: info@peacewomen.org

In response to the unanimous adoption of UNSC Resolution 1325, the Women's International League for Peace and Freedom (WILPF) United Nations Office in New York City developed the PeaceWomen Project in 2001 to monitor and advocate its full and rapid implementation.

Planned Parenthood Federation of America (PPFA)
URL: http://www.plannedparenthood.org
434 West 33rd Street
New York, NY 10001
Phone: (212) 541-7800
Fax: (212) 245-1845
E-mail: actioncenter@ppfa.org

PPFA's affiliated health centers provide reproductive health care and sexual health information to nearly 5 million women, men, and teens each year through family planning counseling, testing, and referrals. Its sexual education community programs include a wide range of information resources and materials about a variety of topics concerning family planning. The organization also sponsors a range of advocacy events to defend reproductive freedom.

Rape, Abuse & Incest National Network (RAINN)
URL: http://www.rainn.org
635-B Pennsylvania Avenue SE
Washington, DC 20003
Phone: (202) 544-1034, (800) 656-4673, ext. 3
Fax: (202) 544-3556
E-mail: info@rainn.org

The nation's largest anti–sexual assault organization has been ranked as one of America's 100 Best Charities by *Worth* magazine. RAINN was founded in 1994 by Scott Berkowitz, who continues as the organization's president.

Revolutionary Association of the Women of Afghanistan (RAWA)
URL: http://www.rawa.org
P.O. Box 374
Quetta, Pakistan
Phone: (92) (300) 8551638
E-mail: rawa@rawa.org

RAWA is the oldest political/social organization of Afghan women involved in education, health, income generation, and politics. It was established in Kabul, in 1977, by a number of Afghan woman intellectuals under the leadership of Meena (1956–87), who was assassinated in 1987 in Quetta, Pakistan. RAWA's objective is to involve an increasing number of Afghan women in social and political activities aimed at acquiring women's human rights and contributing to the struggle for the establishment of a government based on democratic and secular values in Afghanistan.

Roqia Center for Women's Rights, Studies and Education
URL: http://www.kabultec.org
Kabultec
P.O. Box 2079
Falls Church, VA 22042
Phone: (703) 536-6471
E-mail: Kabultec@erols.com

Founded by the Afghan women's rights advocate Nadine Gross in 2002, the Roqia Center provides women's rights seminars, academic information, and

291

adult literacy in Kabul, Afghanistan. The innovative couples literacy program requires husbands and wives to attend class, thereby leveling the playing field for women and helping men experience models of democratic behavior and experience. The organization is the partner of Kabultec, a charity organization in the United States.

Society for Women's Health Research (SWHR)
URL: http://www.womenshealthresearch.org
1025 Connecticut Avenue NW, Suite 701
Washington, DC 20036
Phone: (202) 223-8224
Fax: (202) 833-3472

Founded in the late 1980s by women's health professionals who were convinced that the health of American women was at risk because of biases in biomedical research, SWHR is a not-for-profit research organization that also produces reports on sex-based medicine and identifies areas in which women differ from men in their health care needs. It guarantees that women's health has a voice in the federal government by supporting the women's health offices within agencies such as the Department of Health and Human Services, the Food and Drug Administration, and the Centers for Disease Control and Prevention.

Soroptimist International
URL: http://www.soroptimist.org
1709 Spruce Street
Philadelphia, PA 19103-6103
Phone: (215) 893-9000
Fax: (215) 893-5200
E-mail: siahq@soroptimist.org

Founded in 1921, Soroptimist is an international organization for business and professional women who provide volunteer service to their communities. Almost 100,000 Soroptimists in about 120 countries and territories contribute time and financial support to community-based and international projects benefiting women and girls. The name *Soroptimist* means "best for women." Club projects range from renovating domestic violence shelters, to providing mammograms to low-income women, to sponsoring self-esteem workshops for teenage girls.

Third Wave Foundation
URL: http://www.thirdwavefoundation.org/
511 West 25th Street, Suite 301

New York, NY 10001
Phone: (212) 675-0700
Fax: (212) 255-6653
E-mail: info@thirdwavefoundation.org

The Third Wave Foundation is a feminist activist foundation working nationally to support young women ages 15 to 30. Third Wave creates initiatives, operates specific grant and public education programs, and facilities networking and leadership development opportunities. It is led by a board of young women, men, and transgender activists striving to combat inequalities they face as a result of their age, gender, race, sexual orientation, economic status, or level of education.

United Nations Development Fund for Women (UNIFEM)
URL: http://www.unifem.org, http://www.unifem-eseasia.org
304 East 45th Street, 15th Floor
New York, NY 10017
Phone: (212) 906-6400
Fax: (212) 906-6705

UNIFEM was created in 1976 after the 1975 UN First World Conference on Women in Mexico City. Placing the advancement of women's human rights at the center of all of its efforts, it has worked to help improve the living standards of women in developing countries by providing financial and technical assistance to innovative programs and strategies to foster women's empowerment and gender equality. UNIFEM focuses its activities on four strategic areas: (1) reducing feminized poverty, (2) ending violence against women, (3) reversing the spread of HIV/AIDS among women and girls, and (4) achieving gender equality in democratic governance in times of peace as well as war. UNIFEM also has an East and Southeast Asia Regional Office that covers 13 countries.

United Nations Division for the Advancement of Women (DAW)
URL: http://www.un.org/womenwatch/daw
2 UN Plaza, DC2-12th Floor
New York, NY 10017
Fax: (212) 963-3463
E-mail: daw@un.org

Located within the Department of Economic and Social Affairs of the United Nations, DAW advocates the improvement of the status of women of the world and the achievement of their equality with men, both within and outside the United Nations system. DAW also provides oversight to the Commission on the Status of Women (CSW), established on June 21, 1946, to prepare recommendations and reports to the council on promoting women's rights in political, economic, civil, social, and educational fields. The commission is the vehicle by which the UN is monitoring the Beijing Platform for Action on a yearly basis.

United Nations International Research and Training Institute for the Advancement of Women (INSTRAW)
URL: http://www.un-instraw.org
102-A Santo Domingo, DN, Dominican Republic
Phone: (809) 685-2111
Fax: (809) 685-2117

INSTRAW is a United Nations entity mandated at the international level to promote and undertake research and training programs to contribute to the advancement of women and gender equality worldwide. By stimulating and assisting the efforts of intergovernmental, governmental, and nongovernmental organizations, INSTRAW plays a critical role in advancing the global agenda of gender equality, development, and peace. INSTRAW is funded entirely through voluntary contributions from UN member states and donor agencies; the institute does not have a regular UN budget.

United Nations Population Fund (UNFPA)
URL: http://www.unfpa.org
220 East 42nd Street
New York, NY 10017
Phone: (212) 297-5000

An international development agency that promotes the right of every woman, man, and child to enjoy a life of health and equal opportunity. UNFPA supports countries in using population data for policies and programs to reduce poverty and to ensure that every pregnancy is wanted, every birth is safe, every young person is free of HIV/AIDS, and every girl and woman is treated with dignity and respect.

V-Day
URL: http://www.Vday.org
New York, NY

Started by New York City women's advocate and playwright Eve Ensler, the V-Day movement is a global charity movement to stop violence against women and girls in 76 countries in Europe, Asia, Africa, the Caribbean, and all of North America. V-Day, a nonprofit corporation, distributes funds to grassroots, national, and international organizations and programs that work to stop violence against women and girls, which includes rape, battery, incest, female genital mutilation, and sexual slavery.

Vital Voices Global Partnership
URL: http://www.vitalvoices.org
1150 Connecticut Avenue NW, Suite 600
Washington, DC 20036
Phone: (202) 861-2625
Fax: (202) 861-4290

This nonprofit organization grew out of the U.S. government's successful Vital Voices Democracy Initiative, which was established in 1997 by then–first lady Hillary Rodham Clinton and former secretary of state Madeleine Albright after the United Nations Fourth World Conference on Women in Beijing. With the U.S. foreign policy goal to promote the advancement of women, Vital Voices invests in women who are leading social, economic, and political progress in their countries through development and training initiatives and a global network.

The White House Project
http://www.thewhitehouseproject.org
110 Wall Street, 16th Floor
New York, NY 10005
Phone: (212) 785-6001
Fax: (212) 785-6007
E-mail: admin@thewhitehouseproject.org

The White House Project, a national nonpartisan, not-for-profit organization, aims to advance women's leadership in all communities and sectors, up to the U.S. presidency. Through multiplatform programs, it is trying to create a culture in which women can succeed in all realms and become the critical mass needed to make American institutions, businesses, and government representative of the American population.

Women for Women International
URL: http://www.womenforwomen.org/aocontact.htm
4455 Connecticut Avenue NW, Suite 200
Washington, DC 20008

Phone: (202) 737-7705
E-mail: general@womenforwomen.org.

The organization pairs women willing to provide a year's support (at a cost of $27 per month) with "sisters" in war-torn countries. It was a 2006 Conrad N. Hilton Humanitarian Prize recipient.

Women's Alliance for Peace and Human Rights in Afghanistan (WAPHA)
URL: http://www.wapha.org/index.html
P.O. Box 77057
Washington, DC 20012-7057
E-mail: info@wapha.org

WAPHA is a nonpartisan, nonprofit, and independent organization founded by Zieba Shorish-Shamley, a cultural anthropologist who obtained her degree from the University of Wisconsin–Madison. She is a proponent of Afghan women and girls' human rights and their full participation in the peace processes and future government of Afghanistan. She also advocates women's full participation in every aspect of Afghan sociocultural systems, including education, politics, economics, and medicine.

Women's Environment & Development Organization (WEDO)
URL: http://www.wedo.org
355 Lexington Avenue, 3rd Floor
New York, NY 10017
Phone: (212) 973-0325
Fax: (212) 973-0335
E-mail: wedo@wedo.org

WEDO is an international organization that advocates women's equality in global policy. It seeks to empower women as decision makers to achieve economic, social, and gender justice; a healthy, peaceful planet; and human rights for all.

Women's International League for Peace and Freedom (WILPF)
URL: http://www.wilpf.int.ch
1, rue de Varembe
Case Postale 28
1211 Geneva 20, Switzerland
Phone: (41) (22) 919 70 80

Fax: (41) (22) 919 70 81
E-mail: info@wilpf.ch

Founded in April 1915 in the Hague, Netherlands, among 1,300 women from Europe and North America, among countries at war against each other and neutral ones, WILPF joined in a Congress of Women to protest the killing and destruction of the war then raging in Europe. Led by the Dutch physician Aletta Jacobs, the women issued 20 resolutions, some of immediate importance to end the conflict, negotiate the differences, and others with long-term aims to reduce conflict, prevent war, and lay the foundations for permanent peace. It is recognized as an international NGO with national sections in 37 countries and a New York UN office.

Women's Research and Education Institute (WREI)
URL: http://www.wrei.org
3300 North Fairfax Drive, Suite 218
Arlington, VA 22201
Phone: (703) 812-7990
Fax: (703) 812-0687
E-mail: wrei@wrei.org

WREI identifies issues affecting women and their roles in the family, workplace, and public arena, to inform and help shape public policy on these issues. It is a resource for federal legislators and administrators, and for state and local government officials, women's advocates, corporate policy makers, the media, teachers, and students. It promotes the informed scrutiny of policies regarding their effect on women and encourages the development of policy options that recognize the circumstances of women and their families.

Women Work! The National Network for Women's Employment
URL: http://www.womenwork.org
1625 K Street NW, Suite 300
Washington, DC 20006
Phone: (202) 467-6346
Fax: (202) 467-5366

The network publishes the *Economic Equity Insider* monthly while Congress is in session and is a benefit of membership with Women Work!

10

Annotated Bibliography

This annotated bibliography consists of selected books, articles, Web documents, audiovisual materials, and media agencies organized by subject area. Listings are grouped in the following categories:

Abortion

Affirmative Action

Afghanistan

Africa

China

Contraceptives

Denmark

Document Research

Education

Employment

Encyclopedias

European Union

Family Planning

Female Genital Mutilation

Feminist Literature

Gay and Lesbian Rights/
    Atypical Gender Roles

Gender Roles

Health Care

History

HIV/AIDS

Human Trafficking

International Women's
    Movement

Islam

Kenya

Leadership

Literacy

Literature

Military

Monitoring

Multicultural Issues

Politics

Population

Poverty

Property Rights

Racism

Statistics

Suffrage

Violence

Women's Studies

Within each category, items are listed by type of reference: books, articles, Web documents, television/film/video, or media. Articles include both newspapers and magazines. Articles and reports that are accessible in partial or full-text form on the Internet are listed under Web documents. An item is only listed once, where it is most germane to the subject of women's rights, although it may be relevant to several categories.

ABORTION

Books

Hull, N. E. H., William James Hoffer, and Peter Charles, eds. *The Abortion Rights Controversy in America: A Legal Reader.* Chapel Hill: University of North Carolina Press, 2004. This is a compendium of primary sources related to the abortion controversy. The editors, who are also law professors, have collected relevant briefs, news articles, statutes, and first-person accounts with a strong focus on the development of abortion law in the 1990s.

Torr, James D, ed. *Opposing Viewpoints Series: Abortion.* Farmington Hills, Mich.: Greenhaven Press, 2006. As the title suggests, the Opposing Viewpoints Series is an excellent resource for researching controversial topics. Viewpoints in the abortion book include "Is Abortion Immoral?" "How Does Abortion Affect Women?" and "Should Abortion Rights Be Restricted?"

Articles

Chinni, Dante. "A Shift in Antiabortion Strategy?" *Christian Science Monitor,* 26 July 2005, 9. After years of arguing that *Roe* is a life-or-death issue, antiabortion activists are beginning to argue that the real issue is letting the voter decide about abortion. Abortion opponents can now argue they are not interested in overriding the voters' will but simply want to restore power to the voters.

Mayes, Tessa. "Do Politicians Know the Facts?" *New Statesman,* 21 March 2005, 14. Mayes focuses on various aspects of the topic of abortion and politics in Great Britain. Includes suggestions that politicians decide before election not to make abortion an issue, in reference to the personal views of party leaders, which were published in *Cosmopolitan* magazine. It remains questionable as to whether politicians know their facts. In addition to statistics from the British Pregnancy Advisory Service (BPAS), the survival rates for premature babies are discussed. The safety of early abortions and observations that women do not discover they are pregnant until late are also mentioned, as are the reasons the BPAS turns away 100 women a year.

Sullivan, Andrew. "Life Lesson," *New Republic,* 7 February 2005, 6. Sullivan focuses on the politics and morality of abortion. Although the priority is to reduce the number of unwanted pregnancies, reference is made to a speech by New York senator Hillary Rodham Clinton in which she affirms that abortion should remain legal. She acknowledges the role religious communities have played in encouraging women not to have abortions. The article highlights ways in which the pro-choice movement has damaged its image by not focusing on the moral aspects of abortion.

Web Documents

Ahman, Elisabeth, and Iqbal Shah. "Unsafe Abortion: Global and Regional Estimates of Unsafe Abortion and Associated Mortality in 2000." World Health Organization (WHO), 2004. Available online. URL: http://www.who.int/reproductive-health/publications/unsafe_abortion_estimates_04/index.html. Accessed February 4, 2006. The report takes the position that unsafe abortion is preventable but persists as a significant cause of maternal morbidity and mortality rates in the developing world, where nearly all unsafe abortions occur. Since 1995, the World Health Organization has estimated the regional and global incidences of unsafe abortion and associated mortality rate. Estimates based on figures for the year 2000 indicate that 19 million unsafe abortions take place each year, indicating that approximately one in 10 pregnancies ends in an unsafe abortion, giving a ratio of one unsafe abortion to about seven live births. Unplanned pregnancies, family planning, and the legal framework of abortion as it applies from a global perspective, are also topics covered in this report.

Childress, Sarah. "Abortion Wars: From Internet Campaigns to Cookie Boycotts, Small Pro-Life Groups Are Adopting a Range of Tactics to Fight the Nation's Largest Pro-Choice Organization." *Newsweek*, Web edition (April 18, 2004). Available online. URL: http://www.msnbc.msn.com/id/4733090. Accessed May 5, 2006. Childress chronicles the efforts of pro-life organizations as they mobilize in their fight against legal abortion.

Feldmann, Linda. "A New Federal Move to Limit Teen Abortion." *Christian Science Monitor* (April 27, 2005). Available online. URL: http://www.csmonitor.com/2005/0427/p01s02-uspo.html. Accessed May 5, 2006. Feldmann reports on Congress's latest abortion-related legislation. The Child Interstate Abortion Notification Act, or CIANA, makes it a crime to transport a minor across state lines to obtain an abortion.

Johnsen, Jennifer. "The Difference between Emergency Contraception Pills and Medication." Planned Parenthood, 2006. Available online. URL: http://www.plannedparenthood.org/pp2/portal/files/portal/medicalinfo/ec/fact-contraception-abortion.xml. Accessed March 30, 2006. Contains basic facts and documents that describe the differences in current abortion methods.

Sowti, Naseem. "Abortion: Just the Data: With High-Court Debate Brewing, New Report Shows Procedure's Numbers Down." *Washington Post*, p. HE01 (July 19, 2005). Available online. URL: http://www.washingtonpost.com/wp-dyn/content/article/2005/07/18/AR2005071801164.html. Accessed May 5, 2006. Offers a demographic snapshot about how many abortions are being performed in the United States and who is obtaining them.

Television/Film/Video

Abortion Clinic. 53 minutes. *Frontline*, Public Broadcasting Station, 1983, television documentary (May 2006). Information and documentary are available

online. URL: http://www.pbs.org/wgbh/pages/frontline/twenty/watch/abortion.
html. The program examines the successes of the pro-life movement and its efforts to lobby for and help pass state legislation restricting access to abortion.
It was filmed at a clinic in Chester, Pennsylvania, a small city with a 30 percent
unemployment rate at that time, as a common example of an abortion clinic in
the United States. The clinic offered individual counseling in which the reasons
behind the decision are explored. As are most women who have had abortions
in the United States in the past 30 years, the two whose abortions are shown in
this film are single, white, and young. A 1983 National Academy of Television
Arts and Sciences Emmy Award winner for Outstanding Background/Analysis
of a Single Current Story, the story touches upon the balance between state and
federal authority over Americans' lives and state legislative measures by pro-life
advocates to restrict access to abortion.

The Last Abortion Clinic. Written, produced, and directed by Raney Aronson-Rath.
52 minutes. *Frontline,* Public Broadcasting Station, 2005, television documentary
(May 2006). More information and documentary are available online. URL: http://
www.pbs.org/wgbh/pages/frontline/clinic. In 2005, the *Frontline* documentary
team interviewed abortion providers and their patients, staff at a pro-life pregnancy counseling center, and key legal strategists on both sides of the national
debate in the South, where a growing number of states with regulations limiting
access to abortion states have been trying to restrict abortion. Raney Aronson-
Rath documents the success of the pro-life movement and how this happened
over the past decade, beginning with a critical 1992 U.S. Supreme Court ruling in
a case called *Planned Parenthood v. Casey.* While the Court upheld *Roe v. Wade,* it
changed the standard by which abortion laws would be judged. It allowed states to
regulate abortion so long as they did not place an "undue burden" on the women
seeking the procedure. The page also offers additional tools—statistics, commentaries, a map of state legislation, and access to the documentary itself.

Vera Drake. Directed by Mike Leigh. 125 minutes. Fine Line Features, 2004, film (May
2006). More information is available online. URL: http://www.veradrake.com. For
20 years, an Englishwoman (Imelda Staunton) "with a heart of gold" performs
abortions for fellow working-class girls and women who are pregnant, without
her family's knowledge. Often the women are young girls or are already mothers
of several children. She does this at no charge, although her friend, Lillian Clark,
brokers the appointments for a fee without Drake's knowledge until 1950, when
a girl nearly dies.

AFFIRMATIVE ACTION
Books

Jain, Harish C., Peter Sloane, Frank Horwitz, Simon Taggar, and Nan Weiner. *Employment Equity and Affirmative Action: An International Comparison.* Armonk, N.Y.:
M. E. Sharpe, 2003. Compares similarities and differences of affirmative action/

employment equity practices in six countries (the United States, Canada, Great Britain/Northern Ireland, India, Malaysia, and South Africa).

Articles

Alverson, Marchel. "The Call to Manage Diversity," *Women in Business* 50 (4) (July/August 1998): 34. The author discusses diversity in the workplace and the need for the management of diversity. In his exploration of how minorities, women, seniors, and the disabled can add diversity to the workplace, he includes comments from Connie Aden, president of Aden Management Resources. The article defines diversity training and its importance to a business and what management can do to overcome the differences that divide individuals. He distinguishes between affirmative action and "Equal Employment Opportunity."

Casey, Susan, Albert Kim, and Kostya Kennedy. "The Games Women Play," *Sports Illustrated*, 24 June 2002, 21. The authors focus on how the Title IX legislation has impacted the number of athletic opportunities allotted to women in the United States and addresses the controversy surrounding the law 30 years after its passage and details about the law, which enforces equal opportunity for both sexes in sports that receive federal funding. Opponents attribute the gradual elimination of men's wrestling programs to the bill.

Poltenson, Norman. "Diversity (a.k.a. Affirmative Action) Splits Courts and Country," *Business Journal* (Central New York), 20 April, 2001, 35. Poltenson writes an overview on court rulings in different legal disputes arising from racial diversity issues. He discusses factors that promote racial diversity in U.S. education institutions, which he believes will broaden intellectual and life experiences, but criticizes affirmative action programs.

AFGHANISTAN

Books

Ellis, Deborah. *Women of the Afghan War.* Westport, Conn.: Praeger, 2002. The author, an antiwar and women's rights activist in Toronto, Ontario, Canada, writes an oral history account of the Afghan War as told by women victims. As personal snapshots of the news reports of the Taliban activities in Afghanistan, the accounts provide a historical background to the growth of the Taliban and reveal circumstances of the daily life women must survive in a closed society.

Sunita Mehta, ed. *Women for Afghan Women—Shattering Myths and Claiming the Future.* New York: Palgrave Macmillan, 2002. An attempt to write history, to increase awareness of the issues of Afghanistan and Afghan women, and to promote the agency of Afghan women in issues that impact their lives, the book includes a variety of female voices, highlighting a unifying desire to join as women and share, network, and strategize for change. This desire is focused on Afghan women but is also about global sisterhood and about the importance of feminist activism on an international level. The group of Afghan and non-Afghan women formed in April 2001 and is still committed to the struggle for women's human rights.

Zoya, James R. Follain, John Follain, and Rita Cristofari. *Zoya's Story: An Afghan Woman's Battle for Freedom.* New York: HarperCollins, 2002. Zoya is a young activist who describes how the Taliban publicly cut hands and lashed sick women at hospitals. She chronicles the oblique and subtle resistance of the Kabulites, as women wore makeup under the veils and cursed Taliban under their breath at public places. She also describes the pitiable conditions at the refugee camps in Peshawar, where she was assigned to work by RAWA. She describes the difficulty in operating a school in a camp where most fathers thought a daughter was more useful weaving carpets than acquiring education, which would make her an "infidel." Zoya also speaks about the dangers faced by RAWA members from Taliban supporters in Pakistani cities.

Web Documents

Amowitz, Lynn L. "Women's Health and Human Rights in Afghanistan. A Population-Based Assessment." Physicians for Human Rights (PHR), 2001. Available online. URL: http://www.phrusa.org/campaigns/afghanistan/Afghan_report_toc.html. Accessed December 26, 2005. Based on research undertaken by PHR over a three-month period in the year 2000, the report offers background information and current statistics on humanitarian aid to Afghanistan with the chapter "The Status of Women." It also includes a useful glossary of common terms.

Associated Press. "New Rights, but Afghan Women Still May Face Forced Marriages." *International Herald Tribune* (March 15, 2005). Available online. URL: http://www.iht.com/articles/2005/03/14/news/afghan.php. Accessed June 14, 2006. The story takes as an example of forced marriages 14-year-old Bibi, an Afghan girl who has never seen the father who may earn as much as $7,000 from selling her into marriage with a stranger.

Haidari, M. Ashraf. "Civil Society: Afghanistan's Parliamentary Election Results Confirm Stunning Gains for Women." Eurasianet (October 28, 2005). Available online. URL: http://www.eurasianet.org/departments/civilsociety/articles/eav102805b_pr.shtml. Haidari highlights with statistics the challenges overcome in Afghanistan's first parliamentary elections on September 18, 2005, as the fulfillment to the Bonn Agreement, signed after Afghanistan was liberated from Taliban rule in November 2001. She also speaks of women's returning to political leadership roles.

Human Rights Watch. "Afghan Election Diary." Human Rights Asia (September 19, 2005). Available online. URL: http://www.hrw.org/campaigns/afghanistan. Accessed December 18, 2005. Daily posts from the division researchers Sam Zarifi and Charmain Mohamed that are informative and candid about the challenges in the field during the election process.

———. "The Status of Women in Afghanistan, October 2004." Human Rights Asia. 2004. Available online. URL: http://www.hrw.org/campaigns/afghanistan/facts.htm. Accessed December 19, 2005. A list of facts about women in Afghanistan two years after the end of the Taliban rule.

Kolhatkar, Sonali. "Afghan Women Continue to Fend for Themselves." Foreign Policy in Focus (FPIF) Special Report (March 2004). Available online. URL: http://www.fpif.org/papers/2004afghanwom.html. Accessed December 26, 2006. Kolhatkar points out the various measures and promises by international organizations and the United States to establish equality, democracy, and economic, civil, and political rights for women and for the Afghan population, but "there is little about creating the institutions to uphold or implement these provisions."

Nawa, Fariba. "Afghan Women Debate the Terms of Their Future." Women's E-News (June 30, 2002). Available online. URL: http://www.womensenews.org/article.cfm/dyn/aid/956/context/cover. Accessed October 30, 2005. Afghan women agree that they should play a role in the rebuilding of their country. They are divided, however, on what role Islam should play in the new nation—integral to the new government or a belief system guiding a secular state.

Television/Films/Video

Afghanistan: Exporting the Taliban Revolution. Reported by Mark Corcoran and Ashraf Ali. 24 minutes. Films for the Humanities & Sciences, Princeton, N.J., 1998, documentary. In Afghanistan, the Taliban—militant Sunni fundamentalists schooled in Pakistan—have taken over almost all of the country. Will their jihad spread to the Sunni minority of Iran, igniting a rebellion against that country's Shiite government? Or will Iran strike first, through the Shiite minority living in Afghanistan? This compelling report, filmed by the first crew to enter Afghanistan after America's antiterrorist air strikes in 1998, takes a firsthand look at both the results and the implications of the escalating tensions between Afghanistan and its neighbors.

Afghanistan Revealed. 45 minutes. National Geographic, 2001, documentary film. A vivid portrait of the tumultuous country during the Taliban rule, when it was no longer accessible to journalists and filmmakers. Features in-depth interviews by the author Sebastian Junger and the photographer Reza Deghati of the late Afghan resistance leader Ahmad Shad Massoud, who was assassinated two days before the September 11 terrorist attacks in the United States. Includes exclusive interviews with Taliban soldiers being held by the Northern Alliance. Looks at refugees who speak plainly of their suffering from the effects of Taliban rule and the decrees that are especially harsh for women.

Afghanistan Unveiled. Produced by Aïna Women Filming Group and directed by Brigitte Brault and Aïna. 52 minutes. Public Broadcasting System, 2003, film. Information available online. URL: http://www.pbs.org/independentlens/afghanistan unveiled/index.html. AINA is a nongovernmental organization led by the accomplished photojournalist Reza Deghati, who from July 2002 to August 2003 oversaw the training of 14 young women, several still in their teens, as camera operators and video journalists at the Aïna Afghan Media and Culture Center in Kabul. The first female journalists to be trained in Afghanistan for more than a decade and the first ever to be trained in digital media, most of the trainees had never traveled outside Kabul and had not been able to study or pursue careers while the Taliban controlled their country. Created as the culmination of this unique training program, the film contrasts the harsh lives of the rural women of Afghanistan with those of the film's young camerawomen, who are experiencing newfound freedom and opportunity while attempting to use their work to change the condition of women in their country.

Behind the Veil: Afghan Women under Fundamentalism. 26 minutes. Films Media Group, 2001, documentary film. Information available online. URL: http://www. films.com/id/1860/Behind_the_Veil_Afghan_Women_under_Fundamentalism. htm#. For women living in Afghanistan under repressive Taliban rule, beatings, rape, and enslavement were commonplace occurrences. This program, filmed during the Taliban's regime, describes the human rights abuses that escalated after the withdrawal of Soviet forces, as seen through the eyes of women who survived years of rampant gender and religious intolerance. Resistance activities carried out by women's groups as they fought for freedom and democracy inside the country are also documented. Some content may be objectionable, but check the educational standards scores and view the online media clip.

Media

Afgha.com. Available online. URL: http://www.afgha.com. Accessed May 5, 2006. A Web site with current news stories and editorial opinions from Afghanistan.

Afghan Observer. Available online. URL: http://www.afghanobserver.com. Accessed May 5, 2006. An online daily magazine with stories in Arabic and English and other resources.

Aïna World. Available online. URL: http://www.ainaworld.com/main.html. Accessed May 5, 2006. Founded on August 2, 2001, by the renowned photojournalist Reza, the nongovernmental organization Aïna is working to build and develop a thriving civil society through independent media and culture projects. Aïna offers specialized audiovisual training (filming, photography, journalism, etc.) to women in Afghanistan, encouraging them to speak out and keeping them informed through national information campaigns about important issues such as health, labor rights, and the democratic process.

AFRICA

Media

Feminist Africa. Available online. URL: http://www.feministafrica.org. Accessed July 5, 2006. Feminist Africa is a publication of the African Gender Institute and the continental Feminist Studies Network. Initiated in 2001, and currently hosted at the African Gender Institute at the University of Cape Town, it is produced by an editorial team in conjunction with an international editorial advisory group drawn from the feminist scholarly community.

CHINA

Books

Gilmartin, Christina Kelley. *Engendering the Chinese Revolution: Radical Women, Communist Politics, and Mass Movements in the 1920s.* Berkeley and Los Angeles: University of California Press, 1995. A detailed history of the radical women involved in the revolution and Communist politics from 1920 to 1927.

National Bureau of Statistics. *China Statistical Yearbook.* Beijing: China Statistics Press, 2004. This annual statistical publication covers data in 2003 and some selected data series in historically important years and the most recent 20 years at national level and local levels of province, autonomous region, and municipality directly under the central government, and therefore, reflects various aspects of China's social and economic development.

Web Documents

McCallion, Maureen. "Chinese Women: Incorporating Women into Lessons on China." Primary Source. Available online. URL: http://www.primarysource.org/library/tcus/china_women.pdf (February 2, 2005). A nonprofit Massachusetts organization that works with a number of educational centers, including Harvard University, to create primary source curriculum materials for interdisciplinary social studies classrooms. This document uses examples of the roles of Chinese women in history.

"Population and Family Planning Law of the People's Republic of China." Legislative Affairs Commission of the Standing Committee of the National People's Congress of the People's Republic of China, 2002 (February 2005). Available online. URL: http://www.unescap.org/esid/psis/population/database/poplaws/law_china/china%20pop%20and%20family%20planning.pdf. Accessed January 4, 2006. The official translation of the law adopted on December 29, 2001, which took effect September 2002, enforces family planning as a "fundamental state policy."

"Unbreakable Spirits: Women Breaking Down Barriers in China." Asia Source. Available online. URL: http://www.asiasource.org/arts/unbreaksprts/Daughter.cfm. Accessed April 4, 2006. Short biography of Professor Zheng Xiaoying, the first female conductor in China.

"UN Launches Gender Facility for Research and Advocacy in China." People's Daily Online (May 27, 2005). Available online. URL: http://english.people.com.cn/200505/27/eng20050527_187012.html. Accessed May 5, 2006. Aiming to advance gender equality, the article describes China's launch of the China Gender Facility for Research and Advocacy. Twelve specific areas have been identified as priorities; they include revision of women's law, the collection and use of gender disaggregated data, and sex ratios and girl children.

"Women and Gender in Chinese Studies Network." University of Warwick. Available online. URL: http://www.wagnet.ox.ac.uk. Accessed April 15, 2006. Women's activism in China. The Women and Gender in Chinese Studies Network (WAG) was inaugurated on August 12, 2001, in Berlin. The international network on gender studies offers links to papers, publications, and reading lists specific to Chinese women.

Television/Films/Video

Through Chinese Women's Eyes. Produced and directed by Mayfair Yang. 52 minutes. 1997, documentary film. Distributed by Women Make Movies, New York. The Chinese-American anthropologist Mayfair Mei-hui Yang visits Shanghai to study Chinese women's changing social roles from a Communist to a consumer culture. The documentary includes footage that spans the 20th century, of traditional gender roles, propaganda films from the 1950s, Chinese feminism during the UN world conference on women in Beijing, and recent television shots of teachers and women's rights organizers.

Media/Newspapers

Chinese Women. Available online. URL: http://www.china.org.cn/english/features/cw/139080.htm. Accessed May 21, 2006. The Chinese Women section of an international news agency covering Chinese affairs and international issues in English covers topics of interest to and about Chinese women. The Web site is produced by the China Internet Information Center.

CONTRACEPTIVES

Books

Tone, Andrea. *Devices and Desires: A History of Contraceptives in America.* New York: Hill & Wang, 2001. Tone addresses how the complex story around unwanted pregnancies, quack remedies, and backstreet abortions led to the need for contraceptive choices—from the condoms, pessaries, and douches available in the Victorian era, to the custom-fitted diaphragm and the development of the Pill. Activist Margaret Sanger gained legitimacy for the movement and nurtured the demand for it. The book also deals with related issues: the Pill's health risks, religious objections to it, alleged racism in birth control policy, and the Dalkon Shield tragedy, in which business decisions contributed to the marketing of an unsafe intrauterine device (IUD) in the 1970s.

Articles

Thottam, Jyoti. "A Big Win for Plan B: Wal-Mart's About-Face Expands Access to the 'Morning After' Pill," *Time,* 13 March 2006, 41. Thottam evaluates Wal-Mart's decision to stock the controversial emergency contraceptive Plan B, also known as the morning-after pill, in its 3,700 pharmacies nationwide and what it means for both sides of the abortion debate.

Web Documents

"The Pill: How It Is Affecting U.S. Morals, Family Life." *U.S. News & World Report* (July 11, 1966). Available online. URL: http://www.pbs.org/wgbh/amex/pill/filmmore/ ps_revolution.html. Accessed April 21, 2006. The article reflects how the Pill caused a dramatic change in female attitudes in its first few years on the market.

Television/Films/Video

The Pill. Produced and directed by Chana Gazit. 90 minutes. PBS Home Video, 2004, documentary film. Information available online. URL: http://www.pbs.org/wgbh/ amex/pill/filmmore/index.html. In May 1960, the U.S. Food and Drug Administration approved the sale of the contraceptive pill, a drug that would have an unprecedented impact on American culture. Within five years, more than 6 million American women would make it part of their daily lives; in contrast, a decade earlier, the concept of an aspirinlike pill to prevent pregnancies was inconceivable to the general public. Laws criminalizing the sale of contraceptive devices were still on the books in 30 states around the country. The documentary tells the story of Margaret Sanger and Katharine McCormick, older, defiant women activists who hired and paid the bills of Gregory Pincus, an unknown biologist, to research contraceptive options. He persuaded a pharmaceutical company to risk a possible boycott to put "the Pill" on the market with the aid of John Rock, a well-respected Catholic gynecologist, to conduct the field studies.

DENMARK

Books

Berquist, Christine. *Equal Democracies? Gender and Politics in the Nordic Countries.* Oslo: Scandinavian University Press, 1999. A joint effort of several Nordic scholars specializing in the study of gender and politics. This book reexamines the concept of homogeneity within the region and features of social democracy and extensive equality of the sexes, with two core questions: How equal are women and men in the Nordic countries? How homogeneous are the Nordic countries? The book discusses welfare and gender equality in the Nordic countries, which includes the self-governing islands of the Faeroes, Greenland, and Åland, and characterizes the so-called Nordic model. Berquist also reveals how the Nordic lands differ and shows how different development histories are reflected in diverse strategies with respect to gender equality policy.

Walter, Lynn, ed. "Denmark: Women's Rights and Women's Welfare." In *Women's Rights: A Global View.* Westport, Conn.: Greenwood Press, 2001. Dr. Walter examines the intersections of gender, race, culture, and class in the lives of women in the world and, more particularly, of women in Denmark, in this chapter from her book.

Web Documents

The Danish Research Centre on Gender Equality (CeLi), The Roskilde University. Available online. URL: http://www.celi.dk/template/t09.php?menuId=148. Accessed May 7, 2006. The English-language page of the Danish Web site for the center contains links to its English publications and background information on the relationship of CeLi, which was founded in September 2002, to the Danish National Research Center and Documentation Center on Gender and Equality. Formerly the responsibility of the Gender Equality Ministry, it was transferred to the Ministry for Science, Technology and Innovation.

"Gender Equality." The Danish State, official Web site for Denmark. Available online. URL: http://denmark.dk/portal/page?_pageid=374,520528&_dad=portal&_schema =PORTAL. Accessed November 15, 2000. Historical tracing of information about key figures and events in the women's movement, as well as political acts and treaties that have shaped gender development in Denmark; written in English.

"Report from Denmark by Our Transnational Partner Helle Jacobsen." European Database: Women in Decision-Making (August 2000). Available online. URL: http://www.fczb.de/projekte/wid_db/CoRe/Denmark.htm. Quick facts and statistics about women in politics in Denmark, accompanied by background history and information on women holding political positions.

Television/Films/Video

Babette's Feast. Directed by Gabriel Axel. 102 minutes. 1987. About two young devoutly religious sisters in a Danish fishing village, whose lives are changed by a visiting French woman.

DOCUMENT RESEARCH

Non-Governmental Organizations at the United Nations. Available online. URL: http://habitat.igc.org/ngo-rev/index.html. Accessed May 8, 2006. Links to UN resolutions and International Synergy documents.

United Nations. "United Nations Documentation: Research Guide." Resolutions Adopted by the General Assembly at Its 53rd Session (May 9, 2006). Available online. URL: http://www.un.org/Depts/dhl/resguide/r53.htm. Accessed May 9, 2006. Provides a searchable database of General Assembly resolutions and additional documents.

United Nations Conferences: Selected Materials Available in the Michigan State University Libraries and on the WWW (February 17, 2003). Available online. URL: http://www.lib.msu.edu/publ_ser/docs. Accessed December 18, 2006. Includes links to selected UN conferences, general information about locating UN conferences, and other relevant information.

EDUCATION

Articles

Thornburgh, Nathan. "Dropout Nation." *Time,* 17 April 2006, 30–40. The number of high school students who leave school before graduation is higher than believed. Thornburgh looks inside one town's struggle to reverse the tide and an impressive statistic: Nearly one out of three public high school students will not graduate, and for Latinos and African Americans, the rate approaches 50 percent.

Web Documents

"College Enrollment and Work Activity of High School Graduates." Bureau of Labor Statistics, Current Population Survey (March 24, 2006). Available online. URL: http://www.bls.gov/news.release/hsgec.toc.htm. News releases and data tables with information regarding college enrollment and work activity of 2005 high school graduates. The college enrollment rate for recent high school graduates was a historical high for the series dating back to 1959.

"Digest of Educational Statistics Tables and Figures." National Center for Education Statistics, 2004 (April 2005). Available online. URL: http://nces.ed.gov/programs/digest/d04/tables/dt04_102.asp. Accessed March 1, 2006. With data on educational enrollment at all levels of education between 1995 and 2004, the site also has statistics from 1989 to 2005 in other areas of education, such as the use of libraries and their cooperation with day care services and schools.

"State of the World's Mothers 2005: The Power and Promise of Girls' Education." Save the Children (May 2005). Available online. URL: http://www.savethechildren.org/mothers/report_2005/images/SOWM_2005.pdf. Accessed May 3, 2006. The report explores the connection between girls' education and a more healthy and prosperous future for all children. It highlights the need to reach the 58 million girls who are not attending school. By shining a spotlight on countries that are succeeding in getting and keeping girls in school, it shows that effective solutions to this challenge are affordable, even in the world's poorest countries.

"Title IX: 25 Years of Progress." U.S. Department of Education, June 1997 (July 9, 1997). Available online. URL: http://www.ed.gov/pubs/TitleIX/index.html. Accessed December 14, 2006. Reviews the impact Title IX legislation has had on women in education, sports, and related areas.

Television/Films/Video

Mona Lisa Smile. Directed by Mike Newell. 117 minutes, 2003. A freethinking art professor (Julia Roberts) teaches conservative 1950s Wellesley College girls (including Julia Stiles) to question their traditional societal roles.

EMPLOYMENT

Books

Giele, Janet Zollinger, and Leslie F. Stebbins. *Contemporary World Issues: Women and Equality in the Workplace: A Reference Handbook.* New York: ABC-CLIO, 2003. In spite of notable progress for women in the workplace, why do men continue to have better pay, benefits, status, and opportunities, while working women are still overlooked? This guide to gender equity in the workplace details legal and social progress and the inequalities from World War II to the present and examines sociological and economic implications of inequity. The authors focus mostly on the United States, with comparisons with global issues, to describe the impact of laws and social policies on sex discrimination, equal pay law, affirmative action, and issues of comparable worth.

Articles

Fullerton, Howard N., Jr. "Labor Force Participation: 75 Years of Change, 1950–98 and 1998–2025," *Monthly Labor Review,* December 1999. Available online. URL: http://www.eeoc.gov/federal/fsp2002/part1.html. Accessed November 29, 2005. Women's labor force participation rates have increased significantly over the past 50 years, narrowing the gap between rates for women and men; however, aging will play a dominant role in the rates for 2015 and 2025. This report examines Asian, black, and Hispanic populations of women as well.

Web Documents

Bureau of Labor Statistics (BLS). "NLS Overview." National Longitudinal Study (NLS): Mature and Young Women Cohort Data (March 10, 2004). Available online. URL: http://www.bls.gov/home.htm. Accessed March 1, 2006. The four groups of men and women in the NLS Original Cohorts were first interviewed in the mid- to late 1960s. These cohorts were selected because each faced important labor market decisions, which were of special concern to policymakers. The men's cohort was retired, while respondents in the mature women's and young women's cohorts continue to be interviewed on a biennial basis and have been interviewed for over three decades.

———. "Women in the Labor Force: A Databook." U.S. Department of Labor (May 2005). Available online. URL: http://www.bls.gov/cps/wlf-databook.pdf. Accessed December 2, 2005. Background information and statistical tables on the status of women in the American labor force from 1970 to 2004.

———. "Women's Bureau." U.S. Department of Labor (June 28, 2006). Available online. URL: http://www.dol.gov/wb. Accessed August 1, 2006. Includes quick facts: 20

leading occupations of employed women in 2005, hot jobs for the 21st century, 2004–14; older women workers, ages 55 and over; women in the labor force in 2005; saving for retirement; women in nontraditional jobs; women in nursing.

Institute for Women's Policy Research. "The Gender Wage Ratio: Women's and Men's Earnings" (April 2006). Available online. URL: http://www.iwpr.org/pdf/Updated 2006_C350.pdf. The most recent fact sheet measuring and tracking women's weekly earnings from 1955 to 2005. There is a wealth of U.S. research reports on the status of women and employment at the national and state levels at the IWPR Web site.

International Labour Organization (ILO). "Gender Equality Tool" (March 10, 2006). Available online. URL: http://www.ilo.org/dyn/gender/gender.home. Accessed February 7, 2006. Lists international events, resources, and highlights about the status of women and gender equality in management and the workplace, including tools for men and boys.

———. "Global Employment Trends Brief." Employment Strategy (January 2006). Available online. URL: http://www.ilo.org/public/english/employment/strat/stratprod. htm. Accessed February 7, 2006. A yearly report produced by the ILO that monitors global employment trends.

———. "LABORSTA" (July 2006). Available online. URL: http://laborsta.ilo.org/default _page.html?submit=Home. Accessed February 12, 2006. View and extract data and metadata for over 200 countries or territories from the ILO Bureau of Statistics database on labor.

Women Work! The National Network for Women's Employment. "Chutes and Ladders: The Search for Solid Ground for Women in the Workforce—Update on the Status of Displaced Homemakers and Single Mothers in the United States" (February 17, 2005). Available online. URL: http://www.womenwork.org/issues/chutes.htm. Accessed January 21, 2006. The Women Work! study has found that single mothers and displaced homemakers are not a disappearing phenomenon in the United States. In fact, these family groups are on the increase and likely to be vastly overrepresented in the nation's low-paying service jobs. The report provides an in-depth analysis of 2003 census data and recommendations for intervention and change to support adequately women's transitions into and retention within the workforce. An update of the 1994 report, "Women Work, Poverty Persists."

ENCYCLOPEDIAS

Books

Hannam, June, Mitzi Auchterlonie, and Katherine Holden, eds. *International Encyclopedia of Women's Suffrage.* New York: ABC-CLIO, 2000. This encyclopedia covers the history of women's suffrage throughout the world, enabling the reader to make comparisons among individual countries. The book includes biographies of individual activists and thematic entries covering issues such as suffrage periodicals and newspapers.

Walter, Lynn, editor in chief. *The Greenwood Encyclopedia of Women's Issues World-wide.* 6 vols. Westport, Conn: Greenwood Press, 2003. Europe, edited by Lynn Walter. Sub-Saharan Africa, Aili Mari Tripp, volume editor. North Africa, Bahira Sherif-Trask, volume editor. North America and the Caribbean, Cheryl Toronto Kalny, volume editor. Central and South America, Amy Lind, volume editor. Asia and Oceania, Manisha Desai, volume editor. Covers education, employment, family and sexuality, health, politics and law, religion and spirituality, and violence.

EUROPEAN UNION
Books

García-Ramon, Maria Dolors, and Janice Monk. *Women of the European Union: The Politics of Work and Daily Life.* London and New York: Routledge, 1996. Collects studies to raise questions about the implications of the European Union policies for women. Focusing on different scales of analysis, it includes comparative multinational chapters as well as national case studies and in-depth examinations of urban and rural contexts. The book shows how work, family, and the state function differently in Spain, Italy, Greece, and Portugal than in the countries of northern Europe. Additional perspectives on diversity are provided in chapters addressing discrimination against lesbian women in Denmark and middle-class and suburban couples in the Netherlands.

Snyder, Paula, ed. *The European Women's Almanac.* London: Scarlet Press, 1992. A useful legal reference with statistics and commentary on the socioeconomic position of European women. Indexed by country.

FAMILY PLANNING
Book

Lief, Michael S., and H. Mitchell Caldwell. *And the Walls Came Tumbling Down: Closing Arguments That Changed the Way We Live—from Protecting Free Speech to Winning Women's Suffrage to Defending the Right to Die.* New York: A Lisa Drew Book/Scribner, 2004. Closing arguments of several trials presented in this book are relevant to the issues of sexual reproduction and suffrage rights.

Web Documents

"Family Law." Uniform Law Commissioners (June 18, 2002). Available online. URL: http://www.nccusl.org/nccusl/uniformacts-subjectmatter.asp#family. Accessed July 5, 2006. The National Conference of Commissioners on Uniform State Laws has worked for the uniformity of state laws since 1892. It is a nonprofit unincorporated association, which comprises state commissions on uniform laws from each state, the District of Columbia, the Commonwealth of Puerto Rico, and the U.S. Virgin Islands. Each jurisdiction determines the method of appointment and the number of commissioners actually appointed. Most jurisdictions provide for their commission by statute.

Gillespie, Duff G. "Whatever Happened to Family Planning and, for That Matter, Reproductive Health?" *International Family Planning Perspectives* 30 (March 2004): 34–38. Available online. URL: http://www.guttmacher.org/pubs/journals/ 3003404.pdf. Accessed December 10, 2006. Under the auspices of the Bill and Melinda Gates Institute, senior scholar Gillespie surveys the conspicuous absence of reproductive health issues from major international conferences in recent years.

FEMALE GENITAL MUTILATION
Books

Dirie, Waris, and Cathleen Miller. *Desert Flower: The Extraordinary Journey of a Desert Nomad.* New York: William Morrow, 1998. The journey of a young Somali woman who fled her country's traditional tribal practices to become a supermodel in New York City. As special ambassador to the United Nations, she has as her mission to create awareness of female genital mutilation.

Articles

Hakim, L. Y. "Impact of Female Genital Mutilation on Maternal and Neonatal Outcomes during Parturition." *East African Medical Journal* 78 (2001): 255–258. This article evaluates the impact of female genital mutilation on parturition and to create awareness of its implications for women's and neonates' health. This cross-sectional study took place at the Tikur Anbessa, St. Paul's, and Ghandhi Memorial Hospitals, between January and December 1997.

Web Documents

U.S. State Department. "Female Genital Mutilation (FGM) or Female Genital Cutting (FGC): Individual Country Reports" (June 1, 2001). Available online. URL: http:// www.state.gov/g/wi/rls/rep/crfgm. Accessed May 9, 2006. Individual country reports on FGM or FGC are used as factual background material by Immigration and Naturalization Services (INS) asylum adjudicators. They were developed and released by the Office of the Senior Coordinator for International Women's Issues.

FEMINIST LITERATURE
Books

Anderson, B. S. *Joyous Greetings: The First International Women's Movement, 1830–1860.* New York: Oxford University Press, 2000. Emphasizes the dramatic impact of the Industrial Revolution on western Europe and the United States and the way it ignited an international feminist movement—not just a series of discrete feminist activities in various countries, as other historians have posited. The narrative centers on the contributions of a core group of 20 feminists—American, English, Scottish, French, German, and Swedish—who shared ideas, platforms, and organizing techniques to create political change throughout the United States and western Europe.

de Beauvoir, Simone. *The Second Sex.* New York: Vintage Books, 1989. Originally published in French in 1949, translated into English in 1953. Text on the history of feminism that gives a sense of how far the movement has advanced in the last 50 years and what constituted "radical" feminist thought around 1950.

Freedman, Estelle. *No Turning Back: The History of Feminism and the Future of Women.* New York: Ballantine Books, 2002. Originally published in 1963. Examines issues related to politics, economics, race, relationships, health, sexuality, and violence within the context of feminist history and the creation of different forms of feminism within various cultures.

Friedan, B. *The Feminine Mystique.* New York: W. W. Norton, 1997. Originally published in 1963. A classic and insightful feminist text that voiced the unhappiness felt by women in the West in the 1950s. It is still valued for the way it exposed society's shaping of women's lives and questioned what women take for granted.

Greer, Germaine. *The Female Eunuch.* New York: Farrar, Straus & Giroux, 2001. Originally published in 1970. Greer believed sexual liberation was the key to lifting women's oppression. The book had an impact on sexual relations between men and women that generated debate both outside and inside the women's liberation movement.

Peters, Julie Stone, and Andrea Wolper, ed. *Women's Rights, Human Rights: International Feminist Perspectives.* New York and London: Routledge, 1995. The transformation of human rights from a feminist perspective is crucial to addressing global challenges to human rights in the 21st century.

Rosen, R. *The World Split Open: How the Modern Women's Movement Changed America.* New York: Penguin Books, 2000. A thorough introduction to the modern American women's movement.

Wollstonecraft, Mary. *A Vindication of The Rights of Women* (1792). Amherst, N.Y.: Prometheus's Great Books in Philosophy Series, 1996. Written during a time of revolutionary fervor, when the principle of inalienable rights for all men had caused and was causing political turmoil in the United States, France, and Britain. Wollstonecraft applied the concept of inalienable rights to women as well as men. She addressed the power struggle between the sexes, pointing out that, as with governments, it causes imbalance in both the oppressed and the oppressor. She sought instead an education for women and men that will endow individuals with reason, knowledge, and virtue.

Web Documents

"Documents from the Women's Liberation Movement—An On-Line Archival Collection. Special Collections Library, Duke University" (April 1997). Available online. URL: http://scriptorium.lib.duke.edu/wlm. Accessed February 27, 2006. Documents are arranged by the following categories: general and theoretical, medical and reproductive rights, music, organizations and activism, sexuality and lesbian feminism, socialist feminism, women of color, women's work and roles.

GAY AND LESBIAN RIGHTS/ ATYPICAL GENDER ROLES

Books

Bullough, Vern L., ed. *Before Stonewall: Activists for Gay and Lesbian Rights in Historical Context.* New York, London, and Oxford: Harrington Park Press, 2002. A collection of 49 short biographies of activists in the gay and lesbian rights movement, including Henry Gerber, Pearl Hart, Lisa Ben, and Phyllis Leon.

Curry, Hayden, Denis Clifford, and Frederick Hertz. *A Legal Guide for Lesbian and Gay Couples.* 12th ed. Berkeley, Calif.: Nolo Law for All Series, National Center for Lesbian Rights, April 30, 2005. This guide has been updated frequently since its first edition in 1980 and offers state-by-state legal guidance and information about the forming of domestic partnerships, money management, parenting, health care, and estate planning for gay and lesbian couples.

Donahue, David M. *Lesbian, Gay, Bisexual, and Transgender Rights: A Human Rights Perspective.* Minneapolis: University of Minnesota, Human Rights Resource Center, Human Rights Education Series, 2000. This curriculum guide includes nine lessons that set the struggle for lesbian, gay, bisexual, and transgender (LGBT) rights in a human rights perspective. Using the Universal Declaration of Human Rights as a standard, the lesson plans take students from a gay-straight alliance in Salt Lake City to a prison in Romania in order to improve understanding of the issues confronting LGBT people in today's world.

Endean, Steve, and Vicki Lynn Eaklor, eds. *Bringing Lesbian and Gay Rights into the Mainstream: Twenty Years of Progress.* New York, London, and Oxford: Harrington Park Press, 2006. First-person account of the lesbian and gay movement's early progress in the 1970s and the 1980s, and the legislative and political struggles Endean endured.

Kranz, Rachel, and Tim Cusick. *Gay Rights.* New York: Facts On File, Library in a Book Series, 2000. A concise treatment of the major issues in the gay rights movement. The text has been updated throughout to reflect developments through early 2005.

Web Documents

Human Rights Watch. "Lesbian, Gay, Bisexual, and Transgender Rights" (February 26, 2006). Available online. URL: http://hrw.org/doc/?t=lgbt. Accessed February 26, 2006. The Web site is updated regularly with the latest international news stories relative to LGBT rights. It offers links to information by country and related materials.

International Gay and Lesbian Human Rights Commission (May 8, 2006). Available online. URL: http://www.iglhrc.org/site/iglhrc. Accessed May 8, 2006. Regularly updated with current international news stories pertaining to gays and lesbians.

The National Center for Lesbian Rights (May 8, 2006). Available online. URL: http://www.nclrights.org. Accessed May 8, 2006. Daily updates on news stories and legislation pertaining to lesbian rights.

U.S. State Department. "2005: Country Reports on Human Rights Practices." Available online. URL: http://www.state.gov/g/drl/rls/hrrpt/2005/index.htm. Accessed May 8, 2006. Annual report on human rights fully documents violations against lesbian, gay, bisexual, and transgender people and people who have HIV/AIDS. A number of human rights issues are addressed in a variety of countries.

"World Timeline on Same-Sex Rights." CBS News In-Depth (July 21, 2005). Available online. URL: http://www.cbc.ca/news/background/samesexrights/timeline_world.html. Accessed June 3, 2006. In addition to an international time line of events related to the gay and lesbian movement, the Web page links to newscasts and current legislation.

GENDER ROLES
Books

Ackmann, Martha. *The Mercury 13: The Untold Story of Thirteen American Women and the Dream of Space Flight.* New York: Random House, 2003. In 1961, 13 women were secretly tested in a program to prepare America's first female astronauts, yet it would be 20 years before Sally Ride rode the shuttle into space and another decade before Eileen Collins piloted the shuttle. This is a fascinating and frustrating account of how qualified women were denied their chance by the "Boy's Club" in NASA and on Capitol Hill.

Dowler, Lorraine, Josephine Carubia, and Bonj Szczygiel, eds. *Gender and Landscape: Renegotiating Morality and Space.* London and New York: Routledge, 2005. This volume examines the effect of landscape on women and the "gendering of the landscape," bridging the feminist discussion "of space and place as something 'lived' and landscape interpretations as something 'viewed.'"

Gaughen, Shasta. *Contemporary Issues Companion: Women's Rights.* Westport, Conn.: Greenwood Press, 2003. Explores the transformative force of the modern women's movement, from history, to issues, to its international implications. The book includes writings and speeches by notable individuals, including Margaret Sanger, Gloria Steinem, and Hillary Rodham Clinton. Chapter 1 examines the historical perspective of the movement through these writings, while chapter 2 explores workplace issues for women. Chapter 3 surveys medical and reproductive right concerns, and chapter 4 looks at international rights issues, including female circumcision, sex trafficking, and the changes and challenges for women of Islamic faith.

Hardill, Irene. *Gender, Migration and the Dual Career Household.* London and New York: Routledge, 2002. Addresses labor mobility primarily in Great Britain and examines work and family and dual-career families.

Macy, Sue, and Jane Gottesman. *Play Like A Girl.* New York: Henry Holt, September 1999. Macy, an award-winning young adult author, and Gottesman, a sportswriter, present a collection of quotations, photographs, and excerpts from hundreds of sports books celebrating women in sport; for young adult readers.

Markham, Beryl. *West with the Night.* Boston: Houghton Mifflin, 1942. This part-autobiography, part-memoir describes Markham's exploits as an African bush pilot in 1930s Kenya and as the first person to fly solo across the Atlantic from east to west.

Web Documents

Commission of the European Communities. "Report from the Commission to the Council, the European Parliament, the European Economic and Social Committee and the Committee of the Regions on Equality between Women and Men" (February 14, 2005). Available online. URL: http://www.daadcenter.wisc.edu/events/gende%20equality%20report%202006_71_en.pdf. Accessed November 29, 2005. This second annual report on equality of women and men is the first to cover the enlarged European Union of 25 member states. Equality of women and men is reinforced by the new treaty establishing a constitution for Europe. In addition to the provisions of the current treaty on gender equality, the constitution expressly states that equality is a value of the Union, which should be promoted not only inside the Union but also in its relations with the rest of the world.

HEALTH CARE

Books

Dyck, Isabel, Nancy Davis Lewis, and Sara McLafferty, eds. *Geographics of Women's Health.* London and New York: Routledge, 2001. The book focuses on a range of issues: health and hygiene, women's health services, medical geography, world health, and case studies. Includes bibliographical references and index.

Web Documents

The Henry J. Kaiser Family Foundation (March 2006). Available online. URL: http://www.kff.org/womenshealth/index.cfm. Accessed June 5, 2006. Resources and fact sheets on female health care and contraception, with additional information by ethnicity.

The Office on Women's Health. Quick Health Data Online. U.S. Department of Health and Human Services, 2002. Available online. URL: http://www.healthstatus2010.com/owh/index.html. Accessed May 9, 2006. This system permits those interested in the health status of women and the entire population of the United States to have access to comparative, county-level data for all 50 states, the District of Columbia, and U.S. territories and possessions in 2000 to 2003. Data in the system are available by gender, race and ethnicity, and, to the extent possible, age. Data have been collected from local, state, regional, and national sources, from credible sources at both the national (CDC, U.S. Census Bureau) and local (state health departments) levels. Definitions are consistent across the sources and the data have been compared to other references.

World Health Organization (WHO). "The World Health Report 2005—Make Every Mother and Child Count" (2005). Available online. URL: http://www.who.int/whr/2005/en. Accessed February 4, 2006. In 2005, almost 11 million children under five years of age died of causes that were largely preventable. At the same time, more than half a million women would die in pregnancy, during childbirth, or soon after. Reducing this toll depends largely on every mother and child's having the right to access to health care from pregnancy through childbirth, the neonatal period, and childhood. The report examines the situation in 2005, the obstacles, and strategies to making pregnancy safer and redesigning child care for survival, growth, and development. It also looks at system and policy implications and how to reconcile maternal, newborn, and child health with health system development.

———. "Countries" (March 9, 2006). Available online. URL: http://www.who.int/countries/en. Accessed March 9, 2006. The site, updated regularly, provides statistics by country, including country indicators, health expenditures, health services, current legislation, life summary tables, status of specific disease conditions, and human resources.

———. "International Digest of Health Legislation (IDHL)." Online Database (February 7, 2006). Available online. URL: http://www3.who.int/idhl-rils/frame.cfm?language=english. Accessed February 7, 2006. Contains a selection of national and international health legislation. Texts of legislation are summarized in English or mentioned by their title. Where possible, links are provided to other Web sites that contain full texts of the legislation in question. The electronic version of the digest supersedes the printed version, which was published from 1948 to 1999. It represents the latest stage in the evolution of a service that began in 1909 with the publication of the first issue of the *Bulletin mensuel de l'Office international d'Hygiène publique.* Query the database by country, subject, volume, and issue, or specific keywords.

HISTORY

Books

Chapman, Anne. *Women at the Heart of War: Soldiers without Guns.* Los Angeles: National Center for History in the Schools, UCLA, 1997. This primary source unit documents the multiple ways in which women of diverse regions were affected by World War II. Sections are German Women and Hitler's Ideology, Women's Employment in the United States, Gender Equality in Soviet Combat Forces, and Women's Attitudes about the War in China. Includes activities and discussion ideas, charts, introduction activities, and a time line.

Crawford, Vicki L., et al., eds. *Women in the Civil Rights Movement: Trailblazers and Torchbearers, 1941–1965 (Blacks in the Diaspora).* Bloomington: Indiana University Press, October 1993. This book describes specific times in history when black women played a deciding role in the fight for civil rights, from the Mississippi Delta, Montgomery bus boycott, and the Cambridge movement, to the Boston YWCA.

Gross, Susan, and Marjorie Bingham. *Women in World Area Studies Series.* St. Louis Park, Minn.: Glenhurst, 1983–87. This series of 13 units is now out of print, but some can still be found through used book outlets. This series describes the life of women in different regions and countries of the world and how their social status has changed in history. "Women in Japan," "Women in Latin America from Pre-Columbian Times to the 20th Century—Vols. I and II," "Women in Ancient Greece and Rome," and "Women in Medieval/Renaissance Europe" are recommended.

Himmell, Rhoda. *The Role of Women in Medieval Europe.* Los Angeles: The Regents, National Center for History in the Schools, UCLA, 1992. This work, intended for grades 10 through 12, uses primary sources to establish a historic dramatic moment for students to read, followed by teacher background information and more readings enhanced by questions, role playing, and simulation lessons. Emphasizes Germanic tribes. One section illustrates male attitudes that determined women's place within the framework of medieval society.

Hunter, Lisa, ed. *Sources of Strength: Women and Culture.* Newton, Mass.: Education Development Center, 1980. These individual units provide background information, first-person accounts, and activities that ask students to evaluate the degree of economic, political, and personal power a woman may exercise in a given culture. They look at women's lives in traditional settings and then what happens during periods of change. The Women in Nigeria unit gives information on village life and changes that occurred during European colonization and national independence. The Women in China unit looks at traditional life and continuity and change during the revolutionary years. Other units examine similar themes for women in Chinese-American and African-American history, concluding with a student oral history project.

Ladd, Doris. *Mexican Women in Anahuac and New Spain: Three Study Units.* Austin: Institute of Latin American Studies, University of Texas, 1979. The study unit topics are Aztec roles of women, Women in Mexico City in the 16th century, and the life and writing of Sor Juana Ines de la Cruz. For each, a short introduction is followed by primary documents illustrating the content points. Reflective questions and writing activities end the section.

Mertus, Julie, Nancy Flowers, and Mallika Dutt. *Local Action/Global Change: Learning about the Human Rights of Women and Girls.* New York: UNIFEM, 1999. Each chapter provides information, statistics, and illustrative examples of both human rights abuses and victories and culminates with an exercise in which participants can create a "document" that would protect that right for women. There also are numerous consciousness-raising activities and role playing, that draw attention to the issues around women and their universal rights.

Osolina, Elena, and Ruth Tudor. *Teaching 20th Century Women's History: A Classroom Approach.* Strasbourg: Council of Europe Press, 2000. The historian Elena Osolina uses topics in European women's history to integrate historical skills with knowledge in comparing and contrasting the experiences of women in different political systems across Europe in this high school teacher's guide.

Porter, Cathy. *Women in Revolutionary Russia.* Cambridge: Cambridge University Press, 1987. This is about women active in the revolutionary movement, notably in the Bolshevik Party. It is a thorough look, starting with a descriptive outline of women's place before the revolution, astounding changes during the revolution's early period, and the weakening of women's gains during the 1920s and 1930s. Maps, key dates, and a glossary make this a highly recommended resource.

Read, Phyllis J., and Bernard L. Witlieb. *The Book of Women's Firsts.* New York: Random House, 1992. A book of first achievements by women in the United States and the prerevolutionary colonies that provides a record of lives and events unheralded until the early 1990s.

Reese, Lyn, and Rick Clarke. *Two Voices from Nigeria: Nigeria through the Literature of Chinua Achebe and Buchi Emecheta.* Stanford, Calif.: Stanford Program of International and Cross-Cultural Education (SPICE), Stanford University, 1985. Many teachers use Chinua Achebe's novel *Things Fall Apart* to teach about changes in village society during Western colonial contact. This unit provides excerpts from that novel and others by Achebe, which are coupled with those found in the works of the female author Buchi Emecheta. Through this approach, both male and female views are represented in an exploration of specific Nigerian themes and periods. Critical thinking questions accompany the excerpts. Activities using African proverbs and poems by Nigerian students are included.

Ross, Mandy. *The Changing Role of Women (20th Century Perspectives).* Chicago: Heinemann, 2002. Examines the changing role of women throughout the 20th century in politics, human rights, education, domestic life, work, health care, the arts, fashion, and sports. Primary source materials are included.

Rowland, Debra. *Boundaries of Her Body: A Troubling History of Women's Rights in America.* Naperville, Ill.: Sphinx Publishing, Sourcebooks Inc., August 2004. The legal journalist Rowland analyzes how women's rights have, and have not, evolved since the signing of the Mayflower Compact in 1620. Until the late 19th century, women's rights derived from husbands, fathers, and sons. It was believed that their biology made women incapable of thinking rationally—hence they could not own property, vote, or work as many hours or for as much pay as men, until 1965, when the Supreme Court legalized contraception and other aspects of women's legal lives.

Smith, Bonnie G., ed. *Women's History in Global Perspective.* Vols. 1, 2, and 3. Champaign: University of Illinois Press, 2004–05. These essays, written by some of the pioneering figures in women's history, provide background information, with chronological historical overviews and changing perspectives in the research on women in the era of their expertise. Volume 1: Theory and Practice of Women's History, Family History in Global Perspective, Women and Gender in Judaism, Christianity, and Islam; Gender and Work; Race and Ethnicity; Gender and Nation; and Worlds of Feminism. Volume 2: Women in Ancient Civilizations;

Women in China, Japan, and Korea; Women and Gender in South and Southeast Asia; Medieval Women; Women and Gender in Colonial Latin America; Women in the United States to 1865. Volume 3: Sub-Saharan Africa; The Middle East; Early and Modern Europe; Russia and the Soviet Union; Latin America; North America after 1865.

Sproule, Anna. *Solidarity: Women Workers.* London: Macdonald Press, 1987. Sproule features women who fought for social justice for workers in Britain, the United States, and Japan from the 19th to early 20th centuries, with first-person quotes, "action" sections that raise questions allowing one to interact with the material, "focus" pieces on key personalities, and a useful time chart.

Stanton, Elizabeth Cady, et al. *History of Woman Suffrage.* 6 vols. (1881–1922). Reprint, Salem, N.H.: Ayer, 1985. Many of the activities of the late 19th-century women's movement, including the campaigns of the postbellum years, are recorded in a multivolume work, *History of Woman Suffrage,* authored by Stanton, Susan B. Anthony, and Matilda Josyln Gage. The volumes were later published in 1881, 1882, 1886, and 1902.

Von Drehle, David. *Triangle: The Fire That Changed America.* New York: Grove/ Atlantic, 2003. Of the 146 workers who died in the Triangle Shirtwaist Factory fire in 1911, 123 were young women. This narrative examines the fire and the Jewish and Italian immigrants who poured into New York City and provided the cheap female labor required by the garment industry.

Weiss, Ellen. *Voting Rights Days.* New York: Simon & Schuster, 2002. After going to live with nine-year-old Emily and her family in Washington, D.C., in 1916, Hitty, a well-traveled wooden doll, witnesses the efforts of Emily's aunt and other suffragists to win women the right to vote.

Web Documents

National Women's History Project. News & Events (May 8, 2006). Available online. URL: http://www.nwhp.org. Accessed May 8, 2006. The News & Events alerts readers to special events, such as the Women's History Auction.

Find Your Female Ancestors. Available online. URL: http://www.female-ancestors.com. Accessed May 8, 2006. Several databases of female ancestors, including the entries from the Daughters of Genius (1886); Kansas Women in Literature (1915); a directory of women in New York Women's Clubs published in 1906; early female physicians from "Daughters of America or Women of the Century" by Phebe A. Hanaford, published in 1883; and "History of Stanislaus County California with Biographical Sketches of the Leading Men and Women of the County" by George H. Tinkham, published in 1921.

Gale Free Resources. Women's History. Available online. URL: http://www.gale.com/ free_resources/whm. Accessed May 8, 2006. Thomson Gale has assembled a collection of activities and information to complement classroom topics on women's history. Within this site, teachers and students can read biographies of significant women throughout time, take a quiz based on women and their achievements, follow a time line of significant events in women's history, and enjoy activities to celebrate women's history.

Women in World History Curriculum's Web site. Available online. URL: http://www. womeninworldhistory.com/index.html. Accessed May 8, 2006. Focuses on information about women's history beyond the borders of the United States. This project began in 1985 as the result of a U.S. Department of Education grant to create a secondary-level classroom resource bibliography about women in World History and Global Studies.

Other

Victorian Women's Rights. Society & Culture—Women's History. Available online. URL: http://www.bbc.co.uk/history/society_culture/women/launch_gms_victorian _women.shtml Accessed May 8, 2006. An online game about Victorian women's rights hosted by the British Broadcasting Company (BBC). Play the game to discover how women's rights evolved through the Victorian era: When did women win the right to a university education? When could they keep their earnings for themselves? Play the game by knocking on the doors of Victorian opportunity, but do not expect too much.

HIV/AIDS

Television/Films/Video

Yesterday. Produced and directed by Darrell Roodt. 96 minutes. HBO, 2004, television movie. About a Zulu women (Leleti Khumalo) who copes with the AIDS virus in her rural South African village. After falling ill, Yesterday (Khumalo) learns that she is HIV positive. With her husband in denial and a young daughter to tend to, Yesterday has one goal: to live long enough to see her child go to school.

Web Documents

Human Rights Watch. "Women and HIV/AIDS." Available online. URL: http://hrw. org/women/aids.html. Accessed January 3, 2006. The deadly link between women's rights abuses and the spread of HIV/AIDS is slowly gaining recognition, but not before millions of women have lost their lives to the disease. The Web page provides links to the latest news, publications, and related resources.

Joint United Nations Programme on AIDS (UNAIDS). "UNAIDS/WHO AIDS Epidemic Update: December 2005." Available online. URL: http://www.unaids. org/epi/2005/doc/report_pdf.asp. Accessed May 8, 2006. Although the precise number of people living with HIV is unknown, the report estimates the global penetration of the AIDS epidemic by using a variety of sources—population surveys, medical reports, and the like. The ranges reflect the uncertainty that still surrounds the virus that has been infecting people worldwide since the early 1980s. The report, illustrated with maps and data tables, discusses the impact of

HIV/AIDS by region and has a chapter on prevention as a key strategy for coping with the deadly virus.

HUMAN TRAFFICKING
Web Documents

Human Rights Watch. "Women's Rights—Trafficking." Available online. URL: http://hrw.org/women/trafficking.html. Accessed January 2, 2006. This watchdog organization tracks trends in global sexual trafficking.

United Nations Children's Fund (UNICEF). "Child Protection Information Sheet" (May 9, 2006). Available online. URL: http://www.unicef.org/protection/files/trafficking.pdf. Accessed May 2006. In its work, UNICEF upholds the Convention on the Rights of the Child. The fact sheet specifies the conventions and protocols established along with facts and figures.

United Nations Office of Drug and Crime. "Protocol to Prevent, Suppress and Punish Trafficking in Persons." Available online. URL: http://www.unodc.org/unodc/trafficking_protocol.html. Accessed February 9, 2006. Summarizes the protocol and issues concerning trafficking of women and children. The protocol supplements the United Nations Convention against Transnational Organized Crime. The page also links to collection of documents about human trafficking that include other UN and non-UN organizations coping with trafficking of human beings and background information about the protocol.

U.S. Citizenship and Immigration Services. "Victims of Trafficking and Violence Protection Act of 2000" (March 22, 2006). Available online. URL: http://www.uscis.gov/graphics/services/tempbenefits/antitraf.htm. Accessed March 22, 2006. Includes various agency links to information about VTVPA, implementation of the law, and victim benefits and services as well as research reports on the topic.

U.S. Department of State's Bureau of International Information Programs. "Private, Nonprofit Groups Lead Fight against Human Trafficking: Experts Gather to Discuss Dimension of Issue That Includes Labor Abuses." USInfo.State.Gov (May 5, 2006). Available online. URL: http://usinfo.state.gov/gi/global_issues/human_trafficking.html. The agency acknowledges that the U.S. Trafficking Victims Protection Act would not have passed in 2000 without the support of the faith-based and women's groups that called the issue to the attention of Congress. The site provides news updates on the topic.

U.S. Government (Inter-agency). "Assessment of U.S. Activities to Combat Trafficking in Persons" (September 2005). Available online. URL: http://www.usdoj.gov/ag/annualreports/tr2005/assessmentofustipactivities.pdf. Accessed December 18, 2005. The United States has a significant problem with trafficking in persons, especially as a destination country, with an estimated 18,000 to 20,000 people from other countries entering the country each year to be exploited in involuntary labor. The report includes recommendations for improvement of U.S. government anti-trafficking activities.

"U.S. Immigration and Customs Enforcement: Fact Sheet—Human Trafficking" (July 14, 2004). Available online. URL: http://www.ice.gov/pi/news/factsheets/human traffic_071404.htm. Accessed May 9, 2006. ICE was established in March 2003 as the largest investigative arm of the Department of Homeland Security; it works with state and local law officials to identify human trafficking rings entering and exiting the United States.

World Health Organization (WHO). "World Report on Violence and Health." Available online. URL: http://www.who.int/violence_injury_prevention/violence/world _report/en/index.html. Accessed December 23, 2005. This 2002 report defines the extent of the problem of sexual trafficking on a global level with estimated data from select countries.

Television/Films/Video

Human Trafficking. Directed by Christian Duguay. 240 minutes with commercials. Lifetime for Women movie, 2005, television miniseries. Mira Sorvino and Donald Sutherland play U.S. officers who crack down on an international human-trafficking ring. The story follows several girls and women all over the world who have been abducted and sold into prostitution.

INTERNATIONAL WOMEN'S MOVEMENT
Books

Fraser, Arvonne S., and Irene Tinker, eds. *Developing Power: How Women Transformed International Development.* New York: City University of New York, Feminist Press, 2004. Two activists from the 1970s encourage 27 women who are pioneers from a wide variety of countries and fields to write personal accounts. Through the collection of inspiring and revealing memoirs, they document women's historical accomplishments from the 1970s, from educational development to challenging of international development institutions, and ways women have learned to integrate work and family. Information about the UN conferences for women, the expansion of women's international nongovernment organizations, and major global women's issues is also discussed.

Kahn, Janet, and Susan Bailey. *Shaping a Better World: Global Issues, Gender Issues.* Wellesley, Mass.: Center for Research on Women, 2000. A teaching guide for grades seven to 12 that places women at the center of contemporary concerns about human rights, the global economy (notably sweatshop labor), ethnic conflicts, sustainable development, the environment, and cultural diversity.

Neft, Naomi, and Ann D. Levine. *Where Women Stand: An International Report on the Status of Women in 140 Countries, 1997–1998.* New York: Random House, 1998. This easy-to-read book offers background information, clear charts, and ways to compare the progress of women's issues and status in the global community using United Nations documents.

Pietilä, Hilkka. *Engendering the Global Agenda: The Story of Women and the United Nations.* New York: UN Non-Governmental Liaison Service, 2004. Available online. URL: http://www.unsystem.org/ngls/documents/publications.en/develop.dossier/dd.06/contents.htm. Accessed January 31, 2006. Accessible for downloads in five parts, the book describes how the International Women's Day began with women's roles in the League of Nations and the evolution into a global movement.

Smith, Bonnie, ed. *Global Feminism since 1945.* London: Routledge, 2000. From the West, East, North and South, Smith describes the similarities and differences in women's activism on behalf of equality, liberation, and humane conditions across different countries. Fourteen reprinted essays appear in analyses of nation building, sources of activism, women's liberation, and new waves in the 1980s and 1990s. The collection offers perspectives from 19th- and 20th-century Egypt, Vietnam, South Africa, Brazil, Kenya, Korea, Britain, Japan, Russia, Iran, Germany, and the United States. Of notable interest are discussions of contemporary international movements dealing with women's human rights, Amnesty International, and the "NGO-ization" of feminism, as well as reflections on the world conference on women in Beijing.

Web Documents

U.S. State Department. "Ask the State Department." Online interactive forum (March 10, 2006). Available online. URL: http://www.state.gov/r/pa/ei/59254.htm. Accessed on March 10, 2006. View the transcript of Charlotte (Charlie) Ponticelli, senior coordinator, International Women's Issues, discussing International Women's Day and Women's History Month.

ISLAM

Books

Mernissi, Fatima. *The Forgotten Queens of Islam.* Translated by Mary Jo Lakeland. Minneapolis: University of Minnesota Press, 1993. A Moroccan author analyzes the lives of little-known female leaders within the context of Islamic beliefs about women's place in society. Fascinating stories reveal the meaning of *caliph* and *queen* and the criteria of sovereignty in Islam. A survey of the queens—from those who ruled "behind the throne"; to those, such as the Arab queen Arwa of Yemen, who held great power; to the most numerous, the sultanas of Persia and India—is discussed.

Web Documents

Horace Mann Academic School District (San Francisco, California). "Famous Muslim Women of the Past." Available online. URL: http://www.sfusd.k12.ca.us/schwww/sch618/Women/Women_of_the_Past.html. Accessed May 8, 2006. Brief biographies and links on five famous Muslim women, all closely related to the Prophet Muhammad.

———. "Famous Muslim Women Leaders of Today" (February 20, 2006). Available online. URL: http://www.sfusd.k12.ca.us/schwww/sch618/Women/Muslim_Women_Today.html. Accessed February 20, 2006. Brief biographies and links on four female Muslim prime ministers.

Maryams.net. "Biographical Sketches" (February 20, 2006). Available online. URL: http://www.maryams.net/biog.shtml. Accessed February 20, 2006. Biographical sketches of influential Muslim women.

University of Alberta, Canada. "Women, Class, and Islam." Available online. URL: http://www.humanities.ualberta.ca/ottoman/module2/tutorial2a.htm. Accessed on February 20, 2006. A tutorial on women, class, and Islam during the Ottoman Empire.

Television/Films/Video

Not without My Daughter. Directed by Brian Gilbert. Written by Betty Mahmoody and William Hoffer, 1991. About the American Betty Mahmoody's (played by Sally Fields) escape from Iran, where her Iranian husband has reaffirmed his faith in Islam and will not allow her to leave with her daughter. The film provides a vivid portrayal of women's lives during Ayatollah Khomeini's rule and their attempts to defy tribal customs, beliefs, and manners of living.

KENYA

Books

Abdi, Awa M. "Refugees, Gender Based Violence, and Resistance: A Case Study of Somali Refugees in Kenya." In *Women, Migration, and Citizenship: Making Local, National, and Transnational Connections,* edited by Evangelia Tastsoglou and Alexandra Z. Dobrowolsky. Burlington, Vt.: Ashgate, 2006. Increasing numbers of countries are systematically offering social and political membership to migrants residing outside their territories.

Fox, Diana, and Hasci Naima. *The Challenges of Women's Activism and Human Rights in Africa.* Lewiston, N.Y.: Edwin Mellin Press, 1999. Contains essays written by activists and scholars in a wide range of fields who have conducted research or been involved on a grassroots level in an effort to advance women's human rights.

Luke, Nancy. "Local Meanings and Census Categories: Widow Inheritance and the Position of Luo Widows in Kenya." In *African Households: Censuses and Surveys,* edited by Etienne Van de Walle. Armonk, N.Y.: M. E. Sharpe, 2006. Uses 1989 Kenya census data and local studies to explore the cultural context of widowhood among the Luo ethnic group and confront the stereotype that widows are elderly, celibate, nonproductive dependents.

Sobania, Neal. *Culture and Customs of Kenya.* Westport, Conn.: Greenwood Press, 2003. Presents the contemporary reality of life in Kenya, an important East African nation that has served as a crossroads for peoples and cultures of Africa, the Middle East, and East Asia for centuries.

Articles

Agesa, Richard U., and Jacqueline Agesa. "Sources of Gender Difference in Rural to Urban Migration in Kenya: Does Human Capital Matter?" *Applied Economics Letters* 12 (11) (September 2005): 705–709. Using data from Kenya, this article estimates the urban to rural gender gap in the rate of migration and then analyzes the gap in terms of the gender differences.

Luke, Nancy. "Exchange and Condom Use in Informal Sexual Relationships in Urban Kenya." *Economic Development and Cultural Change* 54 (2) (January 2006). Available online. URL: http://popcenter.uconn.edu/Luke%20Colloquium%20Talk%20 Fall%202004.pdf. Based on data from a project directed by Kaivan Munshi and Nancy Luke, Population Studies and Training Center, Brown University, the study was supported by the National Institutes of Health and the National Institute on Aging.

Web Documents

AfricaBib Database. "Welcome to AfricaBib.org." Available online. URL: http://www. Africabib.org. Accessed May 8, 2006. Two bibliographic databases of Africa's periodical literature (Africana Periodical Literature Database) and women's literature (Africa Women's Database), which includes a comprehensive English-language bibliography on women travelers, explorers, and missionaries to Africa from 1763 to 2004. The database is maintained at the Institute for Economic Advancement, University of Arkansas–Little Rock.

AFROL Gender Profile. "Kenya." Available online. URL: http://www.afrol.com/Catego ries/Women/profiles/kenya_women.htm. Accessed November 13, 2005. English-speaking African news agency that offers an overview of gender issues in Kenya.

Gakii, Carol. "Groups Lobby for Women Rights Protocol." Kenya Broadcasting Corporation (November 11, 2005). Available online. URL: http://www.kbc.co.ke/story. asp?ID=33322. Accessed December 23, 2005. Women's rights lobby groups in the country are asking the government to recognize and respect the women's rights protocol.

Heinrich Böll Foundation. "The Gender Programme: Civic Empowerment of Women in the East and Horn of Africa." Available online. URL: http://www.hbfha.com/ gender.htm. Accessed May 9, 2006. Organizes conferences, publications, and projects about gender issues in Africa.

Human Rights Watch. "Africa-Kenya." Available online. URL: http://hrw.org/ doc?t=africa&c=kenya. Accessed November 11, 2006. Overview of issues of human rights specific to Kenya and archive of news releases.

———. "A Dose of Reality: Women's Rights in the Fight against HIV/AIDS" (March 21, 2005). Available online. URL: http://hrw.org/english/docs/2005/03/21/ africa10357_txt.htm. Accessed May 9, 2006. This briefing paper focuses on the links between HIV/AIDS and abuses of women's and girls' human rights: domestic violence; violations of property and inheritance rights; the harmful traditional practices of bride price, widow inheritance, and ritual sexual "cleansing"; and sexual abuse of girls.

"The Impact of the Global Gag Rule in Kenya." Access Denied—U.S. Restrictions on International Family Planning. Available online. URL: http://www.globalgagrule .org/ pdfs/case_studies/GGRcase_kenya.pdf. Accessed January 2, 2006. The Global Gag Rule has closed clinics in Kenya, curtailed family planning, and aided in making abortion more prevalent as alternative forms of contraception are not available to the vast population that needs them.

Jenda: Journal of Culture and African Women Studies (May 9, 2006). Available online. URL: http://www.jendajournal.com. Accessed May 9, 2006. Full-text articles from the e-journal that has been published since 2001.

Kameri-Mbote, Patricia. "Law of Succession in Kenya: Gender Perspectives in Property Management and Control." Report, Nairobi: Women and Law in East Africa, 1995. Available online. URL: http://www.ielrc.org/content/b9501.pdf. Accessed February 6, 2006. About the laws governing the relationship of marriage and succession in Kenya and the challenge of four different cultural systems of marriage. Download the report from the International Environmental Law Research Centre Web site.

"Kenyans Reject New Constitution." BBC News (November 22, 2005). Available online. URL: http://news.bbc.co.uk/go/pr/fr/-/1/hi/world/africa/4455538.stm. Accessed December 23, 2005. Voters in Kenya emphatically rejected a proposed new constitution in a 2005 referendum. The article highlights what distinguished the constitution in Kenya's first attempt to rewrite its law since independence from the United Kingdom in 1963.

Ministry of Environment and Natural Resources (Nairobi, Kenya). "Republic of Kenya National Assessment Report for the World Summit on Sustainable Development (RIO+10) in Johannesburg, South Africa" (August/September 2002). Available online. URL: http://www.johannesburgsummit.org/html/prep_process/national_reports/kenya_natl_assess3008.pdf. Accessed February 6, 2006. The report examines how strengthening the role of women, youth, and children can impact sustainable development.

U.S. State Department. "Kenya Country Reports on Human Rights Practices—2003" (February 25, 2004). Available online. URL: http://www.state.gov/g/drl/rls/ hrrpt/2003/27733.htm. Accessed November 13, 2005. The report provides detailed facts, figures, recent legislation, and current issues concerning Kenya.

Walsh, Janet. "Double Standards: Women's Property Rights Violations in Kenya." Human Rights Watch (March 2003). Available online. URL: http://www.hrw. org/reports/2003/kenya0303. Accessed January 3, 2006. Report on the inequality of women's property rights with men's and the extent of the impact of property rights violations on poverty, disease, violence, and homelessness.

Television/Films/Video

Disappearing World: Masai Women. Produced and directed by Chris Curling. 52 minutes. 1975, documentary. Focuses on the preparation of young Masai girls for marriage and adult life in Masai society. A candid interview with an older woman probes her feelings about polygamy and the inability of women to own property. Based on the work of the anthropologist Melissa Llewelyn-Davies.

The Maasai and Agents of Change. Produced by Kakuta Ole Maimai Hamisi. 32 minutes. 2001. A rare opportunity to see life among the Masai as filmed by one of their own warriors. The filmmaker and narrator is a Masai who is studying at a U.S. college. He returned to Kenya to film the lifestyles and ceremonies of his people before their culture becomes extinct.

Media/Newspapers

AllAfrica. "Top Women and Gender Headlines" (May 9, 2006). Available online. URL: http://www.allafrica.com/women. Accessed May 9, 2006. Offers daily news updates about women from a variety of African news sources.

Pambazuka News. "Weekly Forum for Social Justice in Africa: Women and Gender." Available online. URL: http://www.pambazuka.org/en/category/wgender. Accessed February 14, 2006. A weekly forum for social justice in Africa with a special section containing news updates about women and gender issues.

Other

Fernando, Priyanthi, et al. "Discovering Technologists: Women and Men's Work at Village Level in East Africa." Nairobi: Intermediate Technology Development Group, Eastern Africa, 2000. This is a training package tool designed to increase the skills of field workers involved in the processes of technology development, working with women and men in local communities. It aims to improve the capacity of men and women field workers to recognize and work with women's existing technical skills. Field workers involved in technology development will find this package a useful reference on methods and tools for developing more gender-sensitive technology interventions. The materials are based on Do It Herself case studies—an ITDG research program that focuses on grassroots technical innovation of women. The program took place in Asia, Africa, and Latin America.

LEADERSHIP

Book

Earnshaw, Doris, ed. *International Women Speak: The Emergence of Women's Global Leadership.* Palo Alto, Calif.: AltaVista Press, 2000. This book is part of Earnshaw's Women's Speak series, which highlights influential women with excerpts from their speeches or writings to present their perspectives on a variety of topics. The author presents 20 women, including Queen Noor (Jordan), Benedita da Silva (Brazil), and Mary Robinson (Ireland), who represent different countries and interests. Each has become a leader, speaking authoritatively on issues such as children, housing, war, peace, and health.

LITERACY

Web Documents

United Nations Educational, Scientific and Cultural Organization (UNESCO). "Global Monitoring Report 2006." Available online. URL: http://portal.unesco.org/educa tion/en/ev.php-URL_ID=43283&URL_DO=DO_TOPIC&URL_SECTION=201. html. Accessed February 24, 2006. The 2006 report aims to shine a policy spotlight on the more neglected goals of literacy—a foundation not only for achieving "education for all" but, more broadly, for reaching the goal of reducing human poverty. The 2006 report is based on data for the 2002–03 school year.

LITERATURE

Books

Cahill, Susan, ed. *Wise Women: Over 2000 Years of Spiritual Writing by Women.* New York: W. W. Norton, 1996. One place to find the ancient and modern voices of women is within the realms of the spiritual. Even in established religious institutions, women have often been "allowed" to express themselves. The writings vary from poems, songs, stories, prayers, letters, excerpts from novels, excerpts from the transcripts of a trials, to short essays. A short biography of the author introduces each piece.

Frederick, Bonnie, and Susan McLeod, eds. *Women and the Journey: The Female Travel Experience.* Pullman: Washington State University, 1993. A series of essays about women travelers or women whose journeys are notably different from men's. A global and historic view includes a discussion of Victorian women's travel dress and how white women prisoners in Argentina and Uruguay were used to heighten colonial and 19th-century fear of Indians, as well as tales of Chinese women in the American West, Ibn Battuta's account of travel by medieval women in Islamic culture, and English women's 20th-century plays. In the section Women and Traditions of Narrative, the editors offer gender perspectives on literature such as the *Faerie Queen, Pilgrim's Progress,* D. H. Lawrence's books, *The Handmaid's Tale,* and stories from the American frontier.

Hirshfield, Jane, ed. *Women in Praise of the Sacred: 43 Centuries of Spiritual Poetry by Women.* New York: HarperCollins, 1994. Hirshfield's anthology of world history poetry contains background information on the author and her times from the hymns of the world's earliest identified author, the Sumerian priest Enheduanna, to a poem written by a Korean Buddhist nun in the 1950s. The poems express major religious traditions from the East and West and several indigenous cultures.

Television/Films/Video

In Black and White. Volume 2: *Gloria Naylor.* Produced by RTSI Swiss TV and directed by Matteo Bellinelli. 22 minutes. California Newsreel, 1992. Information available online. URL: http://www.newsreel.org/nav/title.asp?tc=CN0048-2&s=women. Naylor explains her exploration across the social spectrum of what it means to be black in America in *The Women of Brewster Place* and *Mama Day.*

MILITARY

Books

Carl, Ann Baumgartner. *A WASP among Eagles.* Washington, D.C.: Smithsonian Press, 1999. An account by a test pilot who was among the thousand Women Airforce Service Pilots (WASPs) to ferry and test aircraft or instruct others during World War II for American troops, with little or no publicity and very low status within the force. Includes specifications and costs of the airplanes flown.

Cochran, Jacqueline, and Brinley Maryann Bucknum. *Jackie Cochran: An Autobiography.* New York: Bantam Books, 1987. Excerpts from the late Cochran's own accounts of her flying and life overcoming challenges from poverty to a childhood as an orphan.

Holden, Henry M., with Lori Griffith. *Ladybirds: The Untold Story of Women Pilots in America.* Mt. Freedom, N.J.: Black Hawk, 1993. A history of American women in every aspect of aviation from a woman balloonist of 200 years ago, to the early days of Anne Morrow Lindbergh and Amelia Earhart, to today's commercial women airline pilots (coauthor Lori Griffith is a Boeing 737 captain with USAir).

Articles

Darr, Ann. "The Women Who Flew, but Kept Silent," *New York Times Magazine,* 7 May 1995, SM70-71. Darr describes her experience flying military planes under the director Jacqueline Cochran in the early 1940s [and the quest for WASPs to be recognized for their early feats] by the Air Force. They won veteran status only after much labor in 1977.

Dickerson, Debra. "Was Abu Ghraib Her Fault?" *Elle,* November 2005, 248. Dickerson, who served in the army for 12 years, interviews Janis Karpinski, the first female general to command in a combat zone in the 2002 war in Iraq.

McGirk, Tim. "Crossing the Lines: Though Barred from Combat, Female Troops in Iraq Often Find Themselves in Full-Fledged Battle," *Time,* 27 February 2006, 38–43. An intimate look at the lives of the real "G.I. Janes."

Web Documents

About.com. "Women and World War II." Women's History, Military & War: Women. Available online. URL: http://womenshistory.about.com/od/warwwii. Accessed February 10, 2006. Provides information about international and American women's roles during World War II.

Department of Defense. "Department of Defense Selected Manpower Statistics Fiscal Year 2004." DefenseLINK (May 2006). Available online. URL: http://si adapp.dior.whs.mil/index.html. Accessed May 10, 2006. This report is published by the Washington Headquarters Services, Information Technology Management Directorate (WHS/ITMD). The report provides basic workforce data on active duty military, civilian, retired, and reserve military personnel of the Department of Defense (DoD). This publication is no longer available in a bound, printed edition.

Williams, Rudi. "Military Women Take 200-Year Trek toward Respect, Parity." American Forces Information Service News Articles (January 13, 2003). Available online. URL: http://www.defenselink.mil/news/Aug1998/n08121998_9808123.html. Accessed May 10, 2006. Williams describes the 220 years of trials, tribulations, and indignities women experienced to reach, and benefit, from their present-day positions within the military.

Television/Films/Video

Fly Girls. Written, produced, and directed by Laurel Ladevich. 60 minutes. PBS Movie, 1999, documentary. Full transcript available online. URL: http://womenshistory. about.com. Information about the film available online. URL: http://www.pbs. org/wgbh/amex/flygirls/tguide/index.html. During World War II, more than 1,000 women signed up to fly with the U.S. military. Wives, mothers, actresses, and debutantes who joined the Women Airforce Service Pilots (WASPs) test-piloted aircraft, ferried planes, and logged 60 million miles in the air. Thirty-eight women died in service. But the opportunity to play a critical role in the war effort was abruptly canceled by politics and resentment, and it would be 30 years before women would again break the sex barrier in the skies.

The Life and Times of Rosie the Riveter. Directed by Connie Fields. 65 minutes. Video of motion picture by Clarity Productions, 1980, documentary. During World War II, an unprecedented number of American women responded to government encouragement to enter the high-paying world of war production heavy industry. Women who had worked at pink-collar jobs or in lower-paying women's industrial jobs flocked to war production work as an opportunity to learn new skills and make higher wages. The documentary *The Life and Times of Rosie the Riveter* presents these women's experiences as they developed throughout the war years, and after, when the men came marching home. Some of the valuable elements of the film are interviews with several of the women who entered war production work. When watching the film, pay attention to the juxtaposition of their stories and experiences with government propaganda films that encouraged women to become war workers, described their work on the lines, and then encouraged them to "return to their homes" after the war. The film has been deemed "culturally significant" by the Library of Congress, thereby allowing it to be preserved in the U.S. National Film Registry.

Swing Shift. Directed by Jonathan Demme and written by Nancy Dowd. 100 minutes. 1984, film. A woman (Goldie Hawn) finds romance when she takes a job at an airport plant to help make ends meet after her husband goes off to war. This comedy entertains while it reveals some of the aspects of life for women on the domestic front during World War II.

MONITORING

Books

Flexner, Eleanor, and Ellen Fitzpatrick. *Century of Struggle: The Woman's Rights Movement in the United States.* Cambridge, Mass.: Harvard University Press, 1996. Betty Friedan's review: "A book to be read by every student in this country . . . this account will help us to maintain a truer image of ourselves as we try to finish up the struggle first launched so long ago." The book documents the movement as one of the great social processes in American history.

Mezey, Susan Gluck. *Elusive Equality: Women's Rights, Public Policy, and the Law.* Boulder, Colo.: Lynne Rienner, 2003. This book documents the history of the concerted efforts to equalize women's status in the law—a story marked both by major steps forward and by movement backward, and even inertia. It is in this sense that equality remains elusive.

Van Der Gaag, Nikkie, and Nawal el Saadawi. *The No-Nonsense Guide to Women's Rights.* Market Marborough, U.K.: New Internationalist/Verso, 2004. Although women have progressed—in legal rights, political representation, employment, education, and health—the statistics indicate otherwise. Testimonies from women and men around the world explain why, especially in this postfeminist age, women's rights are still very much an issue for men and women alike.

Women's Rights Project. *Women's Human Rights Step by Step: A Practical Guide to Using International Human Rights Law and Mechanisms to Defend Women's Human Rights.* Washington, D.C.: Women, Law & Development International and Human Rights Watch, 1997. About women's human rights in practice, the analysis describes the concept and content of human rights law and its application to women and to the rights issues of concern to them. As a basic guide to the operation of human rights mechanisms and the strategies at national, regional, and international levels, the manual explains how to use these strategies and mechanisms to uphold women's human rights in different cultural, legal, and political contexts.

Web Documents

The President's Interagency Council on Women (January 8, 2001). Available online. URL: http://secretary.state.gov/www/picw. Accessed April 19, 2006. Launched in 1995 on the eve of the UN Fourth World Conference on Women in Beijing, to "make sure that all the effort and good ideas actually get implemented when we get back home" by presidential executive order. The council was chaired by the Health and Human Services secretary Donna Shalala and the first lady Hillary Rodham Clinton as honorary chair. The activities supporting the agency discontinued when President Clinton left office in 2001, but the Web site still exists for archival purposes.

United Nations. "The World's Women 2005 Progress in Statistics" (January 18, 2006). Available online. URL: http://unstats.un.org/unsd/demographic/products/indwm/wwpub.htm. Accessed January 18, 2006. A report prepared by the

Statistics Division of the UN Department for Economic and Social Affairs (UN-DESA) at five-year intervals starting in 1991. The 2005 issue compiles and analyzes data from national reporting of sex-disaggregated statistics in such areas as demographics, health, education, work, violence against women, poverty, human rights, and decision making. Five years ago, the World's Women report emphasized that the improvement of national statistical capacity—the ability to provide timely and reliable statistics—is essential for improving gender statistics.

———. Division for the Advancement of Women. Available online. URL: http://www.un.org/womenwatch/daw/csw. Accessed January 21, 2006. The Commission on the Status of Women (CSW) was established as a commission of the Economic and Social Council by council resolution 11(II) of June 21, 1946, to prepare recommendations and reports to the council on promoting women's political, economic, civil, social, and educational rights. CSW now monitors progress made in emerging issues from the Beijing Platform for Action on a yearly basis.

———. United Nations Millennium Development Goal Indicators (June 28, 2006). Available online. URL: http://millenniumindicators.un.org/unsd/mdg/Default. aspx. Accessed June 28, 2006. This Web site provides access to the database with the current metadata on the Millennium Development Goal Indicators.

MULTICULTURAL ISSUES

Book

Kramarae, Cheris, and Dale Spender, eds. *Routledge International Encyclopedia of Women: Global Women's Issues and Knowledge.* 4 vols. New York: Routledge, 2000. Provides comprehensive global, multicultural coverage of women's issues and concerns with references and further reading. Selections are cross-referenced. Check the Web site to explore the four-volume resource, from an A–Z list of entries to an extensive selection of excerpts.

Web Documents

The American Civil Liberties Union of Southern California. "ACLU/SC Announces Launch of Latina Rights Project on International Women's Day." Teaching to Change LA (March 8, 2002). Available online. URL: http://www.tcla.gseis.ucla. edu/rights/features/5/attorneylatinarights.html. Accessed June 6, 2006. On International Women's Day, the American Civil Liberties Union of Southern California announced the launch of its Latina Rights Project. The project, a pilot initiative of the ACLU Foundation of Southern California, will utilize model litigation, bilingual/bicultural public education and public advocacy to address priority civil rights issues facing Latina women and girls in Southern California. The article offers interesting statistics about the Latina population in California.

Escobar-Haskins, Lillian, and George F. Haskins. "The AIDS Crisis in Pennsylvania: The Hidden Epidemic among African American and Latina Women." Lulu.com (June 2005). Available online. URL: http://www.lulu.com/content/136980. Accessed May 11, 2006. Study commissioned by the Philadelphia AIDS Coalition that documents the evolution of the AIDS epidemic and issues related to prevention efforts. It focuses on the two segments of the population who are the fastest-growing and highest-risk groups in the HIV/AIDS population: African-American women and Latinas.

MANA, A National Latina Organization (May 8, 2006). Available online. URL: http://www.hermana.org/homfrm.htm. Accessed May 8, 2006. The mission of this non-profit advocacy organization established in 1974 is to empower Latinas through leadership development, community service, and advocacy. MANA fulfills its mission through programs designed to develop the leadership skills of Latinas, promote community service by Latinas, and provide Latinas with advocacy opportunities. Support for these programs is derived from members, corporations, foundations, and government grants.

Mujeres Latinas en Acción. Available online. URL: http://www.mujereslatinasen accion.org. Accessed May 11, 2006. This long-established Chicago organization is a bilingual/bicultural agency that seeks to empower women, their families, and youth. Mujeres Latinas offers counseling, leadership development, and advocacy for program participants. Mujeres Latinas worked with the Chicago Women's Liberation Union (CWLU) to form the Committee to End Sterilization Abuse.

National Organization for Women (NOW). "On Equal Pay Day, NOW Wants Women to 'Get Even'" (April 25, 2006). Available online. URL: http://www.now.org/press/04-06/04-25.html. Accessed April 25, 2006. April 25 is Equal Pay Day—the day when women's average earnings finally catch up with the amount men earned on average in the previous calendar year alone. In 1966, NOW identified the wage gap and its negative impact on women. Forty years later, the gap remained wide and progress had slowed to a crawl. Now, women working full-time, year-round, are paid only about three-quarters as much as men, and African-American women and Latinas receive even less.

Urban League. "Race, Ethnicity, Gender." Available online. URL: http://www.urban.org/race/index.cfm. Accessed July 5, 2006. Web site with a variety of resources for the family, including child support, and immigration information. Sample topics include women and minorities in science fields, the Native American health system, and graduation rates.

Women, Nationality, and Citizenship. Available online. URL: http://www.un.org/women watch/daw/public/jun03e.pdf. Accessed July 5, 2006. This UN report discusses the issue of nationality and women and the significance of the Convention on the Nationality of Women signed at Montevideo, Uruguay, in 1933.

Television/Films/Video

Real Women Have Curves. Directed by Patricia Cardoso. 90 minutes. 2002, film. The story of a first-generation, Mexican-American teenager living in East Los Angeles on the threshold of womanhood. Encouraged by a Latino high school teacher, Ana receives a full scholarship to Columbia University, but her traditional Latino parents feel that now is the time for Ana to help provide for the family, and not go off to college. Ana's yearning to fulfill her potential as a woman and sense of dignity is tempered by her mother's concerns over her portly female attributes. Based on the play by Josefina Lopez.

POLITICS
Book

Reese, Lyn. *I Will Not Bow My Head: Documenting Political Women.* Berkeley, Calif.: Women in the World Curriculum Resource Project, 1995. Over 60 primary sources reveal defiant political acts and the resisting voices of women in diverse periods and places. Background information, follow-up questions, research and activity suggestions, illustrations, and selected bibliography accompany each document.

POPULATION
Web Documents

Population Reference Bureau (PRB). "2005 World Population Data Sheet." Available online. URL: http://www.prb.org/Template.cfm?Section=PRB&template=/Content Management/ContentDisplay.cfm&ContentID=13127. Accessed February 7, 2006. PRB's 2005 World Population Data Sheet reveals persisting global inequalities in health and well-being. The data and frequently asked questions about them can be downloaded directly from the Web site.

United Nations Population Fund (UNFPA). "State of World Population 2005: The Promise of Equality—Gender Equity, Reproductive Health, and the Millennium Development Goals." 2005. Available online. URL: http://www.unfpa.org/swp/2005/pdf/en_swp05.pdf. Accessed February 4, 2006. How do we improve the lives of the nearly 3 billion individuals living on less than two dollars a day? How can we enable all individuals—male and female, young and old—to protect themselves from HIV? How can we save the lives of more than 500,000 women who die each year in childbirth? What will it take to show young people living in poverty that they have a stake in development and a hope for the future? For perhaps the first time in history, questions such as these are not simply rhetorical. They have answers: answers that go to the very heart of what it means to be a woman or a man, wealthy or poor. This comprehensive overview of the state of the world includes a critical examination of poverty, the significant role of human rights, reproductive health issues, implications for youth of all of these aspects, the role men and boys can play, gender-based violence, humanitarian strategies, and empowerment of women and youth to achieve the Millennium Development Goals.

POVERTY
Web Documents

Integrated Public Use Microdata Series Census. Available online. URL: http://www.ipums.org. Accessed July 5, 2006. Microdata for national and international social and economic research. The national census database spanning 1850 to 2004 is maintained by the University of Minnesota and receives major funding by the National Institute of Child Health and Human Development and the National Science Foundation.

World Bank. "World Development Report 2006" (February 2006). Available online. URL: http://www1.worldbank.org/devoutreach/article.asp?id=348#top. Accessed May 24, 2006. The WDR 2006 describes how the opportunities to live a healthy life, learn, work, invest, and innovate vary widely within and across countries on the basis of predetermined characteristics, such as gender, race, and family background. These differences are a clear indication that the world today is far from realizing the ideal of equal opportunities for all.

The World Bank Group. "06 World Development Indicators." Available online. URL: http://devdata.worldbank.org/wdi2006/contents/Section1.htm. Accessed May 24, 2006. Database of progress on poverty and other Millennium Development Goals by country.

PROPERTY RIGHTS
Web Documents

Kameri-Mbote, Patricia. "The Law of Succession in Kenya: Gender Perspectives in Property Management and Control." Report, Nairobi: Women and Law in East Africa, 1995. Available online. URL: http://www.ielrc.org/content/b9501.pdf. Accessed February 6, 2006. Women's property ownership within a marriage circumstance has evolved as a controversial area in gender research and development. The report surveys the history of property ownership; the complex laws of inheritance in Kenya, which are based on four religious systems of marriage; and their relationship to the 1981 Law of Succession Act.

Walsh, Janet. "Double Standards: Women's Property Rights Violations in Kenya." Human Rights Watch (March 2003). Available online. URL: http://hrw.org/campaigns/women/property. Accessed January 3, 2006. The report by Human Rights Watch examines the abuse of women's equal rights to own, inherit, manage, and dispose of property, especially in the sub-Saharan countries, leaving them susceptible to poverty and diseases such as HIV/AIDS. Violation of women's property rights also harms countries' development efforts. The report examines these issues using Kenya as a case study.

RACISM
Book

Blee, Kathleen M. *Women of the Klan: Racism and Gender in the 1920s.* Berkeley and Los Angeles: University of California Press, 1991. A groundbreaking work about the women of the Ku Klux Klan (WKKK), which enrolled hundreds of thousands of recruits in the 1920s and 1930s. The author examines the historical, cultural, and symbolic contexts of the Klan in the United States. From interviews of surviving Klan members, she looks at activities of the women's Klan in Indiana and gives biographical sketches of some of the more prominent women in the Indiana WKKK.

STATISTICS
Web Documents

Organization for Economic Cooperation and Development (OECD). "The Gender, Institutions and Development Data Base (GID)." Available online. URL: http://www.oecd.org/LongAbstract/0,2546,en_2649_201185_36223937_1_1_1_1,00.html (introduction) and http://www.oecd.org/dataoecd/19/28/36223936.xls (database). Accessed February 6, 2006. A tool offered to researchers and policy makers to determine and analyze obstacles to women's economic development. It covers a total of 162 countries and comprises an array of 50 indicators on gender discrimination. The database has been compiled from various sources and combines in a systematic and coherent fashion the current empirical evidence that exists on the socioeconomic status of women. Its true innovation is the inclusion of institutional variables, which range from intrahousehold behavior to social norms. Information on cultural and traditional practices that impact women's economic development is coded so as to measure the level of discrimination. Such a comprehensive overview of gender-related variables and the database's specific focus on social institutions make the GID unique, providing a toolbox for a wide range of analytical queries and allowing case-by-case adaptation to specific research or policy questions.

United Nations Statistics Division. "Statistics and Indicators on Women and Men" (March 27, 2006). Available online. URL: http://unstats.un.org/unsd/demo graphic/products/indwm/default.htm. Accessed March 27, 2006. This Web site provides statistics and indicators on women and men in six specific fields: population, health, work, families, education, decision making.

———. "Millennium Development Goal Indicators Database" (January 18, 2006). Available online. URL: http://unstats.un.org/unsd/mi/mi_goals.asp. Accessed January 18, 2006. A framework of eight goals, 18 targets, and 48 indicators to measure progress toward the Millennium Development Goals was adopted by a consensus of experts from the United Nations Secretariat and IMF, OECD, and the World Bank. Each indicator is linked to millennium data series as well as to background series related to the target in question.

SUFFRAGE
Books

Pankhurst, Emmeline. *My Own Story.* New York: Hearst International Library, 1914 and Kraus Reprints, 1971. Pankhurst's autobiography briefly speaks of her childhood and married life to Dr. Pankhurst, who was considerably older, died, and left her with several children. Mrs. Pankhurst became the leading figure in the British suffragist movement from the turn of the 20th century to World War I, when agitation was suspended for the sake of the war effort, without yet, however, gaining women in Britain the vote, the point where the book's account ends.

Web Documents

Jamieson, Amie, with Hyon B. Shin and Jennifer Day. "Voting and Registration in the Election of November 2000." Current Population Report, U.S. Census Bureau (February 2002). Available online. URL: http://www.census.gov/prod/2002pubs/p20-542.pdf. Accessed December 30, 2005. The report discusses voting and registration of the citizen voting-age population in the November 2000 presidential election. Voting and registration rates historically have been higher in years with presidential elections than in the "off" years. In this report, the 2000 (a presidential election year) data are compared with data for previous presidential election years (1996, 1992, 1988, etc.).

Television/Films/Video

Iron-Jawed Angels. Directed by Katja von Garnier. 125 minutes. 2004, film. Hillary Swank portrays the life of the suffragist Alice Paul from her beginnings in the movement, to her hunger strike, to winning of enfranchisement in 1920.

VIOLENCE
Web Documents

Krug, Etienne G., et al., eds. "World Report on Violence and Health." World Health Organization, Geneva, 2002. Available online. URL: http://www.who.int/violence_injury_prevention/violence/world_report/en. Accessed December 23, 2005. This report examines the types of violence that occur worldwide in the everyday lives of people and that generate much of the health burden imposed by violence. Accordingly, the information has been arranged in nine chapters, covering the following topics: violence—a global public health problem, youth violence, child abuse and neglect by parents and other caregivers, violence by intimate partners, abuse of the elderly, sexual violence, self-directed violence, collective violence, and the way forward: recommendations for action.

Tjaden, Patricia, and Nancy Thoennes. "Full Report of the Prevalence, Incidence, and Consequences of Violence against Women." U.S. Department of Justice. Office of Justice Programs, National Institute of Justice (November 2000). Available online. URL: http://www.ncjrs.org/pdffiles1/nij/183781.pdf#search='Department%20of%20Justice%20statistics%20violence%20women'. Accessed January 23, 2006. These findings from the National Violence Against Women Survey provide a comprehensive overview of violence against women in the United States.

World Health Organization "WHO Multi-Country Study on Women's Health and Domestic Violence against Women" (November 29, 2005). Available online. URL: http://www.who.int/gender/violence/who_multicountry_study/en/index.html.

Accessed May 17, 2006. From 24,000 interviews with women in 10 countries, this study analyzes data and sheds new light on the prevalence of violence against women in countries where few data were previously available. It also uncovers the forms and patterns of this violence across different countries and cultures, documenting the consequences of violence for women's health. This study on domestic violence reveals that intimate partner violence is the most common form of violence in women's lives—much more common than assault or rape by strangers or acquaintances. The study reports on the enormous toll physical and sexual violence by husbands and partners has on the health and well-being of women around the world and the extent to which partner violence is still largely hidden.

Television/Film/Video

No! Produced and directed by Aishah Shahidah Simmons. 94 minutes. 2006, documentary film. Information available online. URL: http://www.newsreel.org/nav/title.asp?tc=CN0187&s=women. Accessed May 18, 2006. About the impact of sexual violence on black women and girls. As the incidents of violence and sexual assault continue on campuses and in communities across the country, this film can be used to support both women and men, regardless of race, as they learn to negotiate the challenging terrain of sexuality—without violence.

WOMEN'S STUDIES

Books

Walker, Mary Edwards, M.D., and Mercedes Graf. *Essays on Women's Rights.* Amherst, N.Y.: Humanity Books, Classics in Women's Studies, 2003. The only woman to receive the Congressional Medal of Honor for her service during the Civil War, Dr. Mary Edwards Walker (1832–1919) was a surgeon, a public lecturer, and an outspoken champion of women's rights. One of the first women in the country to be awarded a medical degree, she served as an assistant surgeon for the Fifty-second Ohio Infantry and was cited for her valor in working behind enemy lines to attend to the sick and wounded.

Articles

Fish, Cheryl J., with Yi-Chun and Tricia Lin. "Women's Studies Then and Now," *Women's Studies Quarterly,* December 2002. Since the launch of the first women's studies courses in the early 1970s, more than 600 programs in the field have been established in the United States and throughout the world. In this special edition, teachers, scholars, activists, and poets examine the historical impact and the new struggles in this dynamic field. Contributors explore intergenerational differences, the effect of new technologies on women's studies curricula, and the challenges of teaching women's studies since September 11, 2001. They speak from community college, undergraduate, and doctoral programs in urban and rural settings.

Chronology

1780 B.C.E.

The Egyptian queen Sobeknefru (ca. 1787–1783 B.C.E.) rules without a king. She is portrayed wearing the royal head cloth and a kilt over female dress.

1750 B.C.E.

The Babylonian Code of Hammurabi protects a woman's right to hold and inherit property.

1500 B.C.E.

During Egypt's Golden Age (the New Kingdom, ca. 1550–1069 B.C.E.), Ahhotep is awarded for bravery in support of her two sons, King Kamose and King Ahmose, and her husband, King Seqnenre-Taa.

1472 B.C.E.

Hatshepsut becomes one of Egypt's most famous queens.

1400 B.C.E.

Queen Tiy becomes the wife of Amenhotep III (1390–1352 B.C.E.) in spite of her provincial origins.

1336 B.C.E.

Queen Nefertiti assists her husband, King Akhenaten, in his restructuring policies. Some believe she ruled as king after her husband died.

1200 B.C.E.

After the death of her husband, Seti II, in 1194 B.C.E., Tawosret takes the throne.

Chronology

51 B.C.E.

The last of Egypt's female pharaohs, the great Cleopatra VII, restores fortune to Egypt until her eventual suicide in 30 B.C.E., marking the end of ancient Egypt.

61–63 C.E.

Boadicea, a Dark Ages hero in the United Kingdom, leads the Iceni Celts to a glorious, but not victorious, war against the Romans in East Anglia.

415

Hypatia, the first noted woman mathematician, is a brilliant lecturer. Her Neo-Platonist philosophy, with religious undertones, leads to her killing by a Christian mob.

527

Theodora, a renowned stage performer, made empress by Justinian in Constantinople, legalizes property inheritance by women and divorce laws and attempts to outlaw prostitution.

1141

Hildegard von Bingen, a German nun and magistra (teacher), has a vision that gives her instant understanding of the meaning of religious texts and commands her to record in writing everything she observes in her visions.

1100s

Mahasty is jailed for speaking her mind about the role women could play in Afghan society.

1327

Twinslayer's Case for abortion in England.

1348

Abortionist's Case in England.

1400s

Queen Gowhar Shad of Heart, ruler of the Afghan empire for 50 years, supports the arts, founds colleges, and enacts laws.

1412–31

Joan of Arc leads the French against the English to chase them out of France.

1558

• *November 17:* Queen Elizabeth succeeds to the throne in England.

1694

The British author and feminist Mary Astell pleads for greater opportunities for women in her *Serious Proposal to the Ladies,* written in two parts between 1694 and 1697. Her work offers a scheme for a women's college, an idea well before its time and the subject of public ridicule.

1700s

Nazo, Zainab, and Zarhgoona are three Afghan wisewomen who advise the state on various matters. Zainab advocates educational rights of women in harems.

1701

The first sexually integrated jury—six men and six women—hears cases in Albany, New York.

1747

In Afghanistan, King Ahmad Shah discontinues the practice of divorce that shames women. Marriage and property rights for widowed women are also protected under his reign, which encourages widows to remarry.

1769

American colonies base their laws on the English common law, summarized in Sir William Blackstone's *Commentaries on the Laws of England* (1765–69): "By marriage, the husband and wife are one person in the law. The very being and legal existence of the woman is suspended during the marriage, or at least is incorporated into that of her husband under whose wing and protection she performs everything."

1777

During the American Revolution, state constitutions bar women from political process. New York passes laws that take away women's right to vote. By 1807, all states disenfranchise women.

1788

Women win the right in the United States of America to stand for election.

1789

The United States Constitution is ratified so the terms *persons, people,* and *electors,* can be interpreted to include men and women.

1792

Mary Wollstonecraft's *A Vindication of the Rights of Woman* is published in England. Educated women begin to promote the equal rights of women to education and work.

1839

The first Married Women's Property Act is enacted in Mississippi, allowing women the right to hold property in their own name, but with their husband's permission.

1840

The World's Anti-Slavery Convention is held in London, England, but the female delegates from the United States, Lucretia Mott and Elizabeth Cady Stanton, are not allowed to participate. They decide to have a women's rights convention when they return home.

1845

Danish women are permitted to take the examination to be heads of schools, allowing them the opportunity to improve teaching and education of girls.

1847

Mary Blackwell attains full status as a physician in the United States.

1848

The New York Married Women's Property Law replaces Mississippi's as a model for other states. The law provides for a married woman to be a sole owner of land and protected from a husband's creditors.

At the Women's Convention in Seneca Falls, New York, 300 women and men sign the *Declaration of Sentiments,* to cease discrimination against women in all aspects of society.

The Boston Female Medical College in Massachusetts opens and eventually merges with Boston University School of Medicine, making it the first coeducational medical school in the United States.

1852

Antioch College in Yellow Springs, Ohio, is the first nonsectarian college to grant women equal rights with men.

1855

In *Missouri v. Celia,* a black female slave is defined as property and without the right to defend herself against a master's act of rape.

Woman's Hospital opens in New York City as the first institution in the world established by women "for the treatment of diseases peculiar to women." It becomes known as the "birthplace of gynecology" and is now part of the St. Luke's hospital complex.

1860s

Indiana State College becomes the first state college to grant equal privileges to women in the 1860s.

1861

Empress Tz'u-hsi becomes ruler of China when her husband dies. She holds the reins of power until 1889.

1862

The Morrill Act of 1862 grants land in the west of the United States for colleges.

1866

The Fourteenth Amendment is passed by Congress to be later ratified by the states in 1868. It is the first time *citizens* and *voters* are defined as "male" in the Constitution.

The American Equal Rights Association (AERA) is founded in New York City with the purpose of securing for all Americans their civil rights irrespective of race, color, or sex. Lucretia Mott is elected president and Susan B. Anthony as secretary.

To test women's constitutional right to hold public office, Stanton runs for Congress, receiving 24 of 12,000 votes cast.

1869

The first U.S. woman suffrage law is passed in the territory of Wyoming.

John Stuart Mills, an English philosopher and economist, addresses the rights of women in his book *The Subjection of Women*, which is immediately translated into Danish.

AERA splits in 1869 as a result of disagreements about the status of equal suffrage rights for blacks, creating three organizations: the National Woman Suffrage Association (NWSA), the American Woman Suffrage Association (AWSA), and the National American Woman Suffrage Association (NAWSA). Anthony and Stanton organize NWSA.

Washington University School of Law (then, St. Louis Law School) in Missouri becomes the first law school to admit women.

The first women's labor organization, Daughters of St. Crispin, holds its first convention at its founding in Lynn, Massachusetts. Chaired by Carrie Wilson, delegates from lodges across New England and the Northeast attend. An economic depression in 1873 causes the organization to disband in 1876.

1870

The Fifteenth Amendment receives final ratification. Its wording does not specifically prevent women from voting: "The right of citizens of the United States to vote shall not be denied or abridged by the United States or by any State on account of race, color, or previous condition of servitude."

The first sexually integrated grand jury hears cases in Cheyenne, Wyoming.

1871

1871, the Dansk Kvindesamfund (Danish Women's Society) is founded, envisioned at first as a division of the International Association of Women, in the Bajer's home in Copenhagen.

1872

Anthony leads a group of women to the polls in Rochester, New York, to test the right of women to the franchise under the terms of the Fourteenth Amendment. Her arrest, trial, and sentence to a fine propel the high-profile case to the U.S. Supreme Court, which decides against her.

1873

In (Myra Colby) *Bradwell v. Illinois,* the U.S. Supreme Court rules that a state has the right to exclude a married woman from practicing law.

The Comstock Act makes it a federal crime to use the U.S. mail to distribute anything considered "obscene, lewd, lascivious, indecently filthy, or vile." The law classifies information about contraception, abortion, and sexual health as obscene in the United States.

The Woman's Crusade of 1873–74 protests alcohol and saloons.

1874

Nielsen Nielsine is among the first women to apply to and be accepted in medical school at the University of Copenhagen in Denmark.

1875

In *Minor v. Happersett,* the U.S. Supreme Court declares that despite the privileges and immunities clause, a state can prohibit a woman from voting. The Court declares women as "persons" but holds that they constitute a "special category of nonvoting citizens."

Danish universities become open to women who successfully pass the physical fitness exams with the same scores as men.

1878

The U.S. Congress passes a constitutional amendment enfranchising women, which the states do not ratify until 41 years later.

The first women's medical society is formed. Later renamed the New England Women's Medical Society, it is initially chaired by Dr. Marie E. Zakrzewska.

1879

Through special congressional legislation, Belva Lockwood becomes the first woman admitted to try a case before the Supreme Court.

1880

Malalai, a Pashtun woman, leads Afghans into war while waving a veil over her head, during the Second Anglo-Afghan War.

1881

Volume 1 of a multivolume series, *History of Woman Suffrage*, written by Susan B. Anthony, Elizabeth Stanton, and Matilda Gage, is published. Volumes are published in 1882, 1886, and 1902.

1885

Bryn Mawr College in Pennsylvania opens and offers graduate programs to women.

1886

The Young Women's Christian Association (YWCA) is founded as a national group in the United States. It began in England in 1855.

The Young Women's Hebrew Association (YWHA) is founded for women and girls of Jewish descent. The YWHAs eventually become Jewish community centers.

1888

The International Council for Women is founded in Chicago, Illinois, and holds its first meeting in Washington, D.C.

1890

The first U.S. state (Wyoming) grants women the right to vote in all elections.

The Daughters of the American Revolution is established in the United States as the first women's patriotic group based on heredity.

1893

New Zealand grants women the right to vote in all elections.

Johns Hopkins Medical School in Baltimore, Maryland, begins to admit women. By 1903, the drive to make medical school coeducational causes a majority of the women-only medical colleges to close.

1896

The National Association of Colored Women is formed, uniting more than 100 black women's clubs. Leaders of the clubs include Josephine St. Pierre Ruffin, Mary Church Terrell, and Anna Julia Cooper.

1897

By 1897, the Women's Suffrage Organization in Copenhagen merges with the Danish Women's Society.

1899

The Danish Women's National Council is founded and associates itself with the Chicago-based International Council of Women (ICW).

1900

Every state has passed legislation modeled after New York's Married Women's Property Act, granting American married women some control over their property and earnings.

1902

Australia grants women the right to vote in all elections but excludes aboriginal women.

ICW holds its board meeting in Copenhagen.

1904

The International Women's Suffrage Alliance (IWSA) is founded to focus on the struggle for suffrage across the globe.

1906

Finland grants women the right to vote in all elections.

Copenhagen is host to an IWSA meeting for suffragists from many countries.

1907

Norway grants women the right to stand for election, which is subject to conditions and restrictions.

1908

The U.S. Supreme Court rules in favor of Oregon's 10-hour workday for women in *Muller v. State of Oregon.*

1909

The IWSA Suffrage Congress takes place in London.

1910

The Camp Fire Girls is founded as the first national nonsectarian, interracial organization promoting character development for girls through indoor and outdoor activities. It holds its first meeting in Maine with a focus on Native American lore. The organization now includes boys and girls.

1912

The Women's Suffragette Alliance is formed in Nanking, China, with women from 18 provinces who rally for equal rights before the national legislature.

1913

In Norway, restrictions are lifted and women can now vote in all elections.

Lucy Burns and Alice Paul organize a demonstration on March 3, 1913, in Washington, D.C., the day President Woodrow Wilson is inaugurated.

1915

Denmark grants women the right to vote in all elections. Iceland also grants women the right to vote in all elections, subject to restrictions.

The Women's Peace Party is formed and chaired by the sociologist Jane Addams, an Illinois native, who goes on to become the first American woman to win the Nobel Prize in peace in 1931 for her work for international peace.

1916

The birth control advocate Margaret Sanger tests the validity of New York's anti-contraception law by establishing a clinic in Brooklyn.

The Congressional Union for Woman Suffrage, founded by Alice Paul and Lucy Burns in 1913, splits from the National American Women Suffrage Association (NAWSA), after differences with its president, Carrie Chapman Catt, and becomes the National Women's Party (NWP).

1917

Canada grants women the right to vote, with restrictions; Netherlands grants women the right to stand for election.

During the Russian Revolution, the February Revolution is triggered by an International Women's Day demonstration.

Russia grants women the right to vote.

1918

Austria and Canada grant women the right to vote, although Canada excludes the Inuit and Indians. In Estonia, Georgia, Germany, and Hungary, women are granted the right both to vote and to stand for election. Ireland grants women the right to vote with restrictions. Kyrgyzstan, Latvia, Lithuania, Poland, the Russian Federation, and the United Kingdom grant women the right to vote with restrictions.

Margaret Sanger wins her suit to allow doctors to advise their married patients about birth control for health purposes in the state of New York.

1919

Belarus grants women the right to vote; Belgium grants women the right to vote, with conditions; Luxembourg grants women the right to vote; the Netherlands grants women the right to vote; New Zealand grants women the right to stand for election; Sweden grants women the right to vote (with conditions); and Ukraine grants women the right to vote.

Women in Denmark win the right to equal pay in the civil service.

The delegates to the International Women's Congress form a new organization, the Women's International League for Peace and Freedom (WILPF), in Geneva, Switzerland.

At the end of World War I, the Paris Peace Conference in 1919 provides proposals for the newly formed Covenant of the League of Nations and the International Labour Organisation (ILO).

1920

Albania grants women the right to vote; Canada grants women the right to stand for election with conditions; the Czech Republic grants women the right to vote; Iceland lifts restrictions; and Slovakia grants women the right to vote.

American women are granted the right to vote with the ratification of the Nineteenth Amendment to the U.S. Constitution. It declares: "The right of citizens of the United States to vote shall not be denied or abridged by the United States or by any State on account of sex."

1921

Armenia grants women the right to vote, and Azerbaijan women are granted the right both to vote and to stand for election. Belgium grants women the right to stand for election, with conditions; Georgia grants women the right to vote; and Sweden lifts conditions on women's right to vote.

1922

In Denmark, the marriage reform acts of 1922 and 1923 establish equal child custody, property, and divorce rights.

The Republic of Ireland grants women the right to vote.

Grace Abbott is the first woman to serve as an unofficial U.S. delegate—the United States is not an official member—to the League of Nations. She serves on the organization's Advisory Committee on Traffic in Women and Children until 1934.

1923

The National Woman's Party proposes a constitutional amendment: "Men and women shall have equal rights throughout the United States and in every place subject to its jurisdiction. Congress shall have power to enforce this article by appropriate legislation."

The Afghan constitution is amended to guarantee equal rights for men and women.

1924

In Kazakhstan, Mongolia, Saint Lucia, and Tajikistan, women are granted the right both to vote and to stand for election.

A New York State case (*Radice v. New York*) upholds a law that forbids waitresses to work the night shift but makes exception for entertainers and ladies' room attendants.

1925

American Indian suffrage is granted by an act of Congress.

The Women's World Fair is organized by Grace Coolidge, wife of President Calvin Coolidge, in Chicago, Illinois. The fair is a demonstration of what women have accomplished up to that time.

1927

During an International Women's Day celebration on March 8, tens of thousands of women gather around a statue of Lenin in Bukhara, near the Afghan border, and throw their burqas into a bonfire. The event is inspired by an earlier one that took place in the 1920s, when Russian women went to Bukhara to introduce revolutionary ideas to the women there.

In Turkmenistan, women are granted the right both to vote and to stand for election.

Involuntary sterilization of Carrie Buck occurs under the Virginia Supreme Court decision on its 1924 eugenics law.

1928

Restrictions are lifted on women's right to vote in Ireland. In the United Kingdom, the second passage of the Representation of the People Act leads to suffrage for both men and women.

Emmeline Pankhurst, the British pioneer of the women's suffrage movement, dies shortly after suffrage is granted in Great Britain.

The Ecole de Mannequins opens in Chicago, becoming the first institution to train young women to be models. At the time, they earn a dollar an hour. Eventually the 6,000 models in Chicago form a union and rally for better pay and hours.

1929

Ecuador and Romania grant women the right to vote (both with conditions).

1930

South African white women are granted the right both to vote and to stand for election. Turkey grants women the right to vote.

1931

Chile and Portugal grant women the right to vote (with conditions). Spain grants women the right to vote. Sri Lankan women are granted the right both to vote and to stand for election.

The All-Asian Women's Conference unites representatives in Lahore from Afghanistan, Burma, Japan, Ceylon (Sri Lanka), and Persia (Iran) with observers from Britain, New Zealand, the United States, and Java (Indonesia) about the achievement of equality and adult franchise.

1932

In Maldives, Thailand, and Uruguay, women are granted the right both to vote and to stand for election.

1932

The National Recovery Act forbids more than one family member from holding a government job; as a result, many women lose their job.

1934

Brazil and Cuba grant women the right both to vote and to stand for election. Portugal grants women the right to vote (with conditions); Turkey grants women the right to stand for election.

1935

Myanmar grants women the right to vote.

Mary McLeod Bethune organizes the National Council of Negro Women, a coalition of black women's groups that lobbies against job discrimination, racism, and sexism.

1936

In *United States v. One Package of Japanese Pessaries* (vaginal suppositories), a Manhattan judge, Augustus Hand, rules that the package ("containing 120 rubber pessaries, more or less, being articles to prevent conception") can be delivered, giving judicial approval of medicinal use of birth control. The ruling weakens the federal Comstock Law, which has prevented dissemination of contraceptive information and supplies since 1873.

1937

The U.S. Supreme Court upholds Washington State's minimum wage laws for women.

Philippines women are granted the right both to vote and to stand for election.

July: The American female pilot Amelia Earhart disappears over the Pacific.

1938

Women of Bolivia and Uzbekistan are granted the right both to vote and to stand for election.

The Fair Labor Standards Act establishes minimum wage without regard to sex in the United States.

1939

In El Salvador, women are granted the right both to vote and to stand for election.

June: The Civilian Pilot Training Program (CPTP) is established by the U.S. government. The program provides pilot training across the country and allows for one woman to be trained for every 10 men.

1940

- **September:** Jackie Cochran writes to Eleanor Roosevelt suggesting the establishment of a women's flying division of the Army Air Forces.

1941

- **June:** Jackie Cochran becomes the first woman to ferry a bomber across the Atlantic.

- *June:* Women are banned from participating in the CPTP.

In Panama, women are granted the right both to vote and to stand for election (with conditions).

1942

In the Dominican Republic, women are granted the right both to vote and to stand for election.

In response to the need for workers in shipbuilding during the war, the International Brotherhood of Boilermakers, Iron Shipbuilders and Helpers, a union of the American Federation of Labor (AFL), opens to women.

1944

Bulgaria and France grant women the right to vote; in Jamaica, women are granted the right both to vote and to stand for election.

1945

Croatia grants women the right to vote; Guyana grants women the right to stand for election. Women in Indonesia, Trinidad, Italy, Japan, Panama, Senegal, Slovenia, and Tobago are granted the right both to vote and to stand for election.

1946

Cameroon, the Democratic People's Republic of Korea, and Djibouti grant women the right to vote. Guatemala, Liberia, and Myanmar grant women the right to stand for election. Restrictions are lifted in both Panama and Romania. The former Yugoslav Republic of Macedonia, Trinidad and Tobago, Venezuela, Vietnam, and Ecuador grant women the right to vote. In Yugoslavia, women are granted the right both to vote and to stand for election.

1947

The Universal Declaration of Human Rights is presented to the General Assembly at the United Nations by Eleanor Roosevelt.

In *Fay v. New York,* the U.S. Supreme Court rules that women are equally qualified with men to serve on juries but are free to be exempted from service.

Women are granted the right both to vote and to stand for election in Argentina, Japan, Malta, Mexico (to vote only), Pakistan, and Singapore.

1948

Belgium lifts restrictions on voting. Women in Israel, Niger, Republic of Korea, Seychelles, and Suriname are granted the right both to vote and to stand for election.

WOMEN'S RIGHTS

1949

Bosnia and Herzegovina grant women the right to vote. Chile lifts restrictions. In China and Costa Rica, women are granted the right both to vote and to stand for election. The Syrian Arab Republic grants women the right to vote with conditions.

Simone de Beauvoir's 1949 *The Second Sex* explores Marxist, Freudian, and Hegelian themes to uncover the sources of the definition of *woman* as the "other" of man.

1950

Susan B. Anthony is elected to the Hall of Fame for Great Americans at Bronx Community College, New York, of the City University of New York.

Barbados and Canada grant women the right to vote. Restrictions are lifted in Haiti and India.

1951

Women of Antigua and Barbuda, Dominica, Grenada, Nepal, Saint Kitts and Nevis, Saint Vincent, and the Grenadines are granted the right both to vote and to stand for election.

Paula Ackerman performs her husband's function as a rabbi of a reform congregation in Meridian, Mississippi, and acts as an interim spiritual leader after he dies.

1952

Restrictions are lifted in Bolivia, and women in Côte d'Ivoire, Greece, and Lebanon are granted the right both to vote and to stand for election.

The General Assembly adopts a resolution urging all member nations to extend suffrage rights to women.

1953

Bhutan and Guyana give women the right to vote. In Mexico, they can stand for election. In the Syrian Arab Republic, restrictions are lifted.

Daoud becomes Afghanistan's prime minister and encourages women to participate in government and employment.

Women's names are used for hurricanes in the Atlantic, Caribbean, and Gulf of Mexico. *Alice* is the name of the first hurricane.

1954

In Belize, Colombia, and Ghana, women are granted the right both to vote and to stand for election.

1955

In Cambodia, Eritrea, Ethiopia, Honduras, Nicaragua, and Peru, women are granted the right both to vote and to stand for election.

Rosa Parks's arrest in December prompts a 13-month civil rights protest, later dubbed the Montgomery bus boycott.

The Daughters of Bilitis (DOB), the first lesbian organization in the United States, is founded. Although DOB originates as a social group, it later develops into a political organization to win basic acceptance of lesbians in the United States.

1956

In Benin, Comoros, Egypt, Gabon, Mali, Mauritius, and Somalia, women are granted the right both to vote and to stand for election.

1957

In Malaysia, women are granted the right both to vote and to stand for election. Zimbabwe grants women the right to vote and lifts restrictions.

March 25: The Treaty of Rome establishes the European Economic Community (EEC) with France, West Germany, Italy, Belgium, the Netherlands, and Luxembourg as the initial members. The name is later changed in 1993 and 2002 to the *EC Treaty*.

Conference for Asian Women takes place in Ceylon, and women from Afghanistan attend.

1958

In Burkina Faso, Chad, Guinea, Lao People's Democratic Republic, and Nigeria (South), women are granted the right both to vote and to stand for election.

Afghanistan sends a female delegate to the United Nations.

1959

Madagascar and San Marino grant women the right to vote. In Tunisia and the United Republic of Tanzania, women are granted the right both to vote and to stand for election.

1960

Canada lifts restrictions for women to stand for election; in Cyprus, Gambia, and Tonga, women are granted the right both to vote and to stand for election. Benin, Burkina Faso, Cameroon, Central African Republic, Chad, Comoro Islands, the Republic of the Congo, the Democratic Republic of the Congo (Zaire), Equitorial Guinea, Gabon, Gambia, Guinea, Ivory Coast, Madagascar, Mali, Niger, Nigeria, and Senegal grant women the right to vote.

The Food and Drug Administration approves the sale of birth control pills.

1961

Bahamas grants women the right to vote (with restrictions). Burundi and El Salvador grant women the right to stand for election. In Malawi, Mauritania, Paraguay, Rwanda, and Sierra Leone, women are granted the right both to vote and to stand for election. Somalia and Tanzania grant women the right to vote.

The U.S. Supreme Court upholds a rule adopted by the state of Florida that makes it less likely for women than men to be called for jury service on the grounds that a "woman is still regarded as the center of home and family life."

In 1961, the first North Atlantic Treaty Organization (NATO) Conference of Senior Women Officers of the Alliance takes place in Copenhagen, Denmark.

President John Kennedy establishes the President's Commission on the Status of Women and appoints Eleanor Roosevelt chairperson until her death in 1962. The report issued by the commission in 1963 documents substantial discrimination against women in the workplace and makes specific recommendations for improvement, including fair hiring practices, paid maternity leave, and affordable child care.

1962

Algeria grants women the right to vote. Australia lifts restrictions, and aboriginal women are allowed to vote. In Monaco, Uganda, and Zambia, women are granted the right both to vote and to stand for election.

1963

In Afghanistan, Congo, Equatorial Guinea, Fiji, Iran (the Islamic Republic of Iran), Kenya, and Morocco, women are granted the right both to vote and to stand for election. Papua New Guinea grants women the right to stand for election.

The Equal Pay Act is passed by Congress, promising equitable wages for the same work, regardless of the race, color, religion, national origin, or sex of the worker.

Betty Friedan publishes her highly influential book *The Feminine Mystique*, which describes the dissatisfaction felt by middle-class American homemakers with the narrow role imposed on them by society. The best seller is a boon to the contemporary women's rights movement.

1964

Bahamas lifts restrictions on women's right to vote. The Libyan Arab Jamahiriya, Papua New Guinea, and Sudan grant women the right to vote.

Title VII of the Civil Rights Act passes; it includes a prohibition against employment discrimination on the basis of race, color, religion, national origin, or sex.

The Equal Employment Opportunity Commission (EEOC) is established to investigate complaints and impose penalties.

1965

In Botswana and Lesotho, women are granted the right both to vote and to stand for election.

The decision in *Weeks v. Southern Bell* challenges labor laws and company regulations, making former men-only jobs available to women, with improved hours and work conditions.

In *Griswold v. Connecticut,* the Supreme Court overturns one of the last state laws prohibiting the prescription or use of contraceptives by married couples.

1966

The National Organization for Women (NOW) is founded by a group of feminists including Betty Friedan. The largest women's rights group in the United States, NOW seeks to end sexual discrimination, especially in the workplace, by means of legislative lobbying, litigation, and public demonstrations.

The International Covenant on Civil and Political Rights (ICCPR) and the International Covenant on Economic, Social and Cultural Rights (ICESCR) are two major international human rights treaties drafted by the United Nations in 1966 but not enforced until 1976.

Indira Gandhi becomes prime minister of India; she rules until 1977 and again from 1980 to 1984.

1967

The Democratic Republic of Congo grants women the right to vote. Restrictions are lifted in Ecuador.

1968

Nauru and Swaziland women are granted the right both to vote and to stand for election.

Executive Order 11246 prohibits sex discrimination by government contractors and requires affirmative action plans for hiring of women.

• *July 22:* Afghan women protest Kabul University's possible prohibition of study in universities abroad by women.

1969

In *Bowe v. Colgate-Palmolive Company,* the court rules that women meeting the required physical requirements can work in many jobs formerly reserved for men only.

California adopts the nation's first "no fault" divorce law, allowing divorce by mutual consent. (Note: By 1985, every state has adopted a similar law. Laws are also passed regarding the equal division of common property.)

1970

In Andorra, women are given the right to vote. In the Democratic Republic of the Congo, women are allowed to stand for election. In Yemen (Arab Republic), women are granted the right both to vote and to stand for election.

In *Schultz v. Wheaton Glass Co.*, a U.S. court of appeals rules that jobs held by men and women need to be "substantially equal" but not "identical" to fall under the protection of the Equal Pay Act. An employer cannot, for example, change the job titles of women workers in order to pay them less than men.

The North American Indian Women's Association, the first of its kind, is founded by Marie Cox.

1971

Women in Switzerland are granted the right both to vote and to stand for election.

The U.S. Supreme Court outlaws the practice of private employers' refusing to hire women who have preschool-age children (*Phillips v. Martin Marietta Corporation*).

Idaho's state law establishing automatic preference for males as administrators of wills is ruled unconstitutional in *Reed v. Reed*. This is the first time a court strikes down a law treating men and women differently. The U.S. Supreme Court finally declares women as *persons*. "Reasonableness" is the criterion rather than making sex a "suspect classification," under the Fourteenth Amendment.

Ms. magazine is first published as a sample insert in *New York* magazine. Over 300,000 copies are sold in eight days. The first regular issue is published in July 1972. The magazine becomes the major forum for feminist voices, and its cofounder and editor, Gloria Steinem, is launched as an icon of the modern feminist movement.

1972

Title IX (Public Law 92-318) of the Education Amendments prohibits sex discrimination in all aspects of education programs that receive federal support.

The Supreme Court decision in *Eisenstadt v. Baird* extends the right to privacy to unmarried persons' right to use contraceptives.

In Bangladesh, women are granted the right both to vote and to stand for election.

Chronology

1973

Andorra and San Marino grant women the right to stand for election; in Bahrain, women are granted the right both to vote and to stand for election. Syria grants women the right to vote.

The U.S. Supreme Court bans sex-segregated "help wanted" advertising as a violation of Title VII of the Civil Rights Act of 1964 as amended, on the basis of its decision in *Pittsburgh Press v. Pittsburgh Commission on Human Relations.*

Roe v. Wade and *Doe v. Bolton* are two cases in which the U.S. Supreme Court declares that the Constitution protects women's right to terminate an early pregnancy, making abortion legal in the United States.

"Call Off Your Old Tired Ethics (COYOTE)" is established to protect rights of women prostitutes and former prostitutes in San Francisco, California. Initially, the organization seeks legalization of prostitution, protection against arrests, and proper legal council for arrests.

1974

Jordan, Solomon Islands, and Guinea-Bissau grant women the right both to vote and to stand for election.

Housing discrimination on the basis of sex and credit discrimination against women are outlawed by Congress.

The decision in *Cleveland Board of Education v. LaFleur* asserts the illegality of forcing pregnant women to take maternity leave on the assumption they are incapable of working because of their physical condition.

The Women's Educational Equity Act funds the development of nonsexist teaching materials and model programs that encourage full educational opportunities for girls and women.

The Equal Employment Opportunity Commission, the Justice and Labor Departments, and AT&T sign a consent decree banning AT&T's discriminatory practices against women and minorities.

The Equal Credit Opportunity Act prohibits discrimination in consumer credit practices based on sex, marital status, age, or receipt of public assistance. It is later amended to include race, religion, national origin, and age.

The first women's professional football league is founded, consisting of seven teams coached by men. Players are paid $25 per game.

1975

International Women's Year is initiated by the United Nations, marking the beginning of the Decade for Women.

March 8 is chosen by the United Nations as International Women's Day in recognition of women's fight for universal rights.

The first of four UN world conferences on women in Mexico City takes place.

The court's decision in *Taylor v. Louisiana* denies the state the right to exclude women from juries.

Angola, Cape Verde, Mozambique, São Tomé and Príncipe, and Vanuatu grant women the right to vote.

On August 1, leaders of 35 nations gather in Helsinki to sign the Final Act of the Conference on Security and Co-operation in Europe (CSCE); the organization will eventually focus on human trafficking and terrorism.

Women can no longer be excluded from juries because of their sex in the United States.

1976

Portugal lifts restrictions on women's right to vote.

In *General Electric Company v. Gilbert,* the Supreme Court upholds women's right to unemployment benefits during the last three months of pregnancy.

The U.S. Supreme Court declares unconstitutional a state law permitting 18- to 20-year-old females to drink beer while denying the rights to men of the same age in *Craig v. Boren.* The Court establishes a new set of standards for reviewing laws that treat men and women differently.

The Equal Pay Act is passed in Denmark.

Barbara Jordan addresses the Democratic National Convention in the United States as the first African-American woman to give the keynote speech.

1977

In Guinea-Bissau, women are granted the right both to vote and to stand for election.

In November 1955, Eritrea was part of Ethiopia when women there were enfranchised. The constitution of sovereign Eritrea adopted on May 23, 1997, stipulates that "all Eritrean citizens, of eighteen years of age or more, shall have the right to vote."

RAWA is founded in Afghanistan by Meena Keshwar.

• *November 3:* The U.S. House of Representatives votes to give the Women's Airforce Service Pilots (WASPs) veteran status.

• *November 23:* President Jimmy Carter signs a bill into law "officially declaring the WASPs as having served on active duty in the Armed Forces of the United States for purposes of laws administered by the Veterans Administration."

1978

In the United States, the Pregnancy Discrimination Act bans employment discrimination against pregnant women. Under the act, a woman cannot be fired or denied a job or a promotion because she is or may become pregnant; nor can she be forced to take a pregnancy leave if she is willing and able to work.

The Equal Treatment Act of 1978 prohibits job discrimination on the basis of sex and provides recourse, such as access to the Equal Status Council, in Denmark.

The National Aeronautics and Space Administration (NASA) names six females of 35 candidates for the space shuttle program, including Margaret Seddon, M.D., from Tennessee, and Sally K. Ride, from California. NASA acknowledges the important role of the women's movement in causing more women to be qualified for the space program.

In Nigeria (North), the Republic of Moldova, and Zimbabwe, women are granted the right both to vote and to stand for election.

Civil war begins in Afghanistan. One reason cited is the Communist Party's fight for women's literacy rights.

1979

In the Marshall Islands, Micronesia (Federated States), and Palau, women are granted the right both to vote and to stand for election.

The Soviet Union invades Afghanistan. Women are emancipated, especially in the cities, and allowed to pursue education and professional opportunities. Other women choose to fight against the Russians with the mujahideen.

December: The UN Convention on the Elimination of All Forms of Discrimination against Women (CEDAW) is adopted by the General Assembly. It becomes known as the "Women's Rights" treaty.

Margaret Thatcher is elected as prime minister of England.

• *May:* The U.S. Air Force issues the first honorable discharges for women serving in the WASPs during World War II.

The U.S. government issues a silver dollar bearing the image of Susan B. Anthony.

1980

In Iraq and Vanuatu, women are granted the right both to vote and to stand for election.

The second of four world conferences on women convened by the United Nations is host to 145 representatives of member states in Copenhagen in 1980. CEDAW is introduced.

- *April 21:* High school girls mount a massive protest in Kabul against Soviet occupation of Afghanistan in what comes to be known as the Children's Revolt.

1981

The U.S. Supreme Court rules that excluding women from the draft is constitutional.

Kirchberg v. Feenstra overturns state laws designating a husband "head and master" with unilateral control of property owned jointly with the wife.

The Law of Succession Act of 1981 proclaims equal consideration of inheritance rights by male and female children in Kenya.

The U.S. Congress passes a resolution establishing National Women's History Week. The week is chosen to coincide with International Women's Day on March 8.

1983

In the United States, the antiporn activist Catherine MacKinnon drafts the Minneapolis antiporn ordinance, which states that all women forced to work in porn can bring a civil lawsuit against producers and distributors.

1984

The Democratic Party presidential candidate Walter Mondale selects Geraldine Ferraro as his vice presidential running mate.

In *Roberts v. U.S. Jaycees,* membership policies of organizations are forbidden to discriminate by sex, giving women access to many previously all-male organizations (Jaycees, Kiwanis, Rotary, Lions).

The state of Mississippi belatedly ratifies the Nineteenth Amendment, granting women the vote.

In *Hishon v. King and Spaulding,* the U.S. Supreme Court rules that law firms may not discriminate on the basis of sex in promoting lawyers to partnership positions.

EMILY's List (Early Money Is Like Yeast) is established as a financial network for pro-choice Democratic Party women running for national political office. The organization has a significant impact on the increasing numbers of women elected to Congress.

Women in Liechtenstein and South Africa (black and Indian) are granted the right both to vote and to stand for election.

1985

The third of four world conferences on women takes place in Nairobi.

Chronology

1986

Women in the Central African Republic and Djibouti are permitted to stand for election.

In *Meritor Savings Bank v. Vinson,* the U.S. Supreme Court holds that a hostile or abusive work environment can prove discrimination based on sex.

Liberia grants women the right to vote.

1987

A U.S. Supreme Court case decision (*Johnson v. Santa Clara County*) rules sex and race can be deciding factors for employment when the number of women or minorities holding a position is in question.

The U.S. Congress expands National Women's History Week to a month. Every year since then, Congress has passed a resolution for Women's History Month, and the U.S. president has issued a proclamation.

1988

The Equity Act for equal opportunities for men and women is passed in Denmark.

1989

In *Webster v. Reproductive Health Services,* the Supreme Court affirms the right of states to deny public funding for abortions and to prohibit public hospitals to perform abortions.

In Namibia, women are granted the right both to vote and to stand for election.

1990

In Samoa, women are granted the right both to vote and to stand for election.

Antonia C. Novello, M.D., is appointed surgeon general of the United States Public Health Service. She is sworn in by the Supreme Court justice Sandra Day O'Connor. She is also distinguished as the first Hispanic and first woman to be appointed surgeon general.

The Convention on the Rights of the Child is established as an international treaty.

1991

Senator Robert Dole introduces the Glass Ceiling Act.

1992

In *Planned Parenthood v. Casey,* the Supreme Court reaffirms the validity of a woman's right to abortion under *Roe v. Wade.* The case successfully challenges

Pennsylvania's 1989 Abortion Control Act, which sought to reinstate restrictions previously ruled unconstitutional.

The Year of the Woman in the United States promotes female political candidates.

The Communist regime in Afghanistan gives way to the Islamic State of Afghanistan, a conservative regime that does not approve of women's education and employment. Women are required to wear headdresses and are forbidden to laugh or wear makeup in public.

- *February 7:* The European Union Treaty (or Maastrict Treaty) is signed in the Netherlands, where the adoption of a single currency is proposed for the member states.

1993

Kazakhstan and the Republic of Moldova grant women the right both to vote and to stand for election.

In *Harris v. Forklift Systems, Inc.,* the U.S. Supreme Court rules that the victim does not need to show that she suffered physical or serious psychological injury as a result of sexual harassment.

In the United States, the Family and Medical Leave Act goes into effect.

The Islamic State of Afghanistan's Supreme Court rules that women need to be completely covered by the veil when not in their home.

The Treaty on European Union is signed at Maastricht.

1994

South African black women and men win suffrage rights.

The African Centre for Women (ACW) organizes a meeting in Kampala, Uganda, to evaluate the establishment of an African bank for women.

The U.S. Congress adopts the Gender Equity in Education Act to train teachers in gender equity, promote math and science learning by girls, counsel pregnant teens, and prevent sexual harassment.

The Violence against Women Act funds services for victims of rape and domestic violence, allows women to seek civil rights remedies for gender-related crimes, provides training to increase police and court officials' sensitivity, and establishes a national 24-hour hotline for battered women.

- *May 26:* Responding to violence against abortion clinics, President Clinton signs the Freedom of Access to Clinic Entrances (FACE) Act, which has become an important legal defense against antiabortion terror.

The Taliban take over Kandahar in November, closing schools for girls and forbidding women to work outside their homes.

Chronology

1995

The fourth UN world conference on women takes place in Beijing.

The Beijing Declaration and Platform for Action is introduced at the UN conference.

- **September:** The Taliban captures the strategic town of Herat in Afghanistan.

1996

In *United States v. Virginia,* the decision acknowledges that the admissions policy of the state-supported Virginia Military Institute, which favors men, violates the Fourteenth Amendment.

The Taliban capture Kabul in September.

1997

With respect to Title IX, the Supreme Court rules that similar numbers of men and women must be involved in college sports programs to qualify for federal support.

Eritrea extends women the right to vote.

In the Bamiyan region of Afghanistan, women fight Islamic fundamentalists and establish a university for women.

1998

Mitsubishi Motor Manufacturing of America agrees to pay $34 million to settle an EEOC lawsuit contending that hundreds of women have been sexually harassed.

In *Burlington Industries, Inc. v. Ellerth* and *Faragher v. City of Boca Raton,* the Supreme Court addresses the balance between employee and employer rights.

1999

The Amsterdam Treaty is entered into force on May 1, 1999, making substantial changes to the Treaty on European Union and defining the contemporary framework of the European Union, which implements a new currency, the euro dollar.

2000

The Equal Status Council and new Equal Status Act are catalysts for further change for women in Denmark.

The United Nations identifies the ambitious Millennium Development Goals to combat poverty, hunger, disease, illiteracy, environmental degradation, and discrimination against women, by the year 2015.

The Dakar Framework for Action is adopted at the World Education Forum in 2000, emphasizing the role UNESCO can play in eradicating poverty through education.

CBS Broadcasting agrees to pay $8 million to settle a sex discrimination lawsuit by the EEOC on behalf of 200 women.

The U.S. Supreme Court renders invalid sections of the Violence against Women Act that allow rape and domestic violence victims to sue their attackers in federal court (*United States v. Morrison*).

- *September 28:* The Food and Drug Administration approves the use of the early abortion pill RU-486 (mifepristone), already available to women in 13 countries. Abortion opponents try to impose restrictions on use of the drug.

- *October:* UN Resolution 1325 on Women, Peace and Security is adopted. The UN International Day for the Elimination of Violence against Women is now celebrated on November 25 each year.

The Trafficking Victims Protection Act is passed by Congress, launching a new visa system for victims of trafficking.

2001

- *November 27:* Afghan women NGOs participate in UN talks on a transitional government for Afghanistan in Bonn, Germany.

- *December 4–5:* The Afghan Women's Summit for Democracy in Brussels convenes at the request of Afghan NGO women's groups, in collaboration with the Office of the Special Adviser on Gender Issues and Advancement of Women and the United Nations Development Fund for Women (UNIFEM).

In China, the Population and Family Planning Law of the PRC is adopted to take effect in September 2003.

The Society for Women's Health Research calls attention to sex-based differences in health care by initiating the landmark study *Exploring the Biological Contribution to Human Health: Does Sex Matter?*

The Children Act of 2001 asserts the rights and welfare of children and guarantees their protection against exploitation for economic purposes in Kenya.

In Kenya, female genital mutilation is outlawed for girls under the age of 16.

Hillary Rodham Clinton is the first former first lady to win elected office when she is sworn in as U.S. senator from New York.

2002

The Domestic Violence Family Protection Bill offers legislation to defend women against violent treatment in Kenya.

President George W. Bush signs the ban against partial birth abortions.

The U.S. government issues a memorandum reminding employers that active duty time of reservists and National Guard members is eligible for benefits under the Family Medical Leave Act.

2003

- *January:* National Council of Women's Organizations publishes statement on the potential war with Iraq ensuing from a disarmament disagreement with Saddam Hussein in late 2002.
- *March 20:* The war of Iraq begins with an invasion by a coalition of multinational military forces against the Iraqi military; the Iraqi government and Saddam Hussein's regime are deposed by April 15.
- *September 25:* A Nigerian court of appeals throws out the case against Amina Lawal, a 32-year-old single mother sentenced to death by stoning for committing adultery.

A crisis is recognized in Darfur, Sudan, where severe forms of violence are being used against women.

2004

- *September:* U.S. Senate Department awards $10 million in grant money through the Iraqi Women's Democracy Initiative to organizations to train Iraqi women to stand for election, vote, develop media and business skills, and establish resource centers for networking and counseling for their upcoming election.
- *November 25:* A worldwide campaign called "16 Days of Activism Against Gender Violence" begins on the International Day for the Elimination of Violence Against Women, and ends on December 10, International Human Rights Day.

2005

- *March:* The Beijing + 10 Conference takes place in New York.
- *September:* Afghanistan's first election since the end of Taliban rule takes place.

In Kuwait, women are granted the right both to vote and to stand for election, to take effect in 2007.

In Saudi Arabia, men take part in the first local elections ever held in the country. Women are not allowed, however, to exercise their right to vote or to stand for election on that occasion.

- *September:* The United Nations World Summit convenes with member states' reaffirming their intention to fulfill objectives of the 1995 Beijing Platform of Action and the 2000 Millennium Development Goals.

The U.S. Senate approves the National Women's History Museum Act of 2005 to create a national women's history museum in Washington, D.C. The museum is expected to attract 1.5 million visitors a year.

WOMEN'S RIGHTS

2006

- *January:* 60,000 to 150,000 march in Milan, Italy, to maintain abortion laws, which had been legal since 1978, countering measures by the Vatican to curb such rights.
- *June:* Kuwaiti women vote and stand in national and local elections for the first time.
- *August:* National and international petitions for women, activists, and groups cause the Iranian government to halt the execution of a mother of four, who had been sentenced to death by stoning for having extramarital sex.
- *August:* U.S. Food and Drug Administration announces the approval of over-the-counter status of Plan B emergency contraception for women age 18 years and older.

U.S. Tennis Association renames the National Tennis Center in New York City after American tennis athlete and women's sports pioneer Billie Jean King at the opening ceremonies of the U.S. Open competition.

Amal Abdullah al-Kubaissi, an Arab female architect, is elected in the United Arab Emirates's first national election, to serve on the Federal National Council. She was one of 438 candidates, including 62 other women, who ran in the election.

Le Livre Noir de la Condition Feminine (The black book on the condition of women), by French sociologist and UN and CEDAW expert François Gaspard, Sandrine Treiner, and Christine Ockrent, is published.

2007

Representative Nancy Pelosi from Illinois becomes the first female Speaker of the U.S. House of Representatives.

Senator Hillary Clinton from New York seeks the presidency by announcing her campaign for the 2008 presidential election.

New Jersey becomes the third state, after Vermont and Connecticut, to legally permit civil unions for same-sex couples.

U.S. study finds one-third of American women by age 24 and one in four American females age 14 to 59 are carriers of the human papilloma virus (HPV), some strains of which cause cervical cancer.

Governor Ricky Perry issues an executive order making Texas the first state to require girls entering sixth grade to receive the HPV vaccine, starting in September 2008.

New medical guidelines issued about preventing heart disease and stroke in women, with specific information about the appropriate use of aspirin in young women.

Glossary

abolitionist   A person who believes that there should be no slavery.

abortion   The intentional intrauterine killing of a fetus.

active duty   Full-time duty in a uniformed service, including duty on the active list, full-time training duty, annual training duty, and attendance while in the active service at a school designated as a service school by law or by the secretary concerned.

affirmative action   Action taken by a government or private institution to compensate for past discrimination in education, work, or promotion on the basis of gender, race, ethnic origin, religion, or disability.

Armed Forces of the United States   Includes the United States Army, Navy, Air Force, Marine Corps, and Coast Guard, and all components thereof.

burqas   Part of the head-to-toe caftan, with a slit left open for the eyes, originally mandated by the Taliban to safeguard women from leering eyes. Made of wool or cotton, often of dark cloth, worn wrapped around the head and usually with a cloak.

civil and political rights   The rights of citizens to liberty and equality; sometimes referred to as first-generation rights. Civil rights include freedom to worship, to think and express oneself, to vote, to take part in political life, and to have access to information.

codification, codify   The process of putting customary international law in written form.

collective rights   The rights of groups to protect their interests and identities.

Commission on Human Rights   Body formed by the Economic and Social Council of the United Nations to deal with human rights. It is considered one of the first and most important international human rights bodies.

concede   Give over; surrender or relinquish to the physical control of another; acknowledge defeat.

conscription military   A military force based on draft or required registration and participation of soldiers from the general population.

convention   Binding agreement between states that is used synonymously with *treaty* and *covenant*. Conventions are stronger than declarations because they are legally binding for governments that have signed them. When the UN General Assembly adopts a convention, it creates international norms and standards. Member states can then ratify the convention, promising to uphold it. Governments that violate the standards set forth in a convention can then be censured by the United Nations.

covenant   Binding agreement between states; used synonymously with CONVENTION and TREATY. The major international human rights covenants are the International Covenant on Civil and Political Rights (ICCPR) and the International Covenant on Economic, Social and Cultural Rights (ICESCR), both passed in 1966.

coverture   Legal concept dating back to feudal Norman customs in England. When a woman married, she became one with her husband and ceased to exist in the eyes of the law. She could not contract for wages, could not own property in her own name, could not sign contracts, and did not have the right to decisions about her own children. In Elizabeth Cady Stanton's words, "with marriage a women is civilly dead." This concept was the driving force in the subordination of women. To understand it is to understand the roots of the women's rights revolution.

customary international law   Law that becomes binding on states although it is not written but rather adhered to out of custom. When enough states have begun to behave as though something is law, it becomes law "by use." This is one of the main sources of international law.

declaration   Document that states agreed upon standards but that is not legally binding. UN conferences, such as the 1993 UN Conference on Human Rights in Vienna and the 1995 world conference on women in Beijing, usually produce two sets of declarations: one written by government representatives and one by nongovernmental organizations (NGOs). The UN General Assembly often issues influential but legally nonbinding declarations.

domestic violence   A pattern of coercive behavior, including physical, sexual, and psychological attacks, as well as economic coercion, that adults or adolescents use against their intimate partners.

Economic and Social Council (ECOSOC)   A UN council of 54 members primarily concerned with population, economic development, human rights, and criminal justice. This high-ranking body receives and issues human rights reports in a variety of circumstances.

economic, social, and cultural rights Rights that concern the production, development, and management of material for the necessities of life. The rights to preserve and develop one's cultural identity, which give people social and economic security, sometimes referred to as security-oriented or second-generation rights. Examples are the right to food, shelter, and health care.

educational attainment The highest diploma or degree, or level of work toward a diploma or degree, an individual has completed.

emergency contraception pills (ECPs) (See MEDICATION ABORTION) ECPs prevent pregnancy. They contain hormones that reduce the risk of pregnancy if started within 120 hours of unprotected intercourse. The treatment is more effective the sooner it begins. Plan B is currently the only product marketed specifically as emergency contraception. Certain oral contraceptives taken in increased doses may also be used as ECPs.

empowerment In feminist literature, sense of personal control over one's destiny.

enfranchisement A statutory right or privilege granted to a person or group by a government (especially the rights of citizenship and the right to vote).

enlisted A person enrolled or conscripted into the military service. Also includes personnel who are officer candidates currently enrolled in an officer training program.

environmental, cultural, and developmental rights Sometimes referred to as third-generation rights, these rights recognize that people have the right to live in a safe and healthy environment and that groups of people have the right to cultural, political, and economic development.

equality The most common definition of equality is that of "formal equality" or "Aristotlean equality." Formal equality requires the same treatment if one is the same but allows different treatment if one is different. Under the formal equality model, men and women should be treated identically because they are considered the same. The formal equality model is problematic for feminists because it does not allow for consideration of the particular role of women in society and therefore often reproduces the inequalities faced by women when treating them as men.

equity Another term for EQUALITY.

eugenics A social philosophy that advocates selective breeding of human beings by improving human hereditary traits through intervention to create healthier, more intelligent people; save society's resources; and prevent human suffering. Methods include prenatal testing and screening, genetic counseling, birth control, selective breeding, in vitro fertilization, sterilization, and genetic engineering. Its scientific reputation tumbled in the 1930s because of the racial policies of Nazi Germany. Although the public and science associated eugenics with abuse, many regional and national governments upheld eugenic programs until the 1970s.

evangelism   Zealous preaching and advocacy of the gospel.

female genital mutilation (FGM)   Female circumcision, also referred to as clitoridectomy or excision. Infibulation is the most extreme form of FGM, involving complete excision of the clitoris, labia minora, and most of the labia majora—followed by stitching to close up most of the vagina.

female infanticide   The killing of female babies, mainly prevalent in China and India and among the North American Inuit. Historically, this was done with both genders in Greek, Roman, French, British, Japanese, Chinese, and Inuit civilizations to fulfill sacrificial purposes; to ward off evil; or to dispose of illegal offspring.

feminist   A man or a woman who supports the development and equality of women in all aspects of living.

gay   Someone who is sexually attracted to persons of the same sex. Homosexual.

gender   The characteristics society expects a person to have on the basis of his or her sex. Economic, social, and cultural roles associated with behavior, attitudes, and characteristics associated with being female or male.

gender mainstreaming   Defined by the United Nations as "the process of assessing the implications for women and men of any planned action, including legislation, policies or programs, in any area and at all levels. It is a strategy for making the concerns and experiences of women as well as of men an integral dimension of the design, implementation, monitoring and evaluation of policies and programs in all political, economic and societal spheres, so that women and men benefit equally and inequality is not perpetuated. The ultimate goal [of mainstreaming] is to achieve gender equality."

gender studies   The theoretical analysis of how gender identities are constructed.

Generation X, Gen X   The generation after the post–World War II baby boom, especially Americans and Canadians, born in the 1960s and 1970s.

Generation Y, Gen Y   The associated labels *millennial* and *echo boomer* are used to describe three types of generational spans: those born in the mid-1970s through early 1980s, the late 1970s through early 1990s, and the early 1980s to the early 2000s.

genocide   The systematic killing of people because of their race or ethnicity.

glass ceiling   Term coined in the 1990s to describe an artificial barrier based on attitudinal or organizational bias that prevents qualified individuals from advancing in their organization into management-level positions.

Global Gag Rule   At the International Conference on Population in Mexico City in August 1984, the U.S. delegation, headed by James Buckley, announced that the United States will no longer fund foreign non-governmental organizations (NGOs) that provide, refer, counsel, or advocate abortion. These restrictions were an executive branch policy in effect until 1993 but never became part of the permanent foreign assistance statute. It became known as the Mexico City Policy and was later dubbed the "Global Gag Rule" by its opponents.

human rights   The rights people are entitled to simply because they are human beings, irrespective of their citizenship, nationality, race, ethnicity, language, gender, sexuality, or abilities; human rights become enforceable when they are codified as conventions, covenants, or treaties, or as they become recognized as customary international law.

human rights treaties   Binding international legal documents outlining the responsibilities of states in regard to the protection, promotion, and fulfillment of human rights. Human rights treaties perform three functions: They guarantee specific rights to individuals, they establish state obligations or responsibilities related to these rights, and they create mechanisms to monitor state compliance with these obligations and/or allow individuals to seek redress for violations of their rights. Since human rights treaties are based on international law, they are only binding when a state voluntarily accepts their terms. In becoming a party to a treaty or ratifying it, a state accepts obligations to apply the provisions of the treaty and to accept international supervision of this compliance. Examples of international human rights treaties are the Convention on the Elimination of All Forms of Discrimination against Women (CEDAW); the International Covenant on Economic, Social and Cultural Rights (ICESCR); and the International Convention on the Elimination of All Forms of Racial Discrimination (ICERD).

inalienable   Refers to rights that belong to every person and cannot be taken from a person under any circumstances.

indigenous peoples   People who are original or natural inhabitants of a country. Native American Indians, for example, are the indigenous people of the United States.

indivisible   Refers to the equal importance of all human rights laws. A person cannot be denied a right because someone decides it is "less important" or "nonessential."

infibulation   (See FEMALE GENITAL MUTILATION) When the clitoris, labia minora, and most of the labia majora are removed and the labia majora (the outer lips of the vagina) then stitched together to cover the vaginal entrance.

interdependent   Refers to the complementary framework of human rights law. For example, persons' ability to participate in government is directly affected by their right to express themselves, to obtain an education, and even to obtain the necessities of life.

intergovernmental organizations (IGOs)   Organizations sponsored by several governments that seek to coordinate their efforts. Some are regional (e.g., the Council of Europe, the Organization of African Unity), some are alliances (e.g., the North Atlantic Treaty Organization [NATO]), and some are dedicated to a specific purpose (e.g., the UN Centre for Human Rights and the United Nations Educational, Scientific and Cultural Organization [UNESCO]).

International Bill of Human Rights   The combination of the Universal Declaration of Human Rights (UDHR), the International Covenant on Civil and Political Rights (ICCPR) and its optional Protocol, and the International Covenant on Economic, Social and Cultural Rights (ICESCR).

International Labour Organization (ILO)   Established in 1919 as part of the Versailles Peace Treaty to improve working conditions and promote social justice, the ILO became a specialized agency of the United Nations in 1946.

legal rights   Rights laid down in law that can be defended and brought before courts of law.

lesbianism   Sexual orientation of a woman toward other women.

loya jirga   Afghan general assembly. It is a traditional decision-making body dating from the 18th century. Prior to the establishment of the Afghan transitional administration, the government of Afghanistan consisted of the interim administration established by the Bonn Agreement.

medication abortion   (See EMERGENCY CONTRACEPTION) Medication that terminates an unwanted pregnancy. Medication abortion is the use of medication that can induce abortion. There are currently two drugs available in the United States for this purpose—mifepristone and methotrexate. Mifepristone can be taken up to 56 days after the first day of the last menstrual period, and methotrexate can be taken up to 49 days after the first day of the last menstrual period. Both are used in conjunction with misoprostol, which is taken after either mifepristone or methotrexate to complete the abortion.

member states   Countries that are members of the international body being referred to, such as the United Nations or the European Union.

misogynism Hatred of women.

moral rights Rights that are based on general principles of fairness and justice; they are often but not always based on religious beliefs. People sometimes feel they have a moral right even when they do not have a legal right. For example, during the Civil Rights movement in the United States, protesters demonstrated against laws forbidding blacks and whites to attend the same schools on the premise that these laws violated their moral rights.

national liberation movement A worldwide movement that began between the first two world wars, growing to massive proportions after 1945, in favor of national self-determination for the colonies of the imperialist powers. The national liberation movement grew out of the resistance of workers in the colonies in the wake of the Russian Revolution, generally inspired and led by the Comintern, and swept across the "third world" after the Second World War, culminating in the defeat of the United States in Vietnam in 1975.

natural rights Rights that belong to people simply because they are human beings.

New Woman A phrase coined in late 1890s novels and magazines to describe confident women who were seeking emancipation in all ways of living, to be self-sufficient.

nonbinding A document, such as a declaration, that carries no formal legal obligations. It may, however, carry moral obligations or attain the force of law as customary international law.

nongovernmental organizations (NGOs) Organizations formed by people outside government. NGOs monitor the proceedings of human rights bodies such as the Commission on Human Rights and are the "watchdogs" of human rights that fall within their mandate. Some are large and international (e.g., the Red Cross, Amnesty International, the Girl Scouts), while others may be small and local (e.g., an organization that is an advocate for people who have disabilities in a particular city or a coalition that promotes women's rights in a refugee camp). NGOs play a major role in influencing UN policy, and many of them have official consultative status at the United Nations.

nonpartisan Orientation of an organization that neither supports nor opposes candidates for office at any level of government.

parity Another term for equality.

parochial Relating to or supported by or located in a parish, such as schools; narrowly restricted in outlook or scope.

partial-birth abortion A late-term abortion in which a physician vaginally delivers, euthanizes, and extracts an unborn child's body.

patrilineal   Based on or tracing descent through the male line.

patrilocal   Of or relating to residence with a husband's kin group or clan.

political rights   (See CIVIL AND POLITICAL RIGHTS) The rights of people to participate in the political life of their communities and society, for example, the right to vote for their government or run for office.

poverty line   The level of personal income defining the state of poverty. The World Bank uses reference lines set at $1 (extreme poverty) and $2 a day.

Prohibition   The period from 1920 to 1933 when the sale of alcoholic beverages was prohibited in the United States by a constitutional amendment.

protocol   A treaty that modifies another treaty by adding procedures or substantive provisions.

quickening   The stage of pregnancy at which the mother first feels movement of the fetus, usually around the 21st week.

race   A social attribute based on skin color and other physical characteristics. The Current Population Survey provides data by race, as specified by the household respondent. Since 2003, respondents are allowed to choose more than one race; previously, multiracial persons were required to select a single primary race. Persons who select more than one race are classified separately in the category *two or more races.* Persons who select one race only are classified in one of the following five categories: (1) white, (2) black or African American, (3) Asian, (4) Native Hawaiian and other Pacific Islander, and (5) American Indian or Alaska Native. Only data for whites, blacks, and Asians are currently published because the number of survey respondents for the other racial categories is not large enough to produce statistically reliable estimates.

ratification, ratify   Process by which the legislative body of a state confirms a government's action in signing a treaty. The formal procedure by which a state becomes bound to a treaty after acceptance.

reservation   The exceptions made by state parties to a treaty, such as provisions that they do not agree to follow. Reservations, however, may not undermine the fundamental meaning of the treaty.

secular   Not religious-based, nor part of the clergy.

Selected Reserve   The Selected Reserve consists of those units and individuals within the Ready Reserve designated by their staff as so essential to initial wartime missions that they have priority over all other Reserves. All Selected Reservists are in an active status.

self-determination   Determination by the people of a territorial unit of their own political future without coercion from powers outside that region.

sex The biological characteristics that make a person male or female, with the distinction that only females become pregnant and menstruate.

sexist Biased toward one sex or the other.

sexual harassment Unwanted sexual attention that intrudes on a person's integrity. This includes requests for sexual favors, unwelcome or demeaning remarks, or touching. It is a form of discrimination and constitutes abuse of power.

signing, sign In human rights the first step in ratification of a treaty; signing a declaration, convention, or one of the covenants constitutes promising to adhere to the principles in the document and to honor its spirit.

Soroptimist The word *Soroptimist,* from the Latin words *soror,* meaning "sister," and *optima,* meaning "best," loosely translates as "best for women." It is in the name of an international organization that acts as a sisterhood.

stand for election When a person can be a candidate in an election.

state Often synonymous with *country.* A group of people permanently occupying a fixed territory, deploying common laws and government, and capable of conducting international affairs.

states party Those countries that have ratified a covenant or a convention and are thereby bound to conform to its provisions.

suffragette The term originated in Britain and was first used to insult members of the suffrage movement. It then became the term to describe the more radical branch of the British suffrage movement.

suffragist A woman or man who is an advocate for a woman's right to vote.

surrogate mother Also called *gestational carrier.* A woman's carrying and giving birth to a child for another woman, by prearrangement. Full surrogacy occurs when the infertile mother's egg is fertilized by the father's sperm and inserted into the surrogate mother's womb. Partial surrogacy occurs when the surrogate mother's egg is fertilized by the father's sperm.

Taliban Islamic fundamentalists who controlled Afghanistan from 1994 to 2002. The literal translation of *Taliban* is "seminary student."

temperance A movement that evolved in the late 1800s to advocate living without destructive excesses such as alcohol; a precursor to the Prohibition era (1920–33) in the United States. Women's groups were strong advocates of both temperance and prohibition.

tenure The right to hold property. Part of an ancient hierarchical system of holding lands.

trafficking Refers to the illegal transport of human beings, in particular women and children, for the purpose of selling them or exploiting their labor. Exploitation can include prostitution of others or other forms of sexual exploitation, forced labor or services, slavery or practices similar to slavery, servitude, or the removal of organs.

treaty   Formal agreement between states that defines and modifies their mutual duties and obligations; used synonymously with CONVENTION and COVENANT. When conventions are adopted by the UN General Assembly, they create legally binding international obligations for the member states that have signed them. When a national government ratifies a treaty, the articles of that treaty become part of its domestic legal obligations.

United Nations Charter   Initial document of the United Nations adopted in San Francisco in 1945 that set forth its goals, functions, and responsibilities.

United Nations General Assembly   One of the principal organs of the United Nations, consisting of representatives of all member states. The General Assembly issues declarations and adopts conventions on human rights issues, debates relevant issues, and censures states that violate human rights. The actions of the General Assembly are governed by the United Nations Charter.

Index

Page numbers in **boldface** indicate major treatment of a subject. Page numbers followed by *f* indicate figures. Page numbers followed by *b* indicate biographical entries. Page numbers followed by *c* indicate chronology entries. Page numbers followed by *g* indicate glossary entries.

A

Abbott, Grace 352*c*
ABC News 137
abolitionists 51–52, 345*c*, 371*g*
abortion(s) **20–22,** 371*g*
  in Afghanistan 116
  banning of 39
  in China 21, 107, 108
  Comstock Act 347*c*
  decline in 80, 101
  in Denmark 101
  Doe v. Bolton 361*c*
  in England 20–21, 343*c*, 366*c*
  forced 108
  in Italy 370*c*
  in Kenya 21, 120, 123
  medication 79–80, 368*c*, 376*g*
  partial-birth 80, **180–184,**
    368*c*, 377*g*
  Planned Parenthood v. Casey
    79, 365*c*–366*c*
  Roe v. Wade 21, **66,** 79,
    176–177, 361*c*, 365*c*
  RU-486 79, 80, 368*c*
  unsafe 21, 116, 123
  in U.S. 21, **79–80**
  Webster v. Reproductive
    Health Services 79, 365*c*
abortion clinics 79, 366*c*
Abortionist's Case (England,
  1348) 20, 343*c*
Abzug, Bella Savitsky 46,
  60–61, 255*b*
accountability 45, 46

ACLU (American Civil Liberties
  Union) 275
active duty (AD) 15, 76, 369*c*,
  371*g*
ACW. *See* African Centre for
  Women
ACWF. *See* All-China Women's
  Federation
AD. *See* active duty
Adams, Abigail 33, 50, 255*b*
Adams, John 33, 50
Adarand Constructors, Inc. v.
  Federico Pena 63
Addams, Jane 37–38, 255*b*, 350*c*
adultery 369*c*, 370*c*
AERA (American Equal Rights
  Association) 346*c*
affirmative action 5, 63, 359*c*,
  371*g*
Afghanistan ix–x, 110–118
  abortion in 116
  Amena Afzali 255*b*
  King Ahmad Shah 344*c*
  Safia Amajan 118, 256*b*
  Amnesty International report
    on **226–229**
  Shukria Barekzai 113, 257*b*
  and Bonn Agreement 368*c*
  and burqas 8
  civil war in 363*c*
  Conference for Asian Women
    357*c*
  continuing women's rights
    movement in 45

  and contraception 19
  current issues in **113–114**
  Muhammad Daoud 356*c*
  divorce in 344*c*
  education in 113, **116,** 118,
    344*c*, 359*c*, 364*c*, 366*c*
  elections in 113, 369*c*
  employment in 9, **116–117**
  equal rights in 352*c*
  family life in **114–115**
  female casualties in 77
  forced marriage in **115,**
    229–230
  future trends in 118
  Fatana Gailani 113, 260*b*–
    261*b*
  Fauzia Gailani 261*b*
  Gowhar Shad of Heart 343*c*
  Nasrine Gross 112, 118, 262*b*
  health care in **115–116**
  inheritance rights in 6, 115
  and international women's
    movement **117–118**
  invasion of vii
  Massouda Jalal 112, 262*b*–
    263*b*
  Rahima Jami 112, 263*b*
  Malai Joya 113, 263*b*
  Meena Keshwar 362*c*
  Mahasty 343*c*
  Malalai 264*b*, 348*c*
  Rona Mansuri 264*b*
  political potential/challenges
    in **111–113**

property rights in **115,** 344c
Sima Samar 112, 268b
sexuality in **114–115**
Suhaila Siddiq 112, 269b
Soviet invasion of 363c, 364c
and UN 357c
violence against women in
114, 118
Sima Wali 271b
and women's as property 15
women's suffrage in 4, 358c,
369c
women's uprising in 37, 352c
"working women" in 9
Mohammad Zahir Shah 111
Zoya 111, 118, 272b
"Afghan Women Debate the
Terms of Their Future"
(Nawa) **226**
Afghan Women's Council
(AWC) 273
Afghan Women's Network
(AWN) 274
Afghan Women's Summit for
Democracy (Belgium, 2001)
117, 368c
AFL (American Federation of
Labor) 355c
Africa. *See also* sub-Saharan
Africa; *specific headings, e.g.:*
Kenya
and abortion 21
access to education in 7
and age of marriage 9
and contraception 18–19
economic activity of women,
2005 251f
female genital mutilation in
23, 24
and HIV/AIDS 17
and human trafficking 28
and reports to UN 32
women's banks in 14
women's studies programs
in 46
women's v. men's earnings
in 250f
African Americans **63–65**
Mary Mcleod Bethune 59, 64,
257b, 354c
and birth control 65
Hallie Quinn Brown 258b
Shirley Chisholm 60, 61,
150–152, 259b
Johnnetta Cole 259b
Anita Hill viii, 74, 262b

and HIV/AIDS 17–18
join the women's movement
54
join women's movement 38
Barbara Jordan 263b, 362c
Coretta Scott King 64–65,
264b
Martin Luther King, Jr. 64
Pauli Murray 62
Rosa Parks 267b, 357c
poverty rate of 74
rights extended only to black
men 52
Maria W. Stuart 51, 270b
suffrage for 35
Vivien T. Thomas 57
Ida B. Wells-Barnett 54
African Centre for Women
(ACW) 14, 366c
African Women's Development
Fund (AWDF) 274
Afzali, Amena 255b
aggression 25, 84
agriculture 10, 122
Ahmad Shah (king of
Afghanistan) 344c
Air Force, U.S. 76, 77, 354c
AJWRC (Asia-Japan Women's
Resource Center) 276
Albright, Madeleine 255b
alcohol 347c. *See also*
temperance
The Alice Paul Institute (API)
274
Alito, Samuel Anthony, Jr. 80
All-China Women's Federation
(ACWF) 104, 109, 274–275
Amajan, Safia 118, 256b
American Booksellers v. Hudnut
84
American Civil Liberties Union
(ACLU) 275
American Equal Rights
Association (AERA) 346c
American Federation of Labor
(AFL) 355c
American Indians 74, 258, 352c
American Revolution 33, 344c
American Woman Suffrage
Association (AWSA) 53,
346c
Amnesty International 45,
226–229, 275
Amsterdam Treaty 43, 367c
Andorra 360c, 361c
Anglican Church 29, 86, 87

Annan, Kofi 46, 117, 190–191,
196–198
Anneke, Mathilda 33, 34, 256b
Anthony, Susan B. 256b
American Equal Rights
Association 346c
as early women's rights
activist 34
elected to Hall of Fame 356c
History of Woman Suffrage
348c
"illegal" voting of 53, 347c
International Council of
Women 36
National American Woman
Suffrage Association 346c
National Woman Suffrage
Association 35, 52
raised Quaker 29
Women's National League 35
antiabortion movement 66, 79
Anti-Apartheid Act of 1986
64–65
anti-gay marriage amendments
82
Antioch College 56, 345c
antipornography laws 24–25,
83, 84, 364c
antiretroviral drugs 17, 18
antiwar movement (Vietnam
War) 41, 61
API (The Alice Paul Institute)
274
*An Appeal to the Christian
Women of the South* (Grimké)
51
Argentina 23, 355c
Armed Forces of the United
States 75–77, 81, 354c, 369c,
371g. *See also* active duty
(AD); conscription military;
military service
Army, U.S. 76, 77
ASCENT (Asian Centre for
Women's Human Rights) 276
Asia. *See also specific headings,*
e.g.: China
and abortion 21
access to education in 7
and contraception 19
economic activity of women,
2005 251f
maternity benefits in 13
women's studies programs
in 46
women's suffrage in 4

Index

women's *vs.* men's earnings
in 250*f*
Asia-Japan Women's Resource
Center (AJWRC) 276
Asian Centre for Women's
Human Rights (ASCENT)
276
assisted reproductive
technologies 20. *See also*
surrogate mother
Associated Press **193–194**
Astell, Mary viii, 32–33, 256*b*,
344*c*
Aston, Louise 33, 34
astronauts 71, 363*c*
AT&T 361*c*
athletics 63, 360*c*, 367*c*
Australia 6, 11, 46, 349*c*, 358*c*
AWC (Afghan Women's
Council) 273
AWDF (African Women's
Development Fund) 274
AWN (Afghan Women's
Network) 274
AWSA. *See* American Woman
Suffrage Association
Ayrton, Hertha 37, 38

B
Baby M case 20, **179–180**
Bahrain 4, 361*c*
Bajer, Fredrik 95, 256*b*
Bajer, Mathilde 95, 96
Bakke case 63
Balkhi, Sediqa 256*b*–257*b*
Bang, Nina 96, 257*b*
Bangladesh 4, 9, 27, 360*c*
banking 13–14, 62, 68, 366*c*
bankruptcy 74, 75
Barekzai, Shukria 113, 257*b*
Baumann, Elisabeth Jerichau
95, 257*b*
BBC News **234–235**
Beauvoir, Simone de 356*c*
Beckenham, Mary 257*b*
beer drinking 362*c*
Beijing Declaration and
Platform for Action (1995)
31–32, 42–43, 45, 109, 125,
207–210, 367*c*, 369*c*
Beijing+5 43. *See also* Women
2000 Conference
Beijing+10 44, 110, 369*c*
Belgium 15, 22, 351*c*–352*c*,
355*c*
Benin, Republic of 14, 357*c*

Bethune, Mary Mcleod 59, 64,
257*b*, 354*c*
Bhutan 4, 356*c*
"Bill of Rights" for women 45.
See also UN Convention on
the Elimination of All Forms
of Discrimination against
Women
`Bingen, Hildegard von 29, 343*c*
"Biobehavioral Responses to
Stress in Females" (Taylor et
al.) **144–145**
biological distinctions between
the sexes 67, 78
biologically determined
behavior 16
birth control. *See also* abortion;
contraception; reproductive
health; sterilization
FDA approves sale of 357*c*
information 347*c*, 354*c*
movement in U.S. **58, 65**
and obscenity 347*c*
Margaret Sanger 21, 58, 65,
268*b*–269*b*, 350*c*, 351*c*
*United States v. One Package
of Japanese Pessaries* 354*c*
birth names 8
birth rates 16, 19
bishops 30, 87, 100, 271*b*
black feminism (in U.S.) **63–65,**
349*c*, 354*c*
Blackmun, Harry 21
Blackwell, Antoinette L. Brown
29, 257*b*–258*b*
Blackwell, Elizabeth 35, 258*b*
Blackwell, Mary 345*c*
Black Women Organized for
Action (BWOA) 64
"blue babies" 57
Boadicea (Boudicca) (queen of
Iceni) 258*b*, 343*c*
Bonn Agreement (2001) 112,
113, 117, 368*c*
Bonnin, Gertrude 258*b*
Bosnia 14, 356*c*
Bosnia-Herzegovina 26, 27
Boston Female Medical College
345*c*
Boudicca. *See* Boadicea
*Bowe v. Colgate-Palmolive
Company* 359*c*
boys, trafficking in 28
Bradwell v. Illinois 347*c*
Brazil 23, 37, 39, 353*c*
Britain. *See* United Kingdom

Brown, Hallie Quinn 258*b*
Bryn Mawr College 56, 348*c*
Buck, Carrie 19, 78, 353*c*
Buck v. Bell 19, 78, **166–169**.
See also 2002 Session, House
Joint Resolution No. 299
*Burlington Industries, Inc. v.
Ellerth* 367*c*
Burns, Lucy 37, 54, 350*c*
burqas x, 8, 111, 114, 352*c*, 371*g*
Bush, George W. and
administration vii, 75, 77,
85, 368*c*
Bush, Laura vii
BWOA (Black Women
Organized for Action) 64

C
California 82, 360*c*
"Call Off Your Tired Ethics"
(COYOTE) 361*c*
Canada
and birth names 8
early women's rights activism
in 34–35
and equal pay 41
and HIV/AIDS 18
same-sex marriage in 22
support for working mothers
in 13
and women in the military 15
women's suffrage in 34–35,
350*c*, 351*c*, 356*c*, 357*c*
cancer 18, 77, 370*c*
Caribbean 10, 17, 46, 250*f*, 251*f*
Carter, Jimmy 362*c*
CASS (Chinese Academy of
Social Sciences) 278
casualties, war 15, 77
Catt, Carrie Chapman 37, 39,
53–55, 58, 258*b*, 350*c*
CBS Broadcasting 368*c*
CCDF (Child Care and
Development Fund) 72
CCP. *See* Chinese Communist
Party
CDC (Centers for Disease
Control and Prevention) 24
CEDAW. *See* UN Convention on
the Elimination of All Forms
of Discrimination against
Women
Center for Health and Human
Rights 276–277
The Center for Women's Global
Leadership (CWGL) 277

The Center for Women Veterans
277–278
Centers for Disease Control and
Prevention (CDC) 24
central Asia 250f, 251f
Chad 23, 24
chadri 111. See also burqas
child abuse 109, 125
childcare 12–13
Child Care and Development
Fund (CCDF) 72
child custody laws 51, 352c
child labor 55, 125
child pornography 83, 84
children
and Convenant of the League
of Nations 38
female infanticide 27
and HIV/AIDS 17, 18
one-child policy in China ix,
21, 27, 107–109
and pornography 25, 84
rape of 83
rights over 34
trafficking in 85, 86, 100,
101
Children Act (Kenya, 2001)
125, 368c
child support 74–75
Child Support Enforcement
Amendments (1984) 75
Chile 353c, 356c
China ix, 102–110
and abortion 21, 107, 108
and contraception 18–19,
107, 225–226
current issues in 104–105
education in 105
employment in 106–107
family life in 105–106
family planning in 107–108
and female infanticide 27
future trends in 110
HIV/AIDS in 17
and homosexuality 23
and human trafficking 28
and idea of the "working
woman" 9
inheritance rights in 6, 105
and international women's
movement 109–110
and maiden/birth names 8
New Culture movement
in 103
one-child policy ix, 21, 27,
107–109

Population and Family
Planning Law x, 107, 108,
223–225, 368c
property rights in 6
sexual freedom in 108
and sexual harassment 12
Tang Junying 263b
Tz'u-Hsi (Cixi) 270b–271b,
346c
violence against women in
108–109
women's suffrage in 103–
104, 350c, 356c
China, People's Republic of
(PRC). See China
Chinese Academy of Social
Sciences (CASS) 278
Chinese Communist Party
(CCP) 102–105
"Chinese Women and Their
Contraceptive Choices"
(Sivelle) 225–226
Chisholm, Shirley 60, 61,
150–152, 259b
Chittister, Sister Joan 259b
"A Chorus of Amens as More
Women Take over Pulpits"
(Murphy) 138–139
Christianity 120, 121
Churchill, Winston 37
Church of Jesus Christ of Latter-
day Saints 87
circumcision 23–24
CIS. See Commonwealth of
Independent States
the Citadel 76
Citicorp 62
civil and political rights 3–7,
22, 51–52, 67–68, 371g
Civilian Pilot Training Program
(CPTP) 354c, 355c
civil partnerships 100
Civil Rights Act (1964) 61. See
also Title VII of the 1964 Civil
Rights Act
Civil Rights movement 41, 61,
357c
civil unions (partnerships) 22,
23, 82, 370c
Civil War (U.S.) 35, 57
Cixi. See Tz'u-Hsi
Clara Raphael (Fibiger) ix, 95
Cleopatra VII (pharaoh of
Egypt) 343c
clergy (female) 29–30, 86–87,
100, 356c

Cleveland Board of Education v.
LaFleur 361c
Clinton, Bill 79, 81, 88, 110,
366c
Clinton, Hillary Rodham 88,
189–190, 368c, 370c
clitoridectomy 23, 24
Cochran, Jacqueline 59–60,
354c
Code of Hammurabi 342c
codification, codify (of
international law) 371g
coeducation 56, 57
Colby, Myra 347c
Cole, Johnnetta 259b
collective rights 371g
college education 7, 56, 68, 69,
105, 346c
college sports 367c
Collins, Susan 89
colonialism 9, 41, 118–119, 121
combat roles 15, 76–77,
141–142
Commentaries on the Laws of
England (Blackstone) 344c
"Comments of the Danish
Women's Society on the
Sixth Periodic Report by the
Government of Denmark
on the implementation of
the CEDAW Convention"
221–223
Commission of Obscenity and
Pornography (1970) 84
Commission on Human Rights
371g
Commission on Pornography
(1986) 84
The Committee on Women in
the NATO Forces (CWINF)
278–279
common law 8, 20–21, 50, 68,
344c
Commonwealth of Independent
States (CIS) countries 10, 28
Communist Party (Afghanistan)
363c, 366c
comparable worth of work 41
computer science 69
Comstock Act 58, 65, 347c, 354c
concede 371g
condoms 19, 58, 80
Conference of American States
202–203
Conference of Senior Women
Officers (NATO) 358c

Index

Congo, Democratic Republic of
359*c*, 360*c*
Congress, U.S. 53, 346*c*, 348*c*
Congressional Union for
Woman Suffrage 54, 350*c*
Connecticut 82, 370*c*
conscription military 54, 66, 76,
177–179, 364*c*, 372*g*
constitution (Afghanistan) 111,
113, 352*c*
constitution (China) 103, 107
constitution (Denmark) 96
constitution (Kenya) 120
Constitution, U.S. 50, 344*c*
constitutions (state) 23
contraception **18–19**
in Afghanistan 115–116
in China 18, 107, **225–226**
and coercion 18–19
Comstock Act 347*c*
declining priority of family
planning 192–193
Eisenstadt v. Baird 65, 66,
175–176, 360*c*
emergency pills for 80–81,
370*c*, 373*g*
Griswold v. Connecticut 58,
65, **170–171,** 359*c*
and HIV/AIDs 19
increase in options for 80–81
in Kenya 124
the Pill 18, 65
Plan B 80–81, 370*c*, 373
post–World War I 38
Margaret Sanger 350*c*
in U.S. 19, **58, 65, 80–81**
use in Denmark 101–102
Convenant of the League of
Nations 38, 351*c*
convention 372*g. See also
specific headings, e.g.:* The
International Convention on
the Elimination of All Forms
of Racial Discrimination
Convention on the
Elimination of All Forms
of Discrimination against
Women. *See* UN Convention
on the Elimination of All
Forms of Discrimination
against Women
Convention on the Rights of the
Child (1989) 25, 365*c*
Coolidge, Calvin 352*c*
Coolidge, Grace 352*c*
Cooper, Anna Julia 63, 349*c*

Costa Rica 356*c*
covenant 372*g. See also specific
headings, e.g.:* International
Covenant on Civil and
Political Rights
coverture 372*g*
Coxe, Marie 360*c*
COYOTE ("Call Off Your Tired
Ethics") 361*c*
CPTP. *See* Civilian Pilot
Training Program
Craig v. Boren 362*c*
credit (consumer) 361*c*
credit (independent) **13–14,** 62,
68, 361*c*
credit card debt 75
Croatia 27, 355*c*
"Crossing the Lines" (McGirk)
141–142
cultural interpretation and
background
and customs 9, 11, 18, 23–24,
50
cultural interpretation or
background
in Afghanistan ix–x, 111,
113–115, 117
in China ix, 105
and domestic abuse 26
and inheritance rights 6
and Kenya 119, 120
in Kenya x, 124
and pace of change 3
and property rights 6
and women's suffrage 4
Curie, Marie 38
customary international law
372*g*
customs (social) 9, 11,
18, 23–24, 50. *See also*
cultural interpretation and
background
CWGL (The Center for
Women's Global Leadership)
277
CWINF. *See* The Committee on
Women in the NATO Forces
Czech Republic viii, 351*c*

D

Dakar Framework for Action 7,
44, 368*c*
The Danish Institute for Human
Rights (DIHR) 279
Danish Women's Council 102,
349*c*

Danish Women's Society (Dansk
Kvindesamfund) 95, 96, 100,
102, 221–223, 279, 347*c*, 349*c*
Daoud, Muhammad 111, 356*c*
data gathering 40, 45
Daughters of Bilitis 60, 357*c*
Daughters of St. Crispin 347*c*
Daughters of the American
Revolution 348*c*
Davis, Paulina Wright 52, 259*b*
DAW. *See* UN Division for the
Advancement of Women
death, causes of 17, 18, 254*f*
deaths, maternal 18, 116, 123
declaration 372*g. See also
specific headings, e.g.:* Beijing
Declaration and Platform for
Action
Declaration of Independence 51
Declaration of Sentiments x, 34,
51, **134–135,** 345*c*
Declaration of the Essential
Rights of Afghan Women 112
decolonization 7
Defense of Marriage Act
(DOMA) (1998) 81–82
De Gouges, Olympia 261*b*
Democratic National
Convention 362*c*
Democratic Party 364*c*
demonstrations 37, 41
Deng Xiaoping 102
Denmark ix, 94–102
abortion in 101
Fredrik Bajer 95, 256*b*
Mathilde Bajer 95, 96
Nina Bang 96, 257*b*
beginning of women's rights
movement in **94–96**
CEDAW implementation
report **221–223**
Danish Women's Society
221–223, 347*c*
education in 95, **97,** 345*c*
employment in **98–99**
equal division of labor in 16
equal pay in 98, 351*c*, 362*c*
Equal Status Act 5, **215–218**
Equal Status Council 367*c*
Equal Treatment Act 363*c*
Equity Act 365*c*
family rights in **99–100**
female clergy in 30
Mathilde Fibiger ix, 95, 260*b*
future trends in **102**
gay rights in 97, **100**

385

Gender Equality Act x,
218–220
gender mainstreaming in 102
health care in **101–102**
human trafficking in 100–101
Line Luplua 264*b*
marriage in 97, 99, 352*c*
maternity benefits in 13
military service in 15
Jutta Bojsen Møller 265*b*
Elna Munch 96, 265*b*
Nielsine Nielsen 36, 97, 266*b*,
347*c*
pornography in 25
religion in **100**
and sexual harassment 12,
98–99
universities in 348*c*
violence against women in
100–101
women's suffrage in 37,
96–97, 98, 350*c*
Nathalie Zahle 271*b*
Department of Defense, U.S.
76–77
Deroin, Jeanne 259*b*
diabetes 77
DIHR (The Danish Institute for
Human Rights) 279
discrimination. *See also*
affirmative action
Amsterdam Treaty 43
AT&T 361*c*
Mary Mcleod Bethune 354*c*
CBS Broadcasting 368*c*
CEDAW **205–207**
in China 106
complaints 62
Declaration of Sentiments
345*c*
in Denmark 98, 363*c*
Executive Order 11246 359*c*
and gay rights 81
and government contractors
61
Hishon v. King and Spaulding
364*c*
in housing 361*c*
in Kenya 120
*Meritor Savings Bank v.
Vinson* 365*c*
and military service 76
National Organization for
Women 359*c*
President's Commission on
the Status of Women 358*c*

at private military academies
76
racial 203–205
Reed v. Reed 360*c*
reverse 5, 63
and sexual harassment 11,
74
Title VII 5, 9, 62, 73–74,
156–159, 358*c*, 361*c*
Title IX 62–63, 68, **159–162,**
360*c*, 367*c*
UN Millennium Summit 44
UN Second World
Conference on Women 41
U.S. legislation against 61
disease 7, 17, 18, 77, 115,
124, 370*c*. *See also* human
immunodeficiency virus/
acquired immunodeficiency
syndrome
divorce
in Afghanistan 344*c*
in China 106
Declaration of Sentiments 51
increasing rates of 16
in Islamic countries 6
"no fault" 360*c*
rise of, during 1950s 60
Theodora 343*c*
doctoral degrees 69
Doe v. Bolton 361*c*
Dole, Robert 72, 365*c*
DOMA. *See* Defense of
Marriage Act
domestic partnership laws 82
domestic violence **25–26,** 372*g*
in Afghanistan 114
in China 106, 108–110
in Denmark 100
as global concern 45–46
in Kenya 124–126, 368*c*
National Coalition against
Domestic Violence 287
in U.S. **82–83**
Violence against Women Act
366*c*, 368*c*
WHO on viii, 46
Domestic Violence Family
Protection Bill (Kenya, 2002)
124, 368*c*
"Don't ask; don't tell" policy 81
double burden (duty) 9, 71–72
Dowd, Maureen 87–88
draft 76, 364*c*
Draft Constitution (Kenya)
232–234, 234–235

draft registration 76, **177–179**
due process clause 76
Duniway, Abigail Scott 53, 260*b*

E

Earhart, Amelia 354*c*
earnings. *See* wages and
earnings
East Asia 10, 250*f*, 251*f*
echo boomers. *See* Generation
Y, Gen Y
economic, social, and cultural
rights 373*g*. *See also* credit
(independent); health care
Economic and Social Council
(ECOSOC) 372*g*
economic development 42,
103, 119
economic independence 33, 34
ECOSOC (Economic and Social
Council) 372*g*
ECPs. *See* emergency
contraception pills
EC Treaty 357*c*
Ecuador 353*c*, 359*c*
education **6–7,** 345*c*. *See also*
higher education; schools
in Afghanistan 113, **116,** 118,
344*c*, 359*c*, 364*c*, 366*c*
in China **105**
Declaration of Sentiments 51
in Denmark 95, **97,** 345*c*
Gender Equity in Education
Act 366*c*
of girls 71, 116, 366*c*
in Kenya 9, **121–122**
Coretta Scott King 65
primary 6, 7, 44, 97, 116
Title VII of the 1964 Civil
Rights Act 62–63
Title IX 62–63, 68, **159–162,**
360*c*, 367*c*
UN Fourth World Conference
on Women 42
in U.S. **6–7, 56–57, 62–63,**
68–69
Women's Educational Equity
Act 361*c*
educational attainment 373*g*
Education Codes of 1972. *See*
Title IX in the Education
Codes of 1972
EEC (European Economic
Community) 357*c*
EEOC. *See* Equal Employment
Opportunity Commission

Index

"EEOC Issues New Guide
on Workplace Bias" (Yen)
136–137
Egypt 23, 262, 342*c*, 343*c*, 357*c*
Eighteenth Amendment 58
Eisentadt v. Baird 65, 66,
175–176, 360*c*
elder abuse 109
elections 67, 113, 344*c*, 364*c*,
369*c*, 370*c*. *See also* stand for
election
Elizabeth (queen of England)
344*c*
El Salvador 354*c*, 358*c*
emergency contraception pills
(ECPs) 80–81, 370*c*, 373*g*
EMILY's List (Early Money Is
Like Yeast) 68, 280, 364*c*
employment (employment
rights)
in Afghanistan 113–114,
116–117
average hours/weeks of paid,
1978, 1998 253*f*
*Bowe v. Colgate-Palmolive
Company* 359*c*
and childcare **12–13**
in China 106, **106–107,** 110
Declaration of Sentiments 51
in Denmark **98–99**
equal opportunities in 5–6
and the ERA 5
Faragher v. City of Boca Raton
367*c*
global increase in 10
*Johnson v. Santa Clara
County* 365*c*
in Kenya 9, 119, 122
*Meritor Savings Bank v.
Vinson* 365*c*
National Recovery Act 353*c*
Pregnancy Discrimination
Act 363*c*
President's Commission on
the Status of Women 358*c*
Reed v. Reed 360*c*
sectors of 10
and social change 7–8
and Title VII 358*c*
in U.S. **55, 61–62, 69–71,**
253*f*
women's roles in **16–17**
and "working women" 7–8,
9–11, 39–40, **70–71**
during World War I 37
worldwide, 2005 251*f*

Employment Non-
Discrimination Act (ENDA)
of 1994 65, 81
empowerment vii, 89, 373*g*
ENDA. *See* Employment Non-
Discrimination Act
enfranchisement 373*g*
England 8, 11, 20–21, 343*c*,
344*c*, 366*c*. *See also* United
Kingdom
enlisted 373*g*
environmental, cultural, and
developmental rights 373*g*
The Environmental Scan (Glass
Ceiling Commission Report)
72
Episcopalians 86, 87
Equal Credit Opportunity Act
(1974) 62, 68, 361*c*
Equal Employment Opportunity
Commission (EEOC) 279–280
and CBS Broadcasting 368*c*
consent decree with AT&T
361*c*
creation of 359*c*
definition of sexual
harassment 73
and discrimination
complaints 62
establishment of 5
and sexual harassment 12,
73–74
equality 42, 373*g*
Equality Act (Denmark, 1998) 5
equal opportunity laws 12, 365*c*
equal pay
in Afghanistan 116–117
continuing challenges of
69–70
in Denmark 98, 351*c*, 362*c*
difficulty enforcing 41
*Schultz v. Wheaton Glass
Co.* 360*c*
and top executive pay 143
Equal Pay Act (Denmark, 1976)
98, 362*c*
Equal Pay Act (U.S., 1963) 61,
87, 360*c*
equal rights 5–6, 40, 42–44,
119, 125, 345*c*
Equal Rights Amendment (ERA)
(1929) 5, 55, **66, 156,** 352*c*
"Equal Rights for Women"
(Chisholm) **150–152**
Equal Status Act (Denmark,
1998) **215–218**

Equal Status Act (Denmark,
2000) 99, 367*c*
Equal Status Council (Denmark)
97, 367*c*
Equal Treatment Act (Denmark,
1978) 12, 98, 363*c*
equity 373*g*
ERA. *See* Equal Rights
Amendment
Eritrea 357*c*, 362*c*, 367*c*
Estate of Thorton v. Calder 86
Ethiopia 357*c*, 362*c*
EU. *See* European Union
eugenics 19–20, 78, 353*c*, 373*g*–
374*g*. *See also* involuntary
sterilization
Europe. *See also* European
Union; *specific headings, e.g.:*
United Kingdom
and contraception 19
early women's rights activism
in 32–33
economic activity of women,
2005 251*f*
and HIV/AIDS 18
and human trafficking 28
managerial positions for
women in 11
maternity benefits in 13
regulation of abortion in 21
and reports to UN 32
support for working mothers
in 13
and surrogate motherhood
20
women's studies programs
in 46
women's *vs.* men's earnings
in 250*f*
European Court of Justice 5
European Economic Community
(EEC) 357*c*
European Union (EU) 367*c*
and affirmative action 5
Amsterdam Treaty 43
managerial positions for
women in 11
and sexual harassment 12,
98, 99
Turkey's admission to vii
evangelism 374*g*
excision 23, 24
Executive Order 11246 359*c*
*Exploring the Biological
Contribution to Human
Health* (SWHR) 368*c*

387

"Exploring the Biological Contribution to Human Health: Does Sex Matter?" (report) 78

extramarital sex 370c

F

FACE Act. *See* Freedom of Access to Clinic Entrances Act

Fair Labor Standards Act 354c

Family and Medical Leave Act of 1993 (FMLA) 77, **162–164,** 366c, 369c

family life 9, 16–17, 105–106, 114–115, 120–121

family planning. *See also* abortion; birth control; contraception; reproductive health; sterilization

in China x, **107–108,** 223–225, 368c

declining priority of 21–22, 192–193

and forced sterilization 19–20

in India 18–20

in Kenya 122–124

Margaret Sanger 21

in U.S. **78–82**

family rights 99–100

Faragher v. City of Boca Raton 367c

Father Knows Best (television show) 60

Fay v. New York 355c

FBI (Federal Bureau of Investigation) 85

FDA. *See* Food and Drug Administration

Federal Bureau of Investigation (FBI) 85

federal contracting 63

federal employees 81

federal funding 21, 79, 365c

Federal Glass Ceiling Commission 72

The Federation of Women Lawyers Kenya (FIDA) 280

FemAid 280–281

female candidates 366c

female circumcision. *See* female genital mutilation

female factory workers 36–37

female genital cutting (FGC) 123

female genital mutilation (FGM) vii, viii, x, **23–24,** 123, 368c, 374g

female heads of state 4

female infant abandonment ix

female infanticide viii, **27,** 107, 374g

female occupations 69, 95

Feminenza International 124, 281

Feminine Mystique, The (Friedan) 60, 358c

feminism

black **63–65,** 349c, 354c

in China 104

The Feminine Mystique 358c

National Organization for Women **62,** 359c

second wave of 67

third wave of 67, **97–89**

in U.S. **60–61,** 62

feminist(s) x, 22–24, 34, 36, 88, 374g. *See also specific headings, e.g.*: Friedan, Betty

feminist spirituality **30–31**

FEMNET 281–282

Ferraro, Geraldine 87, 260b, 364c

fertility 19, 122–123

FGC (female genital cutting) 123

FGM. *See* female genital mutilation

Fibiger, Mathilde ix, 95, 260b

FIDA (The Federation of Women Lawyers Kenya) 280

FIDA (International Federation of Women Lawyers) 124

Fifth Amendment 76, 347c

Final Act of the Conference on Security and Co-operation in Europe (CSCE) 362c

"Finance-Kenya: Small Loans for Men Will Keep Violence against Women Down" (Mulama) **235–236**

financial rights 13–14, 62, 68, 74–75

Finland 37, 349c

first-generation rights. *See* civil and political rights

FMLA. *See* Family and Medical Leave Act of 1993

Folketing 96, 97

Food and Drug Administration (FDA), U.S. 357c, 368c, 370c

football (professional) 361c

footbinding 103

forced sterilization 19–20, **78,** 107, 353c

foreign aid 21

FORWARD (The Foundation for Women's Health, Research and Development) 282

"For Women at the Top, Pay Lags" (McDonald) **143**

Foster, Abigail Kelley 260b

The Foundation for Women's Health, Research and Development (FORWARD) 282

Fourteenth Amendment 35, 52, 53, **154–155,** 346c, 347c, 360c, 367c

France

and burqas 8

civil partnerships in 22

Olympia De Gouges 261b

Jeanne Deroin 259b

early women's rights activism in 33

Joan of Arc 343c

maternity benefits in 13

and sexual harassment 12

Society for the Amelioration of Women's Condition 36

women's suffrage in 37, 355c

working mothers in 13

Freedom of Access to Clinic Entrances (FACE) Act (1994) 79, 366c

free speech viii, 24–25, 83

Friedan, Betty 60, 62, 260b, 358c, 359c

Friedlin, Jennifer 137–138

fundamentalists 23, 24, 66

future trends 102, 110, 118, 126

G

Gage, Matilda Josyln 53, 348c

Gailani, Fatana 113, 260b–261b

Gailani, Fauzia 261b

Gandhi, Indira 19, 359c

Gaspard, Francois 370c

gay 374g

gay rights **22–23,** 65, 81–82, 97, 100, 108. *See also* same-sex marriage

gender 374g

gender balance 40, 44, 67–68, 97, 113

gender equality vii, 42, 46

Index

Gender Equality Act (Denmark, 2002) x, 12, **218–220**
Gender Equity in Education Act (U.S., 1994) 366c
gender mainstreaming 32, 44, **44,** 102, 110, 126, 374g
gender-related crimes 366c
gender roles 16–17, 31, 106. *See also* men's roles; women's roles
gender roles, alternate **22–23, 81–82**
gender stereotyping 99
gender studies 374g
General Electric Company v. Gilbert 362c
Generation X, Gen X 374g
Generation Y, Gen Y 374g
genocide 374g
Georgia (country) 351c, 352c
Germany 33, 34, 39–40, 78, 351c
gestational carrier. *See* surrogate mother
GI bill 57
Gillespie, Duff G. 192–193
Ginsburg, Ruth Bader 256b
girls
  in Afghanistan 116
  Camp Fire Girls 350c
  in China 105
  education of 116
  and female genital mutilation 123
  Gender Equity in Education Act 366c
  in Kenya 125
  marriage of 115
  math/science education for 71
  UN Fourth World Conference on Women 42, 43
  UN Millennium Summit 44
Girl Scouts 32
glass ceiling 72–73, 142–143, 375g
Glass Ceiling Act (1991) 72, 365c
Glass Ceiling Commission **135–136**
Global Gag Rule 21, 123, 375g
globalization of women's movement **40–46**
Goegg, Mary 36, 261b
Goldman, Emma 54, 261b
government contractors 5, 61, 63, 359c

governments
  Afghanistan 112, 113
  Denmark 96, 97
  Kenya 119–120
  U.S. 59, 67–68
Gowhar Shad of Heart (queen of Afghanistan) 343c
graduate education 348c
Graham, Katharine Meyer 261b
Great Britain. *See* United Kingdom
Great Depression 58–59
Green Belt Movement 126, 282
Grimké, Angelina Emily 34, 51, 262b
Grimké, Sarah Moore 34, 51
Griswold v. Connecticut 58, 65, **170–171,** 359c
Gross, Nasrine 112, 118, 262b
The Guttmacher Institute 21, 282–283
Guyana 355c, 356c
gynecology 346c

H

Hamer, Fanny Lou 262b
Hand, Augustus 354c
hard-core pornography 25
Harris, Karen L. 145–147
Harris v. Forklift Systems, Inc. 366c
hate crimes 81, 83
Hatshepsut (pharaoh of Egypt) 262b, 342c
Hazaras 115, 116
head scarves 8, 102, 112, 366c
health care **17–18,** 370c
  in Afghanistan 111–112, **115–116**
  in Denmark **101–102**
  in Kenya **123–124**
  Coretta Scott King 65
  and sex-based differences 368c
  as third wave issue 67
  UN Fourth World Conference on Women 42
  in U.S. **77–78**
health care benefits 22, 77. *See also* maternity benefits
health care workers (male) 10
heart disease 18, 77, 370c
Helms, Jesse 21
"help wanted" advertisements 62, 361c

higher education. *See also* college education; universities
  access to 6, 7, 62
  and affirmative action 63
  in China 105, 110
  demand for 56–57
  in Denmark 97
  mid-19th applications to 35–36
  women enrolled in 57, 68
high school drop outs 68–69
Hill, Anita viii, 74, 262b
Hishon v. King and Spaulding 364c
Hispanics 17–18, 74, 266, 365c
history, religious **31**
History of Woman Suffrage (Stanton, Anthony, and Gage) 53, 348c
history of women's rights (international) 32–46. *See also* women's studies programs
  in early 19th century 33–35
  in late 19th, early 20th century 35–36
  in 20th century **36–40**
  evolution of **45–46**
  first movement in **33–35**
  and gender mainstreaming **44**
  and the United Nations 40–46
  and women's studies programs **46**
history of women's rights (U.S.) 50–66. *See also specific headings, e.g.:* Paul, Alice
  in 1950s **60**
  in 1960s, 1970s **60–61**
  and affirmative action **63**
  and African-American women 63–65
  and birth control **58, 65**
  and civil and political rights **51–52**
  early stirrings in **50–51**
  and education **56–57, 62–63**
  and employment **61–62**
  employment rights **55**
  and Equal Rights Amendment **66**
  and NOW **62**
  property rights **52**
  and *Roe v. Wade* **66**
  and Stock Market Crash of 1929 **58–59**

and temperance movement
57–58
women's suffrage **52–55**
and World War II **59–60**
Hitler, Adolf 39
HIV/AIDS. *See* human
immunodeficiency virus/
acquired immunodeficiency
syndrome
home appliances 56
homemakers 75
Homestead Act 56
homosexuality 81, 108. *See also*
gay; lesbianism
hospitals 346*c*, 365*c*
hostile work environment 365*c*
hours. *See* working hours
House Joint Resolution No. 299
169–170
House of Representatives, U.S.
60–61, 68, 150–152, 370*c*.
See also specific headings, e.g.:
Pelosi, Nancy
"housewife" image 98
housework 16
housing discrimination 361*c*
HPV. *See* human papilloma virus
human immunodeficiency virus/
acquired immunodeficiency
syndrome (HIV/AIDS) 17–18
and China 108
and condoms 19
and Denmark 102
and Kenya 119, 121, **123–
124,** 125
and war/armed conflict 26
human papilloma virus (HPV)
67, 370*c*
human rights **15–16,** 42, 200–
202, 359*c*, 375*g*
human rights treaties 375*g.*
See also specific headings,
e.g.: UN Convention on the
Elimination of All Forms
of Discrimination against
Women
Human Rights Watch 7, 45,
126, 283
human trafficking. *See*
trafficking (human)
hunger strikes 4, 37, 54
hurricanes 356*c*
husbands
assaults/murders by 82
and bank accounts 13
consent of 120

in Kenya 124
Kirchberg v. Feenstra 364*c*
power over wives of 51
using surname of 8
women as property of 15
Hussein, Saddam 369*c*
Hypatia 343*c*
hyphenated surnames 8

I

IAW. *See* International
Association of Women
ICCPR. *See* International
Covenant on Civil and
Political Rights
ICESCR (International
Covenant on Economic,
Social and Cultural Rights)
359*c*
ICW. *See* International Council
of Women
IGOs (intergovernmental
organizations) 376*g*
ILO. *See* International Labour
Organization
immigrants 24, 102, 123
immigration rights 67
"The Impact of Women's Studies
Courses on College Students
of the 1990s" (Harris)
145–147
inalienable 375*g*
incest 21
income 72. *See also* wages
India
and contraception 18–19
and female infanticide 27
forced sterilizations in 19–20
Indira Gandhi 19, 359*c*
HIV/AIDS in 17
women's banks in 14
women's suffrage in 4, 356*c*
indigenous peoples 375*g*
indigenous religions 120, 121
indivisible 375*g*
Indonesia 4, 355*c*
infant mortality rate 123
infibulation 23, 24, 376*g*. *See*
also female genital mutilation
inheritance rights viii, **6**
in Afghanistan 6, 115
in China 6, 105
Code of Hammurabi 342*c*
in Kenya x, 121, 364*c*
Institute for Women's Policy
Research (IWPR) 283–284

INSTRAW. *See* UN
International Research and
Training Institute for the
Advancement of Women
Inter-American Convention on
the Granting of Civil Rights to
Women (1948) **202–203**
interdependent 376*g*
intergovernmental organizations
(IGOs) 376*g*
International Agreement for the
Suppression of the "White
Slave Traffic" (1904) 85,
198–200
International Association of
Women (IAW) 36, 95
International Bill of Human
Rights 376*g*
International Brotherhood
of Boilermakers, Iron
Shipbuilders and Helpers
355*c*
International Conference of
Socialist Women 37, 38
International Conference on
Population and Development
(Cairo Egypt, 1994) 19, 21
The International Convention
on the Elimination of
All Forms of Racial
Discrimination (1969)
203–205
International Council of Women
(ICW) 36, 348*c*, 349*c*
International Covenant on Civil
and Political Rights (ICCPR)
126, 359*c*
International Covenant on
Economic, Social and Cultural
Rights (ICESCR) 359*c*
International Day for the
Elimination of Violence
Against Women 369*c*
International Federation of
Women Lawyers (FIDA) 124
The International Herald Tribune
(newspaper) **229–230**
International Human Rights
Day 369*c*
International Labour
Organization (ILO) 10–12,
38, 41, 125, 284, 351*c*, 376*g*
International Women's Congress
351*c*
International Women's Day 37,
351*c*, 352*c*, 362*c*, 364*c*

Index

international women's movement 32–46. *See also specific countries*
and Afghanistan 117–118
and China 104, **109–110**
evolution of **45–46**
first **33–35**
globalization of **40–46**
and Kenya **125–126**
mainstreaming of **44**
preparation for next wave in **35–36**
in 20th century **36–40**
and the United Nations 40, **41–44**, 45–46
and women's studies programs **46**
International Women's Suffrage Alliance (IWSA) 36, 37, 39, 54, 349*c*, 350*c*
Internet 42, 83
Inter-Parliamentary Union (IPU) 284
intrauterine device (IUD) 18
involuntary sterilization **19–20, 78,** 107, 353*c*
IPU (Inter-Parliamentary Union) 284
Iran 6, 358*c*, 370*c*
Iraq 28, 363*c*, 369*c*
Iraqi Women's Democracy Initiative 369*c*
Iraq War (2003) 15, 28, 77, 369*c*
Ireland 352*c*, 353*c*
Islam. *See also* Muslims
in Afghanistan 110–112, 114–116, 366*c*
in Denmark 102
and property rights 6
Islamic fundamentalists 118, 367*c*
Israel 15, 20, 355*c*
Italy 15, 20, 355*c*, 370*c*
"It's All about Me!" (Bellafonte) **144**
IUD (intrauterine device) 18
IWPR. *See* Institute for Women's Policy Research
IWSA. *See* International Women's Suffrage Alliance

J

Jacobs, Alleta 37–38, 58
Jalal, Massouda 112, 262*b*–263*b*
Jami, Rahima 112, 263*b*
Japan 12, 14, 25, 103, 104, 355*c*

Jiang Zemin 102
Joan of Arc 343*c*
Johns Hopkins Medical School 349*c*
Johnson, Lyndon B. 5, 63
Johnson v. Santa Clara County 365*c*
Jordan, Barbara 263*b*, 362*c*
Joya, Malai 113, 263*b*
Judaism 30, 356*c*
juries 344*c*, 347*c*, 355*c*, 358*c*, 362*c*

K

Kabul, Afghanistan 118, 364*c*
Kabul University 359*c*
Kaggia, Jean 263*b*
Kagunda, Alice 120, 124, 263*b*–264*b*
Karzai, Hamid 112, 113
Kazakhstan 352*c*, 366*c*
Kennedy, John F. 61, 358*c*
Kenya x, 118–126
abortion in 21, 120, 123
Mary Beckenham 257*b*
child abuse/welfare in **125,** 368*c*
current issues in **120**
domestic violence in 124–126, 368*c*
Draft Constitution **232–234**
education in 9, **121–122**
employment in 9, 119, 122
family life in **120–121**
female genital mutilation in x, 24, 123, 368*c*
future trends in **126**
health care in **123–124**
HIV/AIDS in 119, 121, **123–124,** 125
human trafficking in **125**
inheritance rights in x, 121, 364*c*
and international women's movement **125–126**
Jean Kaggia 263*b*
Alice Kagunda 120, 124, 263*b*–264*b*
Wangari Muta Maathai x, 126, **230–232,** 264*b*
marriage in x, 120–121
Millie Akoth Odhiambo 266*b*
Agnes Pareyio 123, 267*b*
property rights in 6, 9, 120, **121,** 126
prostitution in **125**

reproductive rights in **122–123,** 124
small loans for men **235–236**
violence against women in **124,** 125–126, 368*c*
Bishop Margaret Wanjiru 271*b*
women's banking in 14
women's suffrage in **119–120,** 358*c*
and "working women" 9
"Kenyans Reject New Constitution" (*BBC News*) **234–235**
Keshwar, Meena 362*c*
Kibaki, Mwai 120
Kinetz, Erika 194–196
King, Billie Jean 370*c*
King, Coretta Scott 64–65, 264*b*
King, Martin Luther, Jr. 64
Kirchberg v. Feenstra 364*c*
Korea 8, 355*c*
Kubaissi, Amal Abdullah al-370*c*
KULU—Women and Development 101, 284–285
Kuwait 4, 369*c*, 370*c*

L

labor
and demand for education 57
in Denmark 95, 96
equal division of 16
Fair Labor Standards Act 354*c*
global activity 10
Radice v. New York 352*c*
special protection *vs.* equal access in 55
voluntary 39–40
Weeks v. Southern Bell 359*c*
worldwide female, 2005 251*f*
labor force
changes in, 1950–1997 62
decrease of men in 62, 70
and female occupations 69
increase of women in 62, 70
in U.S., 1950–2025 252*f*
women's participation in 70–71, 252*f*
labor market 10, 59–60
labor organizations 41, 347*c*, 355*c*
labor-saving devices 56
land 6, 121

Latin America. *See also specific headings, e.g.:* Brazil
and abortion 21
access to education in 7
economic activity of women, 2005 251*f*
HIV/AIDS in 17
and human trafficking 28
maternity benefits in 13
women's labor activity in 10
women's studies programs in 46
women's v. men's earnings in 250*f*
law enforcement 26, 27, 124
Law of Succession Act of 1981 (Kenya) x, 121, 364*c*
Lawrence v. Texas 81
law schools 11, 69, 346*c*
lawyers 69, 347*c*, 348*c*, 364*c*
LDNs (least developed nations) 19
leaders. *See specific headings, e.g.:* Thatcher, Margaret
League of Kenyan Women Voters (LKWV) 285
League of Nations 39, 352*c*
League of Women Voters 55, 66, 285
"Leaps of Consciousness" (Steinem) **152–153**
least developed nations (LDNs) 19
Lebanon 4, 356*c*
legal rights 6, 50, 67–68115, 376*g*
legislators (female) 67–68, 251*f*. *See also specific headings, e.g.:* Pelosi, Nancy
lesbianism 60, 357*c*, 376*g*
lesbian rights **22–23,** 60, 81–82, 97, 108. *See also* gay rights; same-sex marriage
Lesotho (South Africa) 13, 359*c*
Liberia 27, 355*c*
life expectancy 114, 124
liquor industry 57, 58
literacy
and access to education 7
in Afghanistan 116, 363*c*
in China ix, 105
in Denmark 97
in Kenya 121, 122
Le Livre Noir de la Condition Feminine (Gaspard et al.) 370*c*

LKWV (League of Kenyan Women Voters) 285
loans 13, 14, 107, 235–236. *See also* microcredit
Lockwood, Belva 348*c*
loya jirga 112, 376*g*
Lucretia Mott Amendment 55. *See also* Equal Rights Amendment
lung cancer 18
Luplua, Line 264*b*
Lutheran Evangelical Church 30, 100
Lutz, Bertha 37, 39
Lyon, Mary 56, 264*b*

M

Maasai Girls Education Fund (MGEF) 285–286
Maasai Women for Education and Economic Development (MAWEED) 286
Maastrict Treaty 366*c*
Maathai, Wangari Muta x, 126, **230–232,** 264*b*
MacKinnon, Catherine 84, 364*c*
Maendeleo ya Wanawake Organization (MYWO) 126
maiden name 8
Malalai 264*b,* 348*c*
malaria 124
male dominance 28, 29
male-dominated occupations 70–71
managerial positions
access to 67
and affirmative action 5
in Australia 6
in Fortune 2000 companies 72
in Great Britain 6
increase of women in 10–11
pay for top 143
in the private sector 73
Mansuri, Rona 264*b*
Mao Zedong 102
Marines, U.S. 76, 77
marriage(s). *See also* divorce
in Afghanistan 111, **115,** 344*c*
arranged 105–106, 115
in China 105–106, 108, 110
delaying 16
in Denmark 97, 99, 352*c*
forced 85, **115, 229–230**
and gay rights 81

and human trafficking 85
and keeping surnames 8
in Kenya x, 120–121
minimum age for 9
and property rights 6
same-sex 22, 23, 81–82, 108, 120
married name 8
married women
Bradwell v. Illinois 347*c*
Declaration of Sentiments 51
in labor force 70
New York Married Women's Property Act 349*c*
paid employment of, 1978, 1998 253*f*
post–World War II 40
property rights 345*c*
in U.S. 253*f,* 345*c*
working during World War II 59
Married Women's Property Act (MWPA) 52, 345*c*
Masai people 24, 123
Massachusetts 22, 82
maternal deaths 18, 116, 123
maternity benefits 13, 99, 361*c*
mathematics 69, 71, 343*c,* 366*c*
MAWEED (Maasai Women for Education and Economic Development) 286
Mayer, Diana K. 62, 264*b*–265*b*
McGirk, Tim 141–142
Mead, Margaret 265*b*
Medal of Freedom 57
media 82, 84, 101
Medicaid program 21, 79
medical care. *See* health care
medical schools 11, 35–36, 97, 345*c,* 347*c,* 349*c*
medical treatments 67, 77, 78
medication abortion 79–80, 368*c,* 376*g*
medicine, sex/biology-based 78
member states 376*g*
men 70, 74–75, 235–236, 250*f,* 252*f,* 254*f*
men's roles 8, 16–17. *See also* husbands
men's studies 16
mental illness 23, 26
mentally retarded 19
Meritor Savings Bank v. Vinson 365*c*
methotrexate 80, 376
Mexico 25, 356*c*

Index

Mexico City Policy 21, 123
MGEF. *See* Maasai Girls
 Education Fund
microcredit 14, 107, 122,
 235–236
middle-class women 38, 62
Middle East 6, 10, 250*f*, 251*f*.
 See also specific headings, e.g.:
 Afghanistan
mifepristone 79, 80, 368*c*, 376
military, U.S. *See* Armed Forces
 of the United States
military academies 15, 68, 76,
 367*c*
military service **14–15,** 39–40,
 59–60, 66, 75–77, 177–179.
 See also Armed Forces of
 the United States; women in
 combat
Mill, John Stuart ix, 35, 95,
 265*b*, 346*c*
millennial. *See* Generation Y,
 Gen Y
minimum wage 55, 354*c*
minorities 5, 102
Minor v. Happersett 347*c*
misogynism 28, 377*g*
Mississippi 52, 364*c*
Missouri v. Celia 345*c*
Mitsubishi Motor
 Manufacturing of America
 367*c*
Moldovia 363*c*, 366*c*
Møller, Jutta Bojsen 265*b*
Mondale, Walter 364*c*
monitoring of women's rights
 31–32, 45, 88
moral rights 377*g*
"morning after pill" 80–81
Morrill Act of 1862 56
Morris, Esther 265*b*
mothers
 single 60, 74
 surrogate 16, **20,** 179–180,
 379*g*
 working 12–13, 71–72, 75,
 360*c*
Mother Teresa 29
Mott, James 265*b*
Mott, Lucretia 29, 33–34,
 51–52, 265*b*, 345*c*, 346*c*
Mount Holyoke College 56
Ms. magazine 61, 360*c*
mujahideen 363*c*
Mulama, Joyce 235–236
Muller v. State of Oregon 350*c*

Multinational Programming
 and Operational Centre
 (MULPOC) 14
Munch, Elna 96, 265*b*
Murphy, Caryle 138–139
Muslims. *See also* Islam
 in Afghanistan 111, 114
 in Denmark 102
 feminist x
 in Kenya 120, 121
 and mixed-congregations 30
 and social change 8
Muslim Women's League
 (MWL) 286
MWL (Muslim Women's
 League) 286
MWPA. *See* Married Women's
 Property Act
Myanmar 354*c*, 355*c*
MYWO (Maendeleo ya
 Wanawake Organization) 126

N

NACW. *See* National Association
 of Colored Women
NAF. *See* National Abortion
 Federation
Nairobi Forward Looking
 Strategies for the
 Advancement of Women
 42, 125
Najman, Dina 30
NASA (National Aeronautics
 and Space Administration)
 363*c*
National Abortion Federation
 (NAF) 80, 286–287
*National Abortion Federation v.
 Ashcroft* 80
National Aeronautics and Space
 Administration (NASA) 363*c*
National American Woman
 Suffrage Association
 (NAWSA) 53–55, 346*c*, 350*c*
National Association of Colored
 Women (NACW) 63, 349*c*
National Birth Control League
 58
National Black Feminist
 Organization (NBFO) 64
National Coalition against
 Domestic Violence (NCADV)
 287
National Commission on the
 Status of Women (NCSW)
 (Pakistan) 287

National Consumer's League
 (NCL) 55
National Council of Bishops 79
National Council of Negro
 Women, Inc. (NCNW) 64,
 287–288, 354*c*
National Council of Women's
 Organizations (NCWO) 288,
 369*c*
National Guard 15, 77, 369*c*
Nationalist Kuomintang
 government (China) 104
national liberation movement
 7, 377*g*
National Organization for
 Women (NOW) **62,** 288–289
 and access to the military 75
 and black feminism 64
 and Equal Rights Amendment
 66
 founding of 359*c*
 and gay rights 22–23
 and gender-based "help
 wanted" advertisements 62
 membership of 87
National Policy on Gender and
 Development (Kenya, 2005)
 119, 125–126
National Recovery Act (1932)
 353*c*
National Tennis Center 370*c*
National Woman's Party (NWP)
 54, 350*c*, 352*c*
National Woman Suffrage
 Association (NWSA) 35,
 52–53, 346*c*
National Women's History
 Museum Act 89, 369*c*
The National Women's History
 Project (NWHP) 289
National Women's History Week
 364*c*, 365*c*
National Women's Law Center
 (NWLC) 75, 289
National Women's Political
 Caucus 60, 61, 87, 289–290
National Women's Studies
 Association (NWSA) 89
NATO. *See* North Atlantic
 Treaty Organization
natural rights 377*g*
Navy, U.S. 76, 77
Nawa, Fariba 226
NAWSA. *See* National
 American Woman Suffrage
 Association

NBFO (National Black Feminist Organization) 64
NCADV (National Coalition against Domestic Violence) 287
NCL (National Consumer's League) 55
NCNW. *See* National Council of Negro Women, Inc.
NCSW. *See* National Commission on the Status of Women
NCWO. *See* National Council of Women's Organizations
Nefertiti (queen of Egypt) 342*c*
Neopaganism 31
Netherlands 13, 20, 22, 28, 350*c*, 351*c*
networking (20th century) **36–40**
"new age" spirituality 29–31
New Culture movement (China) **103**
New England Women's Medical Society 348*c*
New Jersey 82, 370*c*
"New Rights, but Afghan Women Still Face Forced Marriages" *(The International Herald Tribune)* **229–230**
New Woman 377*g*
New York Married Women's Property Act (1848) 52, **153–154,** 345*c*, 349*c*
New York State 34, 53, 56, 60–61, 347*c*
New York Times, The (newspaper) **139**
New Zealand 3–4, 46, 349*c*, 351*c*
NGOs. *See* nongovernmental organization
Nicaragua 25, 357*c*
Nielsen, Nielsine 36, 97, 266*b*, 347*c*
Niger 9, 355*c*
Nigeria 363*c*, 369*c*
Nineteenth Amendment 54–55, **155,** 351*c*, 364*c*
Nixon, Richard M. 60
Nobel Peace Prize x, 350*c*
"No Child Left Behind" 69
"no fault" divorce law 360*c*
nonagricultural paid labor 251*f*
nonbinding 377*g*
noncombatant roles 15, 59

nongovernmental organization (NGOs) 377*g*
and Afghanistan 115, 117, 368*c*
and CEDAW 45
in China 110
formation of 39
funding for, and abortions 21
and human trafficking 101
in Kenya x, 119
and rape crimes 27
and UN World Conferences on Women 41, 42
nonpartisan 377*g*
"No One Listens to Us and No One Treats Us as Human Beings: Justice Denied to Women" report (Amnesty International) **226–229**
North Africa 10, 250*f*, 251*f. See also specific countries*
North America 28. *See also* Canada; United States
North American Indian Women's Association 360*c*
North Atlantic Treaty Organization (NATO) 14, 15, 358*c*
Norway 349*c*, 350*c*
Novello, Antonia C. 266*b*, 365*c*
NOW. *See* National Organization for Women
nuns 30, 259
nursing 40
NWHP (The National Women's History Project) 289
NWLC. *See* National Women's Law Center
NWP. *See* National Woman's Party
NWSA. *See* National Woman Suffrage Association
NWSA (National Women's Studies Association) 89

O

Oberlin College 56
objectification x, 84
obscenity 58, 65, 84, 347*c*
occupations 69, 70–71, 95, 106
Oceania 4, 19, 46
Ockrent, Christine 370*c*
O'Connor, Sandra Day 80, 266*b*, 365*c*
The October 2000 UN Resolution 1325 on Women, Peace and Security **210–213**

Odhiambo, Millie Akoth 266*b*
OECD countries 250*f*, 251*f*
officers (female military) 75, 76
one-child policy (China) ix, 21, 27, 107–109
On the Subjection of Women (Mill) ix, 95
opium drug trade 114
oral contraceptives 18, 65
ordination of women 29, 30, 86–87. *See also* clergy (female)
orphans 17, 108, 124, 125
Orthodox Judaism 30

P

Pacific region 250*f*, 251*f*
pacifism 37–39, 41
paid labor 251*f*
Pakistan 4
Pankhurst, Emmeline 37, 38, 54, 266*b*, 353*c*
parade (suffragette) 54
Pareyio, Agnes 123, 267*b*
Paris Peace Conference 38, 351*c*
parity 377*g. See also* equality
Parks, Rosa 267*b*, 357*c*
parliament 111, 113, 119–120
parochial 377*g*
partial-birth abortion 80, 368*c*, 377*g*
Partial-Birth Abortion Ban Act of 2003 **180–184**
part-time employment 98
Pashtuns 113, 115, 116, 348*c*
paternal leave 99
patriarchal society 105
patrilineal 378*g*
patrilocal 378*g*
Paul, Alice 29, 37, 54, 55, 66, 267*b*, 350*c*
payment for surrogacy 20
pay rate ceiling 71
pediatrics 57
Pelosi, Nancy 267*b*, 370*c*
pensions 70
Perkins, Frances 59, 97
Perry, Ricky 370*c*
pessaries 354*c*
Peterson, Esther 61, 267*b*
pharmaceutical companies 65
Philippines 4, 354*c*
Phillips v. Martin Marietta Corporation 360*c*
physical abuse 25, 26
physicians 35, 112, 116, 345*c*, 348*c*

Index

PICW (Presidential Interagency Council on Women) 110

Pill, the 18, 65

pilots, female military 59–60, 354c, 355c

Pittsburgh Press v. Pittsburgh Commission on Human Rights 361c

Plan B (levonorgestrel) 80–81, 370c, 373

Plan for the Gradual Abolition of Slavery, A (Wright) 51

Planned Parenthood Federation of America (PPFA) 58, 65, 80, 290–291

Planned Parenthood Federation v. Ashcroft 80

Planned Parenthood v. Casey 79, 365c–366c

Platform for Action for Improving the Welfare of Women in Kenya (1997) 125

police officers 124. *See also* law enforcement

political participation 42, 119–120

political power 87, 96

political rights 378g. *See also* civil and political rights

politicians. *See specific headings, e.g.:* Clinton, Hillary Rodham

politics 11, 364c

population 103, 107

Population and Family Planning Law (China, 2002) x, 107, 108, **223–225,** 368c

pornography viii, ix, 24–25, 83–85, 364c

Portugal 353c, 362c

poverty
and bankruptcy 74, 75
and contraception 19
and education 7
in Kenya 121–122
and marriage age 9
of single mothers 74
and social security 75
and UNESCO 44
and UN Millennium Development Goals vii
in U.S. 74–75
and violence against women 193–194

poverty line 378g

PPFA. *See* Planned Parenthood Federation of America

Pregnancy Discrimination Act 363c

pregnant women
in Afghanistan 111
Cleveland Board of Education v. LaFleur 361c
in Denmark 99–100
dismissal of 99–100
and domestic abuse 25, 82
endangerment of life of 21
and ERA 5
General Electric Company v. Gilbert 362c
and HIV/AIDS 17, 18
"Presentation to the Third Committee of the Secretary-General's In-depth Study on Violence Against Women" (Annan) **196–198**

presidential candidates 61, 112, 370c

Presidential Interagency Council on Women (PICW) 110

President's Commission on the Status of Women (U.S.) 61, 358c

primary education 6, 7, 44, 97, 116

privacy x, 21, 65, 66, 360c

Privacy Act 76

privatization 6, 75, 101, 121

probate code (Idaho) 171–175

professional workers 8, 9, 117, 251f

Prohibition 57, 58, 378g

property ownership **6,** 104, 105

property rights
in Afghanistan **115,** 344c
Declaration of Sentiments 51
early Egypt 342c
in Kenya 6, 9, 120, **121,** 126
Kirchberg v. Feenstra 364c
Mississippi Married Women's Property Act 345c
New York Married Women's Property Act 345c, 349c
"no fault" divorce 360c
Theodora 343c
in U.S. 34, **52, 68,** 349c

prostitution viii, **28**
in China 109
COYOTE group 361c
in Denmark ix, 100, 101
in Kenya **125**
and sexual trafficking 28, 85, 86, 100, 101
Theodora 343c

Protestantism 29, 86

protests 54, 104, 350c

protocol 378g

Protocol to Prevent, Suppress and Punish Trafficking in Persons, Especially Women and Children 27, 85

public funding 72. *See also* federal funding

public policy 32

public speaking 34, 51

Q

al-Qaeda 113

Quakers 29, 51–52, 86

quickening 21, 378g

Qu'ran 30, 114

R

rabbis (female) 30, 356c

race 378g

racial discrimination 203–205

Radcliffe College 56

Radice v. New York 352c

rape **25, 26**
and abortion 21
in Afghanistan 114
in Denmark 100
in Kenya 124
of slaves 345c
in U.S. **82, 83,** 345c
Violence against Women Act 366c, 368c
as a weapon of war 26–27
WHO studies on viii

Rape, Abuse & Incest National Network (RAINN) 291

ratification, ratify 378g

RAWA. *See* Revolutionary Association of the Women of Afghanistan

Rebel, Lise-Lotte Gauger 100

Redstockings 61, 97

Reed v. Reed 53, **171–175,** 360c

Reform Judaism 30

refugee status vii

Regents of the University of California v. Bakke 63

religion **28–31.** *See also specific headings, e.g.:* Islam
in China 103
and contraception 19
in Denmark **100**
feminist spirituality **30–31**
in Kenya 120, 121
leadership roles in **29–30, 86–87**

male dominance in 28, 29
religious scholarship 29, **31**
spirituality 29–31, 86–87
in U.S. **86–87**
religious freedom 28–29
Religious Freedom and Civil
Marriage Protection Act 82
reports (monitoring) 31–32
reproductive health 21–22, 101,
192–193
reproductive rights **18–19,**
78–81, 107–108, 122–124. *See
also* abortion; birth control
reservation (treaty) 378*g*
reserve (military) 15, 77, 369*c*,
378*g*
retirement issues 87, 194–196
reverse discrimination 5, 63
Revolutionary Association of
the Women of Afghanistan
(RAWA) 118, 291, 362*c*
Rice, Condoleeza 268*b*
Richer, Léon 36
Ride, Sally 71, 268*b*, 363*c*
"Rising above the Stained-
Glass Ceiling" (Van Biema)
142–143
Roberts v. U.S. Jaycees 364*c*
Roe v. Wade 21, **66,** 79, **176–
177,** 361*c*, 365*c*
role models, female 11
Roman Catholicism 21, 30, 87
Romania 353*c*, 355*c*
Rome, Treaty of 357*c*
Roosevelt, Eleanor 40, 59, 61,
268*b*, 354*c*, 355*c*, 358*c*
Roqia Center for Women's
Rights, Studies and Education
291–292
Rose, Ernestine 33, 52, 268*b*
Rosie the Riveter 59
Rostker v. Goldberg 76,
177–179
Ruffin, Josephine 53, 63, 349*c*
RU-486 79, 80, 368*c*
Russia 13, 37, 39, 351*c*, 352*c*
Rwanda 27, 358*c*

S
sacred texts 28, 29, 31
Samar, Sima 112, 268*b*
same-sex marriage 22, 23,
81–82, 108, 120
Sanger, Margaret 21, 58, 65,
268*b*–269*b*, 350*c*, 351*c*
San Marino 357*c*, 361*c*

Saudi Arabia 4, 6, 369*c*
Scandinavia 13, 72
Schlafly, Phyllis 66
scholarship 29, 31, 64
schools
business 11
law 11, 69, 346*c*
medical 11, 35–36, 97, 345*c*,
347*c*, 349*c*
primary 57
single-sex 35
Taliban and 366*c*
theology 30
Schori, Katharine Jefferts 87
Schultz v. Wheaton Glass Co.
360*c*
science 69, 71, 366*c*
Seaman, Barbara 65
"Second and Third Wave
Feminists Clash over the
Future" (Friedlin) **137–138**
Second Anglo-Afghan War
348*c*
second-generation rights. *See*
economic, social, and cultural
rights
The Second Sex (Beauvoir) 356*c*
secular 378*g*
Seddon, Margaret 363*c*
Selected Reserve 77, 378*g*
Selective Service law 76
self-determination 378*g*
self-employment 251*f*
Senate, U.S. 68, 89, 368*c*, 369*c*.
See also specific headings, e.g.:
Clinton, Hillary Rodham
Seneca Falls Convention (1848)
34, 51, 345*c*
sensitivity training 140
September 11, 2001 terrorist
attacks vii
Serious Proposal to the Ladies
(Astell) viii, 33, 344*c*
sex 379*g*. *See also* biological
distinctions between the sexes
sexist 379*g*
sex ratios 107, 108, 110
sexual abuse 25
sexual aggression 82
sexual assault 26
sexual favoritism 98
sexual freedom 33, 84, 108
sexual harassment **11–12,** 379*g*
CEDAW's definition of 12
in Denmark 12, **98–99**
and gays/lesbians 81

Gender Equity in Education
Act 366*c*
*Harris v. Forklift Systems,
Inc.* 366*c*
Anita Hill viii
Mitsubishi Motor
Manufacturing of America
367*c*
and U.S. Navy 76
in U.S. **73–74,** 76
and women in managerial
positions 11
sexuality (in Afghanistan)
114–115
sexually transmitted diseases
(STDs) 17
sexual repression 25
sexual trafficking 27–28. *See
also* trafficking (human)
Shalala, Donna 88
Shaw, Anna Howard 54, 269*b*
Siddiq, Suhaila 112, 269*b*
signing, sign (of documents)
379*g*
Simat, Mary Simalo 269*b*
single mothers 60, 74
single parenthood 16
single-sex schools 35
single women 40
"sister schools" 56
Sivelle, Kristina 225–226
"16 Days of Activism Against
Gender Violence" 369*c*
slaves, rape of 345*c*
Smith College 56
Sobeknefru (queen of Egypt)
342*c*
social change 7–9, 87
socially determined behavior 16
Social Security 70, 75, 87
Society for Women's Health
Research (SWHR) 78, 292,
368*c*
soldiers (female) 14–15. *See
also* military service
"Solitude of Self, The" (Stanton)
147–150
Somalia 23, 26, 357*c*
Song of a German Maiden
(Otto) 34
Soroptimist 379*g*
South Africa 22, 353*c*, 364*c*,
366*c*
South America 41. *See also
specific headings, e.g.:* Brazil
South Asia 10, 27, 46, 250*f*, 251*f*

Index

Southeast Asia 10, 46
Southern Baptist Convention 29, 86
sovereignty, U.S. 45
Soviet Union ix, 111, 363c, 364c
space shuttle program 363c
Spain 13, 22, 353c
special protection 55
spirituality 29–31, 86–87
Sri Lanka 4, 353c
Stalin, Joseph 39
stalking 83
stand for election 379g
stand for election (right to) 379g
  in 1900–1929 349c–353c
  in 1930–1959 353c–357c
  in 1960–1969 357c–360c
  in 1970–1979 360c–363c
  in 1980–1989 363c–365c
  in 1990–1999 365c–367c
  in 2000–2007 367c–370c
Stanton, Elizabeth Cady 269b
  Harriot Stanton Blanch 37
  History of Woman Suffrage 53, 348c
  International Council of Women 36
  National American Woman Suffrage Association 346c
  National Woman Suffrage Association 35, 52
  runs for Congress 346c
  and Seneca Falls Convention 34, 51
  "The Solitude of Self" 147–150
  Troy Female Seminary 56
  Women's National League 35
  World Anti-Slavery Convention 345c
state 13, 379g
"State Secret: Thousands Secretly Sterilized" (ABC News) 137
states party 379g
stature, seeking 10–11
status quo management 11
STDs (sexually transmitted diseases) 17
Steinem, Gloria 61, 152–153, 269b, 360c
sterilization
  2002 Session, House Joint Resolution No. 299 169–170

Carrie Buck 19, 78, 353c
Buck v. Bell 19, 78, 166–169
  in China 107
  as contraception, in U.S. 80
  forced 19–20, 78, 107, 353c
  in U.S. 19, 78, 80
Stock Market Crash of 1929 58–59
Stone, Lucy 53, 269b–270b
Stonewall uprising (1969) 22
stoning 369c, 370c
STOP grants 83
Stowe, Emily Howard 35
Stowe-Gullen, Ann Augusta 35
stroke 77, 370c
Strother, Dora Jean Dougherty 270b
Stuart, Maria W. 51, 270b
The Subjection of Women (Mill) 35, 346c
sub-Saharan Africa. See also specific headings, e.g.: Kenya
  access to education in 7
  and age of marriage 9
  and contraception 19
  female genital mutilation in 23, 24
  HIV/AIDS in 17
  women in major labor sectors, 2005 251f
  women's labor activity in 10
  women's vs. men's earnings in 250f
"substantially equal" pay 360c
Sudan 23, 27, 358c
suffragette 379g
"Suffrage Wins in Senate: Now Goes to States" (The New York Times) 139
suffragist 379g. See also women's suffrage
Sun Yat-sen 104
Supreme Court, U.S.
  and abortion 79, 80
  Adarand Constructors, Inc. v. Federico Pena 63
  and affirmative action 63
  and birth control 65
  Bradwell v. Illinois 347c
  Buck v. Bell 19
  Burlington Industries, Inc. v. Ellerth 367c
  Cleveland Board of Education v. LaFleur 361c
  Craig v. Boren 362c
  Doe v. Bolton 361c

Eisenstadt v. Baird 65, 66, 175–176, 360c
Estate of Thorton v. Calder 86
Faragher v. City of Boca Raton 367c
Fay v. New York 355c
General Electric Company v. Gilbert 362c
Ruth Bader Ginsburg 256b
Griswold v. Connecticut 58, 65, 170–171, 359c
Harris v. Forklift Systems, Inc. 366c
  and "help wanted" advertisements 62, 361c
Hishon v. King and Spaulding 364c
Johnson v. Santa Clara County 365c
  and juries 358c
Kirchberg v. Feenstra 364c
Lawrence v. Texas 81
Belva Lockwood 348c
Meritor Savings Bank v. Vinson 365c
Minor v. Happersett 347c
Muller v. State of Oregon 350c
Sandra Day O'Connor 80, 266b, 365c
Phillips v. Martin Marietta Corporation 360c
Pittsburgh Press v. Pittsburgh Commission on Human Rights 361c
Planned Parenthood v. Casey 79, 365c–366c
  and pornography 84
Reed v. Reed 53, 171–175, 360c
Regents of the University of California v. Bakke 63
Roe v. Wade 21, 66, 79, 176–177, 361c, 365c
Rostker v. Goldberg 76, 177–179
Taylor v. Louisiana 362c
Title IX in the Education Codes of 1972 367c
United States v. Morrison 368c
United States v. Quinton Williams 86
United States v. Virginia 367c
Webster v. Reproductive Health Services 79, 365c
surgeon general 365c
surnames 8

surrogate mother 16, **20,**
179–180, 379*g*
"suspect classification" 360*c*
Swaziland 13, 359*c*
Sweden 351*c*, 352*c*
SWHR. *See* Society for Women's
Health Research
Switzerland 12, 261, 360*c*

T
taboo subjects 17, 22, 60
Tailhook Association 76
Taliban vii, ix, 117, 379*g*
and burqas 8
capture Kabul 367*c*
elections post- 369*c*
fall of 112
and girl's education 116, 366*c*
maternal death rate under
116
and women's as property 15
and women's rights 111
and women's suffrage 4, 113
and "working women" 9
Tang Junying 263*b*
Tanzania 24
Tanzania Gender Networking
Programme (TGNP) 101
Taraki, Nur Mohammed 111
Taussig, Helen Brooke 57, 270*b*
Tawosret (queen of Egypt) 342*c*
Taylor, Shelley E. 144–145
Taylor v. Louisiana 362*c*
teachers 10, 40, 57, 106, 116
technical workers 106, 251*f*
temperance 57–58, 347*c*, 379*g*
10-hour workday 350*c*
tend-and-befriend 144–145
tenure 379*g*
Teresa, Mother 29
Terrell, Mary Church 63, 270*b*,
349*c*
terrorism 15, 362*c*, 366*c*
Texas 370*c*
TGNP (Tanzania Gender
Networking Programme) 101
Thailand 28, 353*c*
Thatcher, Margaret 363*c*
Theodora 343*c*
theology (feminist) 31
Third Annual Women & Power
Conference 152–153
third-generation rights. *See*
environmental, cultural, and
developmental rights
the third wave (in U.S.) **87–89**

Third Wave Foundation
292–293
Thirteenth Amendment 35, 52
Thomas, Clarence viii, 74
Title VII of the 1964 Civil Rights
Act 5, 9, 62, 73–74, **156–159,**
358*c*, 361*c*
Title IX in the Education Codes
of 1972 62–63, 68, **159–162,**
360*c*, 367*c*
Title XIX 81
Tiy (queen of Egypt) 342*c*
Toronto Women's Literary Club
34–35
trade unions 41
traditional custom 9. *See also*
customs (social)
traditionalists 23
Traffic in Women and Children
(1908) 85
trafficking (human) viii, **27–28,**
379*g*–380*g*
Grace Abbott 352*c*
in China ix, 109
and Convenant of the League
of Nations 38
in Denmark 100–101
Final Act of the Conference
on Security and Co-
operation in Europe 362*c*
in Kenya **125**
and pornography 85
and prostitution 28, 85, 86,
100, 101
Protocol to Prevent, Suppress
and Punish Trafficking in
Persons, Especially Women
and Children 27, 85
and U.S. **85–86**
Victims of Trafficking and
Violence Protection Act of
2000 85, **164–166,** 368*c*
transgender people 81–82
treaty 31, 85, 380*g*
"Treaty for the Rights of
Women" 45. *See also*
UN Convention on the
Elimination of All Forms
of Discrimination against
Women
Treiner, Sandrine 370*c*
Troy Female Seminary 56
tubal ligation 19
Turkey vii, 353*c*
Twinslayer's Case (England,
1327) 20, 343*c*

2005 World Summit Outcome
214–215
2002 Session, House Joint
Resolution No. 299 **169–170**
Tz'u-Hsi (Cixi; empress of
China) 270*b*–271*b*, 346*c*

U
Uganda 27
UIFSA (Uniform Interstate
Family Support Act) 74
UN. *See* United Nations
UNDP (UN Development
Programme) 14
unemployment 106, 107, 122,
362*c*
UNESCO. *See* UN Educational,
Scientific and Cultural
Organization
UNFPA. *See* UN Population
Fund
UNIFEM. *See* UN Development
Fund for Women (UNIFEM)
Uniform Desertion and Non-
Support Act 74
Uniform Interstate Family
Support Act (UIFSA) 74
Uniform Marital Property Act
of 1983 68
Uniform Premarital Agreement
Act 68
Unitarians 29, 86
United Arab Emirates 4, 41,
370*c*
United Kingdom. *See also*
England
and Afghanistan ix
employment rights in 6
and Kenya x
military service in 15, 39
Emmeline Pankhurst 37, 38,
54, 266*b*, 353*c*
and sexual harassment 12
support for working mothers
in 13
Margaret Thatcher 363*c*
and Wicca 31
women's suffrage in 4, 37, 38,
351*c*, 353*c*
United Methodist Church 29, 86
UN Charter 40, 55, 380*g*
UN Commission on the Status
of Women 40, 45
UN Committee on the
Elimination of Discrimination
against Women 9

Index

UN Convention against
Transnational Organized
Crime (2003) 27, 85, 110
UN Convention on the
Elimination of All Forms
of Discrimination against
Women (CEDAW) **205–207,**
278
adoption of 363*c*
and China 109
creation of 94
and Denmark 102, 221–223
on property rights 6
and sexual harassment 11–12
and UN Millennium
Declaration 44
UN Second World
Conference on Women 42
UN Decade for Women (1976-
1985) 41, 361*c*
UN Development Fund for
Women (UNIFEM) 27, 41,
109–110, 117, 118, 293, 368*c*
UN Development Programme
(UNDP) 14
UN Division for the
Advancement of Women
(DAW) 293–294
UN Educational, Scientific
and Cultural Organization
(UNESCO) 44, 368*c*
UN First World Conference on
Women (Mexico, 1975) 41,
362*c*
UN Fourth World Conference
on Women (Beijing, 1995) ix,
41–44, 88, 105, 367*c*
UN General Assembly 4, 6,
356*c*, 380*g*
UN International Day for the
Elimination of Violence
Against Women 44, 368*c*
UN International Research and
Training Institute for the
Advancement of Women
(INSTRAW) 14, 41, 294
UN International Women's
Year 361*c*
United Nations (UN) 40–46,
359*c*. See also specific
headings, e.g.: UN Millennium
Development Goals
and Afghanistan 117, 357*c*
and Africa 32
Kofi Annan 117, 190–191,
196–198

and discrimination 41, 44
early work on women's rights
of 40
and education 42
and equal rights 40, 42,
43–44
and European reporting 32
and girls 42–44
and health care 42
International Women's Day
362*c*
and international women's
movement 40, **41–44**
and microfinance loans 14
and NGOs 41, 42
and poverty vii, 44
reports to 31–32
and women's suffrage 4
"U.N. Links Poverty, Violence
against Women" (Associated
Press) **193–194**
UN Literacy Decade (2003-
12) 7
UN Millennium Declaration
43–44
UN Millennium Development
Goals vii, 7, 10, 22, 119,
121–122, 367*c*, 369*c*
UN Millennium Summit (2005)
44
UN Population Fund (UNFPA)
111–112, 118, 294
UN Resolution 1325 on Women,
Peace and Security 44, 368*c*
UN Second World Conference
on Women (Copenhagen,
1980) 41–42, 94, 363*c*
UN Secretary-General 46. See
also Annan, Kofi
"U.N. Secretary-General Kofi
Annan's Women's Day
Message (March 2002)"
(Annan) **190–191**
UN Security Council 112
UN Third World Conference on
Women (Nairobi, 1985) x, 41,
42, 119, 364*c*
UN World Summit (2005)
214–215, 369*c*
United States viii, 50–89. See
also history of women's rights
(U.S.)
in 1950–2025 252*f*
in the 1950s **60**
in the 1960s **60**
in the 1970s **60–61**

in 1978, 1998 253*f*
abortion in 21, **79–80**
affirmative action in **63**
average hours/weeks of paid
employment in 253*f*
birth control movement in
58, 65
causes of death in, by sex,
2002 254*f*
and CEDAW 6, 45
civil and political rights in
67–68
civilian labor force
participation in, 1950-2025
252*f*
civil unions in 370*c*
and the Civil War 35
and comparable worth of
work 41
continuing women's rights
movement in 45
and contraception 19, **58, 65,
80–81**
current situation in 66–89
Declaration of Sentiments x,
134–135
early women's rights
movement in 32–34,
50–51
education in 6–7, **56–57,
62–63, 68–69**
elder abuse in 109
employment/employment
rights in **55, 61–62, 69–71**
Equal Rights Amendment **66**
female clergy in 29
female factory workers in
36–37
and female genital mutilation
24
feminism in **60–61,** 62
financial rights in 13, **68,
74–75**
forced sterilizations 19,
78, 80
gay rights in 23, **81–82**
and glass ceiling **72–73,**
135–136
HIV/AIDS in 17–18
and human trafficking 28,
85–86
legal rights in **67–68**
and maiden/birth names 8
managerial positions for
women in 11
maternity benefits in 13

medical care in **77–78**
military service in 15, 39,
  75–77
National Organization for
  Women **62**
Neopaganism in 31
population of 103
poverty in 74–75
Pregnancy Discrimination
  Act 363*c*
property rights in **52, 68**
rapes/sexual assaults in 26
religion/spirituality in **86–87**
reproductive rights in **78–81**
Roe v. Wade 21, **66**, 79,
  176–177, 361*c*, 365*c*
and same-sex marriage 22, 23
sex ratios in 107
sexual freedom in **73–74**
and sexual harassment 12, 98
Stock Market Crash of 1929
  58–59
support for working mothers
  in 13
and surrogate motherhood 20
the third wave in **87–88**
unemployment in 107
violence against women in
  82–86
women's studies programs
  in 46
women's suffrage in viii, 4,
  34, 35, **52–55**, 346*c*, 351*c*
women's *vs.* men's earnings in,
  1951-2004 252*f*
working mothers in **71–72**
and the "working woman" 9
and World War II **59–60**
U.S. Tennis Association 370*c*
United States v. Morrison 368*c*
*United States v. One Package of
  Japanese Pessaries* 354*c*
*United States v. Quinton
  Williams* 86
United States v. Virginia 367*c*
United Women's Organizations
  (Denmark) 96
Universal Declaration of Human
  Rights (1948) 40, **200–202**,
  355*c*
universities 63, 106, 348*c*, 359*c*,
  367*c*
University of Copenhagen 36, 97
University of Iowa 56
University of Utah 56
unprotected sex 17, 18

unwed women 108
Uruguay 39, 353*c*
Utah 53

V

VA (Veterans Administration)
  77
Van Biema, David 142–143
Vanuatu 362*c*, 363*c*
vasectomy 19, 107
Vassar College 56
VAWA. *See* Violence against
  Women Act
V-Day 294–295
veils 366*c*
Vermont 82, 370*c*
Veterans Administration (VA)
  77
veteran's benefits 362*c*
vice presidential candidates
  364*c*
Victims of Crime Act (VOCA)
  26
Victims of Trafficking and
  Violence Protection Act of
  2000 85, **164–166**, 368*c*
Vietnam viii
Vietnam War 41, 75, 77
*Vindication of the Rights of
  Women, A* (Wollstonecraft)
  ix, 29, 33, 95, **185–188**, 345*c*
violence 4, 11, 84
violence against women viii,
  24–28, 366*c*. *See also*
  domestic violence; female
  genital mutilation; rape
  in Afghanistan **114**, 118
  Kofi Annan's address on
    196–198
  in China **108–109**
  in Darfur, Sudan 369*c*
  in Denmark **100–101**
  female infanticide viii, **27**,
    107, 374*g*
  human trafficking **27–28**
  in Kenya **124**, 125
  and links to poverty 193–194
  and pornography **24–25**
  and prostitution 28
  and small loans for men
    235–236
UN Fourth World Conference
  on Women 42
UN International Day for the
  Elimination of Violence
  Against Women 44

UN Millennium Summit 44
UN Secretary-General's
  report on 46
  in U.S. **82–86**
  and war **26–27**
Violence against Women Act
  (VAWA) (1994) 83, 366*c*,
  368*c*
Virginia Military Institute 76,
  367*c*
Vital Voices Global Partnership
  88, 295
VOCA (Victims of Crime
  Act) 26
voluntary armies 14–15
voluntary labor service 39–40
voting 35, 53, 67–68, 347*c*
voting rights. *See* women's
  suffrage

W

wages and earnings. *See also*
  equal pay
  in Afghanistan 116–117
  in China 106
  in Denmark 98
  disparity in 10, 69–70
  in Kenya 122
  median yearly 70
  men's v. women's 250*f*, 252*f*
  minimum 55, 354*c*
  as percentage of men's 10
  rights over 34
  in U.S., 1951-2004 252*f*
  worldwide 250*f*
waitresses 352*c*
Wali, Sima 271*b*
"Wangari Maathai—Nobel
  Lecture (2004) **230–232**
Wanjiru, Bishop Margaret 271*b*
warlords 114, 115
wars viii, 3, 26–27. *See also*
  specific headings, e.g.: World
  War II
Washington University School
  of Law 346*c*
WASPs. *See* Women's Airforce
  Service Pilots
WCTU (Woman's Christian
  Temperance Union) 34
*Webster v. Reproductive Health
  Services* 79, 365*c*
WEDO. *See* Women's
  Environment & Development
  Organization
Weeks v. Southern Bell 359*c*

Index

"Whatever Happened to Family
Planning and, for That Matter,
Reproductive Health?"
(Gillespie) **192–193**
WHO. *See* World Health
Organization
"Why Your Boss May Start
Sweating te Small Stuff"
(Rawe) **140**
widows 121, 344*c*
WILPF. *See* Women's
International League for
Peace and Freedom
Wilson, Carrie 347*c*
Wilson, Woodrow 54, 350*c*
WITCH (Women's International
Terrorist Conspiracy from
Hell) 61
Wollstonecraft, Mary ix, 29, 33,
95, 185–188, 271*b*, 345*c*
Woman's Christian Temperance
Union (WCTU) 34
Woman's Crusade of 1873–74
57, 347*c*
"womb for hire." *See* surrogate
mother
Women and Power Conference
(NYC, 2004) 118
Women for Women
International 295–296
women in combat 15, 76–77,
141–142
*Women in Conflict with Social
Conditions* (Anneke) 34
Women's Airforce Service Pilots
(WASPs) 59, 362*c*
women's banks 13–14
Women's Bureau (Department
of Labor) 55, 61
women's colleges 56, 57, 69
Women's Educational Equity Act
(1974) 361*c*
Women's Environment &
Development Organization
(WEDO) 61, 296
Women's History Month 365*c*
Women's Hospital 346*c*
Women's International League
for Peace and Freedom
(WILPF) 38, 39, 45, 296–297,
351*c*
Women's International Terrorist
Conspiracy from Hell
(WITCH) 61
women's movement 29, 32,
114. *See also* international

women's movement; women's
suffrage
Women's Peace Party 37, 350*c*
Women's Research and
Education Institute (WREI)
297
women's rights vii, ix, 31–32
"Women's Rights" treaty 363*c*.
See also UN Convention on
the Elimination of All Forms of
Discrimination against Women
women's roles 7–9, 16–17
women's studies programs viii,
46, 88–89, 97
women's suffrage viii, **3–5**. *See
also specific headings, e.g.:*
Anthony, Susan B.
in the 20th century 36–37
in 1900–1929 349*c*–353*c*
in 1930–1959 353*c*–357*c*
in 1960–1969 357*c*–360*c*
in 1970–1979 360*c*–363*c*
in 1980–1989 363*c*–365*c*
in 1990–1999 365*c*–367*c*
in 2000–2007 367*c*–370*c*
in Afghanistan ix, 4, 111, 113,
358*c*, 369*c*
in Belgium 351*c*–352*c*
Margaret Bent 52
in Brazil 37, 39
in Canada 34–35, 350*c*, 351*c*,
356*c*, 357*c*
in China ix, **103–104,** 350*c*,
356*c*
and the Civil War 35
in Denmark 37, **96–97,** 98,
350*c*
and Fifth Amendment 347*c*
in Finland 37, 349*c*
in France 37, 355*c*
in India 4, 356*c*
in Kenya **119–120,** 358*c*
Minor v. Happersett 347*c*
in Netherlands 350*c*, 351*c*
in New York 344*c*
in New Zealand 3–4, 349*c*,
351*c*
in Norway 349*c*, 350*c*
in Sweden 351*c*, 352*c*
and Taliban 4, 113
in United Kingdom 4, 37, 38,
351*c*, 353*c*
and U.S. Congress 53, 348*c*
in U.S. viii, 4, 34, 35, **52–55,**
346*c*, 351*c*
and World War I 37–38, 54

Women's Suffrage Organization
(Denmark) 349*c*
Women's Suffragette Alliance
350*c*
Women's World Fair 352*c*
"Women Taking Charge of
Retirement Purse Strings,
Sort of" (Kinetz) **194–196**
Women 2000 Conference 43,
189–190
Women Workers' Union
(Kvindeligt Arbejderforbund)
(Denmark) 95
Women Work! The National
Network for Women's
Employment 297–298
working hours 55, 253*f*
working mothers 12–13, 71–72,
75, 360*c*
"working women" 7––11, 39–40,
70–71. *See also* employment
(employment rights)
work/life balance 11, 71
workplace, women's roles in
16–17
World Anti-Slavery Convention
(1840) 52, 345*c*
World Education Forum (2000)
44, 368*c*
World Health Organization
(WHO) viii, 18, 25–27, 46,
107
World War I 37–38, 54, 351*c*
World War II viii, 39–40, 59–60
WREI (Women's Research and
Education Institute) 297
Wright, Frances ("Fanny") 51,
271*b*
Wyoming 53, 348*c*

Y
Year of the Family (UN, 1994)
16–17
Year of the Woman 366*c*
Yen, Hope 136–137
Young Women's Christian
Association (YWCA) 348*c*
Young Women's Hebrew
Association (YWHA) 348*c*

Z
Zahle, Nathalie 271*b*
Zainab 344*c*
Zakrzewska, Marie E. 348*c*
Zarhgoona 344*c*
Zoya 111, 118, 272*b*